American
Philosophy

ROYAL INSTITUTE OF PHILOSOPHY LECTURE SERIES: 19
SUPPLEMENT TO PHILOSOPHY 1985

EDITED BY:

Marcus G. Singer

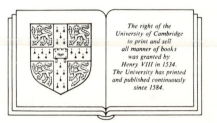

The right of the
University of Cambridge
to print and sell
all manner of books
was granted by
Henry VIII in 1534.
The University has printed
and published continuously
since 1584.

CAMBRIDGE UNIVERSITY PRESS

CAMBRIDGE
LONDON NEW YORK NEW ROCHELLE
MELBOURNE SYDNEY

Published by the Press Syndicate of the University of Cambridge
The Pitt Building, Trumpington Street, Cambridge CB2 1RP
32 East 57th Street, New York, NY 10022, USA
10 Stamford Road, Oakleigh, Melbourne 3166, Australia

© The Royal Institute of Philosophy 1985

Library of Congress catalogue card number: 85-48169

British Library Cataloguing in Publication Data

American philosophy.—(Royal Institute of
  Philosophy lecture series; 19)
  1. Philosophy, American—History
  I. Singer, Marcus G.   II. Philosophy   III. Series
  191   B851

  ISBN 0-521-31048-2

Library of Congress Cataloguing in Publication Data

American philosophy.
  (Royal Institute of Philosophy lecture series; 19)
  "Supplement to Philosophy 1985."
  Bibliography: p. 331
  Includes index.
  1. Philosophy, American—Addresses, essays,
lectures. I. Singer, Marcus George, 1926–   .
II. Philosophy. 1985 (Supplement)   III. Series.
B851.A46 1985 Suppl.   191   85-48169

  ISBN 0-521-31048-2 (pbk.)

Printed in Great Britain by Adlard & Son Ltd, Bartholomew Press, Dorking

Contents

This book is dedicated to Max Fisch
and to the memory of Herbert W. Schneider
in recognition of their
contributions to the study
and the understanding of
American philosophy

Preface

The topic of the Royal Institute of Philosophy lectures delivered in 1984–85 was American Philosophy, an ill-defined and even mongrel subject in which there has been for some time a considerable interest in the United States and in recent years a growing interest elsewhere. The nature of the subject is discussed in the first lecture and in portions of a number of others, as well as in the one by Professor Kuklick. The lecturers were asked to speak to a general audience, not to an audience of specialists; thus to keep technical details to a minimum, and to include biographical and background information not normally included in a philosophical essay; to make it clear why the philosopher under discussion is worth having a lecture on in such a series as this; so far as possible, to present the whole range of the philosopher's thought, making it intelligible how the details fit into a meaningful whole; thus, if need be, to concentrate more on exposition and understanding than on criticism. How well they succeeded, and if they even tried, and whether the advice was well taken, may be left for the reader to decide. The reader only needs to know that each lecturer received a copy of the same set of guidelines, a Prospectus prepared with the aim of imposing some unity of approach and aim on the series as a whole. (More information about this Prospectus and the aims of the series, as it was originally envisaged, is provided in sections 2 and 3 and some later portions of the first lecture.)

The lecturers were also asked to indicate how, if at all, the philosopher under discussion relates to American culture—the history, politics, literature, etc., of the time, and how he conceived himself to be so related. This requires looking at philosophy from a perspective somewhat different from that usual in the philosophic world, in which philosophy is regarded (as, for some purposes, it properly is) as a self-contained autonomous discipline with problems that develop only out of its own exercise. America is unusual in that no other nation has been developed solely by immigrants from so many other places and has at the same time been founded expressly on a basis of philosophical ideas. What effect if any did this have on American philosophy, or on philosophy in America? Some of the lectures address this question directly, others in an ancillary way, in some it is ignored. It is, none the less, one theme, or question, of this volume.

Most of the lectures have been revised for publication, some of them extensively so, and some as printed here are longer than when delivered, but all are in character and in general outline the same as when they were delivered. They are printed here in the order of delivery, since no order that could be imposed on them would work out better than the one arrived at by chance. As it is, the order looks as though it were designed, what with

Preface

Peirce, James, Dewey, and Mead following one another in chronological order, and with Edwards followed by Lewis followed by Thoreau to provide an interesting offset of styles and ideas. But this was all chance and serendipity. Lectures 1 and 9 have a direct bearing on each other and may appear to have been prepared with that in mind; they were not.

There is one serious omission. There is no lecture on Whitehead. If there had been a sixteenth it would have been on Whitehead, though that of course is not much consolation. On the other hand, it might not have been feasible to arrange it. For it would have had to be on Whitehead as an American philosopher, not just as a great speculative philosopher, and that is a bit off the beaten track. It is not always apparent to the interested observer—it had not occurred to me before—that there are difficulties in arranging such a series as this that are not involved in simply commissioning essays for a volume. The person who is just right for a particular topic may not be available at the right time, or the difficulties or the costs of travel may be too great. There were some other philosophers in the United States whom I should have been delighted to have participate in this series but who for one reason or another were unable to. It should be recorded that the Americans who came to London to lecture in this series were not brought over by the funds of the Royal Institute of Philosophy, but had their trips paid for by their own universities, or else by themselves, and the Institute is appropriately grateful for this benefaction.

There are some other omissions worth noting. If this had not been primarily a series of lectures but a volume on the subject, and if space had been no object (but of course it always is), there would be contributions on McCosh and traditional realism, on New and Critical Realism, on W. T. Harris and the idealist tradition in American philosophy (if done well that would bring out how culture was brought to and was present on the frontier, and how law developed out of anarchy, sometimes by anarchic means), on F. J. E. Woodbridge and American Naturalism, on Chauncey Wright and Evolutionism and the origins of Pragmatism, on such figures as Howison, R. W. Sellars, Perry, Lovejoy, and Hocking, and on American philosophy of science. And if I were more prescient than I am I would have seen to it that there were a piece on the philosophical *foundations* of the American Constitution—still a largely unrecognized subject for political philosophy—and on *The Federalist*, as well as one on such founding thinkers, well apprised on philosophical subjects as well as keen reasoners, as Franklin, Jefferson, Paine, Hamilton, Madison, and James Wilson. One criterion, however, I would not have changed—that no lecture be on anyone now alive. The only departure from that rule is in the piece on American legal philosophy, where it is oddly appropriate; in any case lawyers are a law unto themselves.

Some members of the audience were curious why Thoreau was included. The main burden of the answer is provided by Professor

Norton's lecture on Thoreau, but that would not explain why the series was so organized as to have included a lecture on Thoreau at all. Thoreau was included not because he is a famous and influential American literary and cultural figure, and not because he has become the archetype of the Village Philosopher. The explanation is rather this. If any words are vague, 'philosophy' is, and if all words are vague, as some have claimed, then there can be no doubt that 'philosophy' is. Even the most sceptical and cautious philosophers tend to wax dogmatic on this topic and to insist that what *they* are doing is philosophy, or 'real' philosophy, and that whoever is doing anything of a different stripe is not, and there is an oddity in this that bears noting. Thoreau provides a borderline case (I should claim no more than that no matter what Professor Norton claims), and an interesting borderline case. Considering Thoreau as a philosopher helps us test and stretch, and perhaps restrict, our conception of philosophy and of a philosopher and of what is important in philosophy (and in a philosopher). Thoreau provides also a marvellous and striking contrast with, say, C. I. Lewis, and Jonathan Edwards. If all three of them are philosophers, what a remarkable thing philosophy is; and it is. And in the American tradition there is ample precedent for including Thoreau, as an example of a non-academic, even anti-academic, way of thinking that certainly regarded itself as philosophical, and in an important way. Indeed, in some ways the American Transcendentalists can be regarded as interesting forerunners of the Existentialists. Finally, if Wittgenstein was a philosopher, and also Nietzsche and Kierkegaard, then so was Emerson. But if Emerson was a philosopher, and I have no doubt that he was (though to be sure he was also and at the same time a poet), then there is at least a case for considering Thoreau one, or at least for considering him.

Similar questions have been raised about Santayana, and even about Dewey, who is as little known outside America as he is well known in it. (Dewey is the most well-known public figure of all those discussed in this volume. There was recently issued in the United States a John Dewey postage stamp, along with one commemorating Cole Porter.) The devil's advocate here is John Passmore, who expressed these doubts in striking form, especially for a British audience:

> Dewey's great American reputation is still a mystery to the philosophical world outside the United States, and more especially in England . . . many British philosophers would think of Dewey's American reputation as a puzzling form of intellectual aberration, sociologically intelligible but philosophically mysterious, especially as he is well spoken of and seriously discussed by American philosophers about whose ability there is no question. . . .

No one doubts, however, that Dewey is a philosopher; the question, only, is whether he is a good one. In Santayana's case, the doubt cuts deeper; whether with his distaste for and neglect of argument he should not be regarded as a remarkably penetrating sage rather than as a philosopher.[1]

Exactly the same question, of course, has been raised about Emerson, and on the same grounds, that a genuine philosopher, or philosopher 'in the strictest sense of the word' (Passmore, p. 118), lays out and analyzes arguments in a certain way. But it is remarkable that Passmore did not, to my knowledge, apply this criterion to the later work of Wittgenstein, or to Nietzsche or Kierkegaard. In any case, the question as to Dewey and Santayana is answered in this volume in the lectures by Professors Thayer and Sprigge. Indeed, Professor Sprigge's book on Santayana can be taken as a later response to Passmore's question; it was written, edited, and published in Britain, and appeared in 'The Arguments of the Philosophers' series. And the question 'What is philosophy?', like the question whether or not someone is a philosopher, remains a philosophical question (and the latter is only in the rarest and clearest circumstances a simple question of fact). It is one of the questions—philosophy wondering about itself—that the lectures in this volume can throw some light on.

It remains to be noticed that the discussion of Vincent Potter's lecture on Peirce was opened and chaired by Renford Bambrough, of Peter Jones' lecture on James by Sir Alfred Ayer, of Susan Haack's on Lewis by Paul Foulkes, of Andrew Reck's on the background of the American Constitution by Theodore Waldman, and of Professor Singer's two lectures by A. Phillips Griffiths, and I take this opportunity to extend to these gentlemen my thanks for their contributions to the proceedings. For advice on the selection of lecturers I am grateful to Donald Crawford, Bill Hay, Peter Jones, Konstantin Kolenda, John McDermott, Ellen Kappy Suckiel, and Terry Winant, and for especially helpful advice on format and the preparation of the Prospectus I am especially grateful to Peter Jones. I hereby thank Dr Foulkes, Hans Oberdiek, Phillips Griffiths and Professor Waldman for advice on editing some of the papers, Dr Foulkes for his help during the lecture sessions, and Richard Denniss, the Secretary of the Royal Institute, for facilitating my stay at the Institute. I am also grateful to the Research Committee of the Graduate School of the University of Wisconsin for providing the research time and support that enabled me to be in London to conduct the series. Professor Phillips Griffiths has been an immense help in all sorts of ways, which friendship would lead me to take for granted but gratitude obliges me to acknowledge.

M.G.S.

Highgate, London
28 May 1985

[1] John Passmore, 'Philosophical Scholarship in the United States, 1930–1960', in *Philosophy*, by R. Chisholm, H. Feigl, W. Frankena, J. Passmore, and M. Thompson (Englewood Cliffs: Prentice-Hall, Inc., 1964), 122–123.

The Context of American Philosophy

MARCUS G. SINGER

I am, naturally, greatly honoured to have been invited by the Royal Institute of Philosophy to organize and conduct their lecture series on American Philosophy. It has been an interesting if trying experience, and I must say that the process of organizing it has given me a special respect for the patience and administrative capacities of those who have the task year in year out. Of course there were special difficulties in the way of importing so many people from the United States (especially since the Institute does not have the funds needed to bring them over), but if the series was to be on American Philosophy—whatever that is—it seemed especially appropriate that the lectures be given predominantly by Americans who have made a special study of the subject—again, whatever that is. We may, of course, end with the conclusion that there is no such distinctive subject, and that the name 'American Philosophy' is as nominal as a name can be, but that, we should note, is something to be found out, not a conclusion dictated in advance.

I. Autobiographical

I want to begin by telling you how I came to be associated with the study of American philosophy. This is something that not even Professor Griffiths knew about before, and it is time he learned it. I never as a student had a course in American philosophy. I signed up for one once, and then dropped it. Indeed, American philosophy was the only philosophy course I ever dropped, and I dropped all told only two courses my whole time as a student. It was one summer session, I think it was the summer of 1947, that I enrolled in a course entitled American philosophy, which was being taught that session by a Visiting Lecturer at the University of Illinois. I went to two sessions on two successive days, and that was it. I dropped it and took calculus instead. It is curious that I now know a bit more of American philosophy than I do of calculus. Why did I drop it? I had a look at the book, I attended two sessions, I saw sweeping ahead of me more such sessions on the God-intoxicated and Devil-haunted divines from the period of colonization and witch burning, and I decided that this was deadly stuff, and that, if this was philosophy, I wanted no part of it. I had had some philosophy, and it was fascinating, entrancing, not by any means deadly. The conclusion that American philosophy, or what went under that name, was not philosophy, readily formed itself—and ever since I have had some measure of sympathetic understanding for those who say that American philosophy is not philosophy. Some, though not, all told, a great deal, especially if they have not investigated the matter.

Some years later, when I was in my first year of teaching at the University of Wisconsin, I was taken aside by the then chairman of the department and asked if I had any interest in teaching American philosophy. Although my response was not especially enthusiastic, I was none the less given to understand that, be that as it may, if I could not see my way clear to taking on American philosophy I might have to be let go in favor of someone who could, since the person then teaching the course was being let go, and it was necessary that someone teach it. Now I then had the rank of Instructor, a rank that is now largely obsolete. The term of appointment of an Instructor is for only one year at a time, and in those days jobs teaching philosophy were even scarcer than they are now. So after some ten seconds or so of careful meditation I agreed to teach American philosophy. But I was curious why it was so necessary to have someone teach the course, why I should teach that rather than some others somewhat higher up on my list of preferences, such as Philosophy of Language, Symbolic Logic, Political Philosophy, or even Ethics, which I was not to be able to teach for another two years. The answer was illuminating. This was the period of McCarthyism, one of intense interest in inculcating Americanism. The American Legion had some time before been demanding that the University inculcate in the students the principles of patriotism, as understood of course by the American Legion, and that the University accept and fulfil its role in the Americanization of young Americans. The Regents had only a few years before sidestepped this demand, in a way, by requiring that every student in the university take a year of American History and Institutions, and the requirement was such that one course that could be taken towards it was American Philosophy. Hence the very sizeable enrolments in that course.

So I spent the next summer and a good part of the next several years reading and meditating on American philosophy. The question that bothered me most was, what is this course, this subject, all about? What is the rationale for a course in American philosophy? Is there such a subject? Is there, in other words, something worth studying as American philosophy, as distinct from a study of some important philosophers who happened to be Americans? I decided that there is, and that the question is itself an interesting one, which could be dealt with better in this setting than in any other.

Now if it had not been for this fortuitous occurrence, thirty-two years ago, I would not be here today conducting this series of lectures. I do not go so far as to say that you would not be here today. Nor do I say that there would not be this year a series of lectures on American philosophy. But of course it would not be *this* series. As I have been reminded of this occurrence from time to time since, it has led me to reflect on the harm that good men do, or on the good that good manipulative men do in the process of doing harm while thinking they are doing good. So I dedicate this lecture, if not the series as a whole, to the memory of Arthur Campbell Garnett, my late and former colleague and first department chairman, who, in the interest of maintaining enrolments in the philosophy programme at the University of Wisconsin and thus maintaining its budget, made this programme possible.

II. The Series

I now want to tell you what I had in mind in organizing this series of lectures. In organizing it I prepared a Prospectus, which was sent out with each invitation, in which I tried to delineate what I thought lecturers should aim at. Although I do not expect the lecturers to abide by my instructions in any but their own individual ways, I think it useful to let you know what I asked them to aim at and to do.

The Prospectus was prefaced by some passages from Herbert Schneider's *History of American Philosophy*:

American philosophy has continually been given new life and new directions by waves of immigration. In America, at least, it is useless to seek a 'native' tradition, for even our most genteel traditions are saturated with foreign inspirations. Spanish Franciscans, French Jesuits, English Puritans, Dutch Pietists, Scottish Calvinists, cosmopolitan *philosophes*, German Transcendentalists, Russian revolutionaries, and Oriental theosophists have all shared in giving to so-called American philosophy its continuities as well as its shocks. . . .

It is already clear that political, economic, theological, and metaphysical principles have been more closely associated in American thought than we have hitherto been led to believe and that a truly comprehensive history of American philosophy still remains to be written. . . .

A genuine cultural history of the peoples in the United States is taking shape, and it is this kind of history which must be the framework for future histories of philosophy. Since a large part of American philosophizing has been related directly to public affairs and popular culture, this kind of orientation for a history of philosophy comes readily and naturally. But academic philosophy has seemed to historians to exist in a few ivory towers, and there is still

3

much research needed to show how academic systems are related to cultural concerns in the wider sense. . . .[1]

I will return to some of these ideas directly.

I asked lecturers to direct their remarks to a general audience, not an audience of specialists, and accordingly to include biographical and textual details not normally included in a philosophical essay; and also that the lectures not be prepared as if for the pages of a philosophical journal, and not involve minute points of the sort that find their way into *Analysis*. I also suggested that it be made clear why the philosopher in question is worth studying and worth having a lecture on in such a series as this. I furthermore asked lecturers to try, so far as possible given the finite length of the lectures and the conditions of intelligibility, to present or at least to outline the whole range of their subject's philosophy, making it intelligible how the details fit into an ordered meaningful whole, and to make criticism and assessment wait on this. This is, especially with some of the thinkers to be discussed in the series, something enormously difficult to do, and I was gratified that so many of the people I invited agreed with me that it is worth attempting. This is, I am informed, the first time that a series of lectures such as this in the United Kingdom will have been on American Philosophy; accordingly the series aims, in the words of the Director of the Royal Institute of Philosophy, which I have had in mind for some time, to be 'a revelation to the ignorant and an inspiration to the already interested'. These of course are high aims, and so should they be.

III. The Point of American Philosophy

The only reason for having a lecture series on or for studying American Philosophy, as such, is the idea that there is some significant connection between the philosophers in question, identified somehow and on some criterion as American, and the American scene, culture, or setting. Otherwise the philosopher in question, if worth further consideration at the present day, can be studied under some more orthodox heading, such as epistemology, ethics, metaphysics, or logic. And the major figures to be discussed in this series certainly are worth so studying. (Peirce is now in the philosophical pantheon and James is very close to being so; their ideas are coming in for ever-increasing discussion under any variety of headings. If current tendencies continue, Royce may be the next to enter the pantheon, or possibly Dewey.) But under the

---

[1] Herbert W. Schneider, *A History of American Philosophy*, 2nd edn, 1963 (New York: Columbia University Press, 1946), vii–viii, x, xv.

headings for the standard branches of philosophy there would be no reason to treat the philosophers to be covered in this series together. If there is any reason to do so, it must be because of their background, their habitat, their perhaps common assumptions, or else because it is at least plausible to suppose that these factors have played an important role in linking these thinkers together.

Consequently I asked the lecturers in the series to contemplate this matter and to try to address it in one way or another. And an argument to the effect that such a supposition is false is certainly as appropriate as the mere assumption that it is true. So you may expect to hear some speculation and perhaps some evidence on how the American philosopher in question relates to American culture—the history, politics, literature, general assumptions of the time, and also how that philosopher conceived himself to be so related. For this concern was open and avowed on the part of such figures as Dewey, Santayana, and Royce. It is just beneath the surface in Peirce and James, but it is just as much there.

Now it would have been possible—it might even have been easier—to have arranged a series merely on a set of philosophers who happen to be Americans. If chosen, that route would have led us to the inclusion of such philosophers as Quine, Goodman, Davidson, Putnam, Kripke—to mention some in whom at the moment in the philosophical world there is the greatest interest. But what would be the point? That would not have been a series on American philosophy, but rather on a set of contemporary philosophers of language and metaphysicians who happen to be Americans, and would be much more sensibly considered under the heading of Contemporary Philosophy. That they are Americans would seem to have no relevance to their philosophical styles and views except for the extraneous and accidental fact that most of them have worked in contiguous communities and have been able to intersect with some frequency. But there is no philosophical point in discussions of the efficiency of the Boston tram lines.

This the rationale behind this series as so organized. And that is consistent with the way that I, at any rate, understand the purposes and purview of the Royal Institute of Philosophy. I must go by my commission.

There is no unitary tradition in American philosophy. There is not even the illusion of one. There is complex interaction of heterogeneous, even heteronomous, traditions. In that respect even if in no other the path of American philosophy has run parallel to that of American immigration, and it is not too long ago that the bulk of American ideas were imported, along with the bulk of its population. The British philosopher C. D. Broad once observed, in a remark that has become famous, that all good fallacies go to America. What he overlooked is that before too long they go back home, sometimes marvellously transformed and newly packaged, but back home none the less. That curiously is true of some of its philosophies, but few of its people. It is in part owing to this complex heterogeneity of traditions that the question arises whether there is any *characteristically*—or typically, or distinctively, or representative—American philosophy.

Now it is this question that first stimulated my interest in the study of American philosophy. As we shall see, it raises questions about the nature of philosophy as well as questions about the relation of philosophy to culture. It also raises questions about the idea of national character and of 'characteristic' or 'distinctive' national traits. What is also intriguing is that, until very recently, almost until the present generation, the major figures in American philosophy have all, or nearly all, had a self-conscious relation to their times and historical circumstances and to the American experience, which is both unusual and unique. (I do not misuse 'unique', in the current manner, as a value term.) No other nation has been settled and developed solely by immigrants from so many other places and has also been founded expressly on the basis of philosophical ideas. (It can be added that before 1776 or 1789 no other nation had actually been created—before then they had simply grown.[2]) Very few philosophers are given to thinking about philosophy in this way and in this context; most people who have thought on these themes have not been philosophers. But some philosophers have done, and a considerable proportion of those who have have been American philosophers, some of whom have attained prominence, in their time if not for all time. John Dewey, George Herbert Mead, George Santayana, Josiah Royce, W. T. Harris, and James McCosh are examples; so are Morris Cohen and Arthur Murphy, about whom I shall be talking in the last lecture in this series.

There is even some question about who is to count as an *American* philosopher. Is native birth essential? Clearly not. Is having lived most of one's life in America essential? No, not essential. Is having done most of one's work in America essential? Are any of these conditions sufficient? The answer seems clearly no to all these questions. Santayana is still regarded as an American philosopher, even regarded himself as one, in his fashion, although he was born in Spain of Spanish parents and, all told, spent the bulk of his life outside of America. (Although he was a student and teacher at Harvard, his tenure there was a relatively small part of his life, reckoning solely by number of years. As soon as an inheritance made it feasible, he resigned his post and left for England;

[2] This has been observed by Henry Steele Commager, 'The Revolution as a World Ideal', *Saturday Review*, 13 December 1975, 14.

and, when World War I ended, or soon thereafter, he went to live in Italy in the retirement of a convent.) Another example of a philosopher who is on the borderline is Whitehead, who went to America to teach when he was sixty-three and spent the last twenty-three years of his life there. But it was in this period of his career that he emerged as a major speculative philosopher and philosopher of education and culture, and he himself came to think of himself as an American philosopher. With Whitehead one could argue, I suppose, that either he was both a British and an American philosopher, or else that there were two Whiteheads, early and late. Similar questions, as we know, arise about certain literary figures, such as Henry James and T. S. Eliot. Was Eliot an American or an English poet? Some would say, what does it matter?— what matters is that he was a poet. Well, that he unquestionably was, and in the case of Eliot perhaps it does not matter. But it does matter in the case of Henry James, because of the way in which the American theme affects all his novels. And we are now considering the context in which such things do matter.

A question that cuts deeper is whether some writer is a *philosopher*, as distinct from a sage or seer or essayist or publicist. This question is often raised about Emerson and Thoreau, as well as Jefferson, Franklin, and the authors of *The Federalist*. The question whether Emerson or Thoreau is a philosopher can safely be left for the lectures on them (obviously I so regard them or they would not be in this series). (And we must avoid the naive assumption, a form of the fallacy of false disjunction, that if one is a philosopher one is only a philosopher and can be nothing else—that Jonathan Edwards was a theologian does not mean he was not also a philosopher.) About Tom Paine the question is double-barrelled: was he a philosopher, and was he an American philosopher? I think the answer on both counts is yes, but will not argue the matter here, will instead suggest some rough and general criteria (all we can arrive at in the nature of the case) for who is to count as an *American* philosopher. (The question of the nature of philosophy, and consequently what makes a philosopher, I come to later.) I suggest that a philosopher who has spent the major portion of his creative life in America or in connection with American institutions, whose audience has been predominantly or to a large extent American, and who either has had an extensive influence in the United States or has exerted the major portion of his influence, such as it has been, in the United States, may plausibly be regarded as an American philosopher, and in discussions of American philosophy can count as an American philosopher. Of course this is vague—who could have expected it to be anything else? Still, on this criterion Tom Paine (if he is a philosopher), Santayana and Whitehead all count as American philosophers. Even so, this is not to imply that a philosopher coming under this criterion is thereby a typically or distinctively American philosopher or in any way 'representative'. It is to this conception that I now turn.

IV. 'Representative' Philosophers

Josiah Royce, an inventive and original philosopher with great technical facility, had a conception of what a 'representative' philosopher would be, and on the basis of this conception, in 1911, after William James' death, he maintained that there had been up to that time but three representative American philosophers: Edwards, Waldo Emerson, and James. His argument was, as he put it, that 'the conditions that determine a fair answer to the question "who are your representative American philosophers?" are' these: 'The philosopher who can fitly represent the contribution of his nation to the world's treasury of philosophical ideas must first be one who thinks for himself, fruitfully, with true independence, and with successful inventiveness, about problems of philosophy. And, secondly, he must ... give utterance to philosophical ideas which are characteristic of some stage and of some aspect of the spiritual life of his own people.' Royce said of Edwards that 'he spoke not merely as a thinker [and as a thinker Royce gave him very high marks indeed], but as one who gave voice to some of the central motives and interest of our colonial religious life', and that he was, therefore, 'in order of time, the first of our nationally representative philosophers'.

A later phase of our national ideals, says Royce, 'found its representative in Emerson'. Of Emerson he said:

> He too was in close touch with many of the world's deepest thoughts concerning ultimate problems. Some of the ideas that most influenced him have their far-off historical origins in oriental as well as Greek thought, and also their nearer foreign sources in modern European philosophy. But he transformed whatever he assimilated. He invented upon the basis of his personal experience, and so he was himself no disciple of the orient, or of Greece, still less of England and Germany. He thought, felt, and spoke as an American.

And from there Royce goes on to argue that James is the latest successor, for a later time and for ideas characteristic of a later stage and a later aspect of the spiritual life of the American people.

I have dwelt on a brief bit of this account by Royce because, looked at philosophically, it generates problems of interpretation and evidence that I find as puzzling and as intriguing as anything in philosophy. And Royce, unfortunately, though he gives a brilliant account of 'James's thought in so far [as it expresses] the ideas and the ideals characteristic of this phase of [American] national life', does not raise critical questions about the terms in which he couches his account. If he had, of course, it would have been altogether out of order. For he was giving a funeral oration. But he at least helped to raise the questions we will get to presently.

On one matter I feel constrained to present to you something else Royce says. Royce puts the idea of a philosophy of a national civilization in different words, and some are very suggestive indeed. Here is one:

> The essence of a philosophy, *in case you look at it solely from a historical point of view* [I have italicized those words deliberately], always appears to you thus: A great philosophy [Royce has here shifted to speaking of a *great* philosophy, but I think with ample justification] expresses an interpretation of the life of man and a view of the universe, which is at once personal, and, if the thinker is representative of his people, national in its significance. . . .[3]

But what is philosophically puzzling is, how can it be determined that the thinker is representative of his people, and how reliable can the determination be?

To put the matter another way, a representative American philosopher would be one who had given articulate expression to 'the spirit of the age', or what might be called 'the dominant philosophy of the time'. But how is this determined? Is 'the spirit of the age' just an instance of literary loose talk, or is there something determinate in it?

V. Philosophy

I must at this point say something about what philosophy is, in order merely to present the problem about cultural generalizations, of national character, and a national philosophy. There are almost as many different conceptions of philosophy as there are philosophers, and the philosophical differences that go deepest and are the hardest to eradicate are often those that turn on different conceptions of philosophic method and philosophic ends. I hope so far as I can to avoid this impasse and at the same time finesse the general question—with what success, we shall see.

The sense of philosophy I want to call to your attention at the outset is that in which it is something personal. As William James described it, 'the philosophy which is so important in each of us is not a technical matter; it is our more or less dumb sense of what life honestly and deeply means . . . our individual way of just seeing and feeling the total

[3] Josiah Royce, 'William James and the Philosophy of Life', *William James and other Essays* (New York: Macmillan, 1911), 3ff.

push and pressure of the cosmos' (*Pragmatism*, 1907, Ch. 1, 3–4). This is of course not all that philosophy is; if it were we should still be on the level of the barbarian. Philosophy is also a technical discipline, demanding rigorous habits and development of mind, and is the enterprise *Philosophy*, the journal of the Royal Institute of Philosophy, attempts to advance the study of. But, though philosophy is not only that, it is at least that. As Iris Murdoch has put it, 'To do philosophy is to explore one's own temperament, and yet at the same time to attempt to discover the truth'.[4] The peculiarity of philosophy, and the basic ground of its difference from science, is that it claims to be impersonal, and at its best it is; while it denies that it is personal, though at its best it still is. It is because of this characteristic that we can speak, as we do, of Plato's philosophy, Aristotle's, Kant's, or Dewey's, whereas it makes no sense to speak of someone's science. (There is a deviant expression, e.g. Einstein's science, Aristotle's science, or Newton's science, but that does not attribute ownership, only origin.) And no matter how close we come to another in philosophical views there appears always to be this irreducible personal aspect and outlook. It is for this reason that philosophy—though not in the hands of every writer—can claim to be also a branch of literature, and why a philosophy can be expressed in a work of literature; it is also why a philosophical work can also be a work of literature, as some of the great classics are.

Philosophy thus has a double aspect. It has, first, the aspect of something personal, and is thus a fact or a set of events, having causes and effects; it is, foremost, something arguable, discussable, subject to tests of validity and adequacy, and in this aspect it is not merely a set of events having causes and effects, but a set of ideas, having truth value and claiming to be true. (And it is worth repeating that under this aspect ideas are not events with causes and effects.)

But, as has already been suggested, philosophical ideas and the collections of them called philosophies can also be national, can characterize a nation or a culture as they can characterize or even dominate a period, an epoch, or an age.

In his *Science and the Modern World*, the first book he wrote in America, Alfred North Whitehead has some penetrating remarks on this point. 'When you are criticizing the philosophy of an epoch', he said,

> do not chiefly direct your attention to those intellectual positions which its exponents feel it necessary explicitly to defend. There will be some fundamental assumptions which adherents of all the variant systems within the epoch unconsciously presuppose. Such assump-

[4] Iris Murdoch, *The Sovereignty of Good,* (New York: Schocken Books, 1971), Ch. 2, 46.

tions appear so obvious that people do not know what they are assuming because no other way of putting things has ever occurred to them. With these assumptions a certain limited number of types of philosophical systems are possible, and this group of systems constitutes the philosophy of the epoch.[5]

When a long time ago I first read Whitehead's *Science and the Modern World*, with this large and even inspiring conception of philosophy, it was for me an eye-opener. For if there can be a philosophy of an epoch there can be a philosophy of an age and there can be a philosophy of a nation or a national philosophy, and it occurred to me that if there were such a thing as the philosophy of a given nation, which is something somehow different from the philosophies of the individual philosophers of that nation or time, that would be something important and interesting to find out. And it was only a couple of years later that I was called on to try to apply this idea when I was coaxed, as I was, to take on the teaching of American philosophy. I did not find the idea any the less baffling, for the depth of knowledge and the power of insight that the discovery of such a thing seemed to me to call for was enormous, and I have more than once wondered if it were not beyond my powers. But, whether or not I ever succeeded in applying this idea of Whitehead's, I did have it in mind and did try to view the philosophical ideas of the various writers, seers, and savants we considered in the light of it. With a generalization of that amplitude one would have a searchlight of enormous power, if one only knew how to turn it on.

Only a short time later I was called on to face a similar question again, when I was asked to review Morris Cohen's posthumous book on *American Thought*, published just thirty years ago in 1954. Cohen said that the book he had planned 'would focus not on technical philosophy but rather on the general ideas which are taken for granted in various fields of thought and thus come to constitute the philosophy of a period and a country even before they have been systematically articulated'.[6] It is certainly hard, very hard, to pick out these general ideas taken for granted in this inarticulate way, to formulate them and to establish that they are in fact so presupposed. That does not take away from the excitement of the search. It adds to it. If there are such general ideas commonly or generally presupposed in a given nation or culture, they would constitute the philosophy of that culture, and one then could not

---

[5] *Science and the Modern World,* 1932 edn (Cambridge: University Press, 1926), Ch. 3, 61. Cf. Ch. 5, 108.

[6] Morris Cohen, *American Thought* (Glencoe: The Free Press, 1954), 9. Cf. Cohen, *A Dreamer's Journey* (Glencoe: The Free Press; Boston: The Beacon Press, 1949), 195 *et seq.*

adequately understand that culture without being able in this sense to pinpoint and understand its philosophy. This then would be the focal point for the study of American Philosophy, and this in fact is how I conceive it. From this point of view, the study of particular philosophers, such as Peirce, James, and Royce, is subservient to this wider aim—though the temptation is of course great to go off on critical analytical and dialectical binges, and I have succumbed to this temptation with embarrassing frequency. But from this point of view the study of American philosophy is an instance of the philosophy of culture and civilization, and one of the questions of the philosophy of culture is how philosophy relates to culture. This, however, is still philosophy, not intellectual history. The object is not merely to place ideas and move on to the next piece of scenery; the object also is to critique them, to explore their meaning and grounds and implications and validity. The enterprise is not easy; it is hard; but that is one of its rewards.

VI. Cultural Generalizations

I have a special interest in generalization, as some of you know, and it is not restricted to generalization in ethics, may actually extend to generalization in general. I want now briefly to discuss with you generalizations of a special type, as I believe them to be, which I call cultural generalizations. A *cultural generalization* is a proposition to the effect that a certain trait, property, or activity is characteristic, typical, distinctive, or representative of a certain society, culture, or cultural group. Thus, 'X is a distinctively (or typically, or characteristically) American (or British, or French, or Dutch, or Japanese) trait' is a cultural generalization. And statements such as 'So and so (say, Benjamin Franklin) is a typical (or representative) American' thus involve cultural generalizations.

Now we have all heard such generalizations, and I am willing to bet that we all make them. Examples abound. Travel books revel in them. Here is one, supposed to illustrate the British character, for the guidance of us visitors to this land: '"Fancy being born in Iceland", a British guest [is reported to have] said at a party for the Icelandic Ambassador'. Here are some others:

> ... you will find the Spanish are proud with a pride of race. They carry themselves like a proud people ... The greatest of Spanish national virtues is courage. This explains the popularity of Spain's most typical spectacle, the bullfight....
>
> ... the Belgian proclivity for evading the law finds its chief expression in dodging taxes ... When they get behind the wheel of a car, rugged individualism reigns supreme.... Off the road and away

from the tax office, the Belgians are conservative, law abiding, and dignified, even a little sedate and staid ... Generally speaking [strictly speaking, this has all been generally speaking], they do not have the wit, vivacity, and high temperament of the French, whom they regard as frivolous and lazy ...

... the Hollanders [are] a serious, determined, hard-working people of the toughest moral fibre ... they are open, above-board, absolutely trustworthy. ... Cleanliness is a passion with the Hollanders; the whole country looks as though it has been scrubbed with Dutch Cleanser. ...

[The] Finns ... are a fair-skinned, fair-haired, somewhat taciturn but essentially poetic people. The essence of their character may be summed up in a Finnish word *susu*, of which there is no exact English equivalent, but it's a combination of unyielding courage, stamina and fortitude. ...[7]

Of course one does not have to turn to a travel guide to find such generalizations. They are all around, occur constantly. Indeed, I recall seeing more than a few in the pages of *Philosophy*, the journal of the Royal Institute of Philosophy; I didn't bring examples with me, but as I recall they were all about Americans. And here are two observed at random in one day's issue of *The Times*, Tuesday this week. In one, an article reporting the appointment of an advertising man as General Manager of the Metropolitan Opera of New York, it is said that 'the selection represents a particularly American solution to the problem of who is to run an opera house ...'. In the other, a leading article (editorial) commenting on the first debate between Mondale and Reagan, there appears the following astute observation: 'To hear candidates for the most powerful elected office on earth mutually affirming not just their belief in but their daily communication with the deity was a vivid reminder of America's religiosity—an element in the national make-up which America's friends, mesmerized by her material progress, often ignore'.[8]

Now here is a philosophical question of some import: What is the logic of cultural generalizations? That is to say, how are they to be established, what would count as evidence for them and as evidence against them? This has, so far as I know, yet to be examined. I say this because cultural generalizations seem very unlike ordinary factual

[7] *Fodor's Jet Age Guide to Europe 1962* (New York: David McKay Company, 1962), 349, 707, 115, 429, 204.

[8] *The Times* Tuesday 9 October 1984, 14, 17. On Tuesday 16 October 1984, 35, the reader is told that 'Rowan and Martin present a peculiarly American humour show ...'

generalizations. They are not and are not intended to be universal generalizations, of the form 'All Ruritanians are x, y, and z'. Nor are they statistical generalizations, of the form 'Most Erewhonians are t, u, and v', though they may be based on some judgment, or impression, about most Erewhonians or Ruritanians. The key is in the words 'typically' or 'characteristically'. If we try to insert such a qualifier as 'most' or 'all' in such a statement as 'The Erewhonians typically dislike fairhaired people', or 'The Freedonians are characteristically cowardly', we get nonsense. Though it may be false, still it makes sense to say that Americans are characteristically courteous; but it makes no sense to say that *most* Americans are characteristically courteous. Similarly, and typically, it makes sense to say that Spanish people are typically proud; but it makes no sense to say that *all* Spanish people are typically proud. The presence, either actual or implicit, of such terms as 'typically' and 'characteristically' indicates that such generalizations are of a different order.

It is also nonsense to say that they are none of them true. Descriptions of speech patterns and pronunciations can be true though culture-bound, as are languages themselves. And I wonder how many of you have noticed the distinctive way in which an American handles knife and fork when eating, and how it differs from the way in which people here or in Europe do. But that complicated and genteel way of handling knife and fork is a characteristically and may be even a distinctively American trait; it constitutes one decisive break, in a nation of immigrants, with the traditions of the old country. (For those who have never noticed or never had the opportunity to, here is a brief account: an Englishman holds the fork in left hand and knife in right and shovels food on to the fork with the knife; an American slices the food with the knife in right hand and fork in left, places knife on plate, transfers fork from left hand to right, picks up food with fork in right hand and transports food to mouth, lowers right hand and transfers fork from right to left, picks up knife with right hand and resumes process again; withal, Americans do eventually finish eating.) Such examples establish that cultural generalizations are not all false or illusory. Some are true.

Now all assertions about national character involve cultural generalizations. Is there such a thing as national character, or is the idea just a relic of a stereotype? This question cannot be answered without dealing with the logic of cultural generalizations. Further, if all assertions about national character involve cultural generalizations, all references to the American character, the American mind, the American temper, the American make-up involve cultural generalizations, as do references to the British character, the French mind, the German soul, etc.

As I before observed, cultural generalizations lead to the view that there is such a thing as national character, that nations or members of different nations differ from one another in character or personality or dominant traits as they differ in language or dialect or accent or customs, and to the further view that these characteristic national or cultural traits can be investigated and known. I would remind you that it was John Stuart Mill who observed that the study of national character may well be the most important area of social inquiry,[9] and that Hume in his *Essays* has a discourse on national characters. This is not an area that professed empiricists or analytic philosophers must necessarily stay clear of on pain of doctrinal heresy; it has only appeared to be.

VII. Philosophy and Culture

Whether or not Mill is right and such inquiry is the most important area of social inquiry, such inquiry is important, indeed essential, in the consideration of national philosophies, or of philosophy as cultural expression. A culture is an interrelated network of customs, traditions, mores, beliefs, rituals, ceremonies, forms, practices, institutions, ideals, and values. Now to say that a certain philosophy expresses a given culture, or is distinctively of a certain nation (=culture), is to say that the characteristic and dominant customs, traditions, mores, beliefs, practices, ideals, and values of that culture are given theoretical expression in the philosophy and some measure of coherence and even justification (where 'justification' is not used as an achievement word). The philosophy provides the rationale and may even provide the springboard for change and progress, to the extent that it is felt already to answer to the dominant needs and values and to be relevant to the problems of the culture.

Hence a philosophy can be the expression of, an interpretation of, a national character—whether this objective was consciously in the mind or part of the intent of the philosopher or not. It is also true that two philosophies inconsistent with each other can yet be consistent with the national character they each differently express. Thus both Transcendentalism (the philosophy of Emerson and Thoreau) and Pragmatism can be expressions of the American character (supposing there is such a thing), even though they are, as they appear to be, inconsistent with each other.

---

[9] J. S. Mill, *A System of Logic,* 1st edn, 1843; 8th ed, 1872 (London: Longmans, Green, 1949), Bk. VI, Ch. ix, Sec. 4, 590–591.

Take as an analogy the interpretation of a play. Hamlet interpreted as mad, or as indecisive, or as suffering from depression, are all different interpretations of the play, inconsistent with each other yet consistent with the play itself. Again, conflicting interpretations of Shylock in *The Merchant of Venice* can still be consistent with the play as Shakespeare wrote it. And the text is not thereby proved self-contradictory, as a narrow logic would hold, but rather, as we already know it to be, rich in meaning. Why should a culture be any less?

VIII. The Context of American Philosophy

I have all along actually been talking about context, but I want now to talk about it more specifically. The context of American philosophy has been one where, by and large, until recently, philosophical thinking and philosophical thinkers were put to work in the service of causes and for the achievement of objectives not determined by or intrinsic to philosophy itself. Thus, in the Colonial period, philosophical thinking was dominated by the interests of religion and religious leaders, such as the attempt on the part of Puritan divines to establish a theocracy. And thus the God-intoxicated writers who had bedevilled me into dropping that course, so many years ago. Later, philosophical thinking was put to work in the service of first, revolution, and then in making a constitution and a government and a nation. I shall not try to trace out the rest of the story here, will rest with these examples. I note only that there then ensued a period of some sixty years when two philosophical traditions existed side by side with little interaction. There was the academic philosophy of the schools and colleges—there were no universities yet—, and also Transcendentalism, which still exerts so much fascination for so many, which was a rebellion against academic philosophy. It was the Transcendentalists who were expressing something in the culture, not the academic philosophers. Perhaps that is the fate of all of us academics, and we might well ask, what does it matter? Well, philosophers are always being besieged with demands to establish what is quaintly called the relevance of their subject, and a study of its double history might play some role in that endeavor for anyone who thinks it worth taking on.

This special practical bent in American philosophers, which appears very early on and can be found as well in Edwards and the Transcendentalists and idealists like Royce, was perhaps especially prominent in Benjamin Franklin, who has often been said to be a typical or representative American—it is odd that the 'representative person' is the one who stands out. Indeed, I think Franklin may fairly be said to have anticipated pragmatism. We find this tendency in a letter he wrote to Thomas Paine, attempting to persuade Paine not to publish some work of an irreligious tendency. (I do not know if this was *The Age of Reason*—the book, that is; if it was, Franklin was certainly right in his predictions of what would happen to Paine if he published it.) Here is Franklin to Paine:

> By the argument it contains against a particular Providence ... you strike at the foundations of all religion. For without the belief of a Providence, that takes cognizance of, guards, and guides, and may favor particular persons, there is no reason to worship a Deity, to fear his displeasure, or to pray for his protection.... Though your reasonings are subtle, and may prevail with some readers, you will not succeed so as to change the general sentiments of mankind on that subject, and the consequence of printing this piece will be, a great deal of odium drawn upon yourself, mischief to you, and no benefit to others. He that spits against the wind, spits in his own face.
>
> But were you to succeed, do you imagine any good would be done by it? You yourself may find it easy to live a virtuous life, without the assistance afforded by religion; you having a clear perception of the advantages of virtue, and the disadvantages of vice, and possessing a strength of resolution sufficient to enable you to resist common temptations. But think how great a portion of mankind consists of weak and ignorant men and women, and of inexperienced, inconsiderate youth of both sexes, who have need of the motives of religion to restrain them from vice, to support their virtue, and retain them in the practice of it till it becomes *habitual*, which is the great point for its security.... I would advise you, therefore, not to attempt unchaining the tiger, but to burn this piece before it is seen by any other person; whereby you will save yourself a great deal of mortification by the enemies it may raise against you.... If men are so wicked *with religion*, what would they be *if without it*?

A similar theme is struck in a letter to Ezra Stiles, in 1790, near the end of Franklin's life. Stiles had asked Franklin to tell him something of his religion, and Franklin, though a bit surprised by the question, answered it anyway. I read here only this portion of the letter, even though the balance is as pithy:

> As to Jesus of Nazareth, my opinion of whom you particularly desire ... I have, with most of the present Dissenters in England, some doubts as to his Divinity; though it is a question I do not dogmatize upon, never having studied it, and think it needless to busy myself with it now when I expect soon an opportunity of knowing the truth with less trouble. I see no harm, however, in its being believed, if that belief has the good consequence, as probably it has, of making his doctrines more respected and more observed....

Why do I say that Franklin is here anticipating pragmatism? Well, not for ordinary everyday reasons. Notice his belief that if it is useful for something to be believed, then it ought to be believed, which suggests either that it is true because useful or else that the question of truth and falsity is beside the point. Though this is hardly an accurate rendition of pragmatism, it is an account of a version of it that became widely accepted as the message of pragmatism, and it anticipates James' pragmatic theory of truth, which bears some resemblance to it, by quite some number of years.

In the transcendentalist period there was a turning inward, to the improvement of the soul and the spirit. But philosophy was still conceived of as having an essentially practical character—indeed, as being the most important thing on earth, since it relates to the care of one's soul. And it was thought that one could change the world, yes, literally change the world, by changing one's soul. We now live in a period—post-Vietnam—where it is thought that philosophy to justify itself must be applied to all sorts of practical matters, and I gather that that idea has flown across the Atlantic eastwards and is now established in Britain. As I said before, some fallacies come back. (We also live in a philosophical period when it is widely held, by some of the most narrowly influential thinkers, that one's outlook, called a conceptual scheme, determines, literally determines, one's world. This was the import of Transcendentalism, though it was not elaborated and put forward with such highly technical apparatus.)

Now the reason philosophy of culture is so important in the American philosophical tradition is that there was, in most of the most important American thinkers, a conviction that philosophy can and must relate to life and the interests of life, as these are defined outside of philosophical concerns, and for most of them their philosophies were responses to and grew out of reflection on the problems of life. It was Dewey's stated aim to reconstruct philosophy so as to redirect it from the problems of philosophy to dealing with, as he put it, the 'problems of men'. And in this he was not so far off the mainstream. Thus in American philosophy, philosophy of culture and in relation to culture, and consequently philosophy of education, assumed a prominent role, because American thinkers, more than any others I know of, had this interest, felt impelled to have this interest, and thought that philosophy should have such relations. Thus we also find in the context of American philosophy a revival of the ancient idea that a philosophy is something to live by, and that it is unbefitting the dignity of human beings not to have a philosophy to live by. This was not, to be sure, especially true of Peirce, and it was not until later in his life true of C. I. Lewis, but it was true of James, Royce, Dewey (obviously), Santayana (even he) and Whitehead, and many more—until about forty years or so ago. The main stream of the American philosophical tradition has thus been concerned with the philosophy of life and of society, and technical matters were conceived of as subservient, in the end, to this end. Although Peirce is a pronounced exception, even for Peirce the end was the development of concrete reasonableness, and this also was a practical goal. But Peirce is almost unique—he is actually one of the very few philosophers who really and singlemindedly set out to discover the truth, independently of other considerations.

It is especially because American philosophy had this character and developed in this context that there is special appropriateness in considering American philosophy in relation to American culture, and I have tried to indicate not only the cultural relevance of this way of viewing philosophy but also something of its philosophical relevance.

Technical philosophers, who predominate in the recent tradition in the English-speaking world—which, I will remind you, includes America—tend to have no patience with philosophy described in this way and with such distinctions as I have made, even though, oddly enough, distinctions are the life's blood of such a way of doing philosophy. They are likely to say—I have heard it said—that what I have been talking about is not true or real philosophy, but something else under an alias.

Of course highly technical philosophy is not distinctively national in any way. It has the abstract impersonal character of mathematics and physics. And for those who aspire to philosophize only on such heights the idea of a national philosophy or of a philosophy expressing a culture will seem either nonsense or something mischievous. They are none the less ignoring—or trying to escape, for some possibly neurotic reason of their own—something that is distinctively philosophical.

Is Rudolf Carnap an American philosopher? The question is absurd; not because Carnap was a refugee from Nazi oppression who came to America fairly late in life—but because of the sort of philosophy Carnap did and aspired to do and the conception of philosophy he espoused. Similarly for others of the positivist persuasion, though there was a time when that was distinctively Viennese.

In order for the question of the national or cultural bearings of a philosophy to make sense, the philosophy must say something about culture and society—it must have, in other words, a moral or social philosophy, even if only implicitly. If it is only philosophy of mathematics, the question is as odd as any can be. But the philosophy of mathematics, though certainly important, is not the model for philosophy as a whole, which cannot be modelled by anything other than itself.

This sort of study may not be philosophy as philosophy has been understood in Anglo-American analytic circles for some forty or fifty years, and it may not be philosophy as it is understood in the haunts and graveyards of existentialism, but it is philosophy none the less. The standards for evaluating instances of it as good or bad may not be the same as those for evaluating other instances of philosophy. There are such standards none the less, which derive from the activity itself, not from something other than it. The question is not whether the thing in question is philosophy in any standard sense of philosophy current in academic life today, or even whether it conforms to the paradigm handed down by Plato and Aristotle, but whether this thinking is philosophical in character, informed by philosophy even though not directed to standard topics of philosophy. The latter is a subject matter conception of philosophy, which takes it to be the special science of, say, sense data and universals and reference. The former is context and method orientated.

To those who say that this is not philosophy but something else, culture study or intellectual history, or—worse yet—literary criticism, the reply is simple and obvious: there is more in philosophy than is dreamt of in your philosophy, or your simple conception of it, and a good thing it is too.

But I here wax dialectical and contentious, and that was not the spirit in which I started or that I had hoped to inculcate. As Whitehead once observed, philosophy is not—or at least, ought not to be—a ferocious debate between irritable professors.[10]

---

[10] A. N. Whitehead, *Adventures of Ideas* (Cambridge: University Press, 1933), Ch. 6, 125 (Penguin edn, 1942, 121).

Charles Sanders Peirce
1839–1914

VINCENT G. POTTER, SJ

I am honoured and pleased to address you this evening on the life and work of an extraordinary American thinker, Charles Sanders Peirce. Although Peirce is perhaps most often remembered as the father of the philosophical movement known as pragmatism, I would like to impress upon you that he was also, and perhaps, especially, a logician, a working scientist and a mathematician.[1] During his life time Peirce most often referred to himself, and was referred to by his colleagues, as a logician. Furthermore, Peirce spent thirty years actively engaged in scientific research for the US Coast Survey. The National Archives in Washington, DC, holds some five thousand pages of Peirce's reports on this work. Finally, the four volumes of Peirce's mathematical papers edited by Professor Carolyn Eisele eloquently testify to his contributions to that field as well.

These facts are important background to what I have to say this evening. I will talk about Peirce's philosophy, but what I have to say can be properly appreciated only when Pierce's philosophy is understood as growing out of his first-hand experience with experimental science and its methodology. Peirce's pragmatism, I contend, is significantly, even radically, different from that of James or Dewey, because it is the result of his reflections upon his own life in the laboratory and of his thorough, even painstaking, study of logic. Neither James nor Dewey had quite this combination of experience. James was a physician and experimental psychologist, but not a logician. Dewey was a logician but not a working scientist. But Peirce, from his boyhood, lived science, logic and philosophy. From this passionate interest, from this consuming desire to under-

---

[1] See Max H. Fisch, 'Peirce as Scientist, Mathematician, Historian, Logician and Philosopher', *Proceedings of the C. S. Peirce Bicentennial International Congress*, No. 23 Graduate Studies (Lubbock: Texas Tech University, September 1981), 13–34. I want to thank Professor Fisch for his help in preparing this talk. His suggestions and leads to material, historical and philosophical, were invaluable. See Carolyn Eisele, *Studies in the Scientific and Mathematical Philosophy of Charles S. Peirce*, Richard M. Martin (ed.) (The Hague, Paris, New York: Mouton, 1979), 386 pp. See *The New Elements of Mathematics by Charles S. Peirce*, 4 vols (5 books), Carolyn Eisele (ed.) (The Hague, Paris, New York: Mouton, 1976), for Peirce's works on mathematics.

stand the world and our understanding of it, Peirce's pragmatism was born.

The British scientific and philosophical tradition played a major role in shaping Peirce's thought. It is the contribution of those British thinkers, some of whom Peirce knew personally, that I would emphasize this evening, not to flatter this distinguished audience, but because I am convinced that Peirce's distinctive view of pragmatism is in continuity with an authentic British philosophical tradition which antedates the classical empiricist triumvirate of Locke, Berkeley and Hume. We might call this Peirce's 'British Connection'.

Even so, Peirce is not simply a British philosopher who happened to grow up in the Colonies. His pragmatism has a distinctively American spirit about it, although that spirit may be difficult to state succinctly. The so-called 'classical' period of American philosophy is usually said to extend from the end of the American Civil War to just before World War II. During that time, according to some, philosophy in America became American Philosophy.[2] Under the umbrella term 'pragmatism', philosophers in America developed a distinctively American 'spirit', if not a philosophical doctrine. That spirit, put roughly, was that ideas, if they are to merit serious attention, must be practical. They must not remain mere abstractions, but must have some payoff or relevance to the problems of men.

Prior to this classical period, however, philosophy in America was largely a repetition of European thought—mostly British Empiricism but with generous doses of Scottish Commonsensism and a dash of the French Enlightenment. After the Civil War, German thought began to have a major impact on American thinkers. Kant and Hegel gained influence largely through the St Louis Hegelians.[3] About that time too increasing numbers of Americans were going to Germany to study. Among them, for example, was William James. These students returned marked by that experience and enthusiastic to take the German university as the model for the newly born American graduate education. Although Peirce never studied in Germany, he travelled there extensively on scientific business. He knew German philosophical thought through his close study of Kant. Peirce's pragmatism, we might say, was born of British and of German stock. Yet Peirce's 'bantling', as he once called it, had a definite resemblance to its British ancestry in its concern for the empirical. Late in his life, reminiscing about the meetings in Cambridge, Massachusetts, of the 'Metaphysical Club' in the early 1870s, Peirce remarks:

[2] See John E. Smith, *The Spirit of American Philosophy* (New York: Oxford University Press, 1963), vii–xi.
[3] See Woodbridge Riley, *American Thought: from Puritanism to Pragmatism and Beyond* (New York: Peter Smith, 1941), 240–253.

The type of our thought was decidedly British. I, alone of our number, had come upon the threshing floor of philosophy through the doorway of Kant, and even my ideas were acquiring the English accent (CP 5.12).

Only recently has Peirce's work received recognition within the scientific and academic communities in America and Europe.[4] In fact, there have been recent testimonials to his genius which, to some, might seem extravagant. Let me cite just one example. In a paper on Peirce's existential graphs read to the Institute of Mathematics and its Application on 20 January 1981, Professor J. A. Faris, formerly of the Queen's University of Belfast, gave this appraisal of Peirce:

He was a polymath, and because of the extraordinary range of his knowledge and interests, and the great strength and originality of his intellect, I think of him as deserving to be classed along with, for example, Aristotle and Leibniz.[5]

This is to put Pierce in no mean company. If such an appraisal is correct, philosophers, at least, ought not to neglect his views even if only to criticize them.

You may know, too, that recently the German side of pragmatism's family has recognized its descendant. Contemporary German thinkers have taken a more than passing interest in Peirce's semiotic theory and in his understanding of the relation of theory and praxis. I have in mind, of course, among others, the Frankfurt school.[6]

---

[4] See Max H. Fisch, 'The Range of Peirce's Relevance', *The Relevance of Charles Peirce*, Eugene Freeman (ed.) (La Salle, Ill.: Monist Library of Philosophy, 1983), 11–37.

[5] J. A. Faris, 'C. S. Peirce's Existential Graphs', *Bulletin of the Institute of Mathematics and Its Application* **17** (Nov./Dec. 1981), 232.

[6] Thus, for example, in 1976 a two-volume German translation of Peirce by Gerd Wartenberg appeared in Frankfurt. Karl-Otto Apel edited that edition and wrote extensive introductory material. In 1981 an English translation of Apel's book on Peirce, *From Pragmatism to Pragmaticism* appeared in the United States. Finally, it may be surprising that the President of C. S. Peirce Society for the year 1982–83 was Klaus Oehler of Hamburg University, himself a translator of Peirce. No doubt there are many and varied reasons why Peirce has attracted the attention of German thinkers. Apel's reason I find fascinating. He sees Peirce's pragmatism, as distinct from James' and Dewey's, as a dialogue partner for Marxism and from which Marxism has something important to learn. He uses the unusual term 'logical Socialism' to characterize Peirce's theory of inquiry, emphasizing as it does the community of investigators. One wonders whether Apel is searching for an alternative to Marxist 'dogmatic' and unconditioned predictions about the course of history. It might surprise some Americans, I dare say, to think that some aspects of their

While Peirce's recognition by scholarly professionals is perhaps finally assured, still his works are not likely to be read by the general public. William James, Peirce's life-long friend, once described him as full of flashes of brilliance amid Cimmerian darkness.[7] Anyone who has struggled with Peirce's texts knows what James meant. This obscure quality to much of Peirce's writing explains in part the fact that he was in eclipse until relatively recently. Besides, his published papers were few. His voluminous unpublished writings were for many years virtually unavailable. When in the 1930s Charles Hartshorne and Paul Weiss edited the *Collected Papers,* their choice of materials represented only a small part of the manuscripts.[8] A new chronological edition is presently in preparation at the Indianapolis campus of Indiana University which will make available a great deal more of the manuscript material. At present twenty volumes are projected of which two have already appeared[9] and two more are in various stages of preparation. Even this much expanded edition represent only part of the materials which have survived. It is estimated that a complete edition would fill more than a hundred volumes. Still, Peirce's obscure style and the inherent difficulty of his subject matter will most likely keep him off the best-seller list.[10]

---

indigenous philosophy are close enough to Marxism to be an interesting alternative for 'a public, emancipatory mediation of theory and praxis'. Hegel, through Kant, however, is pragmatism's and Marxism's common ancestor. See, *Charles Sanders Peirce: Schriften zum Pragmatismus und Pragmatizismus*, 2nd edn, Karl-Otto Apel (ed.), trans. Gerd Wartenberg (Frankfurt: Suhrkamp, 1976); Karl-Otto Apel, *Charles S. Peirce: From Pragmatism to Pragmaticism*, trans. by M. Krois (Amherst: University of Massachusetts Press, 1981); *Charles S. Peirce: Ueber die Klarheit unserer Gedanken*, trans. by Klaus Oehler (ed.) (Frankfurt a/M: Vittorio Klostermann, 1968).

[7] William James, *Pragmatism: A New Name for Some Old Ways of Thinking* (Cambridge, Mass., and London, England: Harvard University Press, 1975), 10.

[8] *The Collected Papers of Charles Sanders Peirce*, Vols I–VI, Charles Hartshorne and Paul Weiss (eds.) (Cambridge, Mass.: The Belknap Press of Harvard University Press, 1960); Vols VII–VIII, Arthur Burks (ed.) (Cambridge, Mass.: The Belknap Press of Harvard University Press, 1958). I will use the standard convention for reference to these volumes, namely, CP followed by volume and paragraph number: e.g. CP 5.12.

[9] *Writings of Charles S. Peirce: A Chronological Edition*, Vol. 1 (1857–1866) and Vol. 2 (1867–1871) (Bloomington: Indiana University Press, 1982, 1984). The convention for citing from this new Peirce Project Edition is W + arabic volume number + page: e.g. W 1, 12–20.

[10] See Paul Weiss, 'Charles Sanders Peirce', *Dictionary of American Biography* (1934), Vol. 14, 398–403, for an account of Peirce's difficult character and of his divorce in 1883 from his first wife, Harriet Melusina Fay, and his

Now that Peirce's papers have been more thoroughly examined by a growing number of scholars, the close connection between his personal experience of science and his pragmatic philosophy is becoming ever more evident. Let us consider, then, how that connection grew strong and assumed a definite character through his ties, formed by personal acquaintance and by study of their work, to Britain's philosophers and men of science. And to begin, some biographical information may be helpful so that we grasp Peirce's life-long devotion to scientific investigation.

Two hundred years before Charles' birth in Cambridge, Massachusetts, a certain John Pers, then in his forties, left Norwich, England, for Massachusetts.[11] The Peirces prospered in the New World through their having entered the shipping trade of the East India Company. The family moved to Cambridge when Charles' grandfather, Benjamin, left the shipping business and became librarian at Harvard University. His son, Benjamin, Jr, Charles' father, graduated from Harvard and eventually was appointed professor of astronomy and mathematics there. Charles was born on 10 September 1839 in Cambridge a few years before his father's appointment, the second of five children. His father recognized Charles' mathematical genius and introduced him while yet a child, to mathematics, physical science and logic. Charles was constantly in the company of the scientific community at Harvard and learned from them a love and respect for scientific investigation. At the age of eight he took up the study of chemistry on his own with the encouragement of his uncle, Charles Henry Peirce, himself a physician. At thirteen he mastered his older brother's logic textbook (Whately's *Elements of Logic)* and at fifteen entered Harvard College from which four years later he graduated one of the youngest of his class. Charles found the rigid Harvard system of those days something less than a challenge. It was not until Charles studied chemistry at Harvard's Lawrence Scientific School that his academic achievement reflected his natural ability. In 1863 he received his Bachelor of Science *summa cum laude,* the first Harvard student ever to do so.

remarriage to the French woman Juliette Froissy. At about this time Peirce was notified that his appointment at the Johns Hopkins University where he was a part-time logic instructor (the only regular academic post he held) would not be renewed. He retired to the small Pennsylvania town of Milford where he lived in virtual academic isolation until his death from cancer in 1914.

[11] Most of the biographical material which follows comes from the following works of Max Fisch: 'Peirce as Scientist, Mathematician, Historian, Logician, and Philosopher', *Proceedings of the C. S. Peirce Bicentennial International Congress*, 13–34 (cf. note 1); 'The Range of Peirce's Relevance', *The Relevance of Charles Peirce*, 11–37 (cf. note 4); 'Introduction', *Writings of Charles S. Peirce*, Vol. 1, xv–xxxv (cf. note 9); 'Introduction', *Writings of Charles S. Peirce*, Vol. 2, xxi–xxxvi; 'Supplement: A Chronicle of Pragmaticism, 1865–1879', *The Monist* **48** (July 1964), 441–466.

During those years (1861–63) at the Lawrence School, Peirce began to work for the US Coast and Geodetic Survey with which he remained for over thirty years. From 1872 to 1875 he was assistant at the Harvard Observatory during which time he made the astronomical observations, published in 1878 under the title *Photometric Researches,* which won him election to the National Academy of Science in 1877. In 1867 he had already been elected to the American Academy of Arts and Sciences.

While Peirce's training was strongly scientific, he also developed during his Harvard days an interest in philosophy. He tells us that, as an undergraduate, he and his roommate, Horatio Paine, read and expounded to one another, as best they could, Schiller's *Aesthetische Briefe.* At about this time too he came under the influence of Kant, his most important non-British philosophical connection. He read the *Critique of Pure Reason* so many times that he had whole passages committed to memory. By the late 1860s Peirce's philosophical accomplishments were well enough known that Harvard invited him to deliver during the 1869–70 academic year a series of lectures on the British logicians.

Peirce visited England five times between 1870 and 1883 and while there got to know many of the most prominent British scientists, mathematicians and logicians. He also won their esteem for his scientific, mathematical and logical acumen. W. K. Clifford called him the greatest living logician[12] and this high opinion was concretely attested to by his election in 1880 to the London Mathematical Society.

Peirce's five journeys to Europe were all connected with his scientific work with the Coast and Geodetic Survey. His first visit to London was in 1870 when he was sent by the Survey as an advance party to check sites for the observation of the solar eclipse due to occur on 22 December 1870. On his second visit in 1875–76 he visited the newly built Cavendish Laboratory at Cambridge University and consulted with Maxwell concerning the flexure of the pendulum. In 1877 Peirce returned a third time to Europe to deliver a paper to the International Geodetic Association in Stuttgart. It was during this ocean crossing that Peirce wrote his best-known article, 'How to Make Our Ideas Clear' in which he first formulated the so-called pragmatic maxim. In order to practise his French, Peirce composed it in that language and later translated it into English. The English version, however, was published first in *Popular Science Monthly* and about a year later the French version appeared in *Revue philosophique.* This essay was the second in a series of six which appeared in *Popular Science Monthly* under the general title 'Illustrations of the Logic of Science'. It seems that Peirce had hoped to publish all six articles in French and in German as well

---

[12] Edward L. Youmans, editor of the *Popular Science Monthly*, writing from London to his sister in the United States on 29 October, 1877, reports Clifford's remark. Cited by Fisch in 'Supplement', op. cit. (note 11), 461.

as in English. Only the first two articles, however, appeared in French and none appeared in German.

In 1880 and 1883, respectively, Peirce made his final voyages to Europe. Not only was he then elected to the London Mathematical Society but also was a frequent guest of Clifford, Jevons, Spencer and other friends at the Royal Society, the Athenaeum Club and the Metaphysical Society.

So far we have been considering Peirce's lived experience as a working scientist who had established personal and professional ties with British mathematicians, logicians and experimentalists. Before we take a look at how some of the British thinkers shaped Peirce's view of philosophy and of logic as methodology, it may be well to recall Peirce's first formulation, in 1878, of the celebrated pragmatic maxim:

> It appears, then, that the rule for attaining the third grade of clearness of apprehension is as follows: consider what effects, that might conceivably have practical bearings, we conceive the object of our conception to have. Then, our conception of these effects is the whole of our conception of the object (CP 5.402)

Just what Peirce meant by this formulation, I trust, will become clearer as we proceed.

Peirce thought that to do philosophy well, it was absolutely essential to get logic straight. We know from any number of his papers that Peirce greatly esteemed the work of British logicians. One such paper is 'Why Study Logic?' (CP 2.119–216) intended to be part of a book he never published, 'Minute Logic'. In it Peirce contrasts what he calls 'the English position' on reasoning (e.g. Boole, De Morgan, Whewell, J. S. Mill, Jevons, Venn *et al.*) with 'the German position' (Sigwart, Wundt, Schuppe, Erdmann, Bergmann, Husserl *et al.*) and comes down unequivocally on the side of the English. As Peirce sees it, the English consider logic to be objective, while the Germans consider it to be subjective. The English come to logic with their characteristic empirical frame of mind. The 'English position' opposes any doctrine which bases the soundness of reasoning upon a sense of or feeling for rationality. For Peirce, there is neither a logical taste nor a logical instinct nor a logical 'Gefuehl' in terms of which we recognize an argument as sound.[13] He rejects any attempt to reduce logic to intuition or to psychology. In effect, Peirce sees logic as the science of how one *ought* to think, not of how one *must* think. Logic then is a normative science and reasoning is reasoning only if it is subject to critical control. Such critical control is exercised in terms of the purpose of any reasoning, namely, to avoid disappointments and disasters. The hard facts are what we want to know, he writes. The whole motive of

[13] One would infer that Peirce would not have much sympathy with James' 'Sentiment of Rationality'.

one's reasoning is to prepare for them. Reasoning is to be judged sound, therefore, in so far as those hard facts will not and cannot disappoint what reason promises. How one feels about any mode of reasoning has nothing to do with it. 'That is the *rationale* of the English doctrine. It is a perfect as it is simple' (CP 2.173).

I think it worth nothing that Peirce's preference for the 'English position' makes the norm for logical validity *empirical* in two ways: (1) it makes reasoning to consist in the observation and manipulation of diagrams or 'graphs' and (2) it makes reasoning the means of attaining truth, that is, of discovering what is the case independently of what anyone might think or wish or hope. I am convinced that this objectivist view of logic led to two of Peirce's most important and original contributions to the field, namely, his system of existential graphs to diagram his logic of relatives[14] and his broadening the notion of logic to include methodology (or a logic of discovery) by distinguishing inference into adduction, deduction and induction.

Peirce was influenced in his thinking about science and its methodology not only by Britain's men of science and logicians but also by her philosophers. Since it would be impossible in the time which remains to us to treat all the British philosophers whom Peirce had studied, I will select three, each one of whom made a direct and positive contribution to his pragmatism. Two of them, Alexander Bain and William Whewell, were Peirce's contemporaries. The third, John Duns Scotus, flourished more than five hundred years earlier. Scotus inspired Peirce's version of realism; Whewell confirmed his interpretation of scientific method; and Bain furnished his logic with a psychological framework. I suggest that we begin with Scotus.

Peirce considered the nominalist–realist controversy the most important philosophical issue on the solution of which just about everything else depended. In a long letter to Victoria Lady Welby in 1909, after recounting to her his early training, he writes:

> By this time the inexactitude of the Germans, and their tottering logic utterly disgusted me. I more and more admired British thought. Its one great and terrible fault, which my severe studies in the schoolmen rescued me from,—or rather, it was because I suspected they were right about this that I took to the study of them & found that they didn't go far enough to satisfy me,—was their extreme Nominalism. To be sure *all* modern philosophers were nominalists, even Hegel. But I was quite convinced they were absolutely wrong. Modern science, especially physics, is and must be . . . essentially on the side of scholastic realism.[15]

[14] See Faris, op. cit. (note 5), and Don Roberts, *The Existential Graphs of Charles S. Peirce* (The Hague, Paris: Mouton, 1973).

[15] *Semiotic and Significs: The Correspondence between Charles S. Peirce and Victoria Lady Welby*, Charles S. Hardwick (ed.) (Bloomington: Indiana University Press, 1977), 114–115.

28

Scotus defended realism; Ockham championed nominalism. Peirce's account of how the nominalists assumed ascendency in the universities, casting out the Dunces, as they were called, makes it a political rather than an intellectual matter. However that may have been, the important thing is to recall what was at stake, what the issue was between these two British thinkers. Peirce put it this way in one place:

> Roughly speaking, the nominalists conceived the *general* element of cognition to be merely a convenience for understanding this and that fact and to amount to nothing except for cognition, while the realists, still more roughly speaking, looked upon the general, not only as the end and aim of knowledge, but also as the most important element of being. Such was and is the question (CP 4.1)

The earliest published statement of Peirce's siding with the realists in this controversy is the 1868 paper 'Some Consequences of Four Incapacities' in the *Journal of Speculative Philosophy*. There he developed his notions of Truth and of Reality which so far as I can tell he never retracted. Again in 1871 in his critical review of Fraser's edition of the works of Berkeley in the *North American Review* he reiterated and developed his convictions about 'scholastic realism'. When I say that Peirce opted for 'scholastic realism', I am using his own expression. Whether Peirce thought that his realism was indeed that of Scotus, I am not sure. I rather think, however, that he realized that his version was significantly different, for he says that even Scotus was tinged with nominalism (CP 1.560) in his insistence on *haecceitas* contracting the universal to the particular (CP 8.208). Furthermore, he characterized his realism as 'extreme' over against Scotus' more moderate view (CP 5.77, 5.470). Finally, Peirce frequently identified his realism with that proposed by his friend and colleague Francis E. Abbot in his book *Scientific Theism* in which Abbot consciously modified the realism of the scholastics along the lines of modern scientific systems. Abbot called his view 'Relational-ism'.[16] Other commentators, such as John Boler, have suggested other differences.[17] All that the phrase need mean is that Peirce was inspired by the scholastic realists and developed a position something like theirs. They and he held that some general conceptions are real, that is, some are not mere figments of the mind.

According to Peirce, the nominalist would reason something like this. Nothing is immediately present to us but thoughts. Those thoughts,

[16] Francis E. Abbot, *Scientific Theism* (Boston: Little, Brown & Co., 1885).
[17] See John Boler, 'Peirce, Ockham and Scholastic Realism', *The Relevance of Charles Peirce*, 93–106; *Charles Peirce and Scholastic Realism* (Seattle: University of Washington Press, 1963). See also Michael L. Raposa, 'Habits and Essences', *Transactions of the Charles S. Peirce Society* **20** (Spring 1984), 147–167.

however, are caused by sensations which in turn are constrained by something out of the mind. Because this something is out of the mind, it is independent of how we think, and is, therefore, the real. Whatever these external things be they produce sensations which can be embraced under some conception. One can say, for example, that one man is like another, but there is no way in which one can justly claim that two real men have anything in common. One knows only the mental term or thought-sign, 'man', standing indifferently for the sets of sensations caused by the two external realities. Strictly speaking, the sets of sensations do not have anything at all in common either. Such a view makes reality to consist exclusively in bare particulars which, because they are outside of consciousness, are unknowable things-in-themselves.

Peirce, the realist, however, looks at it in quite another way. Although all human thought contains an arbitrary and accidental element which limits it according to the circumstances and powers of the individuals, still human opinion tends, in the long run, to a definite form. If inquiry is pursued long enough and information enough is available to the inquirers, no matter how different (or even erroneous) their initial opinion, and no matter how idiosyncratic their initial circumstances, their final conclusion will be identical. A deaf man and a blind man may witness the same event in very different ways but conclude that they witnessed the *same* event. The realist thinks that there is an answer to every genuine question which is arrived at in the long run, that is, at the *end* of inquiry. Such an answer consists not in the particular sensations of singular men but of the truths about objects expressed in and through general terms. What those truths express is independent, not of thought in general, but of all that is arbitrary and individual in thought. It is quite independent of how you, or I, or any number of men think. This, according to Peirce, is the real and nothing else.

Peirce opines that such a conception of reality is fatal to the idea of the thing-in-itself. There is no reality which is incognizable although there may be much that is not yet actually known by you or me or any number of men. Since the thing-in-itself, according to Peirce, is literally unthinkable, Kant must be corrected.

Peirce's realism is to be understood in terms of his categories and he arrived at his categorial scheme through logic. He was convinced that all predicates were relations and those relations were monadic, dyadic, or triadic. Any higher polyadic relation could be analysed into some combination of those three. Yet those three could not be resolved into simpler components. Hence monad, dyad, triad were both necessary and sufficient to account for any more complex predicate (that is, one with more relatives). But this suggested that the fundamental categories of being were also three and only three which Peirce denominated respectively Firstness, Secondness and Thirdness. Firstness was the category of sheer possibility, a 'may-be' or 'might be'. Secondness was the category of actuality, an 'is' or 'are'. Thirdness was the category of the necessary (in the sense of the destined), a 'would-be' or 'would-do'. Each category is really distinct from and irreducible to every other even though they cannot be separated in our experience. We can distinguish them in thought by precisive abstraction in a definite, non-reversible order. Thus one can prescind Secondness (actuality) from Thirdness (the destined), and First-ness (mere possibility) from Secondness. One can, however, experience neither Firstness nor Secondness without Thirdness. The third category, then, mediates between the airy shadows of mere possibility and the brute force of actuality. It is properly the category of thought, of regularity, or lawlikeness, and so is the category of the Real *par excellence*. Peirce's realism, then, means at least this: 'would-be's' are neither a collection of actuals (no matter how large) nor a mere figment of one's mind (no matter how convenient). The Real is what would be or what would happen if certain conditions were fulfilled—and that independently of what you or I or anyone else might happen to think.

Finally, then, keep in mind that Peirce distinguished the real from the existent. General conceptions are real (they are not figments dependent upon anyone's thinking) but they do not exist. Existence is a distinct category from that of Reality. The former designates brute force, mere action–reaction, while the latter designates regularity, continuity, law. In short, the real is what is destined, that is, what would be in the long run under certain conditions.[18]

I have dwelt upon Peirce's realism at length because he considered it essential to his pragmatism. It is pragmatism's realism which allows it to be empirical but not positivist. Peirce further was convinced that the realist interpretation of pragmatism was the only one which would recommend itself to a working scientist familiar with the history of science who had carefully studied logic as method. James, for example, was a working scientist but had steadfastly avoided logic. Mill, on the other hand, had studied logic but was not a working scientist. Both, according to Peirce, were nominalists.

James dedicated his book, *Pragmatism,* to John Stuart Mill. 'To the memory of John Stuart Mill', he writes, 'from whom I first learned the pragmatic openness of mind and whom my fancy likes to picture as our leader were he alive to-day'.[19] Peirce would certainly not fancy Mill as leader of his kind of pragmatism. If he were to choose such a leader, it would have been another British scientist and logician, William Whewell.

[18] See Vincent G. Potter, SJ, *Charles S. Peirce: On Norms and Ideals* (Amherst: University of Massachusetts Press, 1968), 8–24, for a discussion of Peirce's categories.

[19] William James, *Pragmatism*, dedication.

In the 1840s a lively controversy arose between Mill and Whewell precisely on the nature of scientific inquiry and discovery. Peirce definitely sided with Whewell and always thought of him as the one who pointed the way to a correct undestanding of the nature of scientific investigation. Max Fisch has summed up the matter well:

> Apart from its [Peirce's Harvard lectures on 'British logicians' in the academic year 1868–69] including Peirce's first public exposition of the logic of relations, and showing the fruits of a deeper study of Duns Scotus and of Ockham, the course inaugurates Peirce's lifelong championship of Whewell against Mill in the 'logic of science'. Whewell was himself a scientist (indeed he coined the word); Mill is not. Whewell was also a historian of science; Mill is not. Whewell followed Kant; Mill does not. Whewell was a realist; Mill is a nominalist.[20]

The precise point at issue in this celebrated controversy was the nature of induction. Mill contended that induction is simply the tying together of observed facts while Whewell maintained that such colligation required the introduction of a new Idea. Mill seemed to think that facts are quite independent of theory, while Whewell insisted that fact and theory are relative to each other. Mill contended, for example, that in the case of Kepler's discovering planetary motion to be elliptical, it was simply a matter of Kepler's reporting an observed fact without adding anything to it. Mill asserts that this fact, found in the motion of Mars, was just the sum of the observations. Whewell held that the elliptical orbit was not simply the sum of observations but rather the very hypothesis of the orbit being an ellipse suggested how the observations might be accounted for. The introduction by Kepler of a new idea provided a new perspective from which to interpret the observations. Whewell did not think that Kepler simply imposed an idea on reality. On the contrary, Whewell suggested that Kepler *discovered* the fact that Mars' orbit was elliptical in and through an hypothesis. The point is Whewell realized that science does not discover facts simply by 'reading them off'. Fact in science is more often than not confirmed theory.[21]

Whewell was accused of being a 'mere Kantist' (by Professor Bowen according to Peirce; W 2, 341) dragging '*a priori's*' into science in a very

----

[20] 'Supplement', *The Monist*, 450.
[21] Whewell's major works on inductive method were *History of the Inductive Sciences* first published in 1837 and *The Philosophy of the Inductive Sciences, founded upon their History* first published in 1840. Both went through several editions. For good accounts of Whewell's controversy with Mill, see E. W. Strong, 'William Whewell and John Stuart Mill: Their Controversy about Scientific Knowledge', *Journal of the History of Ideas* 16 (1955), 209–231; C. J. Ducasse, 'Whewell's Philosophy of Scientific Discovery', *Philosophical Review* 60 (1951), 56–69, 213–234.

rationalistic way. In his Harvard lecture on Whewell Peirce defended him against this charge (made, he says, out of ignorance). While Whewell's point may fit in with Kant's analysis, it did not arise *from* Kant's analysis. It arose rather from the history of scientific discoveries. The fact is that scientists do their research in this way. Peirce would have been better satisfied if Whewell had explicitly rejected Kant's *noumenon,* for then the allegation of his being a 'mere Kantist' would not have been made.

That James should have adopted Mill and Peirce, Whewell, as their respective patrons should lead us to suspect that the differences between their understanding of pragmatism involve the difference between a nominalistic and a realistic understanding of human cognition as inquiry. Shortly, I will try to show you that this is indeed the case. But before I do, let us consider Alexander Bain's contribution to Peirce's pragmatic theory.

In the latter half of the nineteenth century Bain's works on psychology were standard treatises.[22] Peirce and James knew them well. Peirce once remarked that pragmatism 'is scarce more than a corollary' from Bain's definition of belief (CP 5.12). According to Bain, belief is that upon which one is prepared to act. Peirce adopted Bain's view of belief in his 1878 version of pragmatism. In fact, it served as the psychological framework for Peirce's logic throughout his career. But in the late 1860s and the early 1870s Bain's position was disputed by John Stuart Mill. In 1869 Mill published a new edition of his father's (James Mill's) *Analysis of the Phenomena of the Human Mind* to which he and Bain added essays critical of James Mill's theory of belief and of each other's. The details of this controversy need not detain us except to say that James Mill thought belief to consist in indissoluble associative bonds and John Stuart thought it consisted in some other mysterious residuum.

Bain's own theory of belief underwent several revisions. These revisions reveal an uncertainty as to whether belief was essentially intellectual or volitional. This waffling is important because it helps explain, I think, the difference Peirce thought he saw between his pragmatism and James' and, besides, helps explain some ambiguity in Peirce's own 1878 version of pragmatism. Permit me to explain.

Bain's problem was to decide whether belief was essentially a fact of intellect or of will. In his 1869 essay for the James Mill re-edition of *Analysis* he called it an error to think of belief as 'mainly a fact of the

[22] Those treatises are: *The Senses and the Intellect* (1855) and *The Emotions and the Will* (1859). A one-volume abridgement appeared in 1868 under the title *Mental Science.* For a careful historical study of what and how the members of the 'Metaphysical Club', at Cambridge at whose meetings Peirce first formulated pragmatism, knew about Bain's definition of belief, see Max H. Fisch, 'Alexander Bain and the Genealogy of Pragmatism', *Journal of the History of Ideas* **13** (June 1954), 413–444, on which I heavily depend for my presentation.

Intellect, with a certain participation of feelings'. There he insisted that belief is essentially a development of our active nature of will. Elsewhere around this time he admitted that belief always contains intellectual elements but they do not constitute the attitude of believing, because nothing in mere intellect makes us act or contemplate action and hence nothing in it makes us believe. In 1872, however, in an appendix to the third edition of his *Mental Science,* he admits it to be an error to make the fundamental nature of belief 'the Spontaneous Activity of the System'. Now belief is 'a primitive disposition to follow out any sequence that has been once experienced, and to expect the result', He now calls it a fact of our intellectual nature and only its energy comes from emotions and will. Again in 1875 in the third edition of *The Emotions and the Will* Bain makes the same move toward intellect even though the chapter on belief contains expressions like these: belief is 'essentially related to Action, that is, volition . . .; Action is the basis, and ultimate criterion, of belief . . .' Peirce criticized James and other pragmatists for making action the be-all and end-all of thought.[23] Without doubt the expressions which gave rise to that criticism are traceable to Bain.

I suspect that Bain's indecision concerning the essence of belief comes from a failure sharply to distinguish the act of believing from what is believed. Belief as an act of adherence to some opinion can plausibly be understood as consisting in one's readiness to act. And it seems unobjectionable to hold that actually acting in a way appropriate to the circumstances is the test of whether one truly believes something or not. But this does not immediately and directly yield a criterion for deciding the meaning of what is believed (or not believed). It is with this second, the meaning of what is believed, that the pragmatic maxim is concerned. The maxim then is not simply a restatement of Bain's definition of belief but, as Peirce thought, a conclusion to be drawn from that definition. That conclusion once drawn, however, will be differently understood depending on whether one thinks the act of believing is volitional (James, perhaps) or intellectual (Peirce, for certain).

But just how did Peirce draw the pragmatic maxim as a corollary from Bain's definition of belief in his 1878 article?[24] He argued as follows: thinking is stimulated by the irritation of doubt and ceases when that irritation is removed by the fixation of belief. Belief is a conscious appeasement of doubt establishing in us a habit or rule of action. Beliefs are distinguished from one another by the modes of action to which they give rise. To determine *what* we believe (not *that* we believe) is to determine what habits the thought in question involves. To determine what habits a thought involves is to determine what sensible result would follow from

[23] CP 5.429, 8.256.
[24] CP 5.394–402.

the action so dictated by the thought under certain specifiable sensible conditions. Hence he concluded:

> Thus our action has exclusive reference to what affects the senses, our habit has the same bearing as our action, our belief the same as our habit, our conception the same as our belief. . . . Our idea of anything *is* our idea of its sensible effects; . . . (CP 5.401).

But this is the pragmatic maxim.

One final note before bidding Bain farewell. By adopting the doubt–belief framework Peirce shifts the emphasis from thought taken as an isolated cognitive incident, to thought taken as an on-going process of discovery. In the series of articles published in *The Journal of Speculative Philosophy* in 1868–69 Peirce argued that there is no intuitive cognition and that all thought is in signs.[25] It followed that there is no first cognition and that a thought is interpreted only by another thought. Peirce never abandoned this position but after adopting Bain's psychology of belief the cognitive continuum was understood as a continuum of inquiry, that is, a continuum of doubt–inquiry–belief.[26]

We have considered the influence on Peirce's pragmatism of Scotus' 'scholastic realism', Whewell's logic of discovery and Bain's analysis of belief. But just how was Peirce's understanding of pragmatism different from other versions which proliferated after James had made the maxim popular? That Peirce thought his was significantly different is clear from the fact that he adopted another term for his, 'pragmaticism', a term, he says, ugly enough to be safe from kidnappers (CP 5.414).

All this time I have been referring to Peirce's pragmatism on the assumption that you know just what it is. I am sure that you all do at least in a general way. Since my next section will compare Peirce's understanding of the pragmatic maxim with James', perhaps it is time to let Peirce tell you what he had in mind by it. In 1906 Peirce wrote:

> I understand pragmatism to be a method of ascertaining the meanings, not of all ideas, but only of what I call 'intellectual concepts', that is to say, of those upon the structure of which, arguments concerning objective fact may hinge (CP 5.467).

Peirce is excluding what he calls 'feelings' from the pragmatic test of meaning. According to him feelings, such as the sensation of red or of blue, have no intrinsic significance beyond themselves. Concepts in the proper sense, however, essentially carry some implication concerning the general behaviour of some conscious being or of some inanimate object.

[25] CP 5.213–357; W 2,193–272.
[26] Fisch, 'Alexander Bain', 438–442, for discussion of Peirce's pre- and post-Bain approach to knowing.

Let us then compare Peirce's and James' version of the pragmatic maxim. Peirce's original fomulation for *Popular Science Monthly* in 1878 goes thus:

> It appears, then, that the rule for attaining the third grade of clearness of apprehension is as follows: consider what effects, that might conceivably have practical bearings, we conceive the object of our conception to have. Then, our conception of these effects is the whole of our conception of the object (CP 5.402).

Here is James' version as expressed in a lecture entitled 'Philosophical Conceptions and Practical Results', delivered at the University of California at Berkeley on 26 August, 1898 (by the way, the first time that the term 'Pragmatism' was used publicly and explicitly attributed to Peirce as its originator):

> To attain perfect clearness in our thoughts of an object, then, we need only consider what conceivable effects of a practical kind the object may involve—what sensations we are to expect from it, and what reactions we must prepare. Our conception of these effects, whether immediate or remote, is then for us the whole of our conception of the object, so far as that conception has positive significance at all.[27]

The general similarity between the two versions is unmistakeable. There is even parallelism in expression and I suppose this is not to be wondered at since James explicitly credits Peirce with the version he just presented. There are differences, however, and in Peirce's mind at least they were crucial.[28] First let us identify some of these differences and then show their significance. In the first place James speaks of attaining 'perfect clearness' while Peirce makes no such statement. In fact in the essay from which Peirce's maxim is taken, 'How to Make Our Ideas Clear', Peirce speaks of grades of clearness. These grades are only relative since there is no such thing as perfect clarity. All conceptions are general signs and so are always to some extent vague.

In the second place James adds a phrase, presumably to clarify what he means by 'conceivable effects of a practical kind', namely, what *sensations* we are to expect. In fact immediately after giving that statement of the pragmatic maxim (rather close to Peirce's) James restates it, expressing it, he says, 'more broadly'. This Jamesian interpretation goes like this:

[27] William James, 'Philosophical Conceptions and Practical Results', *The University Chronical* (Berkeley, California, September 1898); reprinted in *Collected Essays and Reviews* (1920), 406–437.

[28] Vincent G. Potter, 'Peirce's Pragmatic Maxim', *Tijdschrift voor Filosofie* **35** (September 1973), 505–517, where I develop the differences between Peirce and James at some length.

The ultimate test for us of what a truth means is indeed the conduct which it dictates or inspires. But it inspires that conduct because it first foretells some particular turn to our experience which shall call for just that conduct from us. And I should prefer for our purposes this evening to express Peirce's principle by saying that the effective meaning of any philosophic proposition can always be brought down to some particular consequence, in our future practical experience, whether active or passive, the point lying rather in the fact that the experience must be particular, than in the fact that it must be active.[29]

Peirce speaks neither of practical effects nor of sensations nor of particulars. He refers to what 'might *conceivably* have practical bearings', and to 'our *conception* of these effects'. The issue here is what is the concept's interpretant. James seems to think it is sensation, while Peirce seems to think it is another concept for he speaks of the *conceivable* practical bearings the object of our thought might have.

In the third place, the title of James' talk refers to 'practical results' and in the section where he refers to the maxim as Peirce's James calls it 'the principle of practicalism'. Peirce in fact reacted sharply to the use of 'practical' and 'pragmatic' interchangeably. He insisted that he himself, at any rate, distinguished these terms as Kant did[30] and for whom they 'were as far apart as the two poles' (CP 5.412).

There are then at least three points of difference between James' and Peirce's formulation of the pragmatic maxim: (1) perfect clarity in contrast to relative clarity of conceptions, (2) sensations and particulars in contrast to conceptions and generals as interpretants of thought, and (3) practicalism in contrast to pragmatism or pragmaticism. The significance of these differences seems to me to be the following. James' supposition that there is 'perfect' clarity of conceptions entails that they are perfectly definite and determinate. If an idea's definiteness and determinateness were *perfect*, the idea would have no generality and hence would be reduced to a sensation. For Peirce, every general conception, as general, is intrinsically vague, that is, in some respect indefinite and indeterminate.[31] A *perfectly* clear and distinct *general* idea is a contradiction in terms. To think that an idea's meaning is nothing but the sum total of the particulars for which it actually stands is, according to Pierce, a nominalistic error since no number of actual particulars exhaust a concept's meaning. If there are

[29] James, 'Philosophical Conceptions', 412.

[30] Kant, *Anthropologie in pragmatischer Hinsicht* (Leipzig: Modes und Baumann, 1839), Vorrede.

[31] I have discussed vagueness in 'C. S. Peirce's Argument for God's Reality: A Pragmatist's View', *The Papin Festschrift: Wisdom and Knowledge* (Villanova: The Villanova University Press, 1976), 229–230; and in my book *On Norms and Ideals*, 89–90; see, CP 5.505–508, 5.447–408, 3.93–94; 2.357.

general ideas, therefore, they must be to some degree indeterminate and indefinite. Furthermore, what those ideas represent must be real (not mere mental figments), otherwise, Peirce argues, scientific prediction could not be explained.

James' insistence on 'what sensations we are to expect' and on 'some particular turn to our experience' also imply a nominalistic view. In his article on pragmatism in Baldwin's *Dictionary of Philosophy and Psychology* (1902) Peirce remarks that James pushed the pragmatic method 'to such extremes as must give us pause'. He continued:

> The doctrine appears to assume that the end of man is action. . . . If it be admitted, on the contrary, that action wants an end, and that that end must be something of a general description, then the spirit of the maxim itself, which is that we must look to the upshot of our concepts in order rightly to apprehend them, would direct us toward something different from practical facts, namely to general ideas, as the true interpreters of our thought . . . the meaning of the concept does not lie in any individual reactions at all, but in the manner in which those reactions contribute to that development [of concrete reasonableness] (CP 5.3).

For Peirce action cannot be an interpretant of thought because action, that is, the acting itself, is concrete and singular. No one acts in general but performs this or that action. Thought, on the other hand, always has an element of generality. Hence thought and action cannot be identified nor can thought be interpreted by action.[32] Thought and action are certainly intimately related. Thought no doubt *applies* to action in the sense that it is to be interpreted in terms of the *habits* of behaviour or action which call for certain kinds of action under certain conditions. But then this is action as conceived, or thought about, and so generalized.

Finally, the significance of Peirce's insistence on the term 'pragmatism' over against James' interchanging it with 'practicalism' is to be found in Peirce's efforts to eliminate an ambiguity in the whole notion of practical bearings or effects.[33] Certainly the term 'practical' has several meanings. In one sense it simply means action or behaviour. In this sense all human

---

[32] See CP 5.475–493. Peirce gives here a long explanation of what he means by 'interpretant'. He distinguishes three interpretants: emotional, energetic and logical. The emotional is the feeling produced by the sign; the energetic is the effort, mental or physical, elicited by the sign; and the logical is the sign's rational purport. The pragmatic maxim is meant to clarify a sign's rational purport. Pierce concludes that the final logical interpretant of a concept can only be a habit (not another concept, not a desire, not an expectation). Action is not a logical interpretant either. It is thought's energetic interpretant (hence there is a connection between thought and action) but it is not thought's rational purport precisely because it lacks generality.

[33] See Smith, *Spirit of American Philosophy*, 13–17.

action is practical. In a second sense it means the immediate relevance of means to ends—in effect 'what works'. In a third sense 'practical' refers to some purpose we have in mind, some end we wish to achieve, which specifies the kind of behaviour which is appropriate. If two thoughts make no practical difference to the purpose one has in mind then they can be considered to mean the same thing with respect to that purpose. Thus a carpenter can consider two boards to be of equal length if whatever small difference there is between them makes no difference to what he intends to make. Peirce seems to think that James slides from the second to the third sense and back again. Peirce wants to make it clear that he means the third sense and so uses Kant's term 'pragmatic'. The sum total of all the conceivable practical bearings upon conduct is what a conception means. Hence Peirce thinks it essential to consider what ends or purposes are possible for and suitable to human endeavour. These ends or purposes are general and interpret our thought in so far as they become in us dispositions to act (habits or beliefs). If, as James suggests, we must anticipate the sensations we would experience or the particular turn our experience would take if certain thoughts were acted upon, this anticipation would be of *kinds* of sensations and of *kinds* of experience and hence general ideas about those sensations and experiences. Action, and so the sensations which constitute the particular experience as particular, is the upshot of thought not its interpretant nor its purpose.

Consider these restatements of the maxim. In 1903 in his Harvard Lectures on pragmatism, Peirce put it this way (perhaps with tongue in cheek):

> Pragmatism is the principle that every theoretical judgment expressible in a sentence in the indicative mood is a confused form of thought whose only meaning, if it has any, lies in its tendency to enforce a corresponding practical maxim expressible as a conditional sentence having its apodosis in the imperative mood (CP 5.18).

In 1905 in a *Monist* article, 'Issues of Pragmaticism', Peirce restated his maxim in a way he hoped would make clear once and for all what he meant:

> The entire intellectual purport of any symbol consists in the total of all general modes of rational conduct which, conditionally upon all the possible different circumstances and desires, would ensue upon the acceptance of the symbol (CP 5.438).

Peirce, then, thought James to be nominalistic in that he made action the purpose of thought and not merely its outcome or upshot. In that case James implicitly makes some non-thought the ultimate logical interpretant of thought and hence implicitly subscribes to an incognizable (the sensuous flux of experience as proposed in his 'radical empiricism'). For

Peirce, this is the one great sin against logic as method since it blocks the road to inquiry (CP 6.171; 6.273).[34]

To be fair to James, however, I must say that in 1906, Peirce, while still insisting on the differences between his understanding of pragmatism and James', writes in a much more irenic vein:

> The most prominent of all our school and the most respected, William James, defines pragmatism as the doctrine that the whole 'meaning' of a concept expresses itself either in the shape of conduct to

---

[34] Even if we suppose this assessment is correct, to be fair to James we should admit that Peirce's first exposition of pragmatism in the 1878 article 'How to Make Our Ideas Clear' was open to such an interpretation. There he analysed 'hardness' according to the pragmatic maxim (CP 5.403ff.). The results were misleading and later rejected. Imagine a diamond crystallized within soft cotton where it remains until completely burned up. No other substance is ever rubbed against it. Would it be false to say that the diamond was soft? Peirce answers that it would not be incorrect or even false to call it soft since nothing prevents us from saying that all bodies remain soft until they are touched when their hardness increases with the pressure until they are scratched. Such modes of speech 'would involve a modification of our present usage of speech with respect to the words hard and soft, but not of their meaning. For they represent no fact to be different from what it is' (CP 5.403). This passage might be understood in a nominalist or even positivist sense. Again writing to Calderoni, Peirce admitted: 'I myself went too far in the direction of nominalism when I said that it was a mere question of the convenience of speech whether we say that a diamond is hard when it is not pressed upon, or whether we say that it is soft until it is pressed upon. I *now* say that experiment will prove that the diamond is hard, as a positive fact. That is, it is a real fact that it *would* resist pressure, which amounts to extreme scholastic realism. I deny that pragmatism as originally defined by me made the intellectual purport of symbols to consist in our conduct. On the contrary, I was most careful to say that it consists in our *concept* of what our conduct *would* be upon *conceivable* occasions' (CP 8.208). The passage is nominalistic then because it tends to identify the real with the actual. The meaning of 'hardness' is in the actual resistance of the diamond to pressure. Potentiality in the diamond to resist pressure is only a linguistic usage not a matter of a real fact where 'real' means not a figment of mind. Peirce would later (after 1903) put the matter this way: 'would-be's' are real even though they cannot be reduced to 'is's' (if I might be allowed to coin a barbarous expression). 'Would-be's' consist in a reference to the future (*esse in futuro*, as Peirce would say) and as such are general and no number of actual cases exhausts their meaning. Even though Peirce maintained in his letter to Calderoni that he did not intend to fall back into nominalism, none the less the example was unfortunate and could easily have been so understood. And if, mind you if, James was in fact a nominalist already, it is understandable why he attributed to Peirce his own interpretation which Peirce found unacceptable.

be recommended or of experience to be expected. Between this definition and mine there certainly appears to be no slight theoretical divergence, which, for the most part, becomes evanescent in practice (CP 5.466).

Much more could and, no doubt, should be said both about British influences on Peirce and about his pragmatism. I have not said a word about the influence of Herbert Spencer, negative though it was, on Peirce's evolutionary cosmology. I have passed over in silence the positive influence of Charles Darwin whose scientific work Peirce more than admired. I have not touched Peirce's doctrine of the normative sciences and their essential role in understanding pragmaticism. Finally, I have no more than hinted at Peirce's system of categories which he considered to be his one lasting contribution to philosophy and at the correction of Kant which a serious study of logic, as understood by the English, demands. Oddly enough Peirce thought that his corrections of Kant made his own views a resuscitation of Hegel 'in a strange costume' (CP 1.42).[35] Such considerations would bring us to Peirce's tychistic views of cosmology and to the synechistic ontology which grounds his 'scholastic realism'. But all of this will have to wait for another occasion.

I will close with this statement concerning the meaning of pragmaticism by Peirce himself:

> Pragmaticism makes thinking to consist in the living inferential metaboly of symbols whose purport lies in conditional general resolutions to act. As for the ultimate purpose of thought, which must be the purpose of everything, it is beyond human comprehension; but according to the stage of approach which my thought has made to it . . . it is by the indefinite replication of self-control upon self-control that the *vir* is begotten, and by action, through thought, he grows an esthetic ideal . . . as the share which God permits him to have in the work of creation (CP 5.403 n. 3).

[35] Yet see CP 5.38 for a passage in which Peirce denies any conscious influence of Hegel upon his thought.

William James
1842–1910

PETER JONES

He was about five feet eight inches tall, rather thin, and for the last thirty or so years of his life sported a bushy beard and moustache, fashionable for the time.[1] His pleasing low-pitched voice, ideal for conversation, did not carry well to large audiences, and although he was much in demand as a public speaker he rarely spoke from the floor at faculty or professional

The volumes from which quotations have been taken are abbreviated as follows:

Perry: R. B. Perry, *The Thought and Character of William James* (Boston: Little, Brown & Co., 1935).

Letters: H. James, (ed.), *The Letters of William James* (London: Longmans, Green & Co., 1920)

Essays: W. James, *Collected Essays and Reviews* (London: Longmans, Green & Co., 1920).

ERE: W. James, *Essays in Radical Empiricism* (Cambridge, Mass.: Harvard University Press, 1976).

ERM: W. James, *Essays in Religion and Morality* (Cambridge, Mass.: Harvard University Press, 1982).

MT: W. James, *The Meaning of Truth* (London: Longmans, Green & Co., 1909).

PU: W. James, *A Pluralistic Universe* (London: Longmans, Green & Co., 1909).

Pragmatism: W. James, *Pragmatism* (London: Longmans, Green & Co., 1907).

Principles: W. James, *The Principles of Psychology* (New York: Henry Holt & Co., 1890).

Problems: W. James, *Some Problems of Philosophy* (London: Longmans, Green & Co., 1911).

Talks: W. James, *Talks to Teachers* (London: Longmans, Green & Co., 1900).

Varieties: W. James, *The Varieties of Religious Experience* (London: Longmans, Green & Co., 1902).

WB: W. James, *The Will to Believe* (Dover Publications: New York, 1956).

[1] The biographical sketch is derived mainly from Perry, and *Letters*; but see also Henry James, *Autobiography*, F. W. Dupee (ed.) (London: W. H. Allen, 1956).

meetings. As a young man, within the family or with close friends, he was frequently the source and centre of fun, vying with his father in devising practical jokes or in generating lively argument. Like his father he was the victim of his moods, and his own wife and children had much to contend with; typically, he assigned the hour of his evening meal to student consultation, and would refuse to see invited guests if he suddenly felt anti-social. He hated what he called 'loutish' informality in dress, and the American way of eating boiled eggs; he loved bright neckties, animals and hill walking. He had no exotic tastes in food, avoided tea and coffee, and drank no alcohol—one of his brothers became an alcoholic, like their father in his younger days. From his early twenties until the end of his life he experienced, and perhaps savoured, a series of physical and mental depressions; remarkably, so did his father, his four brothers, and even more dramatically, his sister.[2] Like them all he was self-absorbed, and it is no surprise that his philosophy mirrors his self-concern. His first intention was to be a painter and, after spasmodic private schooling in America and Europe, he began to study; but he soon discovered that his talents were modest, his results at best charming, and his interests elsewhere. Thus, at the age of nineteen, in 1861, he turned to chemistry. Three years later he entered Harvard Medical School, and graduated MD from there in 1869. At the age of thirty he began his first job, initially as Instructor, and later Assistant Professor in Anatomy and Physiology at Harvard. He began teaching philosophy in 1879, joining the department formally in the following year and being made Professor in 1885. In 1907, at the age of sixty-five and after seemingly endless prevarication, he finally resigned from all his duties at Harvard: thirty-five years on the Faculty were enough. He died in 1910.

The life and thought of William James take their colour, in the first instance, from the life and thought of his father, Henry James, Sr, but the story begins with the grandfather. William James of Albany, New York, emigrated from Ireland about 1789; he married three times, begat four-teen children, and when he died, in 1832, left three million dollars. Such wealth, acquired during the construction of the Erie Canal, inevitably had a profound effect on his immediate descendants, releasing them from any urgent need to earn their living. Henry James, Sr, fourth child of the third marriage, was born in 1811. He studied at Union College and at Princeton Theological Seminary, although he soon became alienated from the Church and from all formal institutional practices, in a truly 'Calvinistic reaction against Calvin'.[3] Nevertheless, he devoted the whole of his life to an idiosyncratic theology, blended in part from selective reading of

[2] See Jean Strouse, *Alice James* (New York: Houghton Mifflin Co., 1980).

[3] Perry, I, 15.

Swedenborg and Fourier.[4] By all accounts he was unconventional, tender hearted, unstable, restless, impatient—and rich. He dragged his young family to and from Europe, lurching moodily from exhilaration to gloom throughout their travels as reality failed to match his imagination. After a serious boyhood accident one of his legs was amputated above the knee, and this genuine physical disability was to be sympathetically echoed in the ailments of his four children who survived infancy; all had bad backs, poor digestion, and were prone to bouts of severe depression. He was a fervent millennialist, and he counted Emerson and Carlyle among his closest friends. His published works are difficult to follow; as the words flow, the sense departs. What he really loved was a thoroughly good argument, the livelier, the better, and the temper of the man can be conveyed, perhaps, by a letter he wrote to the Editor of *The New Jerusalem Messenger* in 1863, about the attitude of a Swedenborgian congregation:

> judging from your paper, the whole sect seems spiritually benumbed. Your mature men have an air of childishness and your young men have the aspect of old women. I find it hard above all to imagine the existence of a living woman in the bounds of your sect, whose breasts flow with milk instead of hardening with pedantry.[5]

William James, the philosopher, 'derived so much from his father and resembled him so strikingly', according to his own son, writing in 1920, that we shall ignore the influence at our peril.[6] At the age of twenty-three, William interrupted his medical studies at Harvard, ostensibly to seek an improvement in his health, and joined Agassiz on his expedition to the Amazon. In one of his letters from there occurs an idea that was to interest James for the remainder of his life. In 1865 he refers to it under the label of 'American energy'[7]—which he alternately felt he possessed and he lacked—and on the surface he is talking about national differences; at another level, however, he is talking about his own search for identity, for a self he can both tolerate and locate in a complex social matrix. In the following year, and on resuming his medical studies, he wrote to a friend about his belief in the need for each individual to establish an emotional equilibrium in the cycle of moods that all experience. James had been reading Marcus Aurelius, who expresses just such a view, and his letter echoes the Stoic moralist:

---

[4] *ERM*, 5: 'I have often tried to imagine what sort of a figure my father might have made, had he been born in a genuinely theological age'. See also, F. H. Young, *The Philosophy of Henry James, Sr.* (New York: Bookman Associates, 1951); and *PU*, 29.

[5] *Letters*, I, 14.

[6] Ibid., I, 10.

[7] Ibid., I, 66.

each man's constitution limits him to a certain amount of emotion and action, and ... if he insists on going under a higher pressure than normal for three months, for instance, he will pay for it by passing the next three months below par. So the best way is to keep moving steadily and regularly, as your mind becomes thus deliciously appeased.[8]

James's usual response to poor health was to travel, preferably to Europe, but improvement was invariably short-lived, and yielded to a form of homesickness, although not for the past, but for a future that must be better than the present. A change in self, however, could never be effected merely by a change in place. Returning from one such mournful quest, in 1870, James felt that only by finding a philosophy to live by could his spiritual crisis be resolved—he later reported that about this time he was on the continual verge of suicide.[9] He derived initial inspiration from studying and adopting the account of free will set out by the French neo-Kantian philosopher, Charles Renouvier. James recorded in a notebook: 'my first act of free will shall be to believe in free will'.[10] The problem seemed to be that as an empirical scientist he was committed to determinism, and he set himself to harmonize the principal insights of empiricism, as he saw them, and a belief, or a desire for belief, in free will. Philosophy for James was never a dispassionate form of inquiry, or a business, an amusement or academic discipline; above all it was a set of convictions which, in Perry's words, 'reconciled him to life'.[11] Indeed, James was vehemently opposed to academic philosophy as he saw it developing, deplored the German influence over it, talked of 'our damned academic technics and PhD machinery', periodically insisted, in private, that he hated philosophy.[12] An outburst in 1902 is typical: '*vive* the Anglo-Saxon amateur, disciple of Locke and Hume, and *pereat* the German professional!' 'Technicality', he says on another occasion, 'seems to me to spell "failure" in philosophy'.[13] But it was not only in style and mood that James echoed the eighteenth-century moralists who were his mentors, for he entirely agreed with them, as we shall see, that the dominant forces in a man's life are his emotions and his habits. Another significant link is acknowledged in his approval of *ease* as a criterion of choice, by Locke and his successors; in an article of 1879, James calls it 'the aesthetic Principle of Ease'.[14] Initially he took it as an equivalent for his own notion of 'practicalism', but later absorbed the fuller classical sense of an emotional and

[8] Ibid., I, 78.
[9] Ibid., I, 129.
[10] Ibid., I, 147.
[11] Perry, I, 324.
[12] *Letters,* II, 227; Perry, I, 450, 442–443.
[13] *Letters,* II, 165, 79.
[14] *Essays,* 89.

intellectual equilibrium which could be achieved and maintained only by constant effort.

If reflections on free will helped James intellectually, his psychological balance was helped by embarking on a regular teaching career in 1872, and by his marriage, six years later. With a return to a more boisterous frame of mind he berates his brother Henry, just then starting on his literary career, for an element of 'something cold, thin-blooded and priggish' in his style; 'I thought the style ran a little more to *curliness* than suited the average mind'.[15] Like his father, William felt a particular distaste for dogma, priggishness, which he detected in Matthew Arnold, and decadence, all of them being associated, in his mind, with suppression of genuine vitality and energy.[16] His horror of dogma, alongside his deep belief in the influence and ubiquity of habit, partly explains his unease with anything historical or traditional; he did not reject them, and he acknowledged their value, but he sensed their fatal charm and felt that undue attention to them diminished our concentration on the present.[17] Even if our understanding was always of the past, we lived in the present, and it is in the future that we must act. That, at least, is the task confronting every individual. On the other hand, from an early age James held a view well conveyed in this letter, written when he was twenty-six: 'every thought you now have and every act and intuition owes its complexion to the acts of your dead and living brothers. Everything we know and are is through man'.[18]

One other feature of his thought should be mentioned in this introductory sketch. From his mid-twenties until his death James was interested in para-normal phenomena, and he helped to promote in Boston a society parallel to the British Society for Psychical Research. James belonged to a distinctive group of writers in history, not all of whom have been classified as philosophers, who believed that the nature and scope of our feelings escape the grasp of our thought—at least in its formal patterns—that our thought ranges beyond the boundaries of what we say, and that both

[15] Perry, I, 331, 329.

[16] *Letters*, I, 14; Perry I, 407. On 'over-sentimentalism', see *Talks*, 258.

[17] Perry, II, 258: 'The weight of the past world here is fatal,—one ends by becoming its mere parasite instead of its equivalent. This worship, this dependence on other men is abnormal. The ancients did things by doing the business of the day, not by gaping at their grandfathers' tombs,—and the normal man today will do likewise' (1873, from Rome). See also *Talks*, 300: 'those philosophers are right who contend that the world is a standing thing, with no progress, no real history. The changing conditions of history touch only the surface of the show. The altered equilibriums and redistributions only diversify our opportunities and open chances to us for new ideals'.

[18] *Letters*, I, 131. He goes on to say: 'The stoic feeling of being a sentinel obeying orders without knowing the general's plan is a noble one'.

Peter Jones

feelings and thoughts are incompletely or inadequately conveyed in language. Language, in brief, and as traditionally understood, is itself too often a barrier to knowledge.

James published a large number of papers during his teaching career, but only two major books, one of which took several years to complete, and included some of those articles. That book was *Principles of Psychology*, which appeared in 1890. In 1902 came *The Varieties of Religious Experience*. After he retired in 1907 he gathered together some of his earlier papers, and several lecture courses, and the resulting volumes continued to appear after his death three years later. Like most philosophers James never radically changed his views; refinements led to shifts in emphasis, but what strikes one in retrospect is a unity of theme and purpose. Both at the time and later James regarded his early paper on 'The Sentiment of Rationality', published in *Mind* 1879, as an important statement of the direction he intended to take. Philosophers, he says, typically crave for clarity and simplicity, and their theories are precisely designed to simplify what he calls 'sensible diversity'. What must be remembered, however, when we categorize experience, is that 'conceptions, "kinds", are teleological instruments. No abstract concept can be a valid substitute for a concrete reality except with reference to a particular interest in the conceiver.'[19] He insists that a conception 'is a partial aspect of a thing which *for our purpose* we regard as its essential aspect', and a rational conception of things can be negatively characterized as 'strong feeling of ease'. Crucially, 'the whole man within us is at work when we form our philosophical opinions. Intellect, will, taste, and passion co-operate just as they do in practical affairs': 'It is almost incredible that men who are themselves working philosophers should pretend that any philosophy can be, or ever has been, constructed without the help of personal preference, belief, or divination'.

> every philosopher, or man of science either, whose initiative counts for anything in the evolution of thought, has taken his stand on a sort of dumb conviction that the truth must lie in one direction rather than another, and a sort of preliminary assurance that his notion can be made to work.[20]

Such views form the context for the assertion that 'we cannot live or think at all without some degree of faith. Faith is synonymous with working hypothesis.'[21] It is not surprising, moreover, that James always claimed intellectual descent from British, rather than German, thinkers. 'I am happy to say', he remarks in 1898, 'that it is the English-speaking philoso-

[19] *WB*, 70. The versions in *WB* and *Essays* differ: I refer to both.
[20] *Essays,* 86, 84; *WB,* 92–93.
[21] *WB,* 95.

48

phers who first introduced the custom of interpreting the meaning of conceptions by asking what difference they make for life.'[22]

Everyone knows that *Principles of Psychology* is a classic work in introspective psychology. It is equally important to recognize that it further defines James's philosophical stance. He concedes that the psychologist, whatever his metaphysical views may be, 'must assume' '*a thoroughgoing dualism*', of subject and object, mind knowing and thing known. Moreover, viewed from outside, living beings strike us as 'bundles of habits'. From within, however, we must begin with consciousness, recognizing that first, 'it is at all times primarily *a selecting agency*', and second, that from birth it is essentially consciousness 'of a teeming multiplicity of objects and relations'. 'A pure sensation is an abstraction': 'thought is sensibly continuous'.[23] Continuity, diversity, vagueness: these are three essential features of experience which James wishes to underline. But also its particularity. And the general terms in our language mask our recognition of these features. Of course, there is a serious problem over the re-identification of particulars, on such a view, and James agrees that 'if we lost our stock of labels we should be intellectually lost in the midst of the world'.[24] But in casting language as the villain in psychological theory, as much as in philosophical, he is echoing a view espoused by almost every Western philosopher since Francis Bacon. It should be recorded that James nowhere addresses himself to the problems of language by way of an account of the learning, structure and functions of it, nor does he consider the conditions of effective communication, or of the adequate expression of thought and feeling.

In James's view the major fault in traditional British empiricism was adherence to atomism; and however useful this essentially chemical model might have been for thinking about objects, it was disastrous for thinking about thinking. It encouraged the view that ideas must resemble the things they are of, and it even led some philosophers to conflate ideas and things.[25] Removal of such views, however, still allows James to accept a good deal of the old story. For example, Locke and Hume were correct in arguing that a congenitally deaf man 'can never be made to imagine what sound is like', because he can have 'no mental copy' of the appropriate sort. Further, Hume's account of belief is 'essentially correct'; belief is having an idea 'in a lively and active manner'. Defining 'my experience' as 'what I agree to attend to' entitles James to hold, he claims, that 'reality means simply relation to our emotional and active life'; 'in this sense, whatever excites

---

[22] *Essays*, 434.

[23] *Principles*, I, 218, 104, 139, 224, 237; II, 3.

[24] Ibid., I, 444, 463.

[25] Ibid., I, 236, 237, 471. For apparent recognition of the chemical source of the model, *ERE*, 6.

and stimulates our interest is real'. Against this background he is able to characterize doubting as parasitic on believing, in a way that was to be developed later by Wittgenstein. James agrees with the nineteenth-century Scottish philosopher Alexander Bain, who had written of our 'primitive credulity. We begin by believing everything; whatever is, is true'; and he himself insists that 'the primitive impulse is to affirm immediately the reality of all that is conceived'.[26]

During an intriguing discussion on necessary truths, in the final chapter of *Principles*, James remarks that what fundamentally divides philosophies is 'the point of faith' 'that the world *is* rationally intelligible throughout'. Often by 'faith' James means 'working hypothesis', but here his claim is also to be linked with his often repeated contention that 'many of our so-called metaphysical principles are at bottom only expressions of aesthetic feeling'. His view is that philosophical faith is 'bred like most faiths from an aesthetic demand', one of which, as we saw earlier, is the principle of ease.[27] In brief, one adopts those philosophical tenets and positions with which one is least uncomfortable. Reference to such feelings—he sometimes calls them 'needs'—is generally the terminus of his discussion, but it is unclear whether James considers them to be inexplicable, or whether he holds that his successors might have better termini in the light of their—what? research? theory? needs? For example, he declares that 'we have no definite idea of what we mean by cause, or of what causality consists in'; but he also contends that the causal principle (nothing can happen without a cause) 'expresses a demand for *some* deeper sort of inward connection between phenomena than their merely habitual time-sequence seems to us to be'.[28]

The premise from which all his claims derive, the focus from which his theory radiates, is experience; or, later, consciousness, which he insists is not an entity but a function or 'external relation'. It is on such a basis that he asserts that 'classification and conception are purely teleological weapons of the mind'; and that 'there is no property *absolutely* essential to any one thing. The same property which figures as the essence of a thing on one occasion becomes a very inessential feature upon another.'[29] James makes many statements, however, which, as he admits in the last chapter of *Principles*, could not be verified in his or anyone else's experience, and no definition of plausibility in terms of conviction can hide their *a priori* elements. His justly famous, and persuasive, description of a baby's early experiences is essentially a requirement of his theory, and not an astonishing memory report:

[26] *Principles,* II, 44; I, 221: II, 295: I, 402: II, 295: II, 319 and note.
[27] Ibid., II, 677, 672; I, 134.
[28] Ibid., II, 671.
[29] On consciousness see *Principles,* I, 273, 275, 400; *ERE,* 3, 14, 23, 137: on classification see *Principles,* II, 335, 333.

50

the baby, assailed by eyes, ears, nose, skin, and entrails at once, feels it all as one great blooming, buzzing confusion.[30]

James said little about morality in *Principles*, although he records his view that 'life is one long struggle between conclusions based on abstract ways of conceiving cases, and opposite conclusions prompted by our instinctive perception of them as individual facts'. Moreover, 'the most characteristically and peculiar moral judgments that a man is ever called on to make are in unprecedented cases and lonely emergencies where no popular rhetorical maxims can avail, and the hidden oracle alone can speak'.[31] Indeed, as he insisted in the volume of essays published under the title *The Will to Believe*, 'everywhere the ethical philosopher must wait on facts', since 'there is no such thing possible as an ethical philosophy dogmatically made up in advance'. James admits, in that volume, that his defence of free will is neither clear nor stable; 'it gives us a pluralistic, restless universe, in which no single point of view can ever take in the whole scene'.[32] If, strictly speaking, no two persons are the same, and if, even more dramatically, no one individual is the 'same' person through time, the notions of same motives, same actions and same circumstances all become empty and we are unable to formulate causal principles in explanation of what we do. The alleged sting in determinism is drawn. Elaboration of any such view would require an account of how the agent, let alone others, can identify himself and his actions through time; and James needed to supplement his account in *Principles*. He found support for his own gropings in the thought of a philosopher who, by an extraordinary chance, and quite independently, was canvassing views very like James's. The philosopher was Henri Bergson. Later, of course, another writer, Proust, was to explore those same views in his own work.[33] Once James had come across Bergson he generously commended his works and championed them before the English-speaking public.

James himself was constantly being asked to address graduating students, teachers, religious leaders and so on, and in 1892 he gathered together some of those talks, under the title *Talks to Teachers*. Education, he believes, is essentially 'the organization of acquired habits of conduct and tendencies to behaviour'. Rousseau was quite wrong to discourage competitiveness and pugnacity in children, because 'the feeling of rivalry lies at the very basis of our being'. What perennially nourishes the admirable strength of character of the Englishman, he avers, is the national worship of 'athletic outdoor life and sport'; and James suggests that if

[30] *Principles,* I, 488.
[31] Ibid., II, 672, 674.
[32] *WB,* 184, 208, 177.
[33] See my *Philosophy and the Novel* (Oxford: Clarendon Press, 1975), Ch. 4; cf. *Principles,* I, 291–292, 354, 360, 400.

American women take up ski-ing, like the Norwegians, they can anticipate 'a sounder and heartier moral tone', and can expect to take 'the lead in every educational and social reform'. Although the future will ever require 'mental power' rather than 'bare brute strength', James refuses to believe that 'our muscular vigor will ever be a superfluity': 'it will still always be needed to furnish the background of sanity, serenity, and cheerfulness to life, to give moral elasticity to our disposition, to round off the wiry edge of our fretfulness, and make us good-humoured and easy of approach'.[34] The echoes of muscular Christianity in such passages are no illusion. Throughout James's writings, indeed, the dominant metaphor for life itself, for philosophy, and even for aspects of personal relationships, is that of fighting—the preferred form for gentlemen, no doubt, took place in the boxing ring, with the carnage of war as only a last resort. The general notion of a healthy mind and body is ancient, of course, but in James's version it is a fusion of Stoic and Puritan ideals. In another passage, this time reminiscent of John Henry Newman, James upbraids those in education who demand that '"interest" must be assiduously awakened in everything, difficulties ... smoothed away'. He abhors such '*soft* pedagogics': 'it is nonsense to suppose that every step in education *can* be interesting. The fighting impulse must often be appealed to.'[35] Along with all his references to the principle of ease as a criterion of choice, James also believes that only by effort and constant striving can one escape the spiritual death of dogma, inanition, or *ennui*—that siren call of the older moralists. He records his unease at a Teachers' Commune:

> The moment one treads that sacred enclosure, one feels one's self in an atmosphere of success ... in this unspeakable Chautauqua there was no potentiality of death in sight anywhere, and no point of the compass visible from which danger might possibly appear.... But what our human emotions seem to require is the sight of the struggle going on. The moment the fruits are being merely eaten, things become ignoble. Sweat and effort, human nature strained to its uttermost and on the rack, yet getting through alive, and then turning its back on its success to pursue another more rare and arduous still—this is the sort of thing the presence of which inspires us.[36]

It is not surprising that James tells a correspondent that he is 'ceasing to be a psychologist, and becoming exclusively a moralist and metaphysician'.[37] Had he wished, he might have stressed the word *becoming*, since it

[34] *Talks*, 29, 52, 204–205, 206–207.
[35] Ibid., 54–55. See J. H. Newman, 'Discourses on the Scope and Nature of University Education', in *Newman*, G. Tillotson (ed.) (London: Rupert Hart-Davis, 1957), 491, 442–443.
[36] Ibid., 268–272.
[37] Perry, II, 195.

is the condition of *becoming* that he celebrates. Results are closures, ends, deaths; processes, on the other hand, seem full of promise, are changes, and are vital.

In the Preface to the *Talks*, James remarks that 'the facts and worths of life need many cognizers to take them in. There is no point of view absolutely public and universal.'[38] Such sentiments informed the Gifford Lectures, which he delivered in Edinburgh in 1901–2, and published in the second of those years under the title *The Varieties of Religious Experience*. James enjoyed staying in Edinburgh—'surely the noblest city ever built by man'[39]—and was impressed by the attentive and ever increasing audience at his lectures. In several letters he outlines his task:

> The problem I have set myself is a hard one: *first*, to defend (against all the prejudices of my 'class') 'experience' against 'philosophy' as being the real backbone of the world's religious life—I mean prayer, guidance, and all that sort of thing immediately and privately felt, as against high and noble general views of our destiny and the world's meaning; and *second*, to make the hearer or reader believe, what I myself invincibly do believe, that, although all the special manifestations of religion may have been absurd (I mean its creeds and theories), yet the life of it as a whole is mankind's most important function. A task well-nigh impossible, I fear, and in which I shall fail; but to attempt it is *my* religious act.[40]

James was now almost sixty years of age as he embarked on this, his final and most sustained attempt to come to terms with the legacy of his own father's religious views.[41] His defensive report of the lectures to another professional philosopher, F. C. S. Schiller, that they 'are all facts and no philosophy',[42] is entirely misleading. A further letter outlines his thoughts:

> The mother sea and fountain-head of all religions lie in the mystical experiences of the individual, taking the word mystical in a very wide sense. All theologies and all ecclesiasticisms are secondary growths superimposed; and the experiences make such flexible combinations

---

[38] *Talks*, v.

[39] *Letters,* II, 146.

[40] Ibid., II, 127.

[41] *ERM*, 4, 60: James regarded it 'not only a filial but a philosophical duty' to make public his father's ideas. See also a letter of 1891 to his sister: 'These inhibitions, these split-up selves, all these new facts that are gradually coming to light about our organization, these enlargements of the self in trance, etc., are bringing me to turn for light in the direction of all sorts of despised spiritualistic and unscientific ideas. Father would find in me today a much more receptive listener—all *that* philosophy has got to be brought in' (*Letters,* I, 310).

[42] *Letters,* II, 165.

with the intellectual prepossessions of their subjects, that one may almost say that they have no proper *intellectual* deliverance of their own, but belong to a region deeper, and more vital and practical, than that which the intellect inhabits. For this they are also indestructible by intellectual arguments and criticisms. I attach the mystical or religious consciousness to the possession of an extended subliminal self, with a thin partition through which messages make irruption. We are thus made convincingly aware of the presence of a sphere of life larger and more powerful than our usual consciousness, with which the latter is nevertheless continuous.[43]

James finds himself more sympathetic to those who worship, not as Theists do, but rather as the polytheists: 'this more pluralistic style of feeling seems to me to allow of a warmer sort of loyalty to our past helpers, and to tally more exactly with the mixed condition in which we find the world as to its ideals'. The Bible itself seemed to James to be a fatal document against most orthodox theological claims.[44]

In 1904 Professor J. B. Pratt of Williams College sent out a questionnaire on religious beliefs, and James's answers are extremely interesting. An element in religion that he values is 'the social appeal for corroboration, consolation, etc., when things are going wrong with my causes (my truth denied) etc.' And on his notion of God, he wrote:

'God', to me, is not the only spiritual reality to believe in. Religion means primarily a universe of spiritual relations surrounding the earthly practical ones, not merely relations of 'value', but agencies and their activities. I suppose that the chief premise for my hospitality towards the religious testimony of others is my conviction that 'normal' or 'sane' consciousness is so small a part of actual experience.

James confesses that 'I can't possibly pray—I feel foolish and artificial', but that he has come to believe in personal immortality 'more strongly as I grow older'. He categorically denies that the Bible has *authority* in religious matters: 'It is so human a book that I don't see how belief in its divine authorship can survive the reading of it'. On the other hand, he accepts the testimony of those who claim to have felt God's presence directly: 'the whole line of testimony on this point is so strong that I am unable to pooh-pooh it away'.[45]

In *Varieties* itself, James embarks upon a study, not of institutional practices, but of personal religion, defined as 'the feelings, acts, and experiences of individual men in their solitude, so far as they apprehend themselves to stand in relation to whatever they may consider the divine'.

[43] Ibid., II, 149–150.
[44] Ibid., II, 155, 196.
[45] Ibid., II, 213–215.

He derides the dream of 'some direct mark' which would provide an absolute guarantee against error, 'that darling dream of philosophic dogmatists', along with all over-simple theories. In general terms, James takes religion to be 'the belief that there is an unseen order, and that our supreme good lies in harmoniously adjusting thereto'; and what interests him are 'the enormous diversities which the spiritual lives of different men exhibit'. Here, as elsewhere, he holds that 'in the metaphysical and religious sphere, articulate reasons are cogent for us only when our inarticulate feelings of reality have already been impressed in favour of the same conclusion'.[46]

James asserts that 'the original faith in fixing the figure of the gods must always have been psychological. The deity to whom the prophets, seers, and devotees who founded the particular cult bore witness was worth something to them personally. They could use him'; indeed, 'the gods we stand by are the gods we need and can use, the gods whose demands are reinforcements of our demands on ourselves and on one another'.[47] Such views barely differ from those of Hume, in his *Natural History of Religion* published in 1757, and his very language seems to echo his master.[48] Thus, remarking that religious leaders typically attract disciples who then band together and subsequently become 'ecclesiastical institutions with corporate ambitions of their own', James writes: 'the spirit of politics and the lust of dogmatic rule are then apt to enter and contaminate the originally innocent thing'.[49] His sharp comments on institutions underline his overriding concern with religion as a personal experience, but the *a priori* elements in his speculations, both on the origins of personal religion and in the development of institutions, should be noticed: they are no less *a priori* for being constantly repeated, from Cicero onwards, in the secondary sources in which James undoubtedly found them. This aside, he insists that 'personal religious experience has its root and centre in mystical states of consciousness', and he offers four distinguishing marks of such mystical experience: its ineffability, its noetic quality—meaning that it is related to states of knowledge—its transiency and its passivity. He emphasizes that merely being mystical gives no authority to such states, not least because they can be stimulated by alcohol, gases and drugs—with all of which James formally experimented in a modest way, at some time. He concedes that in this context he is defending 'feeling at the expense of reason' and thereby, perhaps, ruling out 'any Theology worthy of the name'.[50]

James suggests that three beliefs typify a religious life:

[46] *Varieties*, 31, 18, 53, 109, 74.
[47] Ibid., 329.
[48] See my *Hume's Sentiments* (Edinburgh University Press, 1982) Ch. 2.
[49] *Varieties*, 334.
[50] Ibid., 379–380, 387, 428, 431.

3

'1. That the visible world is part of a more spiritual universe from which it draws its chief significance;
2. That union or harmonious relation with that higher universe is our true end;
3. That prayer or inner communion with the spirit thereof ... is a process wherein work is really done. ...'

In addition, James adds two psychological characteristics:

'4. A new zest which adds itself like a gift to life. ...
5. An assurance of safety and a temper of peace. ...'[51]

James reiterates his beliefs that 'the world of our present consciousness is only one out of many worlds of consciousness that exist', that beliefs themselves are essentially rules for action, and that the common nucleus of all beliefs is alleviation or solution of uneasiness. Emphasis on feeling naturally allows James to insist again that the aesthetic life plays a part 'in determining one's choice of a religion'.[52]

It is worth recording two passages that James wrote at the end of his life. In the first, published in 1909, he is reflecting on the notion of a godless universe, and he begins by stating that 'framed as we are, our egoism craves above all things inwards sympathy and recognition, love and admiration'. He continues:

Even if matter could do every outward thing that God does, the idea of it would not work as satisfactorily, because the chief call for a God on modern men's part is for a being who will inwardly recognize them and judge them sympathetically. Matter disappoints this craving of our ego, so God remains for most men the truer hypothesis, and indeed remains so for definite pragmatic reasons.[53]

About six months before he died, James wrote an article, 'A Suggestion about Mysticism', in which he described four recent, and overwhelming, experiences—'very sudden and incomprehensible enlargements of the conscious field':

The mode of consciousness was perceptual, not conceptual—the field expanding so fast that there seemed no time for conception or identification to get in its work. There was a strongly exciting sense that my knowledge of past (or present?) reality was enlarging pulse by pulse, but so rapidly that my intellectual processes could not keep up the pace. The *content* was thus entirely lost to retrospection—it sank into the limbo into which dreams vanish as we gradually awake. The feeling—I won't

[51] Ibid., 485–486.
[52] Ibid., 519, 444, 508, 458–461.
[53] *MT,* 189–190 n.

call it belief—that I had had a sudden *opening*, had seen through a window, as it were, distant realities that incomprehensibly belonged with my own life, was so acute that I cannot shake it off today.[54]

In 1907 James published the work by which he is perhaps best known today, at least by philosophers: his lectures on *Pragmatism*. He begins and ends by observing, in a manner very close to Hume and his mentor Cicero, that 'the history of philosophy is, to a great extent that of a certain clash of human temperaments'—which James calls 'the tough-minded' and 'the tender-minded'. The tender-minded thinker, he suggests, is typically rationalistic, intellectualistic, idealistic, optimistic, religious, free-willist, monistic, dogmatical; the tough-minded is empiricist, sensationalistic, materialistic, pessimistic, irreligious, fatalistic, pluralistic, sceptical. Aside from his allegiance to free will, religion, and a form of optimism, there is no doubt that James sees himself as belonging to the camp of the tough-minded.[55]

Pragmatism, he tells us, is 'a method only', not a set of results, and a method in which 'theories become instruments, not answers to enigmas, in which we can rest'. 'Any idea upon which we can ride, so to speak, [is] true instrumentally.'[56] He claims to be elaborating views which C. S. Peirce had explored thirty years earlier, although Peirce intemperately, and typically, dissociated himself from James's version. The avowed link with John Dewey and F. C. S. Schiller provoked no such rejection however. James's explanation of how someone acquires new opinions strikingly anticipates the views of Quine, his distinguished Harvard successor, half a century later:

> The individual has a stock of old opinions already, but he meets a new experience that puts them to a strain. Somebody contradicts them; or in a reflective moment he discovers that they contradict each other; or he hears of facts with which they are incompatible; or desires arise in him which they cease to satisfy. The result is an inward trouble to which his mind till then had been a stranger, and from which he seeks to escape by modifying his previous mass of opinions. He saves as much of it as he can, for in this matter of belief we are all extreme conservatives. So he tries to change first this opinion, and then that (for they resist change very variously), until at last some new idea comes up which he can graft upon the ancient stock with a minimum of disturbance of the latter, some idea that mediates between the stock and the new experience and runs them into one another most felicitously and expediently.
>
> This new idea is then adopted as the true one. It preserves the older stock of truths with a minimum of modification, stretching them just

[54] *Essays,* 504–505.
[55] *Pragmatism,* 12.
[56] Ibid., 51, 53, 58.

enough to make them admit the novelty, but conceiving that in ways as familiar as the case leaves possible.

In brief, 'new truth' 'marries old opinion to new fact so as ever to show a minimum of jolt, a maximum of continuity'.[57] There can be little doubt that such claims are offered as statements of fact, introspectively verifiable in each person's experience; it is not entirely clear, however, in this case or in the others we have already mentioned, what James would say in the face of apparently contrary evidence.

James observes that 'pragmatism tends to *unstiffen* all our theories', tends always to pluralism, and 'converts the absolutely empty notion of a static relation of "correspondence"' between our minds and reality, 'into that of a rich and active commerce . . . between particular thoughts of ours, and the great universe of other experiences in which they play their parts and have their uses'. Because new truths are 'resultants of new experiences and of old truths combined and mutually modifying one another', it is likely that 'very ancient modes of thought may have survived through all the later changes in men's opinions'. James agrees with all those who hold that 'experience merely as such doesn't come ticketed and labelled, we have first to discover what it is'. Moreover, no individual conceptually straightens out more than 'the smallest part of his experience's flux'.[58] It is of the utmost importance, therefore, to recognize that even what we regard as our common-sense categories have histories, undergo change, and may cease to be useful. James does not himself link this claim to his reflections in *Principles* on difficulties in understanding the past.

Critics of *Pragmatism* took great exception to the chapter on truth, so much so, indeed, that James devoted a whole book, in 1909, to answering objections and explaining his position. What upset his readers was his overt flouting of traditional distinctions. Thus, he asserts: 'true ideas are those that we can assimilate, validate, corroborate and verify'; 'truth *happens* to an idea. It *becomes* true, is *made* true by events. Its verity *is* in fact an event, a process: the process namely of verifying itself, its veri-*fication*.' In a colourful passage he explains that

> truth lives, in fact, for the most part on a credit system. Our thoughts and beliefs 'pass' so long as nothing challenges them, just as bank-notes pass so long as nobody refuses them. But this all points to direct face-to-face verifications somewhere, without which the fabric of truth collapses like a financial system with no cash-basis whatever.[59]

[57] Ibid., 59–61. See W. V. O. Quine, 'Two Dogmas of Empiricism' (1951), in *From a Logical Point of View* (Cambridge, Mass.: Harvard University Press, 1961), 42.
[58] *Pragmatism,* 159, 69, 169–170, 172, 178.
[59] Ibid., 201, 207–208.

The point here is that 'in the end and eventually, all true processes must lead to the face of directly verifying sensible experiences *somewhere*, which somebody's ideas have copied'. Our asserted beliefs must take account of three elements in 'reality': the flux of our sensations, the relations between our sensations, and 'the *previous truths* of which every new inquiry takes account'. James agrees with those who hold both that reality exists independently of us, albeit only as 'the merely ideal limit of our minds' which we can never grasp, and that 'what we say about reality . . . depends on the perspective into which we throw it'. Such views are not Kantian, he insists, because it is man himself who makes and constantly modifies his categories, and who breaks the flux of sensible reality at his will. Indeed, we all

> plunge forward into the field of fresh experience with the beliefs our ancestors and we have made already; these determine what we notice; what we notice determines what we do; what we do again determines what we experience; so from one thing to another, altho' the stubborn fact remains that there *is* a sensible flux, what is *true of it* seems from first to last to be largely a matter of our own creation.[60]

In the volume of papers which set out to clarify these doctrines, published under the title *The Meaning of Truth*, James emphasizes that the pragmatist theory of truth is an important element in his own radical empiricism. He distinguishes three features in that doctrine—a postulate, a statement of fact, and a generalized conclusion. The postulate of radical empiricism is that philosophers shall debate only 'things definable in terms drawn from experience'; the factual statement is that conjunctive and disjunctive relations between things are 'as much matters of direct particular experience' as things themselves; the conclusion is that 'the parts of experience hold together . . . by relations that are themselves parts of experience', and no reference to anything 'trans-empirical' is needed. The main obstacle to such a view, James thinks, is the deep-seated rationalist tenet that 'experience as immediately given is all disjunction and no conjunction, and that to make one world out of this separateness, a higher unifying agency must be there'. He does not ask *why* so many thinkers have found such a view more plausible than his; that is, why the rationalist tenet seemed acceptable.[61]

James explicitly asserts that because 'all experience is a process, no point of view can ever be *the* last one. Every one is insufficient and off its balance, and responsible to later points of view than itself'; moreover, 'our fields of experience have no more definite boundaries than have our fields of view. Both are fringed forever by a *more* that continuously supersedes them as life proceeds.' Like Hume, James was constantly accused of confounding

[60] Ibid., 215, 245, 255.
[61] *MT*, xii–xiii

psychology and logic, but he always repudiated the charge by insisting that all relations need a 'psychological vehicle'.[62] He openly lists eight main misunderstandings of his arguments in *Pragmatism*, ranging from the accusation that 'pragmatism is only a re-editing of positivism', to the view that 'no pragmatist can be a realist in his epistemology', that 'pragmatism ignores the theoretic interest' and, moreover, 'is shut up to solipsism'.[63] James insists that pragmatists, like everyone else, use abstractions, but that these must be taken as essentially short-hand devices, possessing no higher grade of reality. To the pragmatist 'all discarnate truth is static, impotent, and relatively spectral, full truth being the truth that energizes and does battle'. And if that sounds more like the proclamation of a moralist than the measured analysis of an epistemologist, we may rest assured in our judgment. For James concedes that his pluralism may not satisfy the needs of 'sick souls'; indeed, the pluralism he seeks to defend 'has to fall back on a certain ultimate hardihood, a certain willingness to live without assurances or guarantees'. In brief, one has to be tough-minded. And the apparent circularity in the position is not a vicious circularity: 'what works is true and represents a reality, for the individual for whom it works'.[64]

If Hegel and Bradley between them stood for all James disliked and rejected, in style and in content, his particular philosophical hero, after the turn of the century, was Bergson. At the outset of his lectures published in 1909 under the title *A Pluralistic Universe*, James laments the German influence on the professional study of philosophy, as a result of which 'all spontaneity of thought, all freshness of conception, gets destroyed'; ideas are typically discussed or approached only through 'the veil of previous philosophers' opinions', and some German philosophers even fear lest their writings prove to be too popular. Hume, however, set the proper tone long ago:

> doesn't David Hume's technique set, after all, the kind of pattern most difficult to follow? Isn't it the most admirable?[65]

Although we 'need a stable scheme of concepts, stably related with one another, to lay hold of our experiences and to co-ordinate them withal', we must recognize that our abstract concepts 'are only moments dipped out from the stream of time, snap-shots taken, as by a kinetoscopic camera, at a life that in its original coming is continuous'.[66] James agrees with a remark attributed to Kierkegaard, that 'we live forward, we understand backward ... and to understand life by concepts is to arrest its movement'. 'To deal

---

[62] Ibid., 90, 117, 153.
[63] Ibid., 182–215.
[64] Ibid., 202, 204, 229, 243.
[65] *PU*, 16–19.
[66] Ibid., 235.

with moral facts conceptually', James continues, glossing Bergson's views, 'we have first to transform them, substitute brain-diagrams or physical metaphors, treat ideas as atoms, interests as mechanical forces, our conscious "selves" as "streams", and the like'. But in the sense of 'giving *insight*', such concepts 'have no theoretic value, for they quite fail to connect with the inner life of the flux, or with the causes that govern its direction'. What conceptual translation leaves out, cannot but leave out, is precisely the change in the flux:

> The essence of life is its continuously changing character; but our concepts are all discontinuous and fixed, and the only mode of making them coincide with life is by arbitrarily supposing positions of arrest therein.[67]

R. G. Collingwood developed a similar view in his *Principles of Art*, published thirty years later in 1938, although he there makes no reference to James. James's own view remained virtually unaltered throughout his life:

> My present field of consciousness is a centre surrounded by a fringe that shades insensibly into a subconscious more. . . . What we conceptually identify ourselves with and say we are thinking of at any time is the centre; but our *full* self is the whole field, with all those indefinitely radiating subconscious possibilities of increase that we can only feel without conceiving, and can hardly begin to analyse.

Exactly thirty years earlier, in his article 'The Sentiment of Rationality', James had written: 'the entire man, who feels all needs by turns, will take nothing as an equivalent for life but the fulness of life itself'.[68]

James published almost nothing on social or political philosophy, although towards the end of his life he spent some time reflecting on the issues of war and peace, and also on the military virtues. In 1897 when James unveiled St Gaudens's striking bronze monument to Col. Robert Gould Shaw, who died leading his black regiment in the Civil War, he spoke of his view that 'man is once for all a fighting animal; centuries of peaceful history could not breed the battle-instinct out of us'.[69] At a peace conference, in 1904, he insists that though 'man lives *by* habits', 'what he lives *for* is thrills and excitements. The only relief from Habit's tediousness is periodical excitement.' A major practical task, therefore, is to 'foster rival excitements and invent new outlets for heroic energy', suitable valves for

---

[67] Ibid., 244, 248, 246, 253.
[68] Ibid., 288–289; *WB*, 69.
[69] *ERM*, 72. James's younger brother Garth Wilkinson (Wilky) was Adjutant of the 54th Massachusetts, and was wounded in the attack on Fort Wagner during which Shaw was killed.

natural aggression. By 1910 he was canvassing the view that 'the martial type of character can be bred without war', and he favoured some form of social service, compulsory if need be. He insists, however, that 'the martial virtues, altho' originally gained by the race through war, are absolute and permanent human goods'; and 'martial virtues must be the enduring cement' of society and the condition of peace among nations.[70]

These reflections allow us to address, however briefly, the question of James's place in American culture, and of his own perception of his place. We have already noted that from his early twenties James was constantly comparing America with Europe—with France, or Germany, Italy, Switzerland or Britain; exhilarated by his nation's 'energy' or 'buoyancy' on the one hand, he deplored, on the other, the 'dreariness' and 'vacuousness' of American life, and the relative ease with which material prosperity could be secured.[71] From the evident security of his own position, some would say, Puritan values gained an added charm, and were easy to commend; in fact, however, he was very far from being sensually self-indulgent, and the simple outdoor life he pursued in the Adirondacks and on his property in New Hampshire seemed genuinely to satisfy his periodic need to play the latterday frontiersman. Returning from one European trip, in 1893, he complains of 'a strange thinness and femininity hovering over all America, so different from the stoutness and masculinity of land and air and everything in Switzerland and England'. He continues: 'But Europe has been made what it is by men staying in their homes and fighting stubbornly generation after generation for all the beauty, comfort and order that they have got—we must abide and do the same'.[72] The key to such passages is to be found in the notions of staying to fight, and of prizes bravely won. On every visit, however, he also swung the other way. In 1901, for example, he laments 'the singular lack of visible *sentiment* in England, and absence of "charm"'; indeed, longing once again for America, he finds England 'ungracious, unamiable and heavy'. One major advantage America has over the older countries, he believes, is 'freedom from all the corrupting influences from on top from which they suffer'. On another occasion he writes: 'we "intellectuals" in America must all work to keep our precious birthright of individualism, and freedom from ... institutions. *Every* great institution is perforce a means of corruption—

[70] *ERM*, 122–123, 170–172.

[71] *Letters*, I, 66; Perry, I, 297, 259.

[72] *Letters*, I, 347. In 1883 he writes from London to his brother Henry: 'Then the theatres, and the hippopotamus-like satisfaction of their audiences! ... Then the determination on the part of all who write ... to do it as amateurs, and never to use the airs and language of a professional; to be first of all a layman and a gentleman, and to pretend that your ideas came to you accidentally as it were, and are things you care nothing about' (Perry, I, 387).

whatever good it may also do. Only in the free personal relation is full ideality to be found.'[73] In his 'Talks to Students'—the second part of *Talks to Teachers*—James deplores what he regards as the *'bad habits'* of 'American over-tension and jerkiness and breathlessness and intensity and agony of expression': they are 'perfectly wanton and unnecessary tricks of inner attitude and outer manner'.[74] Only those privileged to lead can set the right example, and help to inculcate better habits. And, of course, James saw himself as one of the élite. He was a member of the Harvard Faculty throughout the period during which their dynamic President, Charles Eliot, built the college anew, according to his own vision, and established its intellectual pre-eminence in America.[75] James himself, having set up a fully fledged psychology laboratory, then played a significant role in re-building the philosophy department, and in establishing its pre-eminence. In the opening paragraph of his Gifford Lectures, James tells us that the very first philosophy books he read were by Fraser, William Hamilton, Dugald Stewart and Thomas Brown. It is not widely appreciated in Britain how great was the influence on American college education of these Scottish writers; crucially, they introduced the Scottish eighteenth-century notion of philosophy as the ground of every young person's education—it is only within the last decade, indeed, that students at the ancient Scottish universities have been able to study for an arts degree without a compulsory philosophy course of some kind. This aside, there are three elements to be underlined in connection with James. In his posthumously published lectures, *Problems of Philosophy*, he remarks that philosophy 'in one sense of the term is only a compendious name for the spirit in education which the word "college" stands for in America', something to be associated with 'liberal culture'.[76] Discipline, toleration, openness: as he says on another occasion, 'philosophic study means the habit of always seeing an alternative, of not taking the usual for granted'.[77] The second element derived from the Scottish tradition is exemplified in James's attitude to his writing and to his audience. Hugh Blair's *Lectures on Rhetoric*, published in 1783, was enormously popular as a text in American colleges, and alerted readers not only to the proprieties of

[73] *Letters*, II, 152, 100; and 153—'The eternal fight of liberalism has now to be fought by us on much the same terms as in the older countries'.

[74] *Talks*, 212, 215; and 217—'We must change ourselves from a race that admires jerk and snap for their own sakes ... to one that, on the contrary, has calm for its ideal, and for their own sakes loves harmony, dignity, and ease'.

[75] For James's first response to Eliot's election as President in 1869, see Perry, I, 296; for background, B. Kuklick, *The Rise of American Philosophy* (New Haven: Yale University Press, 1977), esp. 131.

[76] *Problems*, 6.

[77] Perry, I, 443.

vocabulary and style, but also to the conditions of effective communication. In 1901 James writes to a friend that 'philosophical discussion proper only succeeds between intimates who have learned how to converse by months of weary trials and failure. The philosopher is a lone beast dwelling in his individual burrow'.[78] He rebukes Peirce for forgetting, or ignoring, the fact that 'a *lecture* must succeed *as such*'; and elsewhere remarks that sketchy philosophical discussion 'alone befits a public lecture'.[79] Now Peirce himself described James's whole procedure as 'slap-dash', and James was well aware that his critics demanded fuller and more detailed explanations of his views.[80] Even a sympathetic modern commentator, A. J. Ayer, feels impelled to insist, within the first half dozen pages of his discussion, that James is 'inattentive to questions of technical detail', and that the early work is 'not of any great technical interest'.[81] James's acerbic sister remarked that he could never stick to anything, and in 1895 he writes: 'as I grow older I get impatient (and incompetent) of details and turn to broad abstractions'.[82] Part of the explanation is surely to be found in the third element that James absorbed from the Scottish tradition, and which he signalled in the very title of his early article 'The Sentiment of Rationality'.

Questions about the respective roles of reason and sentiment absorbed the early empiricists whom James regarded as his chief philosophical mentors. And it was Hume who most prominently canvassed the view that man is influenced less by reason than traditionally claimed, and *driven* by reason, in that sense, not at all—since it has no motor function. Man is a thinking animal, of course, but his judgments are frequently the result of instinct, habit, feelings.[83] James, too, accepts the centrality of feelings in our responses—or of *sentiment*, in the significantly ambiguous term favoured in the eighteenth century. Indeed, by making consciousness the centre of his account he can talk of the experience of thinking as itself a feeling, and avoid explaining how to bridge the dualist gap between sensation and thought. James's psychology, epistemology and metaphysics are explicitly in the tradition of his ancestors, and to this extent he is a *moral philosopher*—in the older sense in which Hume sets out

---

[78] *Letters,* II, 164.

[79] Perry, II, 418; *Pragmatism,* 197; also *Letters,* II, 164, and remarks on Boutroux's lectures at Harvard in the *Nation,* 1910 (W. James, *Essays in Philosophy* (Cambridge, Mass.: Harvard University Press, 1978), 167).

[80] Perry, II, 422.

[81] A. J. Ayer, *The Origins of Pragmatism* (London, 1968), 184–185. On 'technical interests', see *PU,* 14.

[82] Perry, I, 128; II, 189–190. In 1905 he asserts that the humanism he supports 'has to renounce sincerely rectilinear arguments and ancient ideals of rigour and finality'—*ERE,* 247.

[83] See my *Hume's Sentiments, passim.*

to study the *science of man*, and in contrast to the natural philosopher. And as Hume, at least, understood such a role, the moral philosopher undertakes his analyses with a practical end, however distant, in view; he agreed with Cicero that most men will be at ease only if they can link their reflections to practical action in some way, although a few thinkers will have a psychological need to pursue philosophy in the abstract, and to push their ideas to the limit.[84] But Cicero and Hume not only wrote about religion and ethics and politics, but lived an active public life: James did not, could not, would not. His failure to explore any of the social and political implications of his impassioned psychological case for individualism shows that he left half of the moral philosopher's task undone; there are hints that he would repudiate any charge that egoism followed from or was licensed by, his account, but a positive view of the roles of society and of the individual in it is lacking. And it is lacking some would say, in precisely the same way, in his brother Henry's novels. It should be remembered also, in this context, that Cicero and Hume both came to hold that, carried to any great lengths, philosophical reflection was *unnatural*, not only in the sense that most people did not do it, but in the sense that most people did not need it: life goes on, whatever a philosopher says.[85] One source of James's own unease with academic philosophy, and with the institutional life from which he periodically sought escape, is surely to be found in these views of his mentors that he found so congenial.[86]

There is yet another parallel. Hume and James both rejected their stern Calvinist inheritance, although in James, at least, its traces were never covered. 'Our practice is the only sure evidence, even to ourselves, that we are genuinely Christian' he had said, and he agreed with his father that the essence of life is struggle; anxiety must therefore tinge our moments of inactivity, especially where our emotions are engaged:

> There is no more contemptible type of human character than that of the nerveless sentimentalist and dreamer, who spends his life in a weltering sea of sensibility and emotion, but who never does a manly concrete deed. . . . Even the habit of excessive indulgence in music, for those who are neither performers themselves nor musically gifted enough to take it in a purely intellectual way, has probably a relaxing effect upon the character. One becomes filled with emotions which habitually pass without prompting to any deed, and so the inertly sentimental condition is kept up.[87]

[84] *ERE*, 136; *PU*, 15.
[85] James even quotes Cicero in his 1879 article, *WB*, 92.
[86] *Letters*, II, 164.
[87] *Varieties*, 20; *Principles*, I, 125—the first sentence is repeated, *verbatim*, *Talks*, 70; on the *'anti-sexual instinct* . . . of personal isolation' (Ibid., II, 437).

James feared that his views might be judged '*bottomless* and romantic', or even sentimental.[88] But 'for morality life is a war' and it is necessary to keep 'the moral fighting shape' as long as possible—and we all know that 'the athletic attitude tends ever to break down', with death the final victor.[89]

The Scottish moralists who inspired James were intensely self-conscious about their roles in society, and the place of man in nature; new scientific ideas challenged old religious dogmas and seemed to open up a void which threatened to inhibit action of any kind. But man had to act, and a working solution had to be found to the conflicting claims of feeling and thought. The moral philosophers of the eighteenth century were *not* primarily epistemologists, as subsequent commentators have mistakenly thought; their epistemological and metaphysical claims are typically constructed as grounds or explanations of precepts and principles of action. The utility of the speculations is the final, and usually the central, criterion. James, too, with his Scotch-Irish ancestry, was writing as a member of a self-conscious group, in a self-conscious nation, seeking to fuse post-Darwinian thought with the Puritan values of the Founding Fathers, and the philosophical ideals of the Framers of the Constitution. For him, no doubt, the struggle for existence was to be understood spiritually rather than physically, but pragmatism was still a suitable method, and individualism a governing principle. He loved America, as he tells us, for 'her youth, her greenness, her plasticity, innocence, good intentions';[90] unlike Europe, there was, in his view, no past to inhibit decision and stifle the present.

James fully accepts that philosophers are interested in the links between their convictions, and the reasons for them—'the connecting *is* the thinking'; but the benefits of such enquiries have their limits, and philosophers, like everyone else, can go too far: 'the end is after all more than the way'.[91] It is significant that James was frequently uneasy over the proper classification of what he was doing—not psychology, but philosophy; not philosophy of religion but factual description; not epistemology but moral philosophy; or, as his critics insisted, not logic, but merely psychology. Such labels would be inadequate for moral philosophy, in the eighteenth-century sense; they were modern, and they reflected the increasing specialization within philosophy as an institutional practice, which James disliked. He wanted professionalism, for the good of the discipline and of the students being trained for leadership, but a professionalism that sought to strengthen rather than weaken its ability to communicate with an educated public; for what seriousness, he asks, 'what seriousness can possibly

[88] *Letters,* II, 204; *Talks,* v.
[89] *Varieties,* 45, 368, 46.
[90] *Letters,* II, 105; cf. 305.
[91] *Talks,* 143; *PU,* 15.

remain in debating philosophic propositions that will never make an appreciable difference to us in action?'[92] Hume saw himself as a 'Kind . . . of Ambassador from the Dominions of Learning to those of Conversation' and, what is more, looked to America for a general realization of such ideals.[93] James played a similar role a century later, although without any comparable political dimension; but he consciously disguised his learning, and except for *Principles* and *Varieties,* his writings give no indication of his wide reading. Any form of 'scholasticism', he felt, would alienate those whom he hoped to reach, those who normally prefer to surf on the shifting crest of assertion, and it would be false to his own deepest conviction in what can only be called 'personal communion'.[94] The following letter to his ten year old son, written when he was fifty-eight, is pleasantly disingenuous:

> Your Ma thinks you'll grow up into a filosopher like me and write books. It is easy enuff, all but the writing. You just get it out of other books, and write it down.
>
> Always your loving,
Dad.[95]

The concepts that James cherished, over-worked and under-defined as maybe, can all be lifted from their original contexts and weighed in the balance: consciousness, feeling, belief; individualism, pluralism, pragmatism; continuity, diversity, vagueness. And it would be in the spirit of James's philosophy, indeed, to use and test these notions for ourselves. Moreover, since he gives no positive account of language or the conditions of communication—he accepts a degree of relativity in aesthetic judgment—we cannot be sure whether he thought another's views could ever be more than a stimulus to one's own.[96] But, in any case, to examine his concepts separately would give us only the most limited understanding of

[92] *Essays,* 435.

[93] D. Hume, *The Philosophical Works,* Green and Grose (eds) (London: Longmans, Green & Co., 1875), IV, 368; the quotation is from Hume's essay of 1742, 'Of Essay Writing'.

[94] *Letters,* II, 279.

[95] Ibid., II, 129. The coy spelling alludes to his own genuine interest in spelling reform (ibid., II, 319).

[96] Perry, II, 256—'the good thing about a work of art is that it tells all sorts of things to different spectators, of none of which the artist ever knew a word'. Perry surmises that James shrank from discussing aesthetic experiences precisely because he *had* them, but discussed religious experiences because he borrowed already verbalized versions (ibid.). But James certainly had experiences which he regarded as extra-ordinary, and possibly mystical.

James's thought; for that, we need the whole, and the particulars in the whole. It is his own view, after all, that philosophy is reflection on the links between ideas and claims, however much they shift and change; but it is reflection itself consolidated by testing in our own experience. James bequeaths us, as befits a major philosopher, a set of provisional questions and provisional answers, about the nature of philosophy, its role in society, and about the nature of man. By his own statements, anyone is worth studying to the extent that we can use his ideas; but no one can tell, in advance, what might be useful. We cannot know how similar his context is to ours unless we look. James originally intended to begin his Gifford Lectures with the following paragraph; it provides us with a fitting conclusion:

> There is something in life, as one feels its presence, that seems to defy all the possible resources of phraseology. . . . Life defies our phrases, not only because it is infinitely continuous and subtle and shaded, whilst our verbal terms are discrete, rude and few; but because of a deeper discrepancy still. Our words come together leaning on each other laterally for support, in chains and propositions, and there is never a proposition that does not require other propositions after it, to amplify it, restrict it, or in some way save it from the falsity by defect or excess which it contains. . . . Life, too, in one sense, stumbles over its own fact in a similar way; for its earlier moments plunge ceaselessly into later ones which reinterpret and correct them. Yet there is something else than this in life, something entirely unparalleled by anything in verbal thought. The living moments—some living moments, at any rate—have somewhat of absolute that needs no lateral support. Their meaning seems to well up from out of their very centre, in a way impossible verbally to describe. . . . This self-sustaining in the midst of self-removal, which characterizes all reality and fact, is something absolutely foreign to the nature of language, and even to the nature of logic, commonly so-called. Something forever exceeds, escapes from statement, withdraws from definition, must be glimpsed and felt, not told. No one knows this like your genuine professor of philosophy. For what glimmers and twinkles like a bird's wing in the sunshine it is his business to snatch and fix. And every time he fires his volley of new vocables out of his philosophic shotgun, whatever surface-flush of success he may feel, he secretly kens at the same time the finer hollowness and irrelevancy.[97]

---

[97] Perry, II, 328.

John Dewey
1859–1952

H. S. THAYER

It is generally agreed that the most influential philosophers in America are Charles S. Peirce, William James and John Dewey. James's fame came rather suddenly in the latter half of his life—roughly, from 1880 to 1910; it flourished with the appearance of his *Principles of Psychology* (1890) and shortly thereafter with his advocacy of pragmatism and radical empiricism. James was acclaimed in England and Europe as well as in America. Peirce, on the other hand, was almost entirely neglected; his work remained unknown to all but a few philosophers and his chief acknowledgment was as a scientist and logician. His importance began to be recognized and his immense researches and writings studied some twenty-five years after his death. It was otherwise with Dewey. During his long lifetime his ideas not only engaged the reflections and critical discussions of philosophers, he also had a profound and contagious influence on education, the social sciences, aesthetics, and political theory and practice. In this respect his thought has reached a wider audience in America than that of either Peirce or James. In his day lawyers, labour leaders, scientists and several heads of state attested to the vitality of his wisdom.

At the present time we can witness a vigorous and expanding scholarly, philosophic and literary interest in these thinkers. It is worth noticing that all three philosophers were, in their own ways, to share certain fundamental convictions and doctrines: they were the leading spokesmen for a philosophy that became known as *pragmatism*. And early in the present century pragmatism was the leading philosophy in America. Pragmatism has undergone subsequent vicissitudes of fortune; but recently it has been receiving renewed attention.

That pragmatism emerged as a major philosophic movement and that, accordingly, there was some degree of co-operative philosophizing and points of agreement among its spokesmen, has its historical significance. But it would be a serious mistake to view the efforts of Peirce, James and Dewey only in this way as inclining to a common goal or converging to form a school. Each of them produced a large body of philosophic thought relatively independent of the pragmatism with which they were associated.

In what follows, I propose to consider the work of John Dewey. I shall have something to say about his main contribution to pragmatism, his theory of 'Instrumentalism'; a few links with Peirce and James will be mentioned. But the attempt here will be to concentrate on the formative conditions and central themes of Dewey's philosophy on its own, and from the inside, so to speak, and not as contributory to anything other than itself and its own realization.

I

John Dewey was born in Burlington, Vermont, in 1859. He was educated at the University of Vermont and, after an interval teaching high school, he entered Johns Hopkins University in 1882 to undertake graduate study in philosophy. One of the teachers there was Charles S. Peirce under whom Dewey studied logic. But his appreciation of Peirce was to come later. Dewey's main interest at the time was in the history of philosophy and psychology. G. Stanley Hall, a proponent in America of the new psysiological experimental psychology of Wundt, had established a laboratory at Johns Hopkins. Dewey enrolled in all of Hall's courses. Experimental psychology played an especially important part in Dewey's philosophical development. His early writings show a thorough acquaintance with the literature of psychology. Indeed, in these early years of his career, Dewey referred to himself as a psychologist rather than a philosopher.[1]

The teacher who most influenced Dewey at Johns Hopkins was G. S. Morris, an able historian of philosophy and articulate disciple of Hegelian idealism. Dewey had been reared in liberal Christian evangelicalism. The philosophical opinions he had acquired in college before coming to Johns Hopkins were not very strong, but they were disturbing. They did not fit very well with his religious convictions, and they were divisive. Dewey later commented on this sense of intellectual 'divisions' as the 'heritage of New England culture, divisions by way of isolation of self from the world, of soul from body, of nature from God' as causing him 'an inward laceration'. The discovery of Hegelian idealism came as a kind of deliverance. Speaking of its effect on him, Dewey says 'it supplied a demand for unification that was doubtless an intense emotional craving'. And he adds: 'Hegel's synthesis of subject and object, matter and spirit, the divine and the human . . . operated as an immense release, a liberation'.

---

[1] 'Illusory Psychology', *Mind* 12 (1887). Reprinted in *John Dewey, The Early Works* (Carbondale and Edwardsville: Southern Illinois University Press, 1969) 1, see p. 171. This is the definitive edition of Dewey's published writings, Jo Ann Boydston (ed.), chronologically arranged in *Early*, *Middle* and *Later* periods. At present twenty-six volumes, the complete edition will be thirty-three volumes. All references below to Dewey's *Works* are to this edition.

As a sociological and psychological speculation, we might interpret Dewey's 'craving' for unity and his impression of the divisive 'heritage of New England culture', as a reflection of his youth in Burlington, Vermont. The city had a picturesque charm of a New England setting; but there was a sharp contrast between the estates and fine houses of the rich, and a population of poor immigrants and industrial workers. The latter lived in 'haunts of dissipation and poverty' according to one report.[2] Between the two extremes, there was a respectable middle class, such as Dewey's family, sharing with the wealthy the designation of 'old families', the established Americans.

The Hegelian period in Dewey's thought lasted for some fifteen years. This has been a familiar enough topic in historical accounts of Dewey's philosophy ever since he made the matter clear in an autobiographical sketch (in 1930) from which the above quotations are drawn.[3] But there occurs another recollection in the same essay which has received less notice and concerning which, I think, some importance should be assigned. In his junior year in college, Dewey took a 'short course' in physiology. The text used was by Thomas H. Huxley. Dewey records that he found there a kind of unity of subject matter and presentation that attracted him intellectually and provided 'a model of a view of things to which material in any field ought to conform'. There follows the especially significant confession: 'I was led to desire a world and a life that would have the same properties as had the human organism in the picture of it derived from study of Huxley's treatment'.

The fervoured emotional and intellectual demand for unification; the preferred treatment of subject matters as composed of interdependent constituents forming or leading to 'organic unity'; the idea that the parts of a whole, as in the case of the human organism, are to be studied in the light of their relation and contribution to the whole—were latent and powerful, and we will see, permanent traits of Dewey's mind even before he had come to Hegel and idealism.

Dewey was not slow in beginning a life of writing in which he was enormously prolific. (The complete edition of his published writings will comprise thirty-three volumes.[4]) Before entering graduate school he published two articles. During his years as a graduate student he published five articles and wrote a dissertation on 'The Psychology of Kant'.

On graduation from Johns Hopkins, Dewey began teaching at the University of Michigan. But for a year at Minnesota, he remained at

[2] George Dykhuizen, *The Life and Mind of John Dewey* (Carbondale and Edwardsville, Southern Illinois University Press, 1973), 2.

[3] 'From Absolutism to Experimentalism', in George P. Adams and W. P. Montague (eds.), *Contemporary American Philosophy* (New York: Macmillan, 1930), II, 13–27.

[4] See n. 1 above.

Michigan for ten years. There he made lasting friendships with James H.
Tufts (with whom he collaborated on an important volume, *Ethics*
(1908)), and George Herbert Mead. Both men were to remain Dewey's
colleagues when he moved to Chicago.

At the University of Chicago, Dewey was appointed head of the Department of Philosophy and also head of the Department of Pedagogy. His
interest in education was both stimulated by and found direction in the
'Laboratory School' he founded. This was an elementary school in which
philosophical and educational theory could be applied to, and result from,
the facts and observations of practises conducted in a controlled situation.
The 'Laboratory School' rapidly became a famous institution; it served as
a model, often discussed and imitated, elsewhere in the country. The
school was a forerunner of the movement known as 'progressive education'
prominent in the nineteen thirties. One of Dewey's most influential and
widely read books, *The School and Society* (1900), presented the theory
and aim of the school.[5]

In 1904, Dewey left Chicago for Columbia University, in New York,
where he spent the rest of his professional career. He was then forty-five
years old and at the height of his powers, famous as a philosopher and
educator.

In Dewey's Chicago years we can witness the transition in thought and
expression from Hegelian idealism to a naturalism and, as he called it,
'instrumentalism'. There came a growing clarification and distinct direction to his philosophic work. The Columbia period was to issue in his best
known and major philosophical writings. These include numerous articles
on technical philosophical subjects and on general social problems and
some ten books.[6] He travelled in Europe and the Orient and, in 1918,
accepted invitations to lecture in China and Japan. He became renowned
as a leading representative of pragmatism, and an exponent of 'instrumentalism', progressive education, and liberal social thought and action. He
died in 1952.

II

In coming to Dewey's philosophy, we will be helped by recognizing at the
outset the presence of a central and persistent concern expressed and

[5] *The School and Society, Middle Works,* 1, 1–109.
[6] *Ethics* (1908); *How We Think* (1910); *Democracy and Education* (1916);
Essays in Experimental Logic (1916); *Human Nature and Conduct* (1922);
Experience and Nature (1925); *The Public and its Problems* (1927); *The
Quest for Certainty* (1929); *Philosophy and Civilization* (1931); *Art as
Experience* (1934); *Logic: The Theory of Inquiry* (1938). For the first eight of
these books see *Middle Works*, Vols 5, 6, 9, 12, 14, *Later Works*, Vols 1, 2,
4.

reiterated in many writings and occupying much of his thought. This was the acute problem, as he saw it, of finding a way to resolve the destructive cleavage between scientific knowledge and moral beliefs. Of course, there may be cultures in which this problem does not exist. But Dewey's attention was directed to our present Western civilization and its history since the dawn of experimental natural science in the sixteenth century. The problem had earlier antecedents, but it became particularly aggravated as expanding scientific thought began to clash with an inherited body of religious and moral beliefs. Dewey writes:

> The problem of restoring integration and co-operation between man's beliefs about the world in which he lives and his beliefs about values and purposes that should direct his conduct is the deepest problem of modern life. It is the problem of any philosophy that is not isolated from life.

The problem for philosophy, he adds,

> is to work out the relation that exists between beliefs about the nature of things due to natural science to beliefs about value.[7]

In his younger days, Dewey first perceived this problem in a somewhat more narrow and traditional way as a conflict between science and religion. The Hegelian idealism in which he was then immersed, he believed to be entirely compatible, indeed, identical with 'the theological teachings of Christianity'.[8] In one remarkable paper, he took great pains to show that current physiological psychology posed no threat to Christianity. With considerable dialectical ingenuity, he argued that the findings of Helmholtz and Wundt are one with the teachings of Jesus and St Paul on soul and body.[9]

Dewey's initial formulations of psychological theory incorporates Hegelian themes of a universal consciousness entering into finite minds and infusing physical sensations with meaning to direct the individual toward 'self-development' and 'self-realization'. Bodily occurrences and sensations are the means, the stimuli, in the process of living activity; the response and directive factor is supplied by consciousness or soul. The active organic life-process is an interrelated function of both components, body and soul. The life-process is directed to and guided by a higher spiritual end: self-realization; union of finite and universal will, finite and infinite personality. Just as mind and body are taken as fused and co-ordinated features of one organic process, so psychology is assimilated with

[7] *The Quest for Certainty*, *Later Works*, 4, 204.
[8] 'Ethics and Physical Science', *Andover Review* 7 (1887); *Early Works*, 1, 209.
[9] 'Soul and Body', *Bibliotheca Sacra* 43 (1886); *Early Works*, 1, 93–115.

moral theory. Dewey thus commented: 'modern psychology is intensely ethical in its tendencies'.[10] These ideas culminated in Dewey's first book, *Psychology* (1887).[11]

Another influence on Dewey's early work came with his recognition of the implications for psychology and morals of the Darwinian theory of evolution. The basic idea here for psychology, Dewey maintained, is that the nervous system in all of its functions is adjustive and adaptive. Not all events impinging on an organism become converted into stimuli, or call for response; it is rather:

> The stimulus favorable to the well-being of the organism, is selected from the immense number playing upon the organism; others, especially those unserviceable, are inhibited, and then the action results according to the needs, that is, the purpose of the organism itself.[12]

The purposive factor, the psychical, writes Dewey, 'is teleologically immanent in the physical'.[13] The spiritual goals and welfare of the organism, 'self-realization', are hence regarded as in harmony with the theory of evolution. That theory seemed to contribute to and confirm a teleological and purposive interpretation of thought and action.

If the foregoing epitome of the objectives characterizing Dewey's early thought is at all clear, we can notice the emergence of a general theory of thought and action in which knowledge and valuation are not simply juxtaposed, or envisioned as counterparts, but are intimately connected phases in one process of organic activity. Here that desire (as we noticed) which had stirred Dewey as a student in his twenties to find subject matters treated as an 'interrelated unity', like the human organism, begins to be fulfilled.

Fundamental to this theory, and the centre of attention, is the idea of the act, the 'unit of behaviour' as Dewey once captioned it.[14] In its simplest form an organic act is a transition from a state of nervous irritation to some state of recovery or equilibrium. Drawing on his studies in physiological psychology, Dewey states it almost as a cardinal principle: 'every nervous activity is essentially an adjustment'.[15] Among these activities, some may

---

[10] 'The New Psychology', *Andover Review* **2** (1884); *Early Works*, 1, 60.

[11] *Early Works*, 2.

[12] 'Soul and Body', *Early Works*, 1, 103.

[13] Ibid., 103.

[14] His later title for 'The Reflex Arc Concept in Psychology' (1896) when that paper was reprinted with some changes in *Philosophy and Civilization* (New York: Minton, Balch & Company, 1931), 233–248. In the table of contents the title appears as 'The Unity of Behavior'.

[15] 'Soul and Body', *Early Works*, 1, 103. The more complete statement is: 'The simplest nerve action is not so simple as to exclude the adaptive, purposive factor. It is always an adjustment. It is never a mere mechanical result of a stimulus, but always involves selection, inhibition, and response.'

be insignificant and others momentous—relative, always, to the needs and purposes of the organism.

Simple activities—such as adjustment of the eye to light—may become parts of more inclusive activities—such as seeing fire and calling for help. The parts in such cases are co-ordinated with other parts resulting in a whole sequence of behaviour. (But more of this shortly.) Thus it is a basic feature of the behavioural act, as a sequence of component partial acts, to exhibit a developmental history and temporal pattern. In the beginning, there is disturbance, confusion, disequilibrium. Something has gone wrong; previous activity has become disrupted. This constitutes a problem. Subsequent activity is directed to recovering equilibrium, to an integration of activities, restoring order. This is to resolve the problem.

The behavioural act does not, of course, occur in a vacuum; it is not a self-subsistent process. The act has the living organism at its centre, and the responses of the organism qualify every stage and all the stimuli and adjustments making up the act and its outcome. But there is also an environment, physical and cultural, in which the act is situated. There is a continuous interchange between environing conditions and organism, and these sustain the act leading to completion, achievement of purpose, or depletion and failure. So environing conditions become incorporated into the act as among its parts. Just how environing conditions are made to enter into specific functions of living creatures, how a marvel of intricate trading and interchanges of energies occur, cannot be pursued here. But we might note, as part of the complexity of the subject, that in the course of its adjustments and changes the moving organism also imposes adjustments and changes in the environing medium.

In working out his theory of action Dewey came to realize that the framework and vocabulary of Hegelian idealism was impeding his efforts at being clear and accurate. Under the influence of James and Mead, Dewey's idealistic psychology gives way to one increasingly biological and behaviouristic. The Hegelian language of 'universal and finite consciousness', of 'spirit' and 'self-realization', becomes replaced by 'experience' and 'intelligence', 'inquiry' and 'growth'.

The theory of action led Dewey to many positive and original lines of thought in morals, education, logic and, eventually, aesthetics and metaphysics. It also served as the basis for his extensive critical discussions of other influential philosophical views on these subjects.

What I have said so far about this theory has been sketchy in an attempt to avoid distracting details too early. Some further clarification can be gained if we turn to one of Dewey's major—and by now classic—papers in philosophical psychology and the analysis of action: 'The Reflex Arc Concept in Psychology' (1896).[16] The paper was one of the sources of the

[16] *Psychological Review* **3** (1896); *Early Works*, 5, 96–109.

movement known as 'functional psychology' in America.[17] It is also important to us, at the moment, since it contains the seeds and anticipation of most of Dewey's later views on the nature of thought and action, his instrumentalism (or pragmatism), and his interpretation of meaning and purpose.

In the late nineteenth century, critical of an older philosophical analysis of mental activity as a dual play of sensation and idea, or of an association of ideas, psychologists proposed a reflex arc concept. The arc seemed to account for many facts concerning nerve action, stimuli and response. The arc consisted of three parts: sensory stimulus, central activity (or idea), and motor discharge or response. The arc was the joining of these parts to explain how higher animals and humans react to external stimuli.

Dewey criticized this way of representing the data as a disjointed 'mechanical conjunction' of otherwise separate parts. What was needed, he argued (and by now we might have guessed), is a conception of the three parts of the arc, not as separate segments, but as an 'organic unity', as 'divisions of labor' within 'a single concrete whole'.

Dewey considers the example of a child reaching for a candle and getting burnt. According to the reflex arc concept, we have a serial order: the sensation of light is the stimulus, reaching with hand is response; the burn then encountered is the next stimulus, withdrawing of the hand is the response. And so on. Dewey proposed a quite different analysis. We do not begin with sensory stimulus, but with a co-ordination of movements: the movement of the body and of the head, adjustments of the eye muscles, and an 'optical-ocular' activity. These determine the quality of the sensory stimulus and hence are primary. The beginning, Dewey argues, is 'the *act* of seeing', not the sensation of light. The sensation becomes significant, 'it gives the value of the act' while the movement 'furnishes its mechanism and control'.[18] But both sensation and movement lie inside the act of seeing.

The act of seeing may stimulate another, the act of reaching. The acts then become members of a 'larger co-ordination'. Seeing and reaching are interrelated activities; each has come to reinforce and affect the other over time. They become partners in a more general co-ordination. Seeing guides the hand to its object, since both hand and object are in the field of vision. The reaching, in turn, controls the seeing; eyes follow as well as

[17] Edwin G. Boring, *A History of Experimental Psychology*, 2nd edn (New York: Appleton–Century–Crofts, 1950), 554. Also, J. R. Angel, 'The Relations of Structural and Functional Psychology to Philosophy', *Decennial Publications of the University of Chicago*, First Series, Vol. 3, 55–73 (Chicago: University of Chicago Press, 1903). Angel was a student of William James and a younger colleague of Dewey's at Chicago.

[18] 'The Reflex Arc Concept', *Early Works*, 5, 97–98.

guide the hand. What was originally seen is now enlarged into seeing something to be touched.

Finally, there is the burn and pain. This is not simply a new sensation to which withdrawing the hand is the response. The pain is not an isolated experience. If it were, it would be hard to explain how the child learns to avoid that experience in the future. The burn, says Dewey, 'is the original seeing'; the original seeing of light, now 'enlarged and transformed in its value'. The later stage of the act—or co-ordination of acts—has come in to qualify the earlier. The change is between the original seeing of a light and 'seeing-of-a-light-that-means-pain-when-contact-occurs'.[19]

In this view of the circuit of behaviour, the process is teleological. The earlier phases of activity lead to, and into, the later; and the later transforms the earlier in their value and significance. For Dewey, it is the whole co-ordinated act that is to be taken as the primary fact and context in the explanation of behaviour. As we have seen, the distinctions of stimulus and response fall within the act; and they are relative to how we are regarding the act. One and the same phase in the sequence of activities can be designated as stimulus or as response depending on whether we are focusing on it as the beginning of a later phase or the outcome of an earlier one. Stimulus and response are not given and fixed elements; basically they are to be understood as reciprocal changes in the direction and control of behaviour.

To recall once more our child: he has sometimes found pleasure in bright objects and sometimes pain. He sees this bright object. Here the response is initially uncertain; but so is the stimulus. In the preceding stage of activity, the seeing of light was developed into seeing-of-a-bright-object. Now the problem is: what kind of bright object is being seen? Will it yield pleasure or pain when touched? So the problem is how to interpret what is seen with respect to touch, or, with respect to touch, how this object is to be seen.

For Dewey, the most general sense to be made of the notions of 'stimulus' and 'response' is that 'stimulus' denotes the early stage of behaviour which has become problematic, a stage requiring clarification if action is to continue successfully. 'Response' is the later phase of the same process which provides a resolution of those conditions. So Dewey comments:

Just as the discovery of the sensation marks the establishing of the problem, so the constitution of the response marks the solution.[20]

We are brought back to the 'unit of behavior', already discussed, in which the behavioural process is conceived as the organizing and unifying

---

[19] Ibid., 98.
[20] Ibid., 107–108.

of activity according to some purpose or need. We come as well to a point of transition from the psychological part of Dewey's theory of action to the logical: to instrumentalism.

III

Man is a rational animal—or so we have been assured. We have this on the highest authority, namely, from some rational animals who long ago became philosophers. And despite considerable variety of specific doctrines, there was a general consensus among philosophers that reason is not only the distinctive trait of man, it is also the source of knowledge and truth. Either as aided by the senses, or completely independent of bodily organs, it was held that the reasoning mind could discover eternal truths upon which knowledge and moral conduct could be securely based. Thus it was that the task of philosophy was widely envisioned as, in Dewey's words, 'the quest for certainty'.[21] And in this way, it was felt that philosophy might provide a deliverance from the mutable and precarious conditions of life. The authority of reason bore traces of divinity in its constitution and exercise; the divine in man or above him.

Dewey was severely critical of this conception of the office of philosophy. One could appreciate its imaginative vision and artistry—even the awesome confidence by which it had received expression, say, through Plato, or Aristotle, or Spinoza, or Descartes. But it was, in reality, a flight from responsibility and its promise of absolute intellectual security and finality was an alluring deception.

In its natural and normal manifestations reason is addressed, not to eternal truth, but to just those unstable, perilous and changing conditions of existence from which so much philosophy was a retreat. Reason is an agency of change and its role is in the living struggle to improve life. Taking this historical and empirical view of the matter, Dewey was led to argue that the most efficacious form that reason has evolved in performing its natural function is in the experimental method of modern science. One urgent task of philosophy is to gain full understanding of this method so as to suggest how it can be extended to deal with social and ethical problems, problems arising in our changing culture whose underlying problem is the necessity of change.

The recurring challenge to reason is not to try to resist or transcend cultural change, but to give it intelligent direction. If reason (and thought and mind) are rendered in this thoroughly naturalistic fashion, these endowments are understood as much like bodily organs and nerve structure; all are alike instruments of adaptation and control.

[21] *The Quest for Certainty* (The Gifford Lectures).

One of the consequences of this view of the method and vocation of reason was drawn by Dewey and other pragmatists. We do not have to engage in a futile search for a foundation on which to base and guarantee the validity of knowledge and values. The justification of the procedures by which knowledge is attained and responsible moral conduct is practised, is not to be found in a prior philosophy or in metaphysical truths. The justification is in the continued application of those procedures in effecting successful results. A method that regularly (even if not always) leads to satisfactory consequences with respect to specific problems is to that extent justified; justified by its fruits. And Dewey thought that the method which had scored by far the greatest number of successes—and was by far the most likely to do so in the future—was the experimental method of science. For him, then, this was the only method which could rightly be claimed as authoritative.

The experimental method, the method of 'reflective thought', or, as he finally came to call it, 'inquiry', while ordinarily applied to some problem and subject matter, can itself be the subject matter of investigation. This is a reflexive turn, a bit like thinking about thinking. Inquiry occupied a major place in Dewey's thinking. It was the subject matter of many articles and the theme of four books: *Studies in Logical Theory* (1903); *How We Think* (1910); *Essays in Experimental Logic* (1916); and *Logic: The Theory of Inquiry* (1938).[22] Dewey took logic to have as its rightful province the analysis of what inquiry is, how it occurs, and by what means it proceeds to a conclusion, and how the conclusion is validated. This was his instrumental logic. 'Instrumentalism', he writes:

> is an attempt to establish a precise logical theory of concepts, of judgments and inferences in their various forms, by considering primarily how thought functions in the experimental determination of future consequences.[23]

The theory was developed and elaborated carefully and in great detail. Here, once again, the behavioural act is primary; but the focus is now on distinctive intellectual features and operations within the act and as directing its execution. Organic responses and adjustments are now treated as material and occasions for conceptualization, for signs, propositions, and inferences as means to the production of judgment. Judgment is the successful (or unsuccessful) concluding stage of inquiry.

We have already observed that, for Dewey, organic action is a transition through adjustments from a state of imbalance to one of equilibrium.

[22] *Studies in Logical Theory*, Middle Works, 2, 295–375; *How We Think*, Middle Works, 6, 179–356. *Essays in Experimental Logic* (Chicago: Chicago University Press, 1916). *Logic: The Theory of Inquiry* (New York: Henry Holt and Company, 1938).
[23] 'The Development of American Pragmatism', *Later Works*, 2, 14.

Inquiry is now treated in these terms: conditions of arrested activity, of disturbance and doubt, initiate inquiry. And inquiry is the effort to establish a resolution of the troubled conditions and to institute order and integration. (On this point Dewey comes very close to ideas Peirce had advanced earlier; Dewey acknowledged as much, although he had arrived at his position independently.)

Logical forms and the rules and techniques of reasoning have their origin and function within inquiry as means by which warranted conclusions are attained. Eventually, these are generalized as procedures available and to be employed when particular inquiries are conducted. The logical forms of propositions and inferences by which conclusions are suggested and established, function very much like habits of behaviour (a notion also developed earlier by Peirce). The theory reached its most complete formulation in Dewey's *Logic: The Theory of Inquiry*. In that work (in rough paraphrase) 'inquiry' is defined as the controlled transformation of an indeterminate situation so as to convert the elements of the original situation into a unified whole.[24]

Inquiry, like language, is a social art and practise and is conceived by Dewey as a distinctive way of acting; it thus involves changes, a 'transformation' of the environment in which it occurs. Inquiry is a human contribution; but in a very general sense in which reality is in transition, inquiry is one of the ways by which reality makes changes in itself and a way in which knowledge makes a difference in what is 'real'.

When an inquiry is completed and a 'unified whole' situation is realized, the conditions for a final judgment are also established. The judgment, in the form of an assertion, states the solution and resolution of the problem that had provoked inquiry. The judgmental assertion is warranted by inquiry. Dewey calls this the 'warranted assertion', and the warranted assertion is how he understands the meaning of 'truth'. There is a certain kind of correspondence between the warranted assertion and the problematic situation that gave rise to inquiry. The warranted assertion stands to the problematic situation that generated it as a key can be said to 'correspond' to the conditions set by a lock, or as a correct answer corresponds to a question.[25]

I cannot attempt here to venture into the details of this comprehensive theory. But we may note some of the interesting and original implications derived and developed by Dewey from his conception of the nature of organic behaviour and thought. I find nine topics in this connection.

[24] For Dewey's full statement see *Logic: The Theory of Inquiry*, 104–105.

[25] This way of interpreting his conception of truth as a (functional) 'correspondence' theory was advanced by Dewey in a critical exchange with Bertrand Russell. See 'Propositions, Warranted Assertibility and Truth', *Journal of Philosophy* **38** (1946), 169–186.

(1) One of the innovative parts of Dewey's logic is his interpretation of judgment. Traditionally, judgment was regarded as an affirmation or denial of a predicate of a subject. To say 'this is sweet' is to say something is a member of the class of sweet things. Dewey's analysis reflects his reinterpretation of stimulus and response and the act of behaviour. We must not be misled by the grammatical construction of subject and predicate in construing judgment. Subject and predicate, in Dewey's logical theory, represent operations of observing and inferring and experimentation. The subject of judgment is some part of an environing context to which a response is required. The subject at first is a mere *this*, it is not something complete and given. It is *something* noted and pointed out; but what it is remains to be determined. Indication of a *this*, a subject, marks the beginning of a selection. The predicate, like the response in the psychological theory, consists of meanings, or interpretations, suggested as possible determinations of the *this*. The predicate or series of predications represents possible ways in which the subject can act and ways of acting on the subject. The copula is the act of predication; it forms the connection between the *this*-subject and its qualitative significance; it is a 'subjection', a 'constituting of the subject'.[26]

To say 'this is sweet', Dewey argues, is to qualify the initial *this*, by observing that it will function in a certain definite way: it is something that will sweeten other things, such as tea or coffee. Selecting and discriminating that predication is to negate certain others, for instance, that *this* is sour. Other predications, other qualitative discriminations are made in the further inquiry into the *this*. It is white, it is granular, and so on. A more comprehensive and final judgment is arrived at through a series of partial judgments: *this* is sugar. Here the 'logical subject' is determined, says Dewey, and is under control.[27] Each of the predications function as signs of what the *this* will do—or what can be done to it—under certain conditions. The *this*-subject is finally discriminated as the kind of object that possesses certain functional possibilities or dispositional properties. The *this* is now understood as an object that, under certain conditions, when certain interactions with other things and qualities take place, would yield certain consequences. Very roughly stated, the subject is viewed as a means, as a set of possible conditions; and the predicate is the end, representing specific determinations of the possibles.

We may notice here a significant difference between Dewey and the views of most philosophers as to the nature of knowing. In most theories, the primacy of the presence of objects to be known is assumed. The point to be explained is then how we can form accurate beliefs about the objects relying, as we must, on sensory stimulations we (presumably) receive from

[26] *Logic: The Theory of Inquiry*, 132.
[27] Ibid., 128–129.

those objects. Dewey, on the other hand, takes the knowing process to commence, not with objects, but with an immediate qualitative whole and context, the pervasive character of a situation within which discriminations and selections begin to be made. Certain selected qualities are discovered to be signs—thus evidence—of others; white and sweet, for example, are discovered to be signs of the object, sugar. Generally, then, for Dewey, objects, as stable and meaningful subjects of experience, are the outcomes and terminations of the knowing process; they are what is eventually reached and secured and 'constituted' by observation and thought.

The substantial character we attribute to objects is a logical rather than ontological determination, according to Dewey. It is as a result of inquiry that existing things are discovered to be composed of qualities that cohere as reliable signs of what would occur when certain operations are performed. The object is a set of related qualities with specified consequences when encountered and acted on in certain ways. Such is the 'logical' substance: a complex of qualities functioning as signs of what it can do or become. With advances in knowledge familiar objects (such as sugar) may be discovered in time to possess larger numbers of connected qualities (such as extensive physio-chemical properties) and may reveal further consequences when brought into relation with other objects. They are then found to have a more complex constitution. What is more, some objects (such as sugar) can become parts of qualities of more inclusive objects (as when sugar is put into tea or made into candy). And so the partial judgment 'this is sweet', when offered as indicating the presence of sugar, and when made as characterizing tea or candy, will differ in meaning. Thus the specification of just what the nature of a *this*-subject may be, as a quality or object, is relative, always, to the kind of situation in which judgment is initiated and directed and to the particular stages and extent of inquiry.

Objects are not the substances of old, if by 'substance' is meant that which in itself (*per se*) remains unchanged or persists through change. Objects, Dewey is led to argue, as 'logical substances', undergo changes and are transformed in the light of increasing and new information about them.

(2) I have mentioned that, for Dewey, the main predicament of living creatures is how to utilize ongoing interactions between organism and environment as means to controlling and affecting future interactions. To this end knowledge is an indispensable aid. Thought provokes and helps direct the organic adjustments required for continued growth and satisfaction. Hence mind and knowing are included as factors in the interactive process. The knower is not a spectator nor is thinking a mirroring of events. So the recurrent problem of much modern philosophizing as to how the knowing subject is related to objects known, is avoided here. Mind

and knowing are natural functions, ways of responding to and directing organic activity, just as are breathing and digesting. Thus there is no general 'problem of knowledge' for Dewey. There are problems of knowing, those being the problems encountered in specific cases calling for inquiry.

(3) Inquiry that results in knowledge and reliable judgment is also an evaluative process. Adjustments that are made for some purpose are also selections of certain conditions rather than others. Purposes and goals serve as ends to be attained; but the ends also function as means for organizing and directing activity; they activate preferences and choices. That a certain conclusion is arrived at and is warranted, is not simply to say it is true. It is also to say that the actions and procedures that have produced the conclusion were, under the circumstances, correctly taken and directed; they were the acts and procedures that *ought* to have been followed in reaching the end. The end conclusion is what the process was *good* for. The 'unified whole' in its pervasive quality is the consummatory value of the process that produced it, just as it is also the transformation of a doubtful situation.

(4) Scientific experimental method is a paradigm of intelligence. But inquiry is not confined only to the sciences. The process, as Dewey describes it, occurs in all walks of life, private and public, in technology, in crafts and arts, in law, legislation and morals—in short, wherever a problem occasions reflective thinking. The general character and deep nature of inquiry remains the same; different inquiries are distinguished by differences in subject matters rather than in method.

(5) Ethical judgment is, or can be, the product of inquiry. Since any inquiry proceeds in part as an evaluation of means and ends, there is no dichotomy of 'facts' and 'values' or scientific and ethical judgments for Dewey. There are distinctions to be made but not along the well-worn paths of traditional theory. There is a distinction between the abstract and observationally removed objects of scientific inquiry and the more immediate perceptual and emotional qualities of ordinary experience. Ethical judgment is largely concerned with the latter. But one notices then that ethical judgment is not a special kind of *judgment*, nor an isolated sphere of thought. Ethical judgments arise in all kinds of subject matters.

Ethical problems occur whenever questions concerning the regulation of desires and conduct are deliberated. These are questions of what attitude or interest ought to be taken with respect to some subject; questions of how one ought to behave. Exploiting an insight of Plato's,[28] Dewey treats *desire* as a case either of wanting to perpetuate some existing object, or bringing some object into existence. In each case, something is '*wanted*' in both senses of that term: something is felt or judged to be

[28] *Symposium,* 200 A–C.

lacking, and is also prized or esteemed. What is desired then calls for inquiry if a satisfactory resolution of the wanting is to be realized.

Moral conditions or 'values' come to be when some action has to be taken. The fact that action is required means that there are deficiencies or 'evils' in the situation.

Many philosophers have maintained that the essential and most important task of ethical theory is the formulation and establishment of an end, the final object of desire, striving, and obligation, the Good or *summum bonum*. The end is the ultimate standard, then, by which desires and actions can be evaluated and praised or blamed. Virtues, such as honesty, temperance, and justice are treated as means to the end, or as included in the end itself. Various ends have been advocated in the course of history; Pleasure, Happiness, Duty have each been thought to constitute the ultimate Good.

This has been an influential conception of moral experience and values, and espoused alike, if in a medley of forms, by philosophers and kings, saints and revolutionaries, and partisans in a cause. But despite an apparent consensus from an otherwise ill-assorted company, it is an artificial and inaccurate representation of the moral life. So, at least, Dewey argued. Furthermore, there has resulted an interminable controversy, punctuated by outbreaks of violence, over what is *the* true ethical end.

Instead of some one universal and fixed ethical end, as the decisive feature of ethical theory and judgment, Dewey proposed a radical reinterpretation of ends. Contrary to traditional theory, the end is not conceived as a limit or terminal point to which all effort is to be directed. The end is in existing situations and it is discovered and realized there. The end, writes Dewey, is 'the good of the situation'. And this good has to be 'discovered, projected and attained on the basis of the exact defect and trouble to be rectified'. The end, he goes on to say:

> is the active process of transforming the existent situation. Not perfection as a final goal, but the ever-enduring process of perfecting, maturing, refining is the aim of living. Honesty, industry, temperance, justice, like health, wealth, and learning, are not goods to be possessed as they would be if they expressed fixed ends to be attained. They are directions of change in the quality of experience. Growth itself is the only moral 'end'.[29]

(6) When he comes to the arts and aesthetic experience, Dewey again and consistently has the theory of organic behaviour and the process of interaction of the living creature and environment at the centre of his analysis. (The first chapter of his *Art as Experience*, called 'The Live

---

[29] *Reconstruction in Philosophy, Middle Works*, 12, 181.

Creature', is a remarkably suggestive statement of the interactive process.[30]) Works of art are products of such interactions in which materials are selected and organized and made into objects of expressive experience and enjoyment. The activity of production is as 'rational' as in science; and the process is experimental, unless it becomes mere repetition and routine. The goals may differ since scientific thought aims at explanation, prediction, and control. The goal of artistic production is the formation of objects whose unification of energies and materials results (when successful) in a single qualitative whole with consummatory value. These are objects which, in our encounter with them, intensify, purify, and enhance perceptual experience—far more so than in ordinary acts of perception; and the qualitative value of such experience is enjoyed for its own sake.

Artistic production is one in which the skill or controlling factors in the development and forming of materials enter directly into the quality of the product and are elements in its enjoyment. In this sense, science, even knowledge, are also arts. The general process of artistic production, the 'creation' of works of art is, at root, the same behavioural process and temporal pattern: movement from initially discordant and fragmented elements to later phases of increasing coherence and unification. The movement is deliberate and experimental. And if inspiration or intoxication have sometimes played roles in artistic production, it is still the case that they have been allowed those roles as a conscious decision; as means selected for a purpose.

Dewey not only stressed the behavioural process in the production of works of art, he also took the process to be fundamental in our perceptual experience and enjoyment of the arts. In our initial experiencing of the art object, there is first the organic tensions and adjustments in the relating of stimuli and response; an initial disunity of elements and qualities gradually becoming ordered. There is passage from active experiencing to *an* experience, a culmination with its unique, complete, qualitative significance. Our experience and appreciation of a work of art thus has a temporal order and pattern similar to the order of artistic production. The aesthetic experience is an educating of perception; and works of art provide new ways of experiencing life. Thus creativity of a sort is allotted to the audience as well as to the artist.

(7) At this point, it will come as no surprise to the reader to be told that Dewey's educational and social philosophy draws on his theory of the organic process. As always, the analysis is conducted in terms of functions and operations rather than fixed structures. Democracy is accordingly regarded by Dewey not so much as a political and social system and order of persons and powers but as a way of living. Dewey's statement of the

[30] *Art as Experience* (New York: Minton, Balch and Company, 1934).

meaning of 'democracy' is strikingly close to a description of the behavioural process itself. He says,

> Democracy is the belief in the ability of human experience to generate the aims and methods by which further experience will grow in ordered richness.

He continues:

> Democracy is the faith that the process of experience is more important than any special result attained, so that the special results achieved are of ultimate value only as they are used to enrich and order the ongoing process. Since the process of experience is capable of being educative, faith in democracy is all one with faith in experience and education.[31]

The chief problem of democracy is how the institutions of industry, business, and technology are to be directed to promote a co-operative interest in growth of experience, rather than the pursuit of disparate and private ends.

(8) Education is the means by which the experience and values of the past are transmitted to the future. Societies maintain themselves through this process of transmission. The process is made possible through communication of habits of action, thought and feeling, from elders to the young. The school is thus only one of the centres of education; education permeates the whole of society and the existence of society is dependent on educational processes.

The role of the school is thoroughly social in character, since the school is an especially effective instrument by which society as a whole communicates with the young. Taking this view of education, Dewey advanced a number of ideas concerning education and schooling that prompted much controversy early in the present century. He argued that the school cannot be an isolated institution if it is to perform its role. This was not received kindly by educators administering élite and well-endowed private schools. What Dewey meant, however, was that the school must be a community.

> In place of a school set apart from life as a place for learning lessons, we have a miniature social group in which study and growth are incidents of present shared experience.[32]

The physical parts and structure of the school are interpreted in a functional manner by Dewey. Rooms, laboratory, playgrounds not only

---

[31] From an address Dewey delivered on his eightieth birthday, 'Democracy as a Moral Ideal'. For the source and passage, H. S. Thayer (ed.), *Pragmatism: The Classic Writings* (Indianapolis: Hackett Publishing Company, 1982), 261.

[32] *Democracy and Education, Middle Works*, 9, 368.

serve to direct growth; they are means of communication and co-operation, ways of establishing connections and relationships among activities.

Dewey proposed that the activity of learning in the school should be continuous with that outside the school. The walls enclosing the school become corridors so that activities in the school become connected with the interests and life of the community. Experience gained in the school is thus enriched by, and enriches the culture of which it is a part.

One thing to be learned, in school and out, is how to think. Dewey's theory of inquiry describes the temporal phases of the process of thinking. As we have seen, thinking commences with the occurrence of a problem situation. Activities of observation and inference follow and, in due course, there is the elaboration of a hypothetical solution which is then to be tested. Dewey suggested that the course of study in school would be most effectively made material for thinking and learning when it was developed in a similar manner. The method of learning is the same as the natural method of thinking. The learner would begin, first, with a genuine sense of a problem and is then stimulated to acquire information and organize it with observations bearing on the problem. Suggested solutions of the problem occur and some of these will be developed and tested. The testing and conclusion arrived at bring out the full meaning of the original problem and of the previous process of learning.

Much of Dewey's writing was devoted to education. Of several books and many articles, the most rounded expression of his view is *Democracy and Education* (1916).[33] Indeed, this book is an excellent introduction to Dewey's philosophy. There is his work on social psychology, *Human Nature and Conduct* (1922)[34] in which moral and educational doctrines are also to be found.

(9) Consider once more (and for the last time) the behavioural act and inquiry. One final feature of Dewey's view remains to be noticed. We have seen that organic activity is regarded as the passage from real impositions and obstacles to a projected end, an anticipated solution and satisfaction. This is also a passage, then, from the real to the ideal. It is movement from (or through) existing conditions in which desires and aspirations for something better are generated. In a society of persons where such aspirations are shared and communicated, Dewey discerned the religious quality of experience. The projected union of the real with the ideal can be embodied in a symbol charged with feelings and associated values; that symbol is the idea of god.

Dewey distinguished religion as a historical phenomenon and institution, from the *religious*. The latter is not an institution or organization, but the special quality of experience when aspirations and ideals are shared and

[33] *Middle Works*, 9.
[34] *Middle Works*, 14.

stimulate and guide the energies and efforts of the community. The religious quality of experience can occur and find articulation and celebration in diverse social forms and practices. The sense of the religious quality of experience, as discerned and preserved in common ceremonial activities, Dewey called 'a common faith'.[35]

The nine topics surveyed here, I believe, form the main lines and characteristic direction of Dewey's thought with the theory of organic activity and conduct at the core. They are each to a greater or lesser extent (except for the ninth), present in Dewey's major excursion into metaphysics in *Experience and Nature* (1925). Twenty-five years later, when engaged on a new introduction to that book, Dewey proposed to revise his title to 'Culture and Nature'.[36] Reverse the terms to 'nature and culture' and one gains a sense of the order of the work. Dewey shows how certain traits and materials, certain activities and rhythms in nature are appropriated and absorbed into historical and changing cultural institutions. Fundamental among these ways of appropriation is experience and communication, through which issue acts and objects of value and the development of arts. The arts are construed as agencies of production and expression but also, through intelligent selection and arrangement, they are continuations of natural processes and events. Dewey argues that the social arts and institutions of culture have, as their critical office and test, the generation of new values and the growth and improvement of human life.

In this review of Dewey's thought, I have stressed the importance of the theory of organic behavioural process, and inquiry, as affecting and guiding his treatment of philosophic subject matters generally, and as shaping the distinctive features of his outlook. But this emphasis on the theoretical core and principal resource of Dewey's philosophizing runs a risk of misunderstanding. It is well, then, to add that not all human behaviour is occupied with the integration and conversion of originally disturbed and discordant experience. Not every situation is inherently problematic; nor does every situation impose a demand for reflective thinking. The specific quality of any situation is the result of the kind of relations occurring between organic and environing events; but the qualities are multiple and various. Situations may be marked by affection, love, amusement, enjoyment, anger, grief, and may occasion daydreaming, play and romance. None of this is denied by Dewey. Where there are living creatures, there are always processes of organic-environmental adjustments. But not all adjusting becomes problem-solving and material for inquiry. Dewey's concern with the origin and function of successful forms of adjustment in the resolution of problematic situations is due, I

---

[35] *A Common Faith* (New Haven: Yale University Press, 1934).
[36] *Experience and Nature*, *Later Works*, 1, and see p. 361.

think, to what he regarded as the special subject and responsibility of philosophic theory. But even philosophers need not always be philosophizing. So there is no attempt on Dewey's part to reduce or confine all experience to the intellectual operations of inquiry, or to construe all living activity exclusively as an effort to maintain organic equilibrium.

Dewey's work enables us to see familiar objects and ways of thinking in a new and sometimes surprising light. There is a sense of an adventure afoot and discoveries to be made in this attempt at a critical reorientation of philosophic tradition. That spirit animates the text, even if it is sometimes at odds with the scrupulous sobriety of Dewey's style. An unfeigned confidence in the human power of reason to shape the future for the better is omnipresent in his writings. These days we may find it difficult to recapture the purity of this note. But Dewey, after all, was a child of the nineteenth century in which, assuredly, the future was bursting with promise. And while there is here much criticism, there is no contempt for or rejection of the past. Dewey was an informed and astute historian of ideas. However, many hardened philosophic conventions are displaced, and with them many standing quandaries, through a critical method that analyses and assesses thought and things functionally: that is, according to their capacity to produce specific kinds of future consequences.

In all, Dewey's thought commands a comprehensive scope and unity within which is to be found a diversity of special themes. The latter are subjects of many luminous suggestions and compelling argumentation. His analytical and critical discussions, however abstract and difficult, are always tempered by an earnest concern for the relevance of philosophizing to the practical problems of human life. These are the reasons, I believe, that Dewey has been so influential in American philosophy and in the wider sphere of American intellectual history.[37]

[37] I am grateful to Professor Marcus Singer for some valuable critical comments on the penultimate version of this essay.

George Herbert Mead: Philosophy and the Pragmatic Self

JAMES CAMPBELL

George Herbert Mead was born at the height of America's bloody Civil War in 1863, the year of Lincoln's Emancipation Proclamation and the Gettysburg Address. He was born in New England, in the small town of South Hadley, Massachusetts; but when he was seven years old his family moved to Oberlin, Ohio, so that his father, Hiram Mead, a Protestant minister, could assume a chair in homiletics at the Oberlin Theological Seminary. After his father's death in 1881, Mead's mother, Elizabeth Storrs Billings Mead, briefly taught at Oberlin College. (She later served as the president of Mount Holyoke College from 1890 to 1900.) Mead grew to self-consciousness in this educational atmosphere, amidst the conflict between science and religion over the primacy of efficient or final explanations; and he offers us, in some autobiographical comments,[1] a sense of the difficulties felt by one who saw values on either side:

> We wished to be free to follow our individual thinking and feeling into an intelligent and sympathetic world without having to bow before incomprehensible dogma or to anticipate the shipwreck of our individual ends and values. We wanted full intellectual freedom and yet the conservation of the values for which had stood Church, State, Science, and Art.

This theme of the preservation and reconciliation of values, later rooted in a philosophy of social reconstruction, remained a vital part of his thought throughout his life.

Mead graduated from Oberlin College in 1883, after studying the classics and literature in addition to philosophy. He taught primary school for a while, then worked alternatively for a few years as a surveyor on the Wisconsin Central Railroad (in summer) and a tutor (in winter). After a year of further study with William James and Josiah Royce at Harvard, he went to Leipzig and then to Berlin for doctoral study in philosophy and physiological psychology. He married Helen Castle in 1891 and returned to the United States, without completing work on his doctorate, to a

[1] 'Josiah Royce—A Personal Impression', *International Journal of Ethics* XXVII (1917), 168.

position at the University of Michigan. In 1894 he moved to the University of Chicago, where he taught until his death in April 1931.[2]

Mead had at one time intended to become a minister. He later had wanted to run a reformist newspaper; but neither of these professions provided him with sufficient intellectual challenge. He finally settled upon an academic career as a teacher of philosophy, a career that enabled him to integrate his desire for social service with a highly intellectual life. Throughout his long teaching career at the University of Chicago, Mead was an essential element in various of the city's reform efforts: education, labour questions, women's suffrage, the Hull House, the University's Experimental School, the Chicago Physiological School, the Public Education Association, the City Club, and the Immigrants' Protective League, among others.[3] And Mead managed to carry forward all of these reform activities without losing his identity as a professional philosopher.

John Dewey, Mead's close personal and professional friend, wrote of Mead that he 'published but little, and that little was of a comparatively scattered and almost fragmentary character'.[4] Now that many of these published pieces have been gathered together by Andrew J. Reck in *Selected Writings: George Herbert Mead* [SW],[5] readers can see that Dewey overstated his case. Far from being fragmentary, Mead's published writings can be seen to comprise the skeleton of a powerful philosophical

[2] Additional biographical material on Mead and his family can be found in David L. Miller, *George Herbert Mead: Self, Language, and the World* (Austin and London: University of Texas Press, 1973; Chicago and London: University of Chicago Press, 1980), xi–xxxviii; Neil Coughlan, *Young John Dewey* (Chicago and London: University of Chicago Press, 1975), 113–150.

[3] For a further discussion of Mead's work as a social reformer see Robert M. Barry, 'A Man and a City: George Herbert Mead in Chicago', in *American Philosophy and the Future,* Michael Novak (ed.) (New York: Scribners, 1968), 173–192; Darnell Rucker, *The Chicago Pragmatists* (Minneapolis: University of Minnesota Press, 1969), 20–22; Mary Jo Deegan and John S. Burger, 'George Herbert Mead and Social Reform: His Work and Writings', *Journal of the History of the Behavioral Sciences* XIV (1978), 362–373.

[4] 'The Work of George Mead', *The New Republic* 26 July 1936, 329.

[5] *Selected Writings: George Herbert Mead* [SW], Andrew J. Reck (ed.) (Indianapolis: Bobbs-Merrill, 1964; Chicago and London: University of Chicago Press, 1981). A briefer selection of Mead's writings was published under the curious title: *George Herbert Mead: Essays on His Social Philosophy,* John W. Petras (ed.) (New York: Teachers College Press, 1968). The best available bibliography of the published works of Mead has been compiled by John A. Broyer and can be found in *The Philosophy of George Herbert Mead,* Walter R. Corti (ed.) (Winterthur: Amriswiler, 1973), 243–260.

view. Dewey was correct, however, that, compared to the Mead that he knew, the published Mead was no more than a skeleton. Correct as well was Dewey's further observation that Mead's 'intellectual influence upon associates and the students in his classes was so profound as to be revolutionary'.[6] Mead was a powerful extemporaneous lecturer, a professor to whose classroom students often returned year after year to hear the most recent formulations of his ideas on philosophical topics of vital human concern. Regrettably, he published few of his ideas. Mead was, Dewey tells us, 'always dissatisfied with what he had done; always outgrowing his former expressions', and consequently he was 'reluctant to fix his ideas in the printed word . . .'[7] Fortunately for us, however, the powerful impact of these lectures inspired some of Mead's students to have stenographic reports taken; and, after his death, this same impact inspired some of his colleagues and students to see a number of volumes of his ideas into print.

First to appear, in 1932, was *The Philosophy of the Present* [PP], edited by Arthur E. Murphy, drawn from the text of Mead's 1930 Carus Lectures on the role of temporality, and especially of the present, in any understanding of existence. The lectures remained unrevised at the time of Mead's death, but are supplemented by some manuscript materials and two previously published essays. *Mind, Self, and Society from the Standpoint of a Social Behaviorist* [MSS], edited by Charles W. Morris, appeared in 1934. This volume presents Mead's views on social psychology as compiled from stenographic copies of two different sets of lectures on the topic, supplemented occasionally by other related notes and manuscript materials. Two years later, Mead's ideas on the flow of philosophic thought in the previous century, again drawn primarily from stenographic lecture notes, appeared under the title of *Movements of Thought in the Nineteenth Century* [MT], edited by Merritt H. Moore. In 1938, *The Philosophy of the Act* [PA], edited by Morris and others, appeared. It contained unpublished manuscripts derived mostly from the last decade or so of Mead's life that explore a wide range of topics central to human action and thought. And in 1982 *The Individual and the Social Self* [ISS], edited by David L. Miller, appeared. This volume, also drawn primarily from stenographic notes, contains material similar to that found in *Mind, Self, and Society* and *The Philosophy of the Act*, but presented in a different way. All of the original materials for these volumes, as well as other stenographic notes, manuscripts, and some correspondence remain at the University of Chicago.[8]

[6] 'The Work of George Mead', 329.
[7] 'George Herbert Mead', *The Journal of Philosophy* XXVIII (1931), 311.
[8] *The Philosophy of the Present* [PP], Arthur E. Murphy (ed.) (LaSalle: Open Court, 1932; Chicago and London: University of Chicago Press, 1980); *Mind, Self, and Society from the Standpoint of a Social Behaviorist*

These edited volumes flesh out the skeleton of Mead's thought presented in his published works; but, because they are edited volumes, it is necessary to keep in mind that we are not dealing directly with Mead's ideas. They come to us through the filter of students, stenographers and editors. The manuscripts and the stenographic records are of different levels of completeness. Factual errors have been found in the stenographic records—names and titles of books, for example, were misreported—and, no doubt, some of Mead's complex philosophical ideas did not come across exactly as he uttered them. And keeping in mind what Dewey called Mead's reluctance 'to fix his ideas in the printed word', Mead would certainly have wanted to make changes of greater or lesser degree had he seen his lectures and drafts thus fixed.

Still, I think that it is legitimate to consider these volumes as representative of Mead's thought, especially if we remain guided by the skeleton provided by his published essays and reviews and emphasize themes to which he returned again and again. In section II, I would like to offer a broad sketch of his work; I will follow this, in sections III and IV, with a detailed examination of the heart of Mead's thought: his philosophy of human nature. What will emerge from this study is a valuable body of philosophical ideas and a major philosophic figure, both worthy of more serious study.

II

As a modern thinker for whom process and evolution were central issues, Mead's philosophical roots are to be found in Hegel and Darwin. In Hegel's work, Mead found the recognition 'that the world evolves, that reality itself is in a process of evolution' (MT 154). With each new synthesis, something fundamentally new emerges: 'new forms arise out of conflicts of old forms' (MT 145). The achievement of Darwin, as Mead sees it, was to have worked out the mechanism for the resolution of these conflicts, at least on the biological level. Here Darwin saw, Mead notes, 'a life-process, that may take now one, and now another, form' (MT 161; cf. 253), depending upon its reponse to the environmental situation. Evolu-

---

[MSS], Charles W. Morris (ed.) (Chicago and London: University of Chicago Press, 1934); *Movements of Thought in the Nineteenth Century* [MT], Merritt H. Moore (ed.) (Chicago and London: University of Chicago Press, 1936); *The Philosophy of the Act* [PA], Charles W. Morris *et al.* (eds) (Chicago and London: University of Chicago Press, 1938); *The Individual and the Social Self* [ISS], David L. Miller (ed.) (Chicago and London: University of Chicago Press, 1982). The Mead Papers are housed in the Special Collections division of the Joseph Regenstein Library at the University of Chicago.

tion, throughout the range of living things, is, Mead tells us, 'the process of meeting and solving problems' (MT 143). Humans, with their highly developed cultures, address their problems of living through the many institutions that have arisen 'in the social process' (MT 148). Hegel's influence can be found returning here for, as Mead continues, it was Hegel who insisted that 'it is not the human animal as an individual' that 'gets control over his environment'. Rather, 'it is society' (MT 168).

In many ways Mead's work complements that of his more famous colleague Dewey. Each writes within a framework of emergent evolution. Each attempts to understand the importance of human existence while at the same time demonstrating, by means of a purely naturalistic world-view, our rootedness in nature. Each explores the nature of our social existence and the processes by which a society develops and adjusts. And, although each elaborates freely his own point of view, their distinguishable perspectives remain parallel throughout. Let us consider their related views explicitly in two areas and then proceed to a brief characterization of Mead's overall philosophical position.

Their views are clearly distinguishable first of all in the different paths that they take when exploring human attempts to solve problems. Dewey's efforts, as anyone familiar with his writings on this theme will confirm, are directed toward questions of the *method* by which the process of problem-solving is carried out: what the pattern of inquiry is, how many steps this process contains, what the distinct traits of these steps are and the order in which they occur, how problem-solving can be improved, etc.[9] Mead's discussions of problem-solving, on the other hand, focus upon the *model of human life* that stands behind this activity, examining the human factors and traits that make us intelligent problem-solvers. (This topic returns below in section IV.) A second instance of how Mead's and Dewey's views are distinguishable yet parallel can be found in their presentations of social psychology. Here Dewey's focus is upon the roles played in human life by habits, impulses, and intelligence;[10] Mead focuses meanwhile upon the development and nature of self-consciousness, particularly as it reflects the larger society in which individuals develop. (This topic returns below in section III.)

Turning to an exclusive consideration of Mead's work, we see immediately that his fundamental understanding of reality is not one that cuts us off from nature. He sees human experiencing as 'a natural process' (PA 517) like eating or reproducing, and he leaves no room for 'other-worldliness' (PA 515) in his thought. Mead thus aims to offer a

---

[9] See Dewey, *How We Think*, rev. edn (Boston: Heath, 1933), 107–118; Dewey, *Logic, The Theory of Inquiry* (New York: Holt, 1938), 101–119.
[10] See Dewey, *Human Nature and Conduct: An Introduction to Social Psychology* (New York: Modern Library [1922], 1930).

metaphysics that is 'descriptive of the world so far as it comes within the range of our thought', so as to discover 'the essential characters of the world as they enter into our experience . . .' (PA 626).

One of the primary characteristics of the experienced world, for Mead, is that it is made up of enduring physical objects. Mead intends by this claim no simple-minded realism; but he remains committed throughout his work to the viewpoint of the scientist rather than that of the epistemologist. Unlike the latter, whom Mead sees as attempting 'to reach a world outside of the individual's experience' as a means of testing that very experience, the scientist is attempting to solve 'a problem that lies within an unquestioned world of observation and experiment' (PP 108; cf. 140–141; PA 26, 280). 'The attitude of the scientist', Mead writes, 'never contemplates or could contemplate the possibility of a world in which there would be no reality by which to test his hypothetical solution of the problem that arises' (SW 205). In the world that we humans encounter and share with one another, problems arise and are addressed. But, for Mead, these are the problems of the scientist, not those of the epistemologist.

Central to Mead's analysis here is his repeated emphasis upon the importance of human manipulation, upon direct manual contact with the things of nature, for our understanding of the world. We have what he calls 'distance' experiences with our eyes, ears, and noses (PA 142; cf. SW 77); but their 'promise' (PA 103) is fulfilled only in touching. 'The reality of what we see', he tells us, 'is what we can handle . . .' (PA 105; cf. PP 60). By manipulating the things of the world, we are able to avoid the wholesale epistemological problem, Mead tells us, because '[t]he ultimate experience of contact is not subject to the divergencies of distance experience' (PA 281). In a fashion similar to this defence of physical objects, Mead recognizes as well the validity of relativity physics without surrendering to it our legitimate experiential, manipulatory realm: 'For the vast majority of experiences the Newtonian definition of the object that is there in terms of absolute space, time, and mass is adequate' (PA 251).

Mead's understanding of nature, rooted as it is in the methods of the scientist, and concerned to take seriously the reality of temporal processes, emphasizes our need to recognize the emergence of novelty. Although this emergence is often too narrowly construed, Mead maintains that it 'belongs not only to the experience of human social organisms' but is found also 'in a nature which science and the philosophy that has followed it have separated from human nature' (PP 14). Consider a chemical compound: 'When things get together, there then arises something that was not there before, and that character is something that cannot be stated in terms of the elements which go to make up the combination' (PA 641). The compound water, for example, has properties that are different from either of its elements. In more general terms, emergence is a category that allows us to account for temporal continuity in nature without being forced into the straitjacket of determinism. The flow of time in nature is a kind of passage 'within which what is taking place conditions that which is arising', yet these conditions 'do not determine in its full reality that which emerges' (PP 16; cf. 64). Admittedly, as time goes on we rethink our past; and, upon rethinking, we are able to understand more clearly how nature and we reached our present situation. Mead notes that 'new things continually arise, the novelty of whose occurrence is worn down into the reliability of that which becomes familiar' (PP 36–37). This should not blind us, however, to the real novelty of that which has emerged.

Emergence is possible because of another trait of existence that Mead calls 'sociality'. By this term he means 'the capacity of being several things at once' (PP 49). If there is to be continuity without rigid determinism, there must be within nature the ability of the various pieces to participate contemporaneously in different systems. These systems, that he elsewhere calls 'perspectives', have 'objective existence' (PA 114). A stone, for example, is simultaneously in chemical, thermal, gravitational, visual, and perhaps a child's play systems. Mead explains:

> in the present within which emergent change takes place the emergent object belongs to different systems in its passage from the old to the new because of its systematic relationship with other structures, and possesses the characters it has because of its membership in these different systems (PP 65; cf. 76–77).

Mead is careful to emphasize here too that sociality is more than just a human trait. As he puts it, the appearance of human minds capable of occupying their own systems as well as those of others is 'only the culmination of that sociality which is found throughout the universe . . .' (PP 86; cf. 48, 82).

Before we turn to Mead's understanding of human nature, it is important to re-emphasize that his understandings of nature and human nature are very closely related, and that his claims about aspects of nature are often based upon his claims about aspects of human nature. We are, for Mead, truly rooted in nature; and far too often dualistic philosophies have hampered our understanding of ourselves and of our place in nature by portraying properties that are actually found more generally in existence as just human or 'subjective'. Sociality is found in the fact that our lives participate in the lives of others, and also in the fact that nature is a set of systems or perspectives. Emergence is found in the free action of humans, and also in the other processes of nature.

With this continuity of nature and human nature in mind, we can turn to Mead's understanding of human nature. Doing so, we see that he offers us a carefully elaborated and compelling picture of humanity as wholly naturalized—developing and living within nature—and a reinterpretation of our basic ideas and institutions to accommodate this understanding of human nature.

III

From Mead's understanding of human nature, two aspects must be selected for careful examination: we humans are, first of all, social in our innermost being, emergents from and thrivers within the social process; and, secondly, we humans are live, active creatures who attempt to meet and solve the problems of living. In section IV, I shall explore Mead's discussion of the problem-solving aspect of human nature; in this section, his view on the social aspect of human nature.

For Mead, the human self is fundamentally social. I cannot hope to do justice in this space to the full implications of his claim. I cannot even delineate fully the discussion of the evolutionary emergence of self-consciousness that he offers in *Mind, Self and Society*, discussing as he does the arising in a particularly highly developed creature of gesture, significant symbols, the vocal gesture and language. But we will be able to look, however briefly, at some of the factors of Mead's overall understanding of the social aspect of the human self. The first point to make clear about Mead's perspective is that, for him, the human self is ever in process. Although as we shall see Mead values increased human individuality as essential, his is not a ballistic sense of individuality—a sense in which one's course is 'internal' and purely one's own, and in which all influence from 'without' is 'interference' and results in 'deflection' from one's true goal. There is, for Mead, no specifiable target state of human fulfilment, either individually or as a group; there is no status of being 'finally' or 'completely' fulfilled that is safe from setback or relapse. Human individuals remain in process as long as they live: developing, expanding, changing, contracting.

If we go beyond Mead's point that the self is in process to an analysis of the sort of process the self is engaged in, two factors come to our attention: the self is emergent and indirect. Beginning with the former, for Mead, the self emerges. It develops in the course of experience. This point can be made phylogenetically and ontogenetically. On the level of the history of the human race, there would be no humans today if our minds and selves 'had not arisen within or emerged out of the human social process in its lower stages of development ...' (MSS 227). This emergence of human self-consciousness was not according to some preordained plan nor required of simple natural necessity. In a fundamental sense, it just happened. Similarly, on the individual level, a person's self is not something preformed that 'comes out' or is actualized at a certain age. When Mead says that the self emerges, that 'it is not initially there, at birth, but arises' (MSS 135), he means this in the strong sense that the person literally comes into being in the process of living.

The self, for Mead, emerges indirectly or reflexively. It 'arises in the process of social experience and activity' (MSS 135); it develops 'within the social process, within the empirical matrix of social interactions' (MSS 133; cf. ISS 63–65). The individual does not develop a self and then take his or her place within society; the individual develops his or her self by degree and under the influence of his or her society. It is thus true both that it is 'impossible to conceive of a self arising outside of social experience' (MSS 140), and that in the long run we continue to need others: 'Selves can only exist in definite relationships to other selves' (MSS 164).

Let us consider further the reflexive nature of the self. The individual, Mead tells us, 'enters his own experience as a self or individual, not directly or immediately, not by becoming a subject to himself, but only in so far as he first becomes an object to himself just as other individuals are objects to him or in his experience . . .' (MSS 138). That is, before becoming self-conscious, a person must first assume a place within a social group:

> only in so far as he takes the attitudes of the organized social group to which he belongs toward the organized, co-operative social activity or set of such activities in which that group as such is engaged, does he develop a complete self or possess the sort of complete self he has developed (MSS 155; cf. 171, 194).

The role of language as the form of reflexive communication is essential here. As Mead writes, it is impossible that 'consciousness of a self as an object would ever have arisen in man if he had not had the mechanism of talking to himself . . .' (SW 140; cf. 146; ISS 144–145). The reason for this is that 'the individual can hear what he says and in hearing what he says is tending to respond as the other person responds' (MSS 69–70). It is in this responding to himself or herself that self-consciousness emerges. 'It is in addressing himself in the role of an other that his self arises in experience' (PP 168).

With that introduction to Mead's view of the self as a process of reflexive emergence, we are now ready to explore the heart of his understanding of the social self: its duality of 'I' and 'me'. Mead has in mind here no dichotomy of distinct halves within the self, nor a rigid balance maintaining itself throughout life. Rather, he intends a functional distinction between these two 'phases' of the self (MSS 192), both of which are 'essential to the self in its full expression' (MSS 199), and a fluid mutuality in which '[t]he relative values of the "me" and the "I" depend very much on the situation' (MSS 199).

The 'me' is that phase of the self that 'contains' one's society. 'We are individuals born into a certain nationality, located at a certain spot geographically, with such and such family relations, and such and such political relations', Mead explains. 'All of these represent a certain situation which constitutes the "me" . . .' (MSS 182). The 'me' is thus the 'conventional' and 'habitual' phase of the self. The 'me' 'has to have those habits, those responses which everybody has; otherwise the individual could not be a member of the community' (MSS 197). The 'me' is 'essentially a member of a social group. . . . Its values are the values that belong to society' (MSS 214). In fact, we are usually so well integrated into society that '[n]o hard-and-fast line can be drawn between our own selves and the selves of others, since our own selves exist and enter as such into our experience only in so far as the selves of others exist and enter as such into our experience also' (MSS 164).

It is the 'me' that gives the self its 'form' or stability (MSS 209). This means, in part, that the 'me' must itself demonstrate some sort of unity: 'the "me" is the organized set of attitudes of others which one himself assumes' (MSS 175). Of course, there remains a certain amount of diversity in the 'me': it continues to change with the ongoing development of the self and it includes different strands within it, especially in the modern world (for example, the frequently inconsistent values inherent in our conflicting roles as citizens, workers, and family members). However, Mead's emphasis here is primarily upon unity, especially the unity that underlies a self-conscious community. 'The very organization of the self-conscious community is dependent upon individuals taking the attitude of the other individuals', Mead tells us, and accomplishing this in the larger social group 'is dependent upon getting the attitude of the group as distinct from that of a separate individual—getting what I have termed a "generalized other"' (MSS 256; cf. 158). It is at this point that, for Mead, intelligence or rationality becomes possible. 'A human organism does not become a rational being until he has achieved such an organized other in his field of social response', because he can then carry on 'that conversation with himself which we call thought' (PP 87) and he can bring this attitude to bear in his dealings with 'the social problems of various kinds which confront that group or community at any given time . . .' (MSS 156).

The 'I' phase of the human self, on the other hand, Mead tells us 'is the response of the organism to the attitudes of the others. . . . The attitudes of the others constitute the organized "me", and then one reacts toward that as an "I"' (MSS 175; cf. 177). In another formulation Mead puts it this way: 'The "I" is the response of the individual to the attitude of the community as this appears in his own experience' (MSS 196). These passages imply a certain temporal primacy of the 'me', although the two actually develop together. Ontologically, the two phrases are co-equal. As Mead explains, 'there would not be a "me" without a response in the form of the "I"' any more than there would be 'an "I" in the sense in which we use that term if there were not a "me" . . .' (MSS 182).

The importance of the 'I' results from the fact that it is this phase of the self that introduces novelty into our actions. To the extent that an individual is simply a 'me' that person is, as we have seen, habitual and conventional; but the response of the 'I' 'is something that is more or less uncertain' (MSS 176), 'something that is never entirely calculable' (MSS 178). The 'I' is that phase of the self that gives us freedom and initiative and openness to change (cf. MSS 176). It is the 'I' that enables us to break free of our group's set way of thinking, to recognize problems, and to suggest possibilities of change. In this way, the 'I' is responsible for the 'reconstruction of the society, and so of the "me" which belongs to that society' (MSS 214). It is, Mead emphasizes, in the 'reactions of the individual, the "I", over against the situation in which the "I" finds itself, that important social changes take place' (MSS 217).

Mead was conscious of the necessity that in our educational endeavours we take account of these two phases of the self. While we recognize that it is not the job of education to *make* the self social, since it is social already (cf. SW 122), still we can set up our educational goals and procedures to foster social growth by attempting to develop 'the unique characteristic of the human individual—that he can place himself in different perspectives' (PA 182). Instead of attempting to pack the child full of information, it is better to expand his or her 'me' by helping the child enter into the perspectives of others. Literature and the social sciences, for example, are essential to our coming to understand the traditions and beliefs of other peoples. Similarly, we should not attempt to teach natural science without teaching the history of science: the traditions, the personalities, their problems, their struggles and successes, etc. (cf. SW 66–68). We can also attempt to facilitate the development of the 'I', and thereby to enhance the student's sense of his or her need to become an evaluator rather than just a repeater, by attempting to convert instruction into 'an interchange of experience' or a 'conversation' between the instructor and the student, and among the students themselves (SW 118–119).

We have now taken an initial look at Mead's understanding of the social aspect of the self as a duality that grows out of a reflexive and emergent process and at the educational implications of this view. I would like to turn at this point to a consideration of some of the other consequences of his view, and close this examination of Mead's understanding of the social aspect of human nature with a glimpse at some of the implications of this view for the moral life. Mead was explicitly attempting to construct his ethical theory on a social basis, in terms of his social theory of the origin, development, nature and structure of the self (cf. MSS 379). I believe that there are two primary implications: first, the importance of fostering the duality of the 'I' and the 'me', and, secondly, the recognition of our need to choose our 'me'. Let us consider these implications in turn.

First, it is important to foster the duality of the 'I' and the 'me'. As we have seen, Mead maintains that both phases are essential and go hand-in-hand; but he also recognizes that the balance between them changes from situation to situation. Hence, we recognize the importance of the self's striving to remain dual. The 'me' contains the person's set of socially derived values; the 'I' is the reaction to them. It is consequently necessary to be part of the group, but necessary as well to attempt to maintain a critical 'distance'. This is because there are situations, primarily those of a religious or patriotic nature, in which the 'I' and the 'me' can, as Mead puts it, 'in some sense fuse' (MSS 273). These fusion situations, as we all know, are emotionally very satisfying. In Mead's words, they give rise to a 'peculiar sense of exaltation' (MSS 273). When this fusion occurs, when people weld themselves completely to their group and its traditions, they abandon their own individual critical distance and become social automata—a dangerous stance for moral agents.

One way to maintain our critical distance from the group is to recall that, at least in part, we choose our 'me'. This is the second of the primary ethical implications of Mead's understanding of the social aspect of the self. Although far too often we equate 'custom' with 'morality' (MSS 168), individuals in modern pluralistic societies have at their fingertips a great supply of value options resulting from our experiences and our studies. We have a great wealth of possible choices from which to select our moral frame-of-reference. Mead recognizes, of course, that these options are not equally available to all members of society, and that not all individuals are equally able to make use of what is actually available to them. It is for these reasons that Mead puts emphasis upon the social importance of education. And, while we cannot ignore the challenges offered to Mead's belief in the high degree of freedom of the 'I' when faced with contemporary forms of thought 'management',[11] we must remember that Mead's claim is primarily a moral one. We *should*, Mead tells us, see our 'me' as chosen; we have a duty to ourselves and to our communities to evaluate our moral frames-of-reference, to not simply accept them. We can adopt as our moral frame-of-reference the community of scholars and its values, or the community of racists and its values. We can choose to evaluate our actions as adequate or not compared to those of contemporary hedonists or of Mother Theresa. We can claim that our present community has perfect moral values, or we can challenge it by reference to other values that we consider to be superior.

Mead discusses this point in terms of the ethical breadth of the 'generalized other'. He tells us that in moving away from 'a community of a narrow diameter' (MSS 265), really a sub-community like a gang or

[11] See, for example, C. Wright Mills, *The Sociological Imagination* (New York: Grove Press, 1961), 165–176.

clique, or in overcoming any of 'the prejudices of the community', the reformer 'expresses the principles of the community more completely' (MSS 217) than those who stay behind. In this way, the individual, through his or her 'I', has chosen from within the diversity of the 'me' certain ideal values and challenged other persons in the community to abandon their present actions and to live up to their ideals in their social practice. In a still broader sense, we are able to move from what we conceive to be 'a narrow and restricted community to a larger one' (MSS 199) by rejecting the values of our own community and by adopting the better ideals of some other community. In this way, the individual reformer can oppose his or her present community from the point-of-view of a better one, 'from the point of view of what he considers a higher and better society than that which exists' (MSS 389).

It is at this level that the individual is most fully social, in both the descriptive and the moral sense of that term (cf. MSS 304–305). He or she functions as a social critic, fully integrated within the life of the group but calling on the group to live up to its ideals, or even calling on it to abandon them for better ones. The ethical life, the life of social criticism, requires the maintenance of the duality of the 'I' and the 'me' and a commitment to the advance of the group and of the human community. 'All the things worth while are shared experiences', Mead tells us (MSS 385);[12] and, for him, the ideal of democracy is the continued growth in society of pluralism and co-operative participation such that shared experience can be attained (cf. MSS 326). This is a severe standard of morality, no doubt; but it is one rooted in his understanding of human nature as fundamentally social. And, as we shall see, it is the highest standard possible for people whose lives consist of the overcoming of problems.

IV

The second major aspect of human nature in Mead's understanding is that humans are problem-solvers. The human animal lives his or her life, most of the time, in what Mead calls 'the attitude of immediate experience' (PA 14). We live ordinarily 'in a world that is simply there and to which we are so adjusted that no thinking is involved . . .' (MSS 135; cf. 102, 212; PA 368). Our walking, our chewing, our climbing stairs, our greeting of passers-by, our automobile driving—all of these actions are usually carried on automatically, without plan or self-conscious involvement. Of course, this is not always the case; and, in the course of our lives, things do go

---

[12] Compare this comment with Dewey's: 'Shared experience is the greatest of human goods' (*Experience and Nature,* rev. edn (New York: Dover [1929], 1958), 202).

wrong. 'The life in which the human community finds itself inevitably presents a set of problems', Mead writes (PA 79). Problems develop; and, when they do, we are jolted from the habitual realm of immediate experience to the attitude of 'reflective analysis' (PA 14). As Mead tells us, 'reasoning conduct appears where impulsive conduct breaks down' (MSS 348; cf. SW 7). Conflicts inevitably give rise to reflection; and, for Mead, the proper purpose of thinking is problem-solving. 'Reflection is a process of solving problems. . . . We seek a hypothesis which will set free the processes that have been stopped in the situation that we call problematic' (MT 135, 359).

We solve these problems through reconstruction—through the reassessment and reordering of situations. In our ability to reconstruct, Mead sees us as continuous with the rest of nature. Nature's own evolutionary process proceeds 'by reconstruction in the presence of conflicts . . .' (PP 174). Each plant and animal variation results from such a reconstruction in nature. Actions too are reconstructions. In the behaviour of animals, and often in that of people, problems are solved without thought (cf. MSS 92–93; MT 344–346; PA 79, 504; ISS 42–43). But Mead is more centrally concerned with reflective human reconstruction: attempts on the part of an individual or individuals, upon recognizing the existence of a particular problem, to deliberate and experiment until it is possible to effect situational changes sufficient to ameliorate or eliminate the problem.

The key to reflective human reconstruction is our ability to slow down our responses to allow for deliberate experimentation. 'The achievement of the human animal, or rather of human social conduct', Mead notes, 'is the arrest of passage, and the establishment of a "now"' (PA 161). It is in this 'now'—between the recognition of the problem and the hypothetically justified attempt at resolution—that we 'manipulate', a term Mead uses to demonstrate (as we saw above) his recognition of the importance of the human hand:

> man's manual contacts, intermediate between the beginnings and the ends of his acts, provide a multitude of different stimuli to a multitude of different ways of doing things, and thus invite alternative impulses to express themselves in the accomplishment of his acts . . . (MSS 363; cf. PA 16–23; ISS 119–120, 173–175).

Moreover, when we can manipulate such 'elaborations and extensions' of our hands (MSS 363) as books and computers, we can give rise to far more new possibilities. The ability to fashion alternate possibilities through manual contacts would not have been of great use to humans, however, if they did not have a central nervous system that could make use of such possibilities. Ours offers us both a memory and 'the field and the mechanism for selection with reference to distant futures . . .' (PP 66; cf. MSS 98–100, 117). It is in this collapse of past and future into the 'now', in this interrelation of what has happened and what is to come, that Mead again discusses intelligence. In addition to having the internal dialogue made possible by the 'I' and the 'me', the intelligent person now has something about which to converse with himself or herself. 'Intelligence is essentially the ability to solve the problems of present behavior in terms of its possible future consequences as implicated on the basis of past experience ...' (MSS 100).

As with the social aspect of human nature, Mead recognizes that the problem-solving aspect of human nature has educational implications. Because humans can improve their abilities as problem-solvers, it is important that our educational institutions adopt such improvements as one of their goals. This means, Mead writes, a turning away from an emphasis upon the acquisition of 'mere information'—that is, '[w]hatever is stored up, without immediate need, for some later occasion, for display or to pass examinations'—and a turn toward 'knowledge'—whatever 'helps anyone to understand better a question he is trying to answer, a problem he is trying to solve' (SW 69). A good education thus focuses upon the solving of problems. Students can become better at solving problems, moreover, only by becoming more skilled in the use of the scientific method. By this, Mead means nothing esoteric. Rather, using the scientific method to solve problems or answer questions simply means rejecting such other methods of arriving at conclusions as tenaciously holding beliefs without question, relying upon authorities and group discipline to produce unification of belief, and accepting those beliefs that appear self-evidently true, as methods more suited to the accumulation of 'information' than to the acquisition of 'knowledge'. In place of such methods of solving problems and answering questions, Mead would have us develop our students' skills for the long-term co-operative evaluation of problems.[13]

Mead's emphasis upon problem-solving as a fundamental aspect of human nature leads us to have to examine in more detail the role of thought in human life. Let us consider three related strands in turn. One major strand of Mead's analysis is the rootedness of intelligence in action. Our ability to think is not decorative but functional. We are reconstructors—good or poor reconstructors. We are better or worse, more or less intelligent, depending upon the level and quality of our thought. When problems come, we seldom face an easy selection between a good and an evil. Normally we are called upon to evaulate: to determine and choose from a number of conflicting possible courses of action the one that is better. 'All of our impulses are possible sources of happiness', Mead tells us

[13] See Charles S. Peirce, 'The Fixation of Belief', *Collected Papers of Charles Sanders Peirce,* Hartshorne and Weiss (eds), 6 vols (Cambridge: Harvard University Press, 1931–1935), 5.358–5.387.

(MSS 383). Hence the importance of being able to evaluate and choose the better option. We do this by examining possible future consequences:

> there are some impulses which lead simply to disintegration. . . . There are certain of our impulses which find their expression, for example, in cruelty . . . they are not desirable because the results which they bring are narrowing, depressing, and deprive us of social relations. They also lead, so far as others are concerned, to injury to other individuals (MSS 384).

It is in these attempts to prevent harm to ourselves and to others by careful evaluation that we find Mead's emphasis upon the importance of agents keeping their thought rooted in practical concerns.

Another strand of Mead's understanding of the role of thought in life is that it is in large part the problems we face and our responses to them that construct our explicit image of human nature. We can consider this point in the context of our claims about fundamental human rights. What our rights are, and more importantly what these rights mean in a specific rather than a vague sense, are only discoverable, Mead writes, in the addressing of problems. 'The contents' of these rights, he tells us, 'have always been formulated negatively, with reference to restrictions to be overcome' (SW 159). Each particular restatement thus remains only 'a *working* conception' (SW 154) of the ideal. So it is in our response to the particular social problems we face that we discover what we mean *practically* by our claims that people are 'equal' and 'free'. We must discover, in the context of our present problematic situations, what we mean specifically by our claims that, for example, a satisfactory human life requires an effective say in the course of one's life. It is in our ongoing attempts to reconceive these ideals to make them appropriate to new problematic situations that we formulate our explicit understanding of human nature.

A third strand of this emphasis upon problem-solving as a fundamental aspect of human life has to do with how large an aspect of satisfactory living it is. 'Life is a process', Mead tells us, 'of continued reconstruction . . .' (MT 292; cf. SW 331). He goes still farther: 'It is the realization of the problem and its solution that is the whole zest of living . . .' (PA 511). Life, for Mead, *is* problem-solving: preserving our architectural heritage and organizing dinner, making marriages work and paying our bills, phrasing apologies and performing concertos, finding our keys and formulating an adequate metaphysics. Each of these is an instance of problem-solving, some heroic and some mundane; but all of them are illustrations of Mead's view that living is addressing problems. However, this is not to say that, for Mead, solving problems has no value beyond being rid of the difficulty. Mead notes that 'the solution of each problem brings with it a deeper meaning and a richer value in living' (PA 511), a clearer understanding and appreciation of the complexity and interrelations of living and the costs of and reasons for failure, and thus a commitment to further efforts in the future. Thus, for Mead, we should find 'the meaning of life in marshaling all the values that are involved in the problems of conduct and interpretation, and seeking such a reconstruction of them as will motivate conduct that recognizes all the interests that are involved' (PA 512).

Surely Mead's is a severe position. Even if we understand our problems in a rich and variegated way, such that, for example, our understanding of our place in the universe is a problem, some will find Mead's view degrading and deflating. There is no sheltered role for intellectual contemplation, since even 'entirely disinterested knowledge' has a job to do in his analysis: 'Knowledge for its own sake is the slogan of freedom, for it alone makes possible the continual reconstruction and enlargement of the ends of conduct' (SW 210; cf. 69). There is no privileged role for relaxation either, because we have never done enough. Faced with the ongoing reality of social ills, we could always do a bit more. As Dewey writes in this regard, 'the better is too often the enemy of the still better'.[14] We are always called to address our problems, to take an active role in community decision-making. We discover, in our attempts to solve our problems, that we attain higher levels of meaning and self-discovery as members of a co-operative community.

V

In the two prior sections, we have examined what characterizes Mead's understanding of human nature. We human beings, all of us, are fundamentally social and fundamentally problem-solvers. This is what I meant by 'the pragmatic self' of my title.[15] In this section, I want to explore briefly the relationship between this pragmatic understanding of our human nature and philosophy. What is the meaning or the importance of philosophy for such people? What care should such people—we, remember— have for philosophy? The most obvious answer, although clearly the wrong one, is 'none'. Although philosophy in some senses would surely be without value to such pragmatic individuals, philosophy understood in a particular way is of central importance. This importance, and the sense of philosophy that will satisfy it, will take some time to characterize.

Beginning negatively, for Mead philosophy does not have any importance simply as a result of the fact that historically it has been seen as important or as something with which the 'educated' person is familiar.

---

[14] *Liberalism and Social Action* (New York: Capricorn [1935], 1963), 70.
[15] For more on Mead's understanding of pragmatism, the pragmatic theory of meaning, the pragmatic theory of truth, etc., see MT 344–359; PA 360–364; SW 320–344.

Nor is philosophy important if it simply makes us happy or helps us to feel good about living. The importance of philosophy to people like us, Mead maintains, is: first, that we are ever on the frontier of new and serious problems and we need all the help we can get to solve them; and, second, that philosophy can function as an aid in the clarification, evaluation, and solution of these problems.

My introduction of the term 'frontier' here is deliberate. Mead himself makes use of the frontier metaphor with great effect in a 1930 essay entitled 'The Philosophies of Royce, James, and Dewey in Their American Setting' (SW 371–391), and in a companion piece, 'The Philosophy of John Dewey', published posthumously.[16] Mead writes that '[t]he most illuminating conception that has been found for the interpretation of the history of the American community has been that of Professor Turner,[17] that of the Pioneer'. What distinguished the pioneer, the settler of the frontier, Mead writes, was that '[h]e traveled light, and what he carried with him had to be useful enough to justify its transportation'.[18] Mead sees this frontier analysis as offering an explanation for the development in these Western towns and cities of a life within which 'the directive forces in the community' (SW 376), the economic and political forces, operated without a highly intellectualized culture. The America of the pioneers 'abandoned European culture as a vital part of its living'.[19] On the frontier, such culture could not justify itself.

Although the actual open frontier about which Mead was writing closed nearly one hundred years ago, still in Mead's day, and even in our own, the pragmatist sees great value in this frontier analogy. The pioneer is not just the lonesome soul of our past, and the frontier is more than the fringe of unsettled land—the pioneer is us and the frontier, ever dangerous, is here and now. We simply cannot afford to lug around the baggage of a philosophy that we are not using to deal with our social problems. It is important to recognize, however, that this proscription is not of a particular philosopher or of a school of philosophy, but of a mentality—one that sees philosophy as a kind of intellectual decoration and sees us as having time for such fancies.

It would be a mistake to think, however, that because of this position Mead has no place for aesthetics. The aesthetic, for Mead, is a phase of experience that is able 'to catch the enjoyment that belongs to the consummation, the outcome, of an undertaking . . .' (SW 296). But, tied as it is to

[16] The Philosophy of John Dewey', *International Journal of Ethics* XLVI (1935), 64–81.

[17] Mead is referring here to Frederick Jackson Turner (1861–1932), especially his *The Frontier in American History* (New York: Holt, 1920).

[18] 'The Philosophy of John Dewey', 64.

[19] Ibid., 67.

the consummation of actions, to the solution of problems, aesthetic enjoyment must be earned. The aesthetic 'accompanies, inspires, and dedicates common action . . .' (SW 298). In our world of hunger and illiteracy, of unexamined customs and intellectual bankruptcy, the pragmatist has made a decision on moral grounds to forgo philosophy as decoration for philosophy as a tool in the clarification and evaluation of problems.

Mead offers us another phrasing of this same distinction when he considers the difference between the roles played by philosophy when our culture is merely 'an adornment of life' and when it functions as 'an interpretation of life'.[20] For example, in his teaching and writing Josiah Royce offered his students, Mead thought, a philosophy that functioned only within a culture that was second-hand, imported, 'foreign' to their situation (SW 380). Royce's students, and Mead was one of them, 'found in his luminous expositions another cathedral window through which to receive the culture of Europe but no method of living'.[21] Royce's philosophy was a segment in a culture that functioned as 'part of the escape from the crudity of American life', Mead contended, 'not an interpretation of it' (SW 383).[22] Dewey, on the other hand, he wrote, offered 'thought as a method of life';[23] and it is fair to say the same about Mead himself. For both of them, and for other pragmatists of their day and ours, the role of philosophy in life is to foster thinking about and force attention upon fundamental problems, to attempt to understand and thereby to facilitate the amelioration of our shared difficulties. Only then will we have a philosophy that functions as 'an interpretation of life' rather than as an 'adornment'.

Mead's position here has implications for our study of the history of philosophy. If we explore the importance of the history of philosophy, or of history in general, to present day living, we find in Mead's work, as we might expect, a central emphasis upon the role that history plays. Mead cares not at all for the accumulation of 'mere information' (SW 69). He

---

[20] Ibid., 66.

[21] Ibid., 72; cf. 'Josiah Royce—A Personal Impression', 168–170.

[22] It must be recalled here that Mead is writing from the standpoint of Royce's impact on students in the late 1880s. (He himself studied with Royce in 1887–88.) Whether Mead's evaluation should be seen as adequate for an understanding of Royce's whole thought is doubtful, especially if we keep in mind Royce's later work and his 1915 self-evaluation: 'my deepest motives and problems have centred about the Idea of the Community, although this idea has only come gradually to my clear consciousness' ('Words of Prof. Royce at the Walton Hotel at Philadelphia, December 29, 1915', *The Basic Writings of Josiah Royce,* John J. McDermott (ed.), 2 vols (Chicago and London: University of Chicago Press, 1969), Vol. I, 34).

[23] 'The Philosophy of John Dewey', 72; cf. SW 390–391.

cares, rather, for how historical knowledge is *used*. 'History serves a community in the same way as the memory does the individual', he maintains. We use the past 'so as to make our present situation intelligible' (PA 80–81). Consequently, Mead continues, 'the estimate and import of all histories lies in the interpretation and control of the present ...' (PP 28).[24] Thus the evaluation of the history of past philosophy must be in terms of 'the interpretation and control of the present'. So, we must ask ourselves, what is there in the history of philosophy that will do this?

Simply put, what our study of the history of philosophy offers us is a heightening of self-consciousness—it offers us 'a larger self' (MSS 386)—with which to address our problems. The study of the history of philosophy enables us to explore other aspects of our problems and to consider other possible solutions. Among our gains from the study of the philosophical visions of Kant and Aristotle, of Emerson and Bradley, of Wittgenstein and Descartes, are alternative categorial schemes and new challenges to our accepted views. All of this results in a larger self with which to face our problems. But this larger self should not—again, this is a moral claim—be allowed to function as a decoration or simply a means to personal happiness. It must participate in the creation of 'a larger social whole in terms of which the social conflicts that necessitate the reconstruction of the given society are harmonized or reconciled, and by reference to which, accordingly, these conflicts can be solved or eliminated' (MSS 308–309). It is also important to keep in mind that since our social problems are not purely philosophical problems, we cannot hope to effect adequate social reconstruction through the study of philosophy alone. Another way to phrase this same point is to say that the larger self that will make us better social problem-solvers is not derivable from philosophy alone. It can only be gained through a broadly based education including, for example, literature and the social sciences, as we have seen above.

VI

In this concluding section, I would like to offer a brief evaluation of the importance of Mead's work by considering the contribution that a Meadian perspective might make to some contemporary social discussions. If, as Mead says, what the study of philosophy does is to expand our capabilities to function as social problem-solvers, then it seems fitting to evaluate his own work with regard to our social problems. And, when we do so, we find that his thought offers us important insights and suggestions about issues

---

[24] For more on Mead's understanding of the nature of the past, see SW 345–354; PP 1–31; PA 613–616; Miller, *George Herbert Mead,* 172–187.

of vital importance to us today. Let me suggest just three areas of our contemporary social lives where including some of Mead's insights would contribute a great deal to our social discourse.

First, Mead's understanding of human nature as social at its most fundamental level suggests that we have been too quick to accept the dire claims of those who portray the human state as one of alienation and who maintain that humans are by their nature cut off from one another, isolated and alone. Humans are surely separated from one another; tragedies at home and abroad cannot be overlooked. Human community is an ideal that is far from being realized. Recognizing this, however, does not answer the important question of whether, and to what extent, this separateness is *the* human state. To what extent are we humans separated from one another by our 'human condition', and to what extent by custom and enculturation? Are we separated from one another by what we *are* or by what we *have done* and *have failed* to do?

Mead tells us that the isolation and fragmentation we do suffer from in the modern world result in large part from choices that humans have made, especially educational and political choices. We find ourselves giving our support to political systems that are organized on the basis of 'party politics' rather than that of 'the issues' (SW 263), on 'direct personal relationships' rather than on 'the realization of a function in the community' (MSS 316), on attempts at 'realizing one's self by some sort of superiority to somebody else' rather than 'finding out what is to be done and going about to do it' (MSS 314, 316). We find ourselves continuing educational systems that are too often organized to create in each child 'a school self' that expresses 'subordination to school authority and identity of conduct with that of all the other children' (SW 120) so that information can be memorized more quickly. Both our political and our educational systems foster social isolation; and, because of factors like these, we find ourselves without community, lamenting our 'alienated' state. Mead maintains, however, that our situation could be otherwise if we were to make serious political and educational efforts to overcome our separateness through institutional changes. A social institution can be changed, Mead believes, because it is fundamentally an entrenched habit: 'a common response on the part of all members of the community to a particular situation' (MSS 261). So, whether or not we have *created* our social institutions or simply *inherited* them, our habitual responses are what enable them to continue as they are.

This is a strong claim on Mead's part, and I do not know how correct he is. The preponderance of contemporary opinion seems to be against him. In particular, there is the widely held belief that our institutions are more than just our habits, to be modified as we choose. Thus, to many today the degree to which such reforms of our political and educational institutions are possible seems slight. Moreover, we seem less sure than Mead that institutional changes would be able to decrease our separateness anyway. Contemporary understandings place the root of our isolation and fragmentation in a fundamentally alienated human state. Which of these two views is more correct remains to be seen. It is clear, however, that to assume that alienation is *the* human condition is to sanction withdrawal from efforts that might—just might—succeed in advancing human community.

Second, Mead's understanding of human nature as problem-solving at its most fundamental level suggests that we have become too complacent in recent years in our acceptance of unresolved ills. We have been too willing to agree with those who maintain that our problems are beyond human solution and that our efforts and our technology will simply make things worse. It is basically futile, some claim, to get involved trying to ameliorate our inevitable woes. Realistically, they say, we can do no more than watch. For Mead, however, we should not see ourselves as spectators. We are agents, moral agents. We are responsible to do what we can: 'The responsibility of human affairs lies with Humanity, or better, with human society'.[25] He writes that 'society is responsible for the ordering of its own processes and structure . . .' (SW 407); but we have not yet assumed 'the responsibility for our own common ends and purposes'.[26] But, if we were to do so, to use the means available to us, we could have a great impact on our presently unresolved ills.

Again, this is a strong claim, and I do not know how correct Mead is. Surely he thought that our burden would be lighter than it has been; and, out of context, occasional passages from his work sound overly bouyant with regard to our likelihood of success. Consider, for example, the following passage about the power of human intelligence to find its way in our problematic world: 'We, none of us, know where we are going, but we do know that we are on the way' (SW 266). But the context of this and similar remarks in Mead is important. It is his attempt to foster in us a commitment to engage in co-operative activity to attempt to advance the common good at a level beyond that which seems guaranteed to succeed by past experience. His fundamental point remain sound: we are not on the outside looking in—we are involved. In almost all of the problems of human living, our efforts can have some impact; and we cannot know, in advance, when we will fail. We are problem-solvers and we should not allow ourselves to adopt the stance of spectators. In the final analysis, whatever the degree of success legitimately to be anticipated, we can be sure that we will be condemning ourselves unnecessarily to higher levels of unresolved ills if we adopt a spectator stance.

Thirdly, to combine the impact of the problem-solving and social

[25] 'The Philosophy of John Dewey', 80.
[26] Ibid.

aspects of human nature, a Meadian perspective would suggest that we have made some fundamental mistakes in our attempts to understand the present international situation. We continue to be transfixed by an emotionally based nationalism: a combination of 'the sense of superiority to people of other nations',[27] the belief that 'we cannot, as yet, think of ourselves as a self-respecting nation without feeling ourselves ready to fight for grounds of which we ourselves will be the sole censors' (PA 484), and a reluctance to surrender the powerful fusion of our 'complete identification with each other in the whole community'[28] during critical times, a fusion that can make 'the good of the community the supreme good of the individual' (SW 355). Within this nationalistic framework no successful international community is possible because we are binding our nations together by means of 'the union of arms' (SW 365), by means of 'our diaphragms and the visceral responses' (SW 364), by means that preclude thought. We must move, Mead warns, towards 'international-mindedness' (SW 355) and thus international community or we shall die. 'Scientific control of our means [of waging war] has transformed efficient warfare into national or international suicide', Mead recognized (PA 473); and he died, in this regard mercifully, over fifty years ago.

To achieve 'international-mindedness' will not be easy, he writes, primarily because it requires building states upon *thought* rather than *feeling*.

> We are compelled to reach a sense of being a nation by means of rational self-consciousness. We must *think* ourselves in terms of the great community to which we belong. We cannot depend upon feeling ourselves at one with our compatriots, because the only effective feeling of unity springs from our common response against the common enemy (SW 363).

Our success will thus be dependent upon replacing our method of organizing the state based upon hatred for outsiders with a method of organizing the state based upon making the 'common interests' of the citizenry 'the means and the reason for converting diversities into social organization' (SW 366).

Here too, Mead's claim is a strong one; and, again, I do not know how correct his view is. To avoid the paralysis of pessimism, we must believe that the ills of our present international situation can be ameliorated. But are we and our fellows abroad ready to give up the kind of nationalism that gives rise to these ills and to create an international community? As with the other two issues just discussed, in our attempts to ameliorate our

[27] 'The Psychological Bases of Internationalism', in *George Herbert Mead,* John W. Petras (ed.) 157; cf. MSS 207, 284–285.
[28] 'The Psychological Bases of Internationalism', 151; cf. MSS 219–221; SW 235–236.

international problems we seem to be faced with a choice between committing ourselves to efforts toward a goal that we seem unlikely to fully attain, or withdrawing from these attempts to avoid their admitted costs. Is it worth the investment of our time and efforts to attempt to foster international-mindedness when the likelihood of success seems slim? Our answer to this question will depend, no doubt, upon our acceptance or rejection of Mead's prediction about the consequences of abandoning efforts to forestall further international conflicts: 'suicide'.

These are three major contributions of the Meadian perspective to our contemporary situation: a challenge to claims of alienation; a reminder about our responsibility to attempt to address our problems; and a suggestion about how we might reconstruct contemporary international relations. All three contributions arise out of his pragmatic understanding of the human self. All three recognize the existence of as-yet-undiscovered limits to human overcoming. The challenge for us is to come as close as we can to these limits.

George Santayana

T. L. S. SPRIGGE

It would be pleasant to start with a paradox. Santayana was an American philosopher, but he was not an American, and he was not a philosopher. The first of these two qualifying propositions is legally true, the second is a glaring, but sometimes asserted, falsehood.

Let us start with the question of his nationality. Santayana was born, lived and died a Spanish citizen. However, before his mother was married to Santayana's father she was married to an American citizen, by whom she had five children (four of whom survived beyond infancy). After his death she married Augustin Santayana by whom she had one child, Jorge, the philosopher George Santayana to be. Santayana's mother was daughter to the Spanish governor of the small island of Bataan, in the Philippines, and it was in the Philippines that she met both her first husband, George Sturgis, a New England protestant business man, and Augustin Santayana, who, when she first met him (before her marriage to his predecessor) was governor of Bataan in succession to her father. It was, in fact, according to Santayana, to escape the almost inevitable scandal of being an unattached young lady with the young governor as one of the very few Spanish inhabitants that she moved to Manila, where she met George Sturgis, marrying him there and moving to Boston with him. On his death, she returned to Spain where she remet Augustin and married him. Santayana's full account of these events in his autobiography is quite amusing. After five years she returned to Boston to fulfil her pledge to George Sturgis to bring his children up in Boston, while her Spanish son, Jorge, stayed in Spain for the next four years. Finally, when he was nine, his father brought him over to America to grow up with his half brothers and sisters. Augustin returned to Spain, the marriage effectively came to an end, and Jorge, now George, did not return to Spain till he was twenty, and was never there except as a visitor. Thus Santayana lived in America, in Boston and Cambridge to be precise, from the age of nine, and lived there until he retired from his professorship at Harvard in 1911 in his late forties. In the interim, he went to school in Boston, at the Boston Latin School, went up to Harvard as an undergraduate, and stayed thereafter as a member of the philosophy department. As such he achieved early distinction as a poet and a philosopher, but was viewed with a certain uneasiness as a rather alien presence whose influence on students might be adverse to the healthy minded commitment to duty that it was expected that philosophy should promote. After leaving what he found the burdensomeness of his professorship at Harvard he spent the rest of his life, after some years in England, living in hotels and finally at a convent nursing home in Rome, writing his books and living, so far as was possible, the life of pure intuition which he celebrated as the spiritual life. So Santayana was never an American citizen. On the other hand, he lived there from the age of nine till he was forty-eight, was at school there, and a member of the Harvard staff, wrote all his books in English, and developed his philosophy in an American context and had, and even has, something of an American following. Indeed, the interest in him in America has always been enormous even if the appreciation of his strictly philosophic achievement has done it much less than justice. When the Americans entered Rome at the end of World War II, an interview with Santayana was considered a considerable journalistic scoop, and during his post-American years he wrote a good deal about America in a manner that sparked excited controversy. His novel, *The Last Puritan,* published in 1936, which plots the problem of an idealistic American who finds no fit objects for his devotion, was even a best seller and there was much flurry in identifying the orginals of some of his Boston characters. He himself said that it was as an American philosopher that he was to be counted, if he was to be counted at all. Yet he also thought of himself as profoundly un-American in his attitudes, and un-English too, and said that he used the English language to say as many un-English things as possible (un-English meaning Latin as opposed to pertaining to the English-speaking world). Yet though, in my opinion, his best philosophy was written after he left America, the essential ideas were forged in his American years, and I think that it has distinctively American excellences. To me the great years of Harvard, the years of James, Royce, Santayana (with Peirce in the offing) are a real high point of philosophy. For those philosophers form an oustanding group, whose ideas are best understood in relation to each other, from whom there is still much to be learnt, and it is as one of these philosophers that Santayana should be taken.

You will doubtless have already reflected that Santayana's strange family background must have produced problems not only as to which country he belonged to, but as to what his religion was. His father and mother, I think one may say, were unbelieving Catholics. But his mother thought that George would do better in America if he grew up as a Protestant, while his half sister Susanna, who was ten years older than he, became a fanatical Catholic (and for a short time a novice nun) and struggled to keep George one. So he went both to Protestant and Catholic services. Emotionally, Santayana always preferred Catholicism to Protestantism, but he came to an essentially naturalistic view of the world, incompatible with any acceptance of Christian doctrines as literally true, at a very early age. In his eventual philosophy, religion, at its best, was described as a system of symbols which enriched and deepened the experience of living, and which had a certain aptness as a way of adjusting to the world in its true character, but which entirely lacked literal truth. In the light of this Catholicism could be regarded as better than Protestantism, since its symbols were richer and more flexible, and more in tune with nature than Protestantism which, in an attempt to find literal truth, simply impoverished the symbols of Christianity without discarding its falsehoods. Thus Santayana thought that Catholicism provided a better way of life, more spiritually fulfilling for the saintly, and more enriching of natural life for the majority, than Protestantism and since to do this, and not to be true, is the function which reason ascribes to religion, it is to be judged the better type of Christianity. It was this attitude which evoked Bertrand Russell's quip that Santayana believes that there is no God, and that Mary is his mother.

We have seen how far it is true that Santayana was not an American. I would not even bother with the proposition that he was not a philosopher were it not that it gave me a pleasant paradox to start with. However, it has been suggested that Santayana was not really a systematic or analytical thinker, but more a *belles lettres* writer of beautiful philosophic aperçus. He certainly was a great producer of epigrams. His name bulks large in books of quotations, and books have been produced with short nuggets of his wisdom. I shall not dwell on this over-emphasized side of Santayana, for I want to insist on the total falsehood of this conception of him. In fact, he developed one of the most perfectly worked out complex philosophical systems there is, and is a mine of subtle reasoning and distinctions and of insight into the major problems of philosophy. This is recognized by far too few. I have made my own effort to put the record straight, and show his significance for our present day philosophy, in my book on him.

How has the impression ever got around that he is not an exact thinker? There would perhaps be a modicum of justice in it if one considered only the works he wrote before he left the US, for his real system was not formulated until *Scepticism and Animal Faith* (1923) and the four volumes of *Realms of Being* which appeared between 1927 and 1940. The most substantial work which appeared before then, the five volumes of *The Life of Reason* could be held to present a rather impressionistic critique, with a philosophic underpinning, of the nature of human achievement in the construction of common sense, the development of society, and in religion, art, and science, rather than a philosophical system. That work was, for a time, immensely influential, being one of the main documents of American 'naturalism'. But when Santayana published his later system it was received much less enthusiastically in the US, and received little attention in Britain. I think there were several reasons for this. First, it seemed to some of Santayana's original admirers a betrayal of the naturalistic and activist gospel they thought he had taught in *The Life of Reason*.

Second, his complete abandonment of America, and rumoured sympathies with fascism, had a negative effect. Third, he lacked graduate students who would promote his work. Fourth, his thought, though in truth it is systematic, was certainly not in the vein of the analytical and linguistic philosophy which was then coming to be thought the only proper way of doing philosophy, and whose proponents were particularly anxious to avoid anything poetic and dreamy, features which Santayana's writings may certainly suggest to a casual glance.

Upon the whole I would say that it is the most convincing, carefully worked out and comprehensive version of materialism or naturalism that there has been. At a time when so many philosophers are materialists, it is a pity that they do not attend to the one version of materialism which has really found a satisfactory way of dealing with spiritual values and with ethics, and of accounting for mind in a non-reductive way.

I say 'materialism' because Santayana described his own philosophy as materialist, though really it is not materialist in quite the strictest sense (any more than Marxism is). It is, however, as it seems to me, the nearest to materalism which could possibly be true. It is better to talk of 'naturalism', though the expression can sound odd as the name for a philosophic view. The sense in which Santayana is a materialist is that he believes (to put it roughly) that all explanation of how things come about must appeal to physical laws and that the origin and behaviour of animal and human organisms is only a special case of the operation of the physical laws which hold universally. He is also an exponent of the kind of epistemology advocated today by Quine as naturalistic, that is, he thinks one should seek to understand human knowledge as a biological phenomenon, not look for some internal justification of it.

As a materialist Santayana contrasts strikingly with his senior colleagues, who had previously been his teachers, William James and Royce. Santayana was supervised as a graduate student by Royce but he owes much more to James, with whom his personal relations seem to have been somewhat ambivalent. James's description of Santayana's second philosophical book, *Interpretations of Poetry and Religion* as the 'perfection of rottenness' includes the word 'perfection' quite as seriously as the other—he meant that it was a perfect elaboration of an attitude that James found morbid. But there are some very positive references to Santayana in James's work, and Santayana had enormous admiration for James's *Principles of Psychology* which I believe was a main influence on him, and also a highly, if not unqualified, admiration for him as a man and teacher. There is also a strong pragmatist note in Santayana and altogether he probably owed more to James philosophically than he realized.

Santayana's main discussion of Royce and James comes in *Character and Opinion in the U.S.* For his view of Jamesian philosophy the chapter called 'Later Speculations' must be read as well as that expressly on James.

To me it seems that anyone interested in one of the great thinkers, Royce, James and Santayana, best understands them in relation to one another.

A word may be said about Santayana's relation to three other thinkers, first Peirce. Santayana says that a lecture by Peirce sowed some seeds in his mind, but that he knew little of Peirce's thought. This was doubtless true, and I think also that there is not much affinity between them. More significant are Santayana's relations with Bertrand Russell. Russell's elder brother and Santayana were close friends, and this Russell is the original of a main character (Jim Darnley) in Santayana's novel (*The Last Puritan*). It was through him that Santayana knew Bertrand Russell and there was some mutual influence, more of Santayana on Russell, who abandoned the ethical objectivism he had once shared with Moore, under the stimulus of Santayana's criticism, of his and Moore's position, in *Winds of Doctrine*. (See, for example, Russell's note added at beginning of reprint of 'The Elements of Ethics' in *Readings in Ethical Theory*, W. Sellars and J. Hospers (eds) (New York, 1952).) It is worth also mentioning the considerable, though qualified, respect in which Whitehead and Santayana seem to have held each other. Each shows some sense of the affinities which there certainly are between their philosophies, as well as the striking contrasts, especially in general emotional mood. (See, for example, *Process and Reality, passim*—using index—and likewise *The Letters of George Santayana*, D. Cory (ed.) (Scribners, 1955).)

In *Character and Opinion* and elsewhere, Santayana offers a general view of American life and culture. He coined the widely used expression 'the genteel tradition' as a description of certain inadequacies in American literary culture. It referred to a detachment which he thought American writers had from the real forces at work in American life. For Santayana a country had not acquired a genuine culture until its poetry and philosophy expressed ideals which were the implicit goals of the truly active forces in its social, political and industrial life. Although these attitudes of his are closely linked to his philosophical views, I believe that a philosophical audience will prefer me to turn to some exposition of his philosophy.

I shall say something about his philosophical outlook as it expressed itself in three main fields, theory of knowledge, ontology and metaphysics, and ethics. His contributions to aesthetics and political philosophy are of interest, but his most important achievement is in the three areas just mentioned.

So far as epistemology and ontology go, the work previous to *Scepticism and Animal Faith* and *Realms of Being* is much less worked out, and one may as well, in a brief outline, stick mainly to the later work here. But much of his best ethical writing is found in the earlier work and I shall draw on it more in this connection.

I turn now to Santayana's epistemology, as put forward, chiefly, in *Scepticism and Animal Faith*. This work is often misunderstood. It is looked upon as deeply sceptical. On the whole, however, it is directed at showing how a certain concept of knowledge implies that there can be no knowledge, and that since we cannot seriously be such utter sceptics, we should turn to an alternative concept of knowledge which has genuine application, and is what, outside philosophical theory, we normally understand by knowledge in any case. It is a pity it is not more familiar at the present time, when antifoundationalism is the order of the day.

Yet the book does also have as a secondary theme the thesis that an attempt to be sceptics in this sense can lead us to certain positive insights. Firstly, it can be one way in which we become aware of a special realm of being, the realm of essence. Second, it gives us a taste of a special form of life, known as the spiritual life, which is given up to the intuition of essence.

The view of knowledge which leads to scepticism is that for which one can only be said to know that to be true which in some very strong sense one can guarantee to oneself one could not possibly be wrong about. Santayana thinks that if one wants some absolute guarantee, available to one at the very moment when one questions oneself as to what one really knows, one will have to admit that there is no such guarantee that anything exists except that which is present to oneself now in immediate experience. Thus there is no absolute guarantee that one existed a few moments ago, that the physical world as anything other than a sensory presentation to oneself now exists, that other minds exist and so forth. Thus if one only knows what one has an absolute guarantee of, then one knows at most that one is now having certain sensory and other data present to one's mind, that one is experiencing certain coloured shapes, sounds, images and so forth.

This is, of course, a very familiar theme, going back to Descartes. However, Santayana's thought now takes on a more individual twist.

Descartes taught that, until one can build knowledge again on this as a foundation, all one really knows is that one exists, as a mind, living through certain acts of consciousness with certain ideas as their contents. 'I think therefore I am' is the most famous saying in philosophy, though Descartes thought that certainty was not just of the fact that one was thinking or conscious, but that one's consciousness was of a certain definite character and with certain immediate contents.

Santayana holds that one who really succeeds in doubting all that can be doubted will have no belief in his own existence, for a mind must exist over time and one has no guarantee that there is any reality other than that of this moment. He holds, further, that what would be 'this moment' if it were flanked by other moments is not a moment in time at all, if the reality which fills it does not occur in any wider context. If this moment is the only reality we believe in, we are not taking it as a moment at all, but as something belonging to no time or place.

What, then, is this reality which is all that is certain for one if one believes in nothing not guaranteed in some absolute fashion? It is a kind of picture of what might be, but it is not taken as a picture of anything actual. The most obvious part of it is likely to be what might be called the perceptual field, a pattern of sensible forms. It might seem, then, that Santayana holds that what is indubitable is typically an act of awareness of some kind of sensory pattern, an act of awareness which does not necessarily pertain to any continuing self. But Santayana goes further than this. He claims that one cannot be directly aware of an act of awareness. What one is directly aware of is the sensory pattern, also probably of some emotional qualities with which it is suffused. To think of this pattern as being the object of an act of awareness is to think of it as being one item in a sequence of such patterns which follow each other in a temporal flux or stream of consciousness. But one is not in a position to believe that this pattern is a member of any such series if one is doubting all that can be doubted. Therefore, once one has discarded all dubitable beliefs one has discarded the idea that *this* scene is the object of any act of awareness.

So what is this scene? Santayana calls it an essence, a complex essence. By this he means that it is a definite pattern, with its own individual character, but it is not, or at least is not known to be, an element in any real world, for a real world is one which things occur as phases in some sort of historical process. Thus this scene or essence, at least in the aspect of it the reality of which is guaranteed to us, is something which has a kind of *being,* but which does not exist in any ordinary sense.

Santayana's argument turns here on a view he has as to what it is for a possible form of being to *exist.* He holds that if something exists, there must be contingent truths about it, or, what he sees as the same thing, it must be related to other things in ways not merely a matter of its own character. That is, it must stand to other things in what are called external relations. If all that is true of something is that it is what it essentially is, then it is a possible form of being, but not an existence. Now this scene, as revealed to a consciousness which takes nothing on trust, is just the very pattern it is, and does not, so far as thus revealed, relate to anything else. Thus, so far as we are concerned, it is a being which does not exist.

So, according to Santayana, if one managed to doubt everything not absolutely guaranteed one would not be cognizant of any fact about what exists at all, but would simply be aware of an essence or pattern in its own inherent character.

Someone might object that the various elements in the scene manifestly do stand in external relations to one another. Santayana's reply is that they are simply elements in the total pattern with an affinity, but no real identity, to certain elements in other patterns, and that it is part of the very nature of these elements that they are parts of that pattern.

It is to be noted that Santayana claims that when one returns from the sceptical stance one will carry with one the recognition that the essences immediately given to consciousness have being but no existence. To this it may be objected that all he has shown is that we can reach a state in which only their being, and not their existence, is evident to us. However, Santayana's answer is that when we revert to our ordinary state we will come to believe that our acts of consciousness of these essences are in external relations, but will still see that the essences themselves cannot be, for each is complete in itself and not continuous with anything else. It is different with the essences actualized in physical processes which must be supposed to flow into each other in some problematic way.

We see, then, that a consciousness which doubted everything not guaranteed to it would simply be aware of certain patterns which do not really exist. It would not be aware of its own awareness of these patterns, nor of any real physical world of which these patterns provide a picture. Thus one will be intuiting, as Santayana puts it, pure essences and will have no beliefs at all, and *a fortiori* no factual knowledge. Of course, if one reached this state, as the result of an attempt to doubt all that can be doubted, one would have lost all awareness that one had ever made such an attempt (though some essence might figure as a kind of after image of it) but that does not mean one would not have reached one's goal.

However, we may be sure that no human mind will remain in this state for long—'sure', that is, in the form of the more practicable kind of knowledge to which we shall be coming shortly. Some external stimulus will soon be so psychologically compelling that it will prompt an active response, and this active response will bring with it a stock of ordinary beliefs. Thus as I rest in pure intuition a knock on the door will evoke the automatic response of tidying myself and saying 'Come in' and my whole state will be that of believing that I have someone to deal with.

Santayana concludes that we have in our minds a whole stock of beliefs which are psychologically, ultimately biologically, imposed on us, without our having any ultimate grounds for them. The acceptance of the facts specified by these beliefs is what Santayana calls 'animal faith' and he holds that a practicable concept of knowledge must allow that the stable aspects of such faith constitute it. He contends that knowledge, in this practicable and proper sense, is true belief which has been generated by processes which do, in fact, standardly lead to true, not false, belief. Of course, from one point of view it is only my belief that some of my beliefs constitute knowledge in this sense, and this belief is not logically guaranteed. But that does not mean that it is not true or even knowledge in the present sense. You will know that a view of knowledge along these lines has recently become quite popular among philosophers but its novelty then made it difficult for people to grasp that Santayana was not a sceptic.

One main conclusion which Santayana draws from this encounter with scepticism is that philosophical systems which justify themselves as only appealing to what is indubitably there are ill founded. This disposes of the rationale of most reductionisms. Once we get away from the search for some impossible absolute certainty we will accept in our philosophy what we cannot help accepting as true in practice. In doing this, we are simply being honest and making our philosophy, not a kind of dreamy, if disciplined, alternative to the beliefs we hold in daily life, but a rationally organized and clarified version of the system of these beliefs.

So let us now turn to the view of the world which Santayana presents, in this spirit, in the four volumes of *Realms of Being*. The four realms are (1) essence; (2) matter; (3) truth; (4) spirit.

An essence, as we have begun to see, is a quality or a form which might either come before a mind as its immediate object of attention or might pertain to a physical reality as its present character or as an element thereof. There are, perhaps, other essences which do not come under this description but they are essences because their mode of being is of the sort to which we can best draw attention by considering such qualities and forms.

Suppose I sniff a flower and smell a beautiful scent. Could you smell the same scent? Santayana thinks that that which I am finding beautiful is a quality which could certainly be presented to another mind as a result of chemical processes stemming from a different source. It would be possible even that after the destruction of life on this earth life might arise on another planet and one day a consciousness emerge which, on some occasion, savoured the beauty of this very same sensory quality.

Thus what one is appreciating is not some private sensation but a quality which could in principle swim into a consciousness existing at any time. As such it is eternal and out of time. It could not be destroyed, for it remains eternally available. Moreover, even if no one had ever experienced it, and it had had no other standing in the temporal world, it would have still been an item in the realm of essence. For it would be a definite truth about the world that no one was then experiencing it, and this would be a different truth from the truth that no one was experiencing some other scent. But there could not be these two different truths if these two scents were not different, and to be different they must *be*.

We have already seen how one path to the discrimination of the special kind of being pertaining to essences is through sceptical doubting. But this is only one such path. It is in the delight in beauty, above all, that one appreciates an essence simply for its being the eternal form or quality it is, though it is only some essences that easily lend themselves to the kind of wrapt attention which is the experience of them as beautiful.

Presence to consciousness as its immediate object is not the only way in which essences can enter into the flux of existence. Every part of the physical world has a form and quality which could pertain to some other part of it, then or at another time, and which, if it had not thus pertained to any part of the physical world would still be a definite form of being whose absence from the world would be a different fact from the absence of some other such form.

Thus essences can slip from the eternal realm of pure being, in which things are present simply because they are what they are, into the temporal flux of the existing world in two different ways. They can occur there as the characteristics of some reality, such as a part of the physical world, or they can occur there as immediate objects of some mind's act of attention. Some essences can play either of these roles, others only one.

Essences play a particularly important part in Santayana's account of what knowledge is. (His development of this theme became the uniting dogma of a school of American philosophers known as 'critical realists' who published a manifesto in 1920.) We have seen that for Santayana knowledge in the most useful sense is appropriately generated true belief. But Santayana thinks that such knowledge is of two different kinds, the literal and the symbolic.

Whenever one has any kind of knowledge of a *fact* (which, as Santayana uses the term, means some chunk of the existing world) one is, as a physical organism, in some way directed on to that fact in the sense that some physical process of adjustment to or preparation for encounter with it is going on within one. (It may be to a fact in the very distant past, e.g. to Julius Caesar. In explaining how my mental reference is to particulars via causal chains Santayana, in opposition to Royce who thought the Absolute must mediate such connections, adumbrates a view we now associate with Saul Kripke.) This process, moreover, has produced a mental act of intuition of an essence which is one's conscious registering of the fact's existence and nature. If one's knowledge is literal, this essence will be the very same essence as was present in the fact as its character, or as an element thereof, while if one's knowledge is symbolic, this essence will, in one or other of various possible ways, be an appropriate symbol in human terms for something of the real character of the fact. It is to be noted that when essences are intuited in such acts of knowledge, they are not merely contemplated, as they are by the perfect sceptic, but felt about in a way indicative of one's physical processes of adjustment or preparation.

Santayana's view that our knowledge of nature is largely symbolic is crucial to his whole way of thinking. In the light of it he can say that both in science and in religion, we think about the world in terms of essences which are not part of the literal truth about it, but which may still be an apt way of conceiving it, as bringing out something about our relation to it, of what it has to offer us or how it threatens us. The essences present to our minds in scientific thought help adjust us to the finer details of the world process so that we can act more effectively, while religion, at its best, deals in symbols which arouse emotions suitable to our place in the scheme of things such as gratitude to the great mysterious powers that produced us.

It is here that Santayana is very close to pragmatism. Most human belief is to be judged true or false according to its effects in adjusting us to, and helping us make the best of, the reality we are in the midst of and ourselves a part of. But he thought that the formulation of pragmatist doctrine by William James was too apt to call in question the very notion that there is a real literal truth about how things are, however limited our access to it. He thought this both destructive of clear thinking and of a proper respect for the world as it is independently of what humans make of it.

This is the place to deal briefly with Santayana's realm of truth. By truth he does not mean the property which pertains to true beliefs, but that by relation to which beliefs are either symbolically or literally true. Truth, for him, consists in essences qua being the characters of parts of reality.

This they can be in two different ways. Some of them may be actualized in a kind of all at once way in certain ultimate facts, such, perhaps, as what for science are sub-atomic events. Others of them are actualized in more diffuse ways. For example, if you consider such long processes as the development of life on the planet, or the French Revolution, each of these, considered as a whole, has a certain complex character which is the truth about it. Yet this character or essence is not actualized all at once as are the characters of ultimate units of process and that means a certain contrast between the essence which is the truth about the process and the way in which the process itself actualizes essences. The contrast is that the truth about the process is an essence in which all elements are so synthesized as to be in internal relations to one another, that is, they are individually coloured by their role in the whole, while the process as it unravels exemplifies these elements piecemeal, so that they stand only in external relations to each other.

The realm of matter, to which I now turn, comprises the whole flux of physical process. This is constantly changing, but it abides by certain fixed laws and habits, and has sufficient continuity from moment to moment for each to be describable as the same physical world transformed with mostly the same objects. That there is, and will continue to be, this regularity and continuity is part of that system of psychologically compulsory beliefs which constitute our animal faith. There must, in any case, be some such continuity between moment and moment or the moments would not be phases in the history of the same world, and would be in no relation to each other at all.

As we seek to clarify what our animal faith commits us to in regard to these matters, we will see that there must be, to each part of the physical world, an aspect which we can never characterize clearly to ourselves. Nor is this simply a limitation of our minds, it is a limitation inevitable for any mind, even if there were one which came as near to omniscience as possible. This is because mind must characterize things to itself in terms of essences. But even if we knew the precise essence actualized as the quality and form of some isolable element in the flux, there would be something about that element not a matter of the essence it actualizes. For this element must be related to other elements in the flux, to its predecessors, successors and contemporaries, and related in ways which are not a matter simply of the affinities and contrasts, that is the ideal or internal relations, between these essences. These external relations of one element to another will always be falsified by any essences by which a mind seeks to characterize them, though it can get a dim sense of them from its own sense of being carried along in the general bustle of only half comprehended events. One traditional and helpful way of characterizing the external relations between one such element and its successor is to say that each such element contains a portion of the substance or energy of the world which it transmits to the next one, the substance taking in each case a slightly modified form.

There is a certain affinity—rather despite itself—in some of what Santayana says about the flux of physical existence to aspects of James's thought.

James, regarding himself here as in alliance with Bergson, thought that there was an aspect to the flux of experience (which, for him, was as much as to say, the total flux of existence) which could not be characterized in concepts. Concepts split up the world into discrete pieces and aspects, whereas in reality everything flows into other things without sharp boundaries. This real flux can only be known by an intuition based on submergence in it. Santayana's view that the flux of physical process cannot be captured in essences, since these are distinct synthesizing totalities, and that such sense as we have of it comes from our sense of simply being carried along in the rush of things, is surprisingly close to this. Surprisingly, because much of what Santayana says seems to point in other directions. Perhaps the key to it is that Santayana sees it as, so to speak, the role of mind to crystallize the flux by contemplating the eternal essences unstably present in it, and does not at all celebrate the worth of the kind of unintellectual submergence in things to which James thought that the philosopher was now called.

Let us now turn to spirit, which is Santayana's word for consciousness, as he conceives it.

Spirit is to be distinguished from what Santayana calls the psyche. An animal organism, in particular each human, has, according to Santayana, a principle of organization within it which he calls the psyche. This is a power lying within it to produce behaviour which will keep the organism as close as possible to some inherited ideal plan as present circumstances allow. This power is a resultant of purely physical laws, but it calls for special consideration as being a very special such resultant.

The psyche is more truly what one is, is one's very self, than is one's consciousness. One's consciousness is simply one aspect of the psyche's operations, and not the most important as a force in the world.

Indeed, spirit is not a force in the world at all. According to Santayana, at the level of ultimate explanation everything a human being does—in intersubjectively accessible ways—is a physical process having an entirely physical explanation, ultimately probably by the laws of physics and chemistry, though at a rather less ultimate level by reference to the psyche.

Spirit, or consciousness, is an expression or fruition of the physical life and behaviour of the organism. My present speaking is a physical activity with purely physical causes in my brain states, and so is the physical registration and processing of this in your brains, but my conscious sense of the noises I am making, and of their meaning, as well as your conscious attention, are generated by these processes. They do not, however, react upon them. Santayana is thus what is called an epiphenomenalist.

Rather than try to give Santayana's reasons for holding this view, I shall say something as to the obvious appeal it has for him.

He thinks that there is a strong tendency, in many thinkers, especially in pragmatists, to value things only for the work they do. Thus the tendency is to think that consciousness has no proper role in the world unless it does some work there. But this is to fail to grasp that it is only as generating spirit that anything in the world possesses value. Spirit is not a force acting in the world but it is what alone gives point to it. One can say that for Santayana epiphenomenalism highlights what is the true importance of spirit, as being the fruition of life, and the seat of all value. To see its point as lying in work it does in preserving the organism is to miss this. There is no value, as such, in the preservation of organisms. All that matters is the spirit they generate.

[I do not find Santayana's arguments for the truth of epiphenomenalism altogether convincing, but this moral which he draws from it seems to me just. Moreover, I will say this for epiphenomenalism as a putative truth about the world. There are many today who think, like Santayana, that all physical events, including all human action and speech, have an adequate explanation at the purely physical level, just as the print-outs of computers and the movements of robots. If this is so, then either epiphenomenalism is true or consciousness must somehow itself simply *be* a brain process. To me it appears evident that the latter is an incoherent supposition, unless perhaps—as in fact I hold to be so—the physical world is somehow psychic in its inner being. For those who do not take this view epiphenomenalism is the only coherent alternative. It is thus a much more promising theory of mind—or rather of consciousness, for mind covers much more than this— than most of those current today. Santayana's particular version of it, and the way in which it fits in with his general scheme of things and of values, should be of particular interest at the present time.]

So Santayana postulates four basic realms of being. The world as a whole is a physical system governed by physical laws. Spirit or consciousness is an outgrowth of this which brings some of the truth about the world into the light of awareness and brings value into nature. This truth consists in essences which are illustrated in the flux of nature (including such consciouness as is generated in that flux) or which apply to it as suitably symbolic of it. These essences are only a selection from an eternal realm of essences which have being whatever may or may not exist. Spirit is aware of a wider range of these essences than are ever illustrated in nature, because nature generates spirit which not only knows something of the truth of nature but also contemplates alternative possibilities in imagination. The essential good of spirit is to contemplate essences which are true or beautiful, these being the essential forms of the good which can only have lodging in the world as forms under which spirit contemplates things. Incidentally, to complete the picture I should note that spirit has its own essence which is not to be identified with the essences it contemplates. Even when it contemplates its own essence, its actualization of the essence of spirit, by being a spirit, is a different fact from its contemplation of this essence.

That gives you a rough outline of Santayana's ontology, or theory of what there is. I shall conclude with some remarks on his views on three topics, ethics, religion and time.

The prime texts for understanding Santayana's ethical views are *The Life of Reason* and the section called 'Hypostatic Ethics' in *Winds of Doctrine,* though there is much else that is important.

For Santayana, all action inspired by conscious choice is action for the sake of the good. When we aim at something it presents itself to our consciousness as falling under the form of the good, that is as possessing a quality of goodness. Goodness is an essence consisting in a kind of glow or sparkle which some things wear for us. However, they only wear that glow or sparkle for us because unconscious psychic forces are propelling us towards what seems to possess it, so that quite different states of affairs possess the quality of goodness as they present themselves to different people. Thus Santayana is an ethical relativist, things are good for me or you, not as they are in themselves. The same, of course, goes for the various forms of badness which pertain to what our psyches propel us to avoid, spurn, or destroy so far as possible; but, as I have done already, and as Santayana tends to do, I shall ignore the point that action is sometimes more concerned with avoiding the bad than possessing the good.

Santayana's relativism is of a very special kind, since most ethical relativists would not recognize that there is any such essence or quality as good. More striking still, Santayana's ethical relativism actually issues in the end in a more absolutistic point of view, though he does not put it in quite this way. That is because he thinks that to the extent that I manage really to understand another person's point of view, the situations he views as good will come to present themselves to me also as, at least in the aspect of them which I think of as concerning him, *good* too. Thus the more I understand the variety and relativity of people's value systems, the more I will come to endorse only those policies which maximize the extent to which people obtain what appears under the form of the good to them.

This thesis is closely related to Santayana's view of reason, which he usually understands in the sense of practical reason rather than theoretical reason, though what he says could be extended to the latter.

Reason is essentially an organizing principle in the psyche, an urge to develop a steady and stable pattern of life, values and beliefs in which all our initial impulses are given as much of a head as is compatible with their being organized into a coherent unity. The life of reason is one in which no human impulse is condemned as essentially wicked, but all are respected as bringing with them a vision of the good, which should certainly be endorsed if it stood alone. However, many of our impulses are wavering and there is much conflict between different impulses. Reason, therefore, seeks to prune and modify the different impulses so that in combination they drive us to a richly comprehensive and stably coherent pattern of living. If one takes into account the fact, just mentioned, that as one learns about the goals and values of others one will endorse them as desirable objectives for them, it will appear that the impulses which the reason of one individual strives to organize will include the impulse to let, perhaps assist, others find their good too.

To the question why one should try to be resonable in one's system of values and in one's way of life, Santayana usually answers that there is no ultimate reason why one should, beyond the fact that the specific impulse of reason is strong within us. We do most of the time seek more or less successfully a life in which we do not simply swing hopelessly from one feeling or impulse to another, so that our lives, and at the social level our communities, have no overall structure or plan. Reason, then, is an impulse in its own right, though it is an impulse to organize other impulses, and it has its own vision of the good, one in which all other goods are organized so as to assist and enhance each other. Yet though it has no justification outside itself, Santayana does appear to think that there is a sort of inevitability in the development of some sort of reason, on account of the fact, just mentioned, that simply in knowing something of the impulses of others, or of one's own presently less dominant impulses, one inevitably develops a wish that the goals of all these impulses should be attained if possible.

Although reason is a pervasive aspect of human endeavour, it successes in human history and in our individual lives have never been more than partial and precarious. The five volumes of *The Life of Reason* try to discuss the extent to which reason has been successful, and what its future possibilities may be, in common sense, society, religion, art and science. That vast undertaking is one which Santayana pursues in a confident often epigrammatic way, with barely a footnote recording his sources. Much of it, inevitably, is very dated but much of it is also very wise. Santayana thought of his project as akin to Hegel's *Phenomenology of Spirit,* but one in which the history of reason as a natural propensity in man replaces the history of the coming to consciousness of absolute spirit.

In one respect, Santayana's ethics sounds a distinctively American note. The doctrine that one cannot understand what another's vision of the good is without sharing it, is crucial to Royce's early ethical theory and also to James's fairly slight enagagement with issues in moral philosophy. One should not confuse this view with that urged by many today, that one can only understand a culture to which one belongs, originally or by slow adoption. The endorsement of an alien culture's or individual's values is, for these American philosophers, a resultant, not a prerequisite, of understanding their way of feeling. It should be stressed that in spite of this shared premise the ethical outlook to which it leads Santayana is fairly different from Royce's, putting less emphasis on good works and more on imaginative creativity.

Santayana did not think that a life of reason is the only goal a reflective person can set himself. Besides rational morality, there are pre-rational and post-rational moralities. The former, which rests on a collection of accidentally generated superstitious dogmas need not detain us, but the second requires some comment. A rational ethic assists us organize our life, or at a social level, our community, so that as many sides of our nature find their good as possible. A post-rational ethic is one which organizes life around one single over-riding aim—it might, for example, be the increase of scientific knowledge. The post-rational ethic which especially interests Santayana is that grounding what he calls the spiritual life. This is a life of pure contemplation in which qualities and forms, in short, essences, become the focus of an intense meditation. In extreme cases, as with certain sorts of mystic, all life comes to centre round the attempt to achieve an ecstatic absorption in the contemplation of pure being.

The relations between the life of reason and the spiritual life are a recurrent theme in Santayana. His basic view is that the spiritual life is simply one human ideal the satisfaction of which is given considerable, but not unlimited, weight in rational personal and social policies.

The spiritual life is one ingredient in the complex of phenomena which come under the heading of religion. Santayana says many things about religion which it is somewhat difficult to hold together in one's mind. One thing which is beyond doubt is that he regarded religious ideas as lacking literal truth. Since, however, he often says the same about science, asserting that both have a different sort of symbolic truth, the force of this point may not seem too strong. However, it is clear that he thinks science can come much nearer to the literal truth about things than can religion taken as concerning actual fact.

Yet he does think that religion at its best has real value. (See *Reason in Religion* and *The Idea of Christ in the Gospels*.) First, its symbolic truth, provided the mythical details are not taken as descriptive of particular observable episodes in history, is sometimes great, expressive of great moral, psychological and even cosmic truths. This is true of much of Christianity, for example. For it tells man that he is a finite dependent being, and tells him what is truly valuable about himself, namely the pure spirit within him which is tied down by petty fears, struggles and ambitions which a wider more steady view of things can dispel. Secondly, it formulates in a mythical manner the ideal to which our impulses point and focuses our aspirations so that our life becomes more purposeful and coherent. Thirdly, religion is to be valued for the sheer enrichment of life it provides. Santayana has a strong affection for Greek religion, especially on its more Apollonian side, where the myths of the gods of Olympus and the rites associated with them add a depth to the standard events of life by associating them with evocative and sometimes illuminating stories which also serve to link the generations one with another. He thinks Catholicism, with its cult of the saints, adds beauty and dignity to the recurring patterns of life, and provides the right kind of conditions for prayer. And 'in rational prayer', says Santayana, 'the soul may be said to accomplish three things important to its welfare: it withdraws within itself and defines its good, it accommodates itself to destiny, and it grows like the ideal which it conceives.' *(Reason in Religion,* 43). This view of prayer is close to that Iris Murdoch talks of in *The Sovereignty of the Good.* Thus religion, as part of the way of life of a community, may be a vital aspect of the patterns of fulfilling living which it provides. It was because he thought that a main value of religion lay in its dignifying, and casting a poetic glow over, and emphasizing the essential values of, the great standard events of human life, birth, marriage, death, repentance, forgiveness, reconciliation, gratitude for life, that Santayana disliked James's approach to religion in *The Varieties of Religious Experience,* which he described as spiritual slumming, and which he thought identified religion too much with the isolated and the abnormal.

Thus for Santayana religion could be an instrument and aspect of the life of reason and of the spiritual life as reason endorsed it. However, it has serious drawbacks. At least in modern times, it stands in the way of intellectual honesty, it confuses aspiration towards fulfilment of our ideals with piety to the sources of our being, and it too often fills us with false guilts and images of horror. He expresses no very certain view as to how far a religious consciousness might develop which retained only religion's positive elements. It must be admitted, I think, that he was not always generous to those who, like some of the American humanists, seemed to

T. L. S. Sprigge

take a somewhat similar view to his, though this sprang from his great distrust for the more distinctively protestant kind of Christinanity, which, he thought, preserved the basic illusions of religion while throwing out the enriching and moralizing poetry.

It may be interesting to note that he found Royce's approach to religion particularly unattractive, as it grounded the being of God or the Absolute on evil and error. Santayana was particularly repelled by any attempt to claim that the suffering in the universe is somewhat essential to its goodness. It is instructive to compare the responses of Royce and Santayana to Shelley's picture in *Prometheus Unbound* of a mankind redeemed from suffering and evil. Royce saw Shelley's vision as a revelation of the insipidity of a world of pure goodness, while Santayana saw it as Shelley's special gift to picture the ideal, however feeble his grasp of how it might be achieved.

I shall conclude with a nod towards what I think one of Santayana's greatest achievements, his treatment of time and eternity. He holds that from an ultimate point of view the events of every moment of time are simply there each in its own spatial and temporal position. There is a real flux of events in the sense that it is of the very essence, to put it paradoxically, of what makes an event an event, and not a mere essence, that it is unstable and in passage to what follows it. Yet ultimately every such event is eternally present in its own time, and past and future only in relation to other events. Thus the concepts or essences of past and future are in a manner illusory, since Julius Caesar's deeds and thoughts, as they are in themselves, as opposed to the perspective in which they appear to us, are as much in the present as are our present thoughts and actions. Some find this claim—for which Santayana provides, I believe, a compelling proof—an odd way of stating the obvious, others as totally opaque or obscure. For me it is a deep truth, the significance of which is often not grasped, even when it is granted in words.

Bibliographical Note

Santayana wrote many major works. The essentials of his final system are in *Scepticism and Animal Faith* (1923), *The Realm of Essence* (1927), *The Realm of Matter* (1930), *The Realm of Truth* (1938), *The Realm of Spirit* (1940). The five volumes of *The Life of Reason* (1905–6) are also key works. The shortened version which appeared in 1954 is best avoided. There are many other important and delightful works. A good volume to convey the general feel of Santayana's thought is *Soliloquies in England and Later Soliloquies* (1922), though no one should form a conclusion as to his constructive philosophical ability on the basis of it. There are not very many full-length commentaries. My own study of his thought is *San-*

tayana: An Examination of his Philosophy (1974). Some valuable articles on him are collected in *Animal Faith and Spiritual Life* ed. John Lachs (1967). The volume *The Philosophy of George Santayana* ed. P. A. Schilpp (1940) is of value mainly for Santayana's own contributions. A Santayana newsletter is published at Waterloo University, Canada (where many of his papers are held) edited by Angus Kerr-Lawson, and a new scholarly edition of his works is in preparation under the general editorship of Professor Herman J. Saatkamp. Jr, to be published by MIT Press.

Emerson and the Virtues

ELLEN KAPPY SUCKIEL

Ralph Waldo Emerson, whose life spanned most of the nineteenth century, is widely regarded as one of the greatest sages in the history of American thought. Among educated American citizenry, Emerson is probably the most commonly read indigenous philosopher—and for good reason. Emerson presents a vision of human beings and their place in the universe which gives meaning and stature to the human condition. His profound, even religious, optimism, gives structure and import to even the smallest and apparently least significant of human activities. The inspirational quality of Emerson's prose, his willingness to travel far and wide to lecture, his ability to help people transcend the difficulties of the times, all led to his very great national as well as international significance.

Emerson stands as the key figure in American Transcendentalism, the most influential intellectual movement in America in the nineteenth century. Transcendentalism as a movement began early in the 1830s, when a number of mostly young people in New England joined together to exchange ideas and discover ways of helping to ameliorate what they regarded as the profound difficulties of the age. In 1836, the 'Transcendental Club' was formed. Its members included Emerson, Henry David Thoreau, Theodore Parker, Margaret Fuller, William Ellery Channing, and others. While meetings were irregular and lasted only four years, the club provided the main springboard and nourishment for the birth of the transcendentalist movement in nineteenth-century America. The purpose of the club was to counter and reverse the increasing commercialism in the public consciouness, and to re-establish a sense of idealism and commitment to spiritual values. The members of the Transcendental Club also shared a common feeling that the reigning Christian (and by this they usually meant Unitarian) doctrine and practice were impoverished. They wanted to transform and revitalize a religious world-view which had become for them cold, vacant and out of touch. They promulgated an affirmative, optimistic philosophy, nowhere so evident as in their magazine, the *Dial,* which was published for four years, and which testified to the editors' intention to raise the populace to a higher and more joyous sensibility.

The members of the Transcendental Club had no desire to funnel their individual views into a single common philosophy. They were highly independent and sometimes idiosyncratic thinkers who had too strong a sense of their own individualities to submerge themselves into conformity with the thoughts of others. They did, however, have certain fundamental broad intellectual viewpoints in common. They were all metaphysical idealists who attempted to grasp beyond the physical world to the moral and spiritual truths they felt occupied an ideal realm beyond. They held a common belief in the basic goodness of humankind. In general, they were romantics, both morally—in proclaiming the profound dignity and value of the individual; and epistemologically—in relying more on feeling or intuition than on reason or empirical evidence. Most importantly, the transcendentalists shared a common desire to celebrate God's divinity in human beings, rather than His separation from them, and they sought to understand the implications this would have for our daily lives.

My particular concern in this paper is Emerson's conception of virtue. I mean to focus not so much on the traditional litany of virtues: courage, temperance, wisdom, justice and the like; but rather on a certain central configuration of related moral qualities which Emerson thought every person should possess. He had in mind an ideal human type—a coherent set of excellences—which throughout his works he exhorts us to fulfil. Emerson was trained and ordained as a Unitarian minister, and although he renounced the ministry early in life, he retained throughout his life the sense that he had moral wisdom to impart. Emerson's moral philosophy is in turn nurtured by and rooted in his religious and metaphysical theories; and it is with these that I shall begin.

Emerson considers the divine spirit—or as he calls it, the oversoul—to be part of the natural world. The oversoul expresses itself in human beings and nature, pervading and giving meaning to all aspects of existence, suffusing it with moral and religious significance. Natural laws, such as pertain to gravitation, inertia, and the like, for Emerson, are no different from the morally laden metaphysical laws emanating from the divine presence. Indeed, every aspect of existence—every entity, law, event—is merely a particular form which the universal spirit takes, and by which it expresses itself. For Emerson, 'the universe is represented in an atom, in a moment of time'.[1]

Human beings participate fully in these divine laws as full embodiments of the oversoul. In a manner reminiscent of Leibniz, Emerson holds that each individual embodies and expresses the entire universe from his or her own unique point of view. Each one of us is all of existence. Moreover, each particular action which any of us performs is itself a full expression of

---

[1] *The Complete Works of Ralph Waldo Emerson,* Edward Waldo Emerson (ed.), 12 vols (Boston and New York, 1903–4), vol. II, 297. (Hereafter all reference to Emerson's *Complete Works* will be in abbreviated form, thus: II,297.)

the oversoul, thus bearing ultimate moral significance. Emerson puts it dramatically when he proclaims:

> Every occupation, trade, art, transaction, is a compend of the world and a correlative of every other. Each one is an entire emblem of human life. . . . And each one must somehow accommodate the whole man and recite all his destiny.[2]

Emerson's metaphysics is paralleled by his epistemology. Given the ultimacy of our mission as the expression of the divine force in the universe, we must have the commensurate ability to discern the divine element in ourselves. For Emerson, no mere ratiocinative capability is enough. Drawing a distinction between 'reason' and 'understanding', he uses the term 'understanding' for our ordinary common-sense mode of apprehension. Our understanding enables us to negotiate through the world and deal with the mundane details of our lives. It is also the mechanism by means of which we generate theories in science, mathematics, history, and the like. But the most important, indeed the only genuinely meaningful relation the individual has to the universe, is not through understanding, but through 'reason'. 'Reason', however, is not the best word for what Emerson has in mind. For 'reason' as Emerson uses the term stands for precisely the opposite of what we ordinarily mean by reasoning, or logic, or discursive thought. 'Reason', for him, is the faculty of transcendental intuition, or as he sometimes calls it, 'instinct'. When using 'reason', or transcendental intuition, we delve deeply into our own centres, and subjectively discover truths by a process not polluted by the distinctions, hesitations and indirectness of discursive thought.[3]

Transcendental intuition, for Emerson, though private, personal and subjective, is not supposed to be in any way unreliable or idiosyncratic. Indeed it is the only genuinely reliable source of knowledge, affording us direct access to the oversoul:

> Place yourself in the middle of the stream of power and wisdom which animates all whom it floats, and you are without effort impelled to truth, to right and a perfect contentment.[4]

Since Emerson holds that this direct, intuitive apprehension is the only genuine means of knowing, he denigrates any knowledge which comes

[2] II,101.

[3] Emerson claims to have acquired the term 'transcendental' from Kant (I, 339–340). But as Morton White, among others, points out, Emerson's transcendental intuition ultimately reduces to feeling, and has little to do with Kant's conception of transcendental understanding (*Science and Sentiment in America* (Oxford, 1972), 98–99).

[4] II,139.

second-hand. He goes so far as to reject any reliance on books or other persons for gaining knowledge. In his most dramatic, and indeed even caricatured expression of the ideal of transcendental intuition, Emerson pictures himself as follows:

> Standing on the bare ground,—my head bathed by the blithe air and uplifted into infinite space,—all mean egotism vanishes. I become a transparent eyeball; I am nothing; I see all; the currents of the Universal Being circulate through me; I am part or parcel of God.[5]

It seems odd that Emerson rejects books and other persons as important sources of knowledge. For even if he were right that 'reason' in his sense were to give us the highest—that is to say, divine—knowledge, he must have recognized that we need more than that to negotiate our way through the world. A single person, isolated from most of the collective knowledge of the race, may indeed think, and thus learn about God and him or herself, but he or she will be unable to learn much else. In any case, the truths which Emerson found of genuine significance were the moral and religious ones. And it is upon the position of human beings at the epistemic and moral centre of the universe that Emerson builds his picture of the ideal human type.

Emerson's concept of the ideal person involves the characteristics of grandness and nobility. Self-reliance, for Emerson, is the paramount human excellence. In his most stirring essay, entitled 'Self-Reliance', Emerson issues a ringing call for heroic individualism. By 'self-reliance' he means the free development and expression of the individual, who goes by his or her own judgments and follows his or her own lights, unfettered by either the demands of society or the opinions of others. Since each individual contains in microcosm the entirety of the oversoul, he or she should act from the knowledge, certitude and confidence that comes from the indwelling presence of the divine. Emerson repeatedly denies any conception of life and morality in which the individual conforms to social conventions or moral rules. He distrusts social institutions, and considers society to be oppressive and otiose, a source only of restricting the individual's creativity and self-expression. 'Society', he objects, 'everywhere is in conspiracy against the manhood of every one of its members.'[6] For Emerson, the person is in no way responsible to the opinions of others. For each individual embodies the universal spirit from his or her own point of view, and no one else is in the same privileged position—epistemic and moral—to say what is right from that point of view.

Emerson here may be assuming, optimistically, if not naively, that all points of view, no matter how they may seem to conflict, genuinely do

[5] I,10.
[6] II,49.

reconcile themselves ultimately into a single system. Or else—and perhaps this is more likely—he may simply be uninterested in any contradictions between points of view that may arise. I must say I find it hard to imagine a society of Emersonians. The agreement and coherency of major assumptions and goals, not to mention social controls, which are required for group living, are simply absent from Emerson's world-view.

Emerson encourages his readers to shun not only the constraints of other persons' judgments upon them, but equally any of their own self-imposed limitations on their choices. The person need not critically examine the principles of his or her action, because what comes from his or her genius is always, and necessarily, right. 'Trust thyself: every heart vibrates to that iron string', Emerson proclaims.[7] 'The only right is what is after my constitution; the only wrong what is against it.'[8] Indeed Emerson takes this so far as to hold that the individual has no responsibility even to maintain consistency of his or her own opinions over time. In perhaps his most famous injunction, Emerson proclaims that 'a foolish consistency is the hobgoblin of little minds.... With consistency a great soul has simply nothing to do.'[9] Consistency is not of benefit to the individual. For the mandate to be consistent, Emerson holds, really comes down to a command of mediocrity and conformity. Since others rely on your past actions and stated beliefs in their attempts to understand you, it is only not to frustrate or disappoint them that consistency has a function. But the genuine individual has no responsibility to keep others from being frustrated, and need have no commitment to his or her past, if he or she has outgrown it and is no longer represented by it.[10]

Conformity is similarly inimical to the true expression of the individual. To attempt to be like others only dissipates our unique energies and talents. Men and women who mimic someone else are inauthentic: 'not false in a few particulars, authors of a few lies, but false in all particulars'.[11] Whatever the expectations and needs of others, they are secondary. For the divine principle itself is at work in the individual's self-expression. It is this fact, or alleged fact, which lends such force and legitimacy to Emerson's ringing injunction that 'nothing is at last sacred but the integrity of your own mind'.[12]

Emerson's individualism is not limitless, however, the way it is, say, for some existentialists. Sartre, for instance, holds that the individual must create him or herself in the context of infinite possibilities, from a position

[7] II, 46.
[8] II, 50.
[9] II, 57.
[10] II, 55–58. See II, 67.
[11] II, 55.
[12] II, 50.

of having no essence, no fundamental human nature or pre-determined vantage point upon which to base, guide or evaluate his or her choices.[13] In contrast, Emerson holds, very much like the ancient Stoics, that the individual's self-expression occurs within the context of his or her proper role and life-scheme.[14] For Emerson, each person has his or her own role to play and perspective to uphold in the overall expression of humanity, and in the full expression of the oversoul. Our task is to be clear about this role and to enact it energetically, with commitment, and with joy. We should think of ourselves not as isolated individuals, performing and reduced to our own special activities, but rather as the embodiment of an archetype, as one aspect of the universal 'Man' ('Human' would have been a better term). In his famous Phi Beta Kappa address of 1837, 'The American Scholar', Emerson argues that an individual is not just a farmer, but 'Man on the farm'; the scholar is not a mere thinker, rather he is 'Man Thinking'.[15] From this point of view our life and work are infused with ideal meaning. The seemingly trivial tasks to which we frequently must address ourselves become contextualized and sanctified. All aspects of our lives are purified and idealized, in that they incorporate and reflect the full significance and value of the oversoul.

This is a beautiful and edifying conception of the meaning of life, yet one which, paradoxically, in some ways obstructs rather than enhances self-perfection. For what of a person in a role which he or she finds unfulfilling, or oppressive? Or what of roles that are less than admirable? 'Man Farming' and 'Man Thinking' are attractive images. But what of 'Man Burgling' or 'Man Mopping Up?' Put another way, Emerson seems to commit no small error in his conservatism—idealizing whatever it is one does, if one but approach it right, as necessarily a worthwhile and legitimate expression of the divine. Emerson incautiously jumps headlong into this precarious position:

> Let a man believe in God, and not in names and places and persons. Let the great soul incarnated in some woman's form, poor and sad and single, in some Dolly or Joan, go out to service and sweep chambers and scour floors, and its effulgent daybeams cannot be muffled or hid, but to sweep and scour will instantly appear supreme and beautiful actions, the top and radiance of human life.[16]

The problem with Emerson here is that he really has two ideas in mind when he talks about a person's calling, and his teetering between them causes a great deal of difficulty in interpreting and assessing his proposals.

[13] *Being and Nothingness,* trans. Hazel E. Barnes (New York, 1956).
[14] See, for example, Epictetus, *The Encheiridion*.
[15] I, 83–84.
[16] II, 165–166.

Much of the time he is thinking of a person's calling as defined by his or her social role. When he thinks this way, the problem arises as to how Emerson genuinely can enjoin the individual to flourish in a given social position if by its nature it constrains, prevents, distorts, or even renders unintelligible that person's self-expression and fulfilment. But superimposed on this image is the idea of a person's calling not as his or her concrete vocation or occupation, but rather as a kind of metaphysical programme, which, if that person lives life correctly, he or she will act out. This programme is rather like the daimon or indwelling personal spirit posited by the Greeks. When Emerson is thinking along the lines of the latter image, he enjoins his readers not merely to accept their current roles, but rather actively to discover and select the paths most fitting for them, and also continually to perfect themselves in their proper paths.[17]

In 'Spiritual Laws', for instance, an essay impressive for its inspirational impact if not always for its literal truth, Emerson proclaims that each person has his own vocation. He must follow his talent. This depends on his organization, 'or the mode in which the general soul incarnates itself in him'.[18] But what this means concretely Emerson never reveals. How does one discover one's personal divine principle, and how does one identify the ways in which it might be fulfilled? What is its relationship to one's social role? In thinking about Emerson, I am reminded of William James's discussion in *Pragmatism* of what he calls the 'sentimentalist fallacy'—viz. 'to shed tears over abstract justice and generosity, beauty, etc., and never to know these qualities when you meet them in the street, because there the circumstances make them vulgar'.[19] Emerson encourages us each to follow our call, but he never explains concretely what it means to do so, or how our call actually relates to our particular conditions.

In most instances Emerson seems to *identify* one's metaphysical role with one's concrete social position. In dealing with the pervasive imperfections of common life, Emerson holds that if individuals find themselves in positions they consider unacceptable, the solution is not for them to change the external situation, but rather to change their own perceptions and attitudes towards it. Emerson resembles the Stoics in his belief that the key to life and freedom lies ultimately in the way one interprets one's situation, rather than in any pre-existent and unmalleable facts of the situation itself. He maintains that no matter what our concrete tasks, we can, and should, elevate them by our attitude. 'If the labor is mean', Emerson proclaims, 'let him by his thinking and character make it liberal.'[20] Here his Stoicism and conservatism are in full force.

[17] VI, 276–277.
[18] II, 141.
[19] *Pragmatism* (Cambridge, 1975), Lecture VI, 110.
[20] II, 142.

There is considerable truth to the notion that a person's psychological approach can ameliorate his or her condition. Often much of a person's apparent victimization by external circumstances is due instead to that person's own feelings, attitudes and beliefs, and can be overcome. The Stoics did make a good case for this. Nevertheless to place the responsibility for bettering one's situation back upon one's own attitudes makes sense only in situations where one genuinely has no ability to make concrete improvements in one's material circumstances. A paradigm situation in which Emerson's recommendation is germane has been discussed more recently by Victor E. Frankl. In his book, *Man's Search For Meaning,* Frankl shows how even prisoners in German concentration camps could regain an important measure of control over their lives, in a central moral sense at least, by controlling their beliefs, attitudes, and feelings.[21] The way in which each prisoner viewed his or her situation considerably affected that person's health, chances of survival, and moral sensibilities. It is important, then, to recognize the considerable control we do have over our lives, even given the many things that are not up to us. But granting this, it must be said that Emerson's view is still extreme. His point of view, at bottom, seems to be that all social evils are ultimately merely degradations of, infringements upon, or failures of the spirit, and that the solution to social problems lies merely in changing one's personal point of view. He says that once a person recognizes the oversoul:

> He will cease from what is base and frivolous in his life and be content with all places and with any service he can render. He will calmly front the morrow in the negligency of that trust which carries God with it and so hath already the whole future in the bottom of the heart.[22]

Given the degree of oppression and injustice, human frustration, social exploitation, enslavement, corruption and other moral evil in this world, it will not do to respond with any prescription that locates the solution to these problems exclusively in the personal sphere. Quiescence based on metaphysical intuition, although it may seem grand and profound in some ways, also seems quite shallow in the face of these conditions. Emerson's political conservatism must be judged as less than realistic as a social philosophy.

Looking at Emerson's social conservatism from a somewhat different perspective, he dismisses any obligation the individual might have towards others, because he is confident of the individual's right, as well as primary obligation, to fulfil his or her own inner call. Thus in 'Self-Reliance', Emerson rejects social action to help others because it dilutes one's own self-development. His claims are striking in their unqualified and direct nature:

[21] New York, 1959.
[22] II, 297.

> Do not tell me ... of my obligation to put all poor men in good
> situations. Are they *my* poor? I tell thee, thou foolish philanthropist,
> that I grudge the dollar, the dime, the cent I give to such men as do not
> belong to me and to whom I do not belong.[23]

Harsh words. But does Emerson, as he suggests here, at least preserve
the idea that we have special obligations to those, in his terminology, to
whom we *do* belong? Not even this is altogether clear, since he rejects the
idea that we have special duties, say, to our families—a paradigm case, I
should think, of persons to whom, on some moral dimension, we do
'belong':

> I shun father and mother and wife and brother when my genius calls
> me. I would write on the lintels of the door post, *Whim*. I hope it is
> somewhat better than whim at last, but we cannot spend the day in
> explanation. Expect me not to show cause why I seek or why I exclude
> company.[24]

Emerson's further lack of interest in the amelioration of social and
political problems is apparent in 'Spiritual Laws', where he argues that
material goods have no genuine significance, and that only the full expression of the individual counts toward the worthiness of his or her life.[25]
While it is clear that material advantages by themselves cannot overcome
the impoverishment of the spirit, still Emerson needs more fully to
recognize the ways in which adverse material conditions so frequently
obstruct our spiritual and intellectual possibilities.

In the light of Emerson's social philosophy, it is interesting to note the
respects in which his life did or did not synchronize with his formal
thought. We know, for example, that Emerson refused to join the com-
munitarian social reform movements of other transcendentalists, because
he thought all social groupings to be a diminishment of the individual. On
the other hand, in his home of Concord, Massachusetts, he held a political
office, served as a volunteer fireman, helped maintain a public reading
room, and contributed in numerous other ways to the intellectual vitality
of the town. Slavery was the major political issue of the day. For a long
while Emerson resisted becoming involved, on the grounds that his
obligation was only to develop his own spirit, not to protect anyone else's.
But in 1850 the Fugitive Slave Law was passed—a law which prevented
people from aiding escaped slaves, and which could require them to form
posses to chase the fugitives. At this point Emerson found the situation to
be intolerable, and from then on energetically worked for the cause of
abolition. In spite of the considerable benefits of Emerson's philoso-

---

[23] II, 52.
[24] II, 51–52.
[25] See II, 143.

phy—as a ringing call for independence and individualism—we have seen that it also seems to represent a less than adequate social sensibility. It is gratifying to see Emerson personally more involved than his philosophy enjoins.

One may wonder at Emerson's show of callous egocentricism in his philosophical rejection of all social obligations to others. How could a civilized, cultured man from nineteenth-century New England, a former minister of good breeding, be so blind—at least in his written philosophy—to our obvious social responsibilities? Emerson's position becomes, if not ultimately more justified, at least more understandable, when seen within the broader context of his metaphysics. In his famous doctrine of compensation, articulated in an address of that same name, Emerson argues that from the point of view of material benefits or misfortunes, the universe balances itself out. Every materially good event or object in one's life will be balanced by some cost, and every misfortune balanced by a benefit. Thus, there is no point to feeling responsible for those less fortunate than ourselves, no need to help the disadvantaged, since whatever evils they experience must ultimately be balanced by corresponding goods.

Emerson does not go into a concrete account or explanation of how this might be so. It might have helped for him to have tried to do so. For as it stands, it seems clear that his position would topple upon observation of real conditions. Emerson's lack of interest in the concrete facts may have stemmed from an even deeper doctrine in his metaphysics, going beyond mere compensation—where after all there does exist some evil to compensate for good—to a thoroughly optimistic world-view. Ultimately, for Emerson, the universe is thoroughly beneficent. Like Augustine, he holds that evil is only privative—it is the absence of being. If one, then, seems to perceive evil, it is due ultimately to a flaw in one's own point of view. Thus it is the challenge of a courageous, self-reliant individual to uphold an optimistic spirit.

In a fine essay on Emerson, William James defends him, saying 'his optimism had nothing in common with that indiscriminate hurrahing for the Universe with which Walt Whitman has made us familar'.[26] While I think James is right in reference to some aspects of Emerson's philosophy, and while Emerson's 'hurrahing for the Universe' is not entirely indiscriminate, it does raise serious questions. How do we judge the truth of a metaphysical system? What sort of evidence could one have to support a metaphysical optimism, in spite of considerable empirical evidence to the contrary? We have already seen that Emerson's transcendentalist epi-

[26] 'Address at the Emerson Centenary in Concord', in *Emerson: a Collection of Critical Essays,* Milton R. Konvitz and Stephen E. Whicher (eds) (Westport, Connecticut, 1978), 22.

stemology is founded on personal intuition. But if intuited metaphysical 'truths' contradict more ordinary empirical evidence, which source of knowledge shall we trust? To ignore concrete evils and refrain from ameliorating them because they are supervened by a personally intuited metaphysical principle leaves immense epistemological and moral problems in its wake.

Let us return to Emerson's philosophy of the person. In providing a metaphysical basis for morality, the doctrine of the oversoul affects the meaning of Emerson's recommendations in interesting ways. On the level of practical/moral injunction, as we have seen, Emerson encourages a heroic individualism, where each person in nobility and strength is enjoined to develop and express him or herself unhampered by social conventions and the opinions of others. At the same time on a deeper, metaphysical level, through self-expression, the individual is the medium for the expression of the oversoul. Emerson's pluralism of self-fulfilled individuals, then, on a more fundamental level, reduces to a thoroughgoing monism, in which only the oversoul expresses itself, via its many facets. For Emerson, ultimately, self-reliance and the flourishing of the individual, however important they may be as personal ideals, are most important as expressions of the divine principle. In this sense there is in Emerson's thought a recurring desire for unity, and also a surprising level of depersonalization. Parenthetically, I might add that the idea of the oversoul itself is relatively depersonalized in comparison to a theistic conception of God.

I should point out that Emerson's celebration—indeed deification—of the individual, is subject to certain qualifications. Emerson does believe that we are all embodiments of the oversoul, that we all partake equally in the divine principle. At the same time, however, he is cynical about, and even disdainful of most persons, regarding them as not having fulfilled their potential—indeed, as not even coming close. He calls those persons 'ripe' or 'finished' who have achieved the self-development necessary for becoming unified with the oversoul. But he feels, based on his experience, that most persons neither have tried nor succeeded in accomplishing the self-development and union with the oversoul that is their natural birthright.[27] He refers to the mass of people as a 'maudlin agglutination'.[28] Thus in spite of Emerson's buoyant democratic individualism, on the one hand, he also believes that noble self-reliant individuals constitute a kind of *de facto* aristocracy.

The main ideals of Emerson's philosophy of self-reliance, the importance of personal nobility and strength on the one hand, and the impor-

[27] VI, 54, 249–253; II, 213.
[28] Quoted by Daniel Aaron, 'Emerson and the Progressive Tradition', in Konvitz and Whicher, op. cit., 89. This is an excellent article which shows nicely the aristocratic elements of Emerson's thought.

tance of unification with the divine on the other, recur often throughout his work. We find them, for example, in his view of sympathy and prayer, and in his analyses of friendship and love. Self-reliant individuals exhibit heroism and self-control, and have mastery over their choices and their lives as a whole. They stand above the ordinary travails of the human condition, remaining emotionally detached from human problems and weaknesses, even their own. Emerson denigrates prayer, for example, when it is used as a response to personal needs or desires. He claims that prayer as personal supplication, 'as means to effect a private end, is meanness and theft'.[29] The only acceptable kind of prayer is the celebration of the oversoul—'the contemplation of the facts of life from the highest point of view'.[30]

Emerson never removes the armour provided by union with the universal, and hence the depersonalized oversoul. In thinking about friendship, he begins from the premise that human relations, unless carefully controlled, are typically a diminishment of the individual. In his words, 'almost all people descend to meet'.[31] He considers the society of others, even the 'virtuous and gifted' to be a 'perpetual disappointment'.[32] Indeed, Emerson unequivocally rejects involving oneself in daily intimacies with one's friend. His aim seems genuinely to eliminate any personal element. He asks:

> Why insist on rash personal relations with your friend? . . . Leave this touching and clawing. Let him be to me a spirit. . . . Should not the society of my friend be to me poetic, pure, universal and great as nature itself?[33]

On this count, Emerson did in fact come close to living in accord with his austere philosophy. While he generously provided help for his friends when needed, nevertheless, much to his friends' disappointment, he withheld intense personal involvement.[34] So far as he could, he maintained friendships at a highly intellectualized level. There is in fact an amusing story that when Margaret Fuller, a friend and also a transcendentalist, once visited Emerson at his home, she and Emerson spent the entire visit communicating in writing, via letters delivered back and forth by Emerson's son.[35]

[29] II, 77.
[30] Ibid.
[31] II, 199.
[32] II, ibid.
[33] II, 210.
[34] See Hubert H. Hoeltje, *Sheltering Tree: A Story of the Friendship of Ralph Waldo Emerson and Amos Bronson Alcott* (Durham, NC, 1943); Sherman Paul, *Emerson's Angle of Vision* (Cambridge, 1952), Ch. 6.
[35] See Paul F. Boller, Jr, *American Transcendentalism, 1830–1860* (New York, 1974), 94.

Following out the theme of friendship as a relationship between two noble, independent natures, Emerson holds that a person's imperfections are an overwhelming impediment to friendship. He claims that 'men cease to interest us when we find their limitations',[36] and even holds that anyone who accepts a friend in spite of his or her limitations is by that fact unworthy of the friend's reciprocated affection. We know that Nietzsche was genuinely taken with Emerson. Indeed, there are striking similarities between Emerson's self-reliant individual (particularly the heroic individual) and Nietzsche's *übermensch*. The following passage on friendship is also reminiscent of Nietzsche:

> We search for approbation, yet cannot forgive the approver. . . . If I have a friend I am tormented by my imperfections. The love of me accuses the other party. If he were high enough to slight me, then could I love him, and rise by my affection to new heights.[37]

The end-point, in every instance, is not intimacy, but the oversoul. 'There can never be deep peace between two spirits, never mutual respect, until in their dialogue each stands for the whole world.'[38] Genuine friendship is not ultimately a personal relationship between its participants. It transcends the mundane details of life. 'Reverence is a great part of it.'[39] 'It demands a religious treatment.'[40]

In sum, then, friendship is a religious, rather than a personal relationship. It is a meeting and celebration of two (or more) grand natures, each cognizant of the divine element in him or herself, as well as the other. The pattern of Emerson's thought is becoming clear. Just as self-reliance, for Emerson, is at bottom unification with the oversoul, so also is friendship. In the final analysis, in perfect friendship, the personal and the individual become absorbed in the absolute.[41]

Emerson's conception of love parallels exactly his notion of friendship. As with friendship, love should never be desecrated to a level of mere prudence—it 'def[ies] all attempts at appropriation and use'.[42] Romantic love—with its deep personalization, mundane emotionalism, and particular involvement with one human being—is, for Emerson, an immature form. He sees it as just a beginning point, a training ground, for achieving a purified and noble love for the highest qualities of the loved one. But

---

[36] II, 307–308.
[37] II, 307. See Nietzsche, *Thus Spoke Zarathustra,* Part I. Sec. 14; *Menschliches, Allzumenschliches,* Sec. 376.
[38] II, 211.
[39] II, 209.
[40] Ibid.
[41] See, for example, II, 216–217.
[42] II, 179.

at the other extreme of the spectrum, maintaining that the nature of personhood is necessarily social—that the very nature of the individual is intelligible only by reference to his or her relation with others. But most philosophers in the American tradition—Dewey and James are good examples—stand somewhere between these two extremes. They share Emerson's individualism, but reject the isolationism so prevalent in his social philosophy.

Accompanying individualism among most traditional American philosophers is a democratic spirit of egalitarianism. Emerson, we have seen, is somewhat ambivalent on this issue. On the one hand he holds that all persons, potentially at any rate, participate equally in the oversoul. Indeed, on the basis of this doctrine Emerson has been celebrated by many as the philosopher of equality. One the other hand, we have seen that he holds the view, less well-recognized, that there is a kind of aristocracy of those persons who have exercised and developed the divine element in themselves—a notion resembling, in certain key elements, Jonathan Edwards' doctrine of the 'elect'.

Emerson shares with other major American philosophers the cultural characteristic of optimism. But while others, like James and Dewey, approach evil with a healthy sense of our ability to be strong, good, pertinacious and committed enough to overcome it, we have seen that Emerson denies that there is really any problem of evil at all. James represents the more typical American attitude in his statement that it is 'not the absence of vice, but vice there, and virtue holding her by the throat, [that seems] the ideal human state'.[52] We find this attitude even more pronounced in Dewey, who was so caught up with the process of achieving moral betterment that he neglected adequately to specify the goods to be achieved. But for Emerson, as we have seen, while we must strenuously develop our own self-reliance, ultimately we may rest in the knowledge that the benevolence of the universe is divinely quaranteed.

The purpose behind Emerson's philosophy as a whole is profoundly American. For the most part, American philosophers have not been interested in system-building, or abstract metaphysics or epistemology for their own sakes. Thinking is valued not as an abstract enterprise, but rather as a tool for the improvement of the concrete conditions of life. Even Emerson, in the context of his grand transcendental metaphysics, approaches his theory with a motive which is quite directly moral. It is not the nature of the universe *per se* which most concerns him, but how that finds expression in and affects the life of the individual.

It has been clear for over a century that Emerson is a great American thinker—respected in all quarters as one of the most stimulating, edifying,

---

[52] William James, 'The Dilemma of Determinism', in *The Will to Believe* (Cambridge, 1979), 131.

influential and articulate representatives of American culture. But an enigmatic question lingers: is he really a philosopher?

As we have seen, Emerson denigrates discursive reasoning, and deliberately—indeed on principle—refuses to engage in it. But can anyone count as a philosopher who really believes that 'a foolish consistency is the hobgoblin of little minds', and who defines as 'foolish' any consistency which the individual does not currently choose to uphold?

This is the problem. As you might expect, the solution is not straightforward, for the question, 'What is a philosopher?' is itself a philosophical question. Whether we want to honour someone with the appellation 'philosopher' is as much a decision as a discovery. Let us look at some of the relevant criteria.

First and foremost a philosopher's work is cognitive. That is to say, philosophy's function is not primarily to illustrate, manifest or embody truths (the way fiction, poetry, visual art, and even music can do) but cognitively to present them. A philosopher sets out to discover truths and then to explain and state them in an illuminating way. The philosopher's enterprise is to set out propositional claims which he or she regards as worthy of intellectual assent. Philosophy may also have emotional effects, but they must be secondary to, and primarily arise from, its cognitve import. Applying this criterion, I would say that Walt Whitman, when he proclaims in his poetry 'I celebrate myself, and sing myself',[53] illustrates some of the same points that Emerson cognitively presents. They both inspire many of the same feelings. But on the criterion I have set out here, Whitman is not a philosopher, while Emerson is.[54]

A second mark of a philosopher is that the questions he or she mainly deals with are ultimately non-empirical. It is true that a philosopher often does and should use empirical data in order to articulate and understand the deeper issues. It is also true that philosophical claims should function to explain the phenomena of the empirical world, or at least should be consistent with them. Still, on final analysis, the philosopher's questions cannot be decided by scientific test, or any other methods of ordinary observation. By inquiring into the most fundamental reality, the question of the good life, and the relation of human beings to the universe, Emerson certainly qualifies as a philosopher *par excellence* on this criterion.

A third mark of a philosopher, at least in the judgment of most contemporary professional philosophers, is that his or her work must be critical. This criterion is intended to enable us to distinguish philosophy in the full sense from wisdom literature. If a philosophy is to be critical, bald

---

[53] 'Song of Myself', *Leaves of Grass* (New York, 1950), 23.
[54] This is not to deny that Emerson is also a poet, and that his writing is, and is designed to be emotionally stimulating. It is only to say that his primary aim is cognitive: to state and communicate truths.

statements or conclusions are not sufficient. Rather, reasons must be given in justification of claims. A critical philosopher develops rigorous and well-reasoned arguments in support of his or her conclusions, or at least suggests ways in which those arguments could be developed. He or she regards the claim of inconsistency as a rebuke, and accepts the responsibility of providing, or at least being able to provide, rational and discursive support for his or her claims.

In this sense, as we have amply seen, Emerson is not a philosopher—at least not a critical philosopher. Indeed he rejects critical philosophy, as he rejects discursive reason as a means to truth. His supporters would say that he is able to make the most use of his highly evocative literary talent precisely because he does not restrain his insights with the fetters of critical rigour and proof.

Shall we then, finally, consider Emerson a philosopher? I do not think the question can survive in this simple form. The themes in Emerson's work are profound and he aims for his readers' intellectual assent—in these respects he is a philosopher. But Emerson is not critical—in this respect he is not a philosopher. If I needed to use one word to categorize Emerson, I would say first and foremost he is a preacher. On final analysis, Ralph Waldo Emerson never left the ministry—he just substituted his own more sophisticated and well-integrated doctrines for the traditional ones. Emerson does indeed offer much of philosophical value. His sermons are philosophical in their cognitive import, the profundity of their topics, and the breadth of their scope. They are typically American in their optimism, moral purpose, and faith in the individual. Finally, they rank high among America's most buoyant and most edifying instances of self-expression; and from a literary point of view, they are among the most masterful of all contributions to America's intellectual tradition.[55]

[55] I would like to thank Joseph W. Suckiel for the stimulating discussions we have had about Emerson, and for his insightful comments on this paper; and also Marcus G. Singer for his numerous helpful suggestions.

Josiah Royce's Philosophy of the Community: Danger of the Detached Individual

JOHN J. McDERMOTT

The popular mind is deep and means a thousand times more than it knows.[1]

I

It is fitting that the Royal Institute of Philosophy series on American philosophy include a session on the thought of Josiah Royce, for his most formidable philosophical work, *The World and the Individual*, was a result of his Gifford lectures in the not too distant city of Aberdeen in 1899 and 1900. The invitation to offer the Gifford lectures was somewhat happenstance, for it was extended originally to William James, who pleaded, as he often did in his convenient neurasthenic way, to postpone for a year on behalf of his unsettled nerves. James repaired himself to the Swiss home of Theodore Flournoy, with its treasure of books in religion and psychology, so as to write his Gifford lectures, now famous as *The Varieties of Religious Experience*. In so doing, however, James was able to solicit an invitation for Royce to occupy the year of his postponement. Royce accepted with alacrity, although this generosity of James displeased his wife Alice, who ranted, 'Royce! ! *He* will not refuse, but over he will go with his Infinite under his arm, and he will not even do honour to William's recommendation.'[2] Alice was partially correct in that Royce, indeed, did carry the Infinite across the ocean to the home of his intellectual forebears, although on that occasion as on many others, he acknowledged the support of his personal and philosophical mentor, colleague and friend, William James.

We note a philosophical irony in Royce's lectures in Scotland, for if ever there were a book to arouse the wrath of the great Scottish philosopher, David Hume, it was *The World and the Individual*, representing as it did the acme of the metaphysics destined for the Humean bonfire. Fortunately for Royce, Hume was dead and as yet unrecovered, else his Gifford

[1] Josiah Royce, in *The Letters of Josiah Royce,* John Clendenning (ed.) (Chicago: University of Chicago Press, 1970), 586.
[2] Gay Wilson Allen, *William James* (New York: Viking Press, 1967), 387.

lectures would have been severely challenged. Instead, they have fallen into comparative neglect, although they represent one of the most ambitious philosophical attempts to ground the existence of the individual self within the context of an all-knowing Absolute Mind. I shall return to an analysis of that effort by Royce, but first let us place Royce in the setting of classical American philosophy and detail his personal and philosophical journey.

II

Most commentators agree that classical American philosophy is comprised of six figures: Charles Sanders Peirce (1839–1914), William James (1842–1910), Josiah Royce (1855–1916), John Dewey (1859–1952), George Herbert Mead (1863–1931) and George Santayana (1863–1952). All but Santayana were native born. He was born in Spain and did not come to America until he was eight years of age. Santayana lived in America until 1912, when he retired to Europe, permanently. Some commentators include Alfred North Whitehead (1861–1947) who was born in England and did not come to America until 1924 at the age of sixty-three. It is true that Whitehead, when in America, wrote in the tradition of James and was fond of the thought of Mead, but he more properly belongs to the later period known as the Silver Age of American philosophy, rather than the Golden Age as herein described.

As in all great philosophical clusters of the past, and this one was truly distinguished, one can trace strands of continuity among the group and one can elicit profound philosophical differences in their thought, one against the others. As an instance of commonality, I point to the fact that with the exception of John Dewey, the classical American philosophers either studied or taught at Harvard University. The abiding presence of Harvard in this tradition is extraordinary, as has been detailed by Bruce Kuklick in his brilliant and contentious book, *The Rise of American Philosophy*.[3] In keeping with the Cambridge ambience, the thought of Ralph Waldo Emerson was very influential on these philosophers.[4]

Differences abound, as, for example, the influence of Hegel. Royce and Dewey began as neo-Hegelians, with Royce maintaining that position until mid-career. James and Peirce, to the contrary, had nothing but contempt for Hegel. All but Royce adopted a pragmatic epistemology and

[3] Bruce Kuklick, *The Rise of American Philosophy: Cambridge, Massachusetts, 1860–1930* (New Haven: Yale University Press, 1977).

[4] See John J. McDermott, 'Spires of Influence: The Importance of Emerson for Classical American Philosophy', *History, Religion and Spiritual Democracy,* Maurice Wohlgelernter (ed.) (New York: Columbia University Press, 1980), 181–202.

fought against idealism, although idealist tendencies remain in the work of James and Dewey.

The upshot of this set of relationships is that classical American philosophy resembles a many-coloured mosaic, something like a wall painting by Marc Chagall. The strident differences in their philosophical views are held together by their constant refraction of the American scene, often enthusiastic, often critical, but distinctively American in their pluralism, meliorism and temporalism. Even Royce, long an Absolute Idealist, adopts these American strategies for a creative philosophical future.

III

Focusing now on Royce, it is notable that he alone among the six philosophers was neither born nor raised in the northeast. In fact, he was a child of the frontier, a Californian by birth and by deepest inclination. One cannot understand America without understanding the frontier experience and one cannot understand the life and thought of Josiah Royce without a grasp of his version of that experience. Despite the influential hegemony of the northeast and especially New England on the intellectual life of America, the long-standing experience of westering and trekking is a far deeper factor in the evolution of American self-consciousness.

In detailing this experience we must be aware that despite the presence of the Spanish and the French, America was founded by English Calvinist Puritans. The fathers and founders of America are not Jefferson and Adams, but John Winthrop, Roger Williams and Thomas Hooker. It was they who bequeathed the congregational insight of a covenanted community to the forbidding rigours of the wilderness, that is, of western Massachusetts and in turn, West Virginia, western New York, the original northwest territory of the Great Lakes, the plains, Texas, the northwest of Lewis and Clarke, California and finally, the interior west of Oklahoma in 1907. This dramatic odyssey lasted for two centuries and it left a permanent deposit on the American soul.

The English Puritans were masters of the interior life. They recorded the struggle of their anxiety for a conversion experience as taking place within their own self-consciousness. Their diaries and letters are exquisite testaments to their introspective sophistication and their description of false conviction, self-deception and hypocrisy which richly limns the thicket of the inner personal wilderness. In the early seventeenth century, some of those English Puritans became children of the new world, of America. It soon became clear, as in clearing, that the wilderness existed, but it was spatially external and it lay to the immediate west, rather than festering within the breasts of Puritan men and women.

The conquering and cultivation of the land became the major sign of conversion as the itinerant and trekking Baptist and Methodist ministers replaced the staid, fixed congregations of the Presbyterians. A dialectic soon set up between the systemic loneliness of the frontier and a developing sense of possibility, to be realized over the next hill, across the next river, atop the next mountain. The experience of the inner wilderness of the depraved Calvinist soul gave way to the potential fertility of the American settler, always on the move, perennially restless, while searching for the signs of salvation, on, in, of and about the land.

Just as the founding and/or invention of the new world rendered the European world old, so too did the American West find itself in relationship to the East coast. The Europeans interpreted America variously: as barbarians over against their long-standing civilization; as children over against the parentage of the mother country; as noble savages over against their jaded ways; as a source of hope over against their cynicism; and finally as physical paradise over against their intractable inner wilderness. It is striking that these polarities are duplicated in the relationship between the western settlers and the Brahmins of American East Coast sensibility. The transition from spiritual transformation to agrarian realization is put well by Charles Sanford.

> ... The most popular doctrine in the colonies was that America had been singled out, from all the nations of the earth, as the site of the Second Coming; and that the millennium of the saints, while essentially spiritual in nature, would be accompanied by a paradisiac transformation of the earth as the outward symbol of their inward state. ...[5]

Josiah Royce was born amidst the high point of the trek west, namely, the Gold Rush of 1849 and the immediately subsequent years. His mother, Sarah Royce, was a remarkable woman, literate, educated and deeply religious in the best tradition of American puritanism. She detailed the perilous family journey in a memoir,[6] written at Royce's request when he was preparing his history of California in the 1880s. Leaving Iowa in April of 1849, the Royce family made their way across the plains, the Nevada desert and the high Sierra mountain range until in October of 1849 they arrived in a California mining camp, named Hangtown, for therein thieves were regularly hung on recognizance. It was in a similar mining camp at Grass Valley, California, in the Sierra mountains, that Josiah

---

[5] Charles Sanford, *The Quest for Paradise: Europe and the American Moral Imagination* (Urbana: University of Illinois Press, 1961), 82.

[6] Sarah Royce, *A Frontier Lady* (New Haven: Yale University Press, 1932). The editor of *A Frontier Lady,* Ralph Henry Gabriel, tells us that Josiah Royce had asked his mother to recount her journey overland to California, so as to assist him in his writing of the history of California, which he published in 1886. It is an informal document, but then all the more does it convey the authenticity of those exciting, courageous and treacherous days as lived by the Westward settlers of 1849.

Royce was born in 1855. Some sixty years later on 29 December 1915, less than a year before his death, Royce recalled the message of his childhood.

> My earliest recollections include a very frequent wonder as to what my elders meant when they said that this was a new community. I frequently looked at the vestiges left by the former diggings of miners, saw that many pine logs were rotten, and that a miner's grave was to be found in a lonely place not far from my own house. Plainly men had lived and died thereabouts. I dimly reflected that this sort of life had apparently been going on ever since men dwelt in that land. The logs and the grave looked old. The sunsets were beautiful. The wide prospects when one looked across the Sacramento Valley were impressive, and had long interested the people of whose love for my country I heard much. What was there then in this place that ought to be called new, or for that matter, crude? I wondered, and gradually came to feel that part of my life's business was to find out what all this wonder meant.[7]

Assisted by the *Recollections* of his mother, Royce movingly details the terror and the spiritual quality of the trek west, from wilderness to the alleged paradise of California.

> On the plains journeyed, meanwhile, in the summer of 1849, and in a number of subsequent summers, vast crowds of weary emigrants, who faced disease, hunger, and Indians for the sake of the golden land.... As my own parents were of this great company, I have taken a natural interest in following their fortunes, and have before me a manuscript, prepared by my mother for my use, wherein, as an introduction to her own reminiscences of early days in San Francisco and elsewhere in California, she has narrated, from her diary of that time, the story of the long land journey....
>
> The route taken and the general sequence of events in the early part of the journey do not vary much in her account from the ordinary things narrated by all the emigrants of that year. There was the long ascent of the Rocky Mountains, with the cholera following the trains for a time, until the mountain air grew too pure and cool for it. A man died of cholera in my father's wagon. There were also the usual troubles in the trains on the way, among such emigrants as had started out in partnership, using a wagon in common, or providing, one a wagon, and another the oxen or mules. Such partnerships were unstable, and to dissolve

---

[7] Josiah Royce, 'Words of Professor Royce at the Walton Hotel at Philadelphia, December 29, 1915', *The Hope of the Great Community* (New York: Macmillan Company, 1916), 122–123. (Cited hereafter as *HGC*.) Reprinted in John J. McDermott, *The Basic Writings of Josiah Royce*, 2 vols (Chicago: University of Chicago Press, 1969), I, 31–32. Hereafter cited as McDermott, *Royce*.

them in the wilderness would usually mean danger or serious loss to one of the partners. In settling these and other disputes, much opportunity was given to the men of emigrant trains for showing their power to preserve the peace and to govern themselves. There was also the delight at length, for my mother as for everybody, of reaching the first waters that flowed towards the Pacific Ocean. And then there was the arrival at Salt Lake, the meeting with the still well-disposed Mormons, and the busy preparation for the final stage of the great undertaking.

From Salt Lake westward my parents, with their one child, my eldest sister, then but two years old, traveled apart from any train, and with but three men as companions. Their only guide-book was now a MS. list of daily journeys and camping-places, prepared by a Mormon who had gone to California and back in 1848. This guide-book was helpful as far as the Sink of the Humboldt, but confused and worthless beyond. The result was that, after escaping, in a fashion that seemed to them almost miraculous, an openly threatened attack of hostile Indians on the Humboldt River,—an attack that, in their weakness, they could not for a moment have resisted,—they came to the Sink, only to miss the last good camping-place there, by reason of their vaguely-written guide-book, to find themselves lost on the Carson desert. They erelong became convinced that they had missed their way, and that they must wander back on their own trail towards the Sink. It was a terrible moment, of course, when they thus knew that their faces must be turned to the east. One was confused, almost stupefied, for a while by the situation. The same fatal horror of desolation and death that had assailed the Donner party in the Truckee pass seemed for a while about to destroy these emigrants also. They knew themselves to be among the last of the great procession. Many things had concurred to delay and to vex them. It was now already October, and there was not a moment to waste. To turn back at such a crisis seemed simply desperate. But the little water carried with them was now nearly exhausted, and their cattle were in hourly danger of falling down to die. Dazed and half senseless, the company clustered for a while about their wagon; but then a gleam of natural cheerfulness returned. 'This will never do', they said, and set about the work of return. On the way they met by chance another lonesome little party of emigrants, who, with very scant supplies, were hurrying westward, in fear of the mountain snows. These could not help my father, save by giving him a few new directions for finding water and grass at the Sink, and for taking the right way across the desert. As the slow wagon neared the long-sought camping-place, my mother could not wait for the tired oxen, but remembers hurrying on alone in advance over the plain, carrying her child, who had now begun to beg for water. In her weariness, her brain was filled with nothing but one familiar Bible story, which she seemed to be dreaming to the very life in clear and cruel detail. But the end of all this came, and the party rested at the little pasture-ground near the Sink.

These details I mention here, not for their personal interest, but because they are so characteristic of the life of thousands in the great summer of 1849. My mother's story goes on, however, to yet another characteristic experience of that autumn. Once supplied at the Sink, my parents, still as nearly alone as before, set out once again across the forty-mile desert, and, after more hardships and anxiety, reached the welcome banks of the Carson. But the mountains were now ahead, the snows imminent, and the sand of the Carson Valley, under the wagon-wheels, was deep and heavy. On October 12, however, they were opportunely met by two mounted men deatailed from Captain Chandler's detachment of the military relief party which General Smith had sent out to meet and bring in the last of the emigration. The new-comers, riding at full speed, seemed to my mother, in her despair, like angels sent from heaven down by the steep, dark mountains that loomed up to the westward. They were, at all events, men of good mountaineering experience and of excellent spirit, and they brought two extra mules, which were at once put at my mother's own service. By the peremptory orders of these relief men, the wagon was forthwith abandoned. What could be packed on the still serviceable animals was taken, and the rest of the journey was made by the whole party mounted. They arrived safely in the mines a little before the heavy snows began.

Socially considered, the effect of the long journey across the plains was, of course, rather to discipline than to educate; yet the independent life of the small trains, with their frequent need of asserting their skill in self-government, tended to develop both the best and the worst elements of the frontier political character; namely, its facility in self-government, and its over-hastiness in using the more summary devices for preserving order. As for the effect on the individual character, the journey over the plains was, at least as a discipline, very good for those who were of strong and cheerful enough disposition to recover from the inevitable despondency that must at first enter into the life of even the most saintly novice in camping. Where families were together, this happy recovery happened, of course, more quickly. One learned, mean-while, how to face deadly dangers day by day with patience and coolness, and to strongly religious minds the psychological effect of this solitary struggle with the deserts was almost magical. One seemed alone with God in the waste, and felt but the thinnest veil separating a divine presence from the souls that often seemed to have no conceivable human resource left. This experience often expresses itself in language at once very homely and very mystical. God's presence, it declares, was no longer a matter of faith, but of direct sight. Who else was there but God in the desert to be seen? One was going on a pilgrimage whose every suggestion was of the familiar sacred stories. One sought a romantic and far-off golden land of promise, and one was in the wilderness of this world, often guided only by signs from heaven,—by the stars and by the sunset. The clear blue was almost perpetually overhead; the pure mountain winds were about one; and again, even in the hot and parched deserts, a mysterious power provided the few precious springs and streams of water. Amid the jagged, broken, and barren hills, amid the desolation of the lonely plains, amid the half-unknown but always horrible dangers of the way, one met experiences of precisely the sort that elsewhere we always find producing the most enthusiastic forms of religious mysticism. And so the truly pious among these struggling wanderers gained from the whole life one element more of religious steadfastness for the struggle that was yet to come, in early California, between every conservative tendency and the forces of disorder.[8]

Royce's search for the meaning of his childhood in the mining camp became an obsession for him, personally, morally and philosophically. His adolescence was difficult, especially as his physiognomy and body image lent themselves to mockery. He was short of stature, rotund, with orange hair, an enormous forehead and a high-pitched voice. Shall we say simply that he was the butt of much abuse, some of it physical, on the part of his more macho peers. Money was hard to come by for Royce and he began his life much as he finished it, under financial pressure for one reason or another. He did manage to attend the brand-new University of California at Berkeley where he became competent in Greek literature, although overall his grades were not outstanding. Yet he impressed sufficiently to be given assistance to study philosophy in Germany in 1875–76. Imbued with the thought of German idealism, he returns to the first graduate pro-gamme in America at Johns Hopkins University where he completes his PhD degree in 1878. His only opportunity is to return to Berkeley as a lecturer in the Department of English. Cut off from his European experi-ence as well as the intellectual excitement of Hopkins, where, among others, he met William James, Royce became very depressed in California.

Actually, Royce was of two minds, for he had an abiding 'loyalty' to California and he treasured its topography and physical beauty.[9] Yet,

[8] Josiah Royce, *California from the Conquest in 1846 to the Second Vigilance Committee in San Francisco: A Study of American Character* (Boston: Houghton Mifflin Company, 1886), 240–246 (excerpted). (Cited hereafter as *CAL.*) For literature on the final destination of the forty-niners, the mining camps, see Remi Nadeau, *Ghost Towns and Mining Camps of California* (Los Angeles: Ward Ritchie Press, 1965) and Charles Howard Shinn, *Mining Camps: A Study in American Frontier Government* (New York: Charles Scribner's Sons, 1884).

[9] See e.g. Royce's address of 1898 'The Pacific Coast: A Psychological Study

distant from philosophical conversation, he became increasingly lonely, insecure and even alienated from himself. Two texts reveal this Picasso-esque 'boy in the mirror' image of the reflective Royce. The first is on behalf of California, written in 1879 as a hymn to the Golden Gate, that is, to the magnificent promontory which from on high affronts the entrance to San Francisco Bay by the vaunted majesty of the Pacific Ocean. The text is as follows:

'MEDITATION BEFORE THE GATE'

I am a Californian, and day after day, by the order of the World Spirit (whose commands we all do ever obey, whether we will it or no), I am accustomed to be found at my tasks in a certain place that looks down upon the Bay of San Francisco and over the same out into the water of the Western Ocean. The place is not without beauty, and the prospect is far-reaching. Here as I do my work I often find time for contemplation. . . .

That one realizes the greatness of the world better when he rises a little above the level of the lowlands, and looks upon the large landscape beneath, this we all know; and all of us, too, must have wondered that a few feet of elevation should tend so greatly to change our feeling toward the universe. Moreover the place of which I speak is such as to make one regret when he considers its loveliness that there are not far better eyes beholding it than his own. For could a truly noble soul be nourished by the continual sight of the nature that is here, such a soul would be not a little enviable. Yet for most of us Nature is but a poor teacher.

Still even to me, she teaches something. The high dark hills on the western shore of the Bay, the water at their feet, the Golden Gate that breaks through them and opens up to one the view of the sea beyond, the smoke-obscured city at the south of the Gate, and the barren ranges yet farther to the left, these are the permanent background whereon many passing shapes of light and shadow, of cloud and storm, of mist and of sunset glow are projected as I watch from my station on the hillside. The seasons go by quietly, and without many great changes. The darkest days of what we here call winter seem always to leave not wholly without brightness one part of the sky, that just above the Gate. When the rain storms are broken by the fresh breezes from the far-off northern Sierras, one sees the departing clouds gather in threatening masses about the hilltops, while the Bay spreads out at one's feet, calm and restful after its little hour of tempest. When the time of great rains gives place to the showers of early spring one scarcely knows which to delight in the more,

---

of the Relations of Climate and Civilization', *Race Questions, Provincialism and other American Problems* (New York: Macmillan Company, 1980), 169–225. (Cited hereafter as *RQP*.) See also McDermott, *Royce*, I, 181–204.

whether in the fair green fields, that slope down gently to the water, or in the sky of the west, continually filled with fantastic shapes of light and cloud—nor does even our long dry summer, with its parched meadows and its daily sea winds leave this spot without beauty. The ocean and the Bay are yet there; the high hills beyond change not all for any season; but are ever rugged and cold and stern; and the long lines of fog, borne in through the Gate or through the depressions of the range, stretch out over many miles of country like columns of an invading host, now shining in innocent whiteness as if their mission were but one of love, now becoming dark and dreadful, as when they smother the sun at evening. So, while the year goes by, one is never without the companionship of nature. And there are heroic deeds done in cloud-land, if one will but look forth and see them.

But I have here . . . to speak not so much of Nature as of Life. And I shall undertake to deal with a few problems such as are often thought to be metaphysical (whereby one means that they are worthless), and are also often quite rightly called philosophical (whereby one means that it were the part of wisdom to solve them if we could). With these problems I shall seek to busy myself earnestly, because that is each one's duty; independently, because I am a Californian, as little bound to follow mere tradition as I am liable to find an audience by preaching in this wilderness; reverently, because I am thinking and writing face to face with a mighty and lovely Nature, by the side of whose greatness I am but as a worm.[10]

On another occasion, however, in the very same year as the 'Meditation', 1879, Royce writes the following letter to William James.

There is no philosophy in California—from Siskiyou to Ft. Yuma, and from the Golden Gate to the summit of the Sierras . . . Hence the atmosphere for the study of metaphysics is bad, and I wish I were out of it. On the other hand, I am at home and so among good friends; and further, as to my work, I am entirely free to arrange my course as I please, and to put into it a little philosophy. . . . I trumped up a theory of logical concepts last term and preached it to the seniors. It was a kind of hybrid of Hume and Schopenhauer, with an odor of Kant about it. It was somewhat monstrous, and, in this wilderness with nobody to talk with about it, I have not the least idea whether it is true or not. . . .[11]

---

[10] Josiah Royce, 'Meditation Before the Gate', *Fugitive Essays by Josiah Royce,* Jacob Loewenberg (ed.) (Cambridge: Harvard University Press, 1920), 6–7. (Cited hereafter as *FE*.)

[11] See Ralph Barton Perry, *The Thought and Character of William James* (Boston: Little, Brown and Company, 1935), I, 781. The complete letter, longer by far, is found in *The Letters of Josiah Royce,* John Clendenning (ed.) (Chicago: University of Chicago Press, 1974), 66–68.

William James, ever responsive to a plaintive cry, soon arranged for a temporary appointment for Royce in the Harvard University philosophy department. Royce arrived in 1882 and did not leave until his premature death in 1916, some thirty-four years later. Royce, the indigenous Californian found himself among the New England Brahmins. Try as he might, he never quite fitted that august, precious and self-serving intellectual world. A rocky marriage to Katharine Head and a severe mental collapse by his oldest son increased the tensions in Royce's life. His other two children did not fare very well and he had the burden of a severely retarded grandchild. Money problems often plagued Royce and he seemed caught in a tangle between paying his creditors and struggling to obtain a public reputation judged worthy of a Harvard professor. George Herbert Palmer, a mainstay of the Harvard philosophy department, stated that Royce was visited by 'afflictions sorted, anguish of all sizes'.[12] Royce had fled the loneliness and alienation of the sparse intellectual life on the Pacific rim of California, only to have these deep self-doubts reappear in the cosy but yet forbidding interpersonal terrain of New England high culture. In 1888, when under severe mental strain, Royce took a year away from Harvard and sailed around the world, with a prolonged intermediate stay in Australia and New Zealand. From 1882 until 1888, Royce had taught full-time at Harvard and at an earlier version of Radcliffe, as well as having published three books: *The Religious Aspect of Philosophy* (1885);[13] *California* (1886);[14] and *The Feud of Oakfield Creek: A Novel of California Life* (1887).[15] With financial assistance from Harvard and from his friend, Charles Rockwell Lanham, Royce attended to his breakdown by leaving home, a routine he was to adopt periodically in the future. Some commentators, such as Frank Oppenheim, see Royce's trip to the South Seas as extraordinarily important for the development of his mature philosophical position.[16] We do know that he returned to Harvard refreshed and anxious to once again take on his many duties and begin to fashion a metaphysical response to the always underlying theme of his life, why suffering?

[12] George Herbert Palmer, 'Josiah Royce', *Contemporary Idealism in America* (New York: Macmillan Company, 1932), 9.

[13] Josiah Royce, *The Religious Aspect of Philosophy* (Boston: Houghton Mifflin Company, 1885). (Cited hereafter as *RAP*.)

[14] Royce, *California*.

[15] Josiah Royce, *The Feud of Oakfield Creek: A Novel of California* (Boston: Houghton Mifflin Company, 1887). (Cited hereafter as *FOC*.)

[16] See Frank M. Oppenheim, *Royce's Voyage Down Under: A Journey of the Mind* (Lexington: University Press of Kentucky, 1980).

IV

In a famous statement of the moral quandary which results from the existence of evil, Dostoevsky sharpens the issue by involving us in the death of an innocent child. Surely such a tragic occurrence makes necessary the existence of an all-good God who will in the canopy of eternity make right this flagrant injustice. Yet Dostoevsky holds simultaneously that given such an event, an all-good God could not exist, for if He did and did not prevent this outrage, then that God would be evil. In my reading of Royce, I have come to believe that this moral dilemma is at the centre of his life and thought. Further, I believe that he takes a double route to resolve the problem. The first is metaphysical and, in turn, the utilization of modern mathematics and logic. The second way is through social philosophy, laced with homilies and a plea for tolerance and the willingness to develop a community. The most notorious single obstacle to the building of a great and beloved community, according to Royce, is the existence of the detached individual. That person who lacks loyalty and concern is fair game for seduction by those nefarious movements which seek to wreck the community on behalf of some political, social or religious ideology, all of them self-aggrandizing. Royce seeks to overcome this loneliness of the detached individual, a characteristic of his own life, experientially learned and observed in mining camp childhood. The parallel strategies of Royce to deal with this matter find him concentrating on metaphysics and logic, on the one hand, and a philosophy of community, on the other hand. They are not brought together until the publication of the *Problem of Christianity* in 1913. A breakout of this parallel, citing the major writings of Royce, looks as follows [see table on facing page].

If we weave together a commentary on each of the two approaches taken by Royce, the development of his thought takes on the following cast. The young Royce is very taken by the seamy side of human life. In 1879, after having returned to California, he writes an essay on 'The Practical Significance of Pessimism'. In a remarkably pessimistic text, Royce delineates the human condition from his perspective.

> Contemplate a battle field the first night after the struggle, contemplate here a vast company the equal of the population of a great town, writhing in agony, their groans sounding at a great distance like the roar of the ocean, their pain uneased for many hours, even death, so lavish of his favors all day, now refusing to comfort; contemplate this and then remember that as this pain to the agony of the world, so is an electric spark drawn from the back of the kitten to the devastating lightning of many great storms; and now estimate if you can the worth of all but a few exceptional human lives, such as that of Caius.

Briefly and imperfectly I state the case for pessimism, not even

Social Philosophy	Metaphysics and Logic
Fugitive Essays (on Pessimism and Romanticism)—1879–1880 (FE)	*The Religious Aspect of Philosophy*—1885 (RAP)
California—1886 (CAL)	*The Spirit of Modern Philosophy*—1892 (SMP)
The Feud of Oakfield Creek—1887 (FOC)	*The Conception of God*—1897 (CG)
Studies of Good and Evil—1898 (SGE)	*The World and the Individual*—1899–1901 (WI)
The Philosophy of Loyalty—1908 (PL)	*The Conception of Immortality*—1900 (CI)
Race Questions, Provincialism, and other American Problems—1908 (RQP)	*Lectures on Modern Idealism*—1906 (1919) (LMI)
William James and other Essays on the Philosophy of Life—1911 (WJO)	*The Principles of Logic*—1913 (PrL)
The Sources of Religious Insight—1912 (SRI)	

The Problem of Christianity—1913 (PC)

The Hope of the Great Community—[17] 1916 (HGC)

[17] Citations for works not cited above are as follows: Josiah Royce, *Studies of Good and Evil: A Series of Essays upon Life and Philosophy* (New York: Appleton, 1898). (Cited hereafter as *SGE*.) Josiah Royce, *The Philosophy of Loyalty* (New York: Macmillan Company, 1908. (Cited hereafter as *PL*.) Josiah Royce, *The Sources of Religious Insight* (New York: Charles Scribner's Sons, 1912). (Cited hereafter as *SRI*.) Josiah Royce, *The Spirit of Modern Philosophy* (Boston: Houghton Mifflin Company, 1892). (Cited hereafter as *SMP*.) Josiah Royce, *The Conception of God,* with 'Comments' by S. E. Mezes, J. LeConte and George Holmes Howison (Berkeley: Philosophical Union, 1895). Second edition, with 'Supplementary Essay' by Royce, 1897. (Cited hereafter as *CG*.) Josiah Royce, *The World and the Individual,* 2 vols. (New York: Macmillan Company, 1899, 1901). (Cited hereafter as *WI*.) Josiah Royce, *The Conception of Immortality* (Boston: Houghton Mifflin Company, 1900). (Cited hereafter as *CI*.) Josiah Royce, *Lectures on Modern Idealism,* J. Loewenberg (ed.) (New Haven: Yale University Press, 1919). (Cited hereafter as *LMI*.) Josiah Royce, 'The Principles of Logic', *Logic (Encyclopedia of the Philosophical Sciences),* 1 (London: Macmillan Company, 1913), 67–135. (Cited hereafter as *PrL*.) Josiah Royce, *The Problem of Christianity,* 2 vols. (New York: Macmillan Company, 1913). Reprinted with new introduction by John E. Smith, in a one-volume edition (Chicago: University of Chicago Press, 1968). (Cited hereafter as *PC*.)

touching the economical and social argument, drawn from a more special consideration of the conditions of human life. Such then, is our individual human life. What shall we call it and whereunto shall it be likened? A vapor vanishing in the sun? No, that is not insignificant enough. A wave, broken on the beach? No, that is not unhappy enough. A soap bubble bursting into thin air? No, even that has rainbow hues. What then? Nothing but itself. Call it human life. You could not find a comparison more thoroughly condemning it.[18]

For the next five years, Royce attempts to overcome this perspective by appealing to his philosophical conviction that the doctrines of Absolute Idealism can successfully account for evil and error, sufficient to render it meaningful. The fruition of these reflections is published in 1885 under the title of *The Religious Aspect of Philosophy*. Royce was never pollyanna about the existence of evil, stating in his essay on 'The Problem of Job', that 'I regard evil as a distinctly real fact, a fact just as real as the most helpless and hopeless sufferer finds it to be when he is in pain'.[19]

The epistemological version of evil is the existence of error. Royce sees this perennial human activity as potentially undermining of any philosophical effort to ground religious truth, such that one could account for evil. Consequently, before addressing the problem of evil in *The Religious Aspect of Philosophy,* Royce attends to the problem of error. Holding that we cannot ascribe error to any judgment, unless it be compared to an Absolute Truth, Royce sees error as a torso, a fragment of the seamless garment of Truth. He writes:

That there is error is indubitable. What is, however, an error? The substance of our whole reasoning about the nature of error amounted to the result that in and of itself alone, no single judgment is or can be an error. Only as actually included in a higher thought, that gives to the first its completed object, and compares it therewith, is the first thought an error. It remains otherwise a mere mental fragment, a torso, a piece of drift-wood, neither true nor false, objectless, no complete act of thought at all. But the higher thought must include the opposed truth, to which the error is compared in that higher thought. The higher thought is the whole truth, of which the error is by itself an incomplete fragment.[20]

---

[18] Royce, *Fugitive Essays,* 152.

[19] Royce, *Studies of Good and Evil,* 16. McDermott, *Royce,* II, 845.

[20] Royce, *The Religious Aspect of Philosophy,* 431. McDermott, *Royce,* I, 350–351.

What is intriguing here is that Royce is pursuing an inductive argument, to wit, the existence of error as a particular, empirical antifact is able to be so judged if, and only if, a total fabric exists in which all of the possibilities extant are known, by someone, somewhere, somehow, somewhen. This latter capacity must exist because we do come to know about counterfactuals. Thus, from a single miscreant event, claim, or judgement, we can conclude to a wider, all embracing whole which gives credibility to our decision on the veritability of the particular in question.

Turning from epistemological error to moral and metaphysical evil, Royce attempts the same strategy, namely, to turn the very existence of particular evil into a proof for the existence of Absolute Good. For Royce, the acknowledgment that an act is morally evil is a sign that it is being overcome on behalf of a good will. Such a designation, Royce calls a 'moral insight'.

> ... The moral insight condemns the evil that it experiences; *and in condemning and conquering this evil it forms and is, together with the evil, the organic total that constitutes the good will.... I here directly experience how the partial moral evil is universal good*; for so it is a relatively universal good in me when, overcoming myself, I choose the universal will. The bad impulse is still in me, but is defeated. In the choice against evil is the very life of goodness, which would be a pale, stupid abstraction otherwise ...[21]

Frankly, even for sympathetic students of Royce, these arguments are not convincing. In the first place, the prose of *The Religious Aspect of Philosophy* is bloated, much like an English language redaction of what William James used to call, condescendingly, teutonic metaphysics. Secondly, the claim of Royce that particulars, be they judgments, acts, or events are meaningful only if they are understood as parts of a whole, is plausible but not apodictic. It is possible, after all, that William James is right in holding that totality and finality are constructs of an insecure human temperament. Third, and in his deeper, more reflective less cerebral self, Royce knows it to be true that systemic evil is not whitewashed or even made acceptable by philosophical principles of accountability. Yet, during this period from 1878 until 1885, Royce walks the double path of acknowledging the existential presence of pessimism, the violence perpetrated in the struggle for a human community, as, for example, on the California frontier, and the philosophical attempt to render the entire scene, all for the good, *sub specie aeternitatis*.

In that decade of the late nineteenth century, few, if any, commentators, knew that Royce was treading a double path, of experiential, empirical reportage of evil and of a complex intellectual attempt to render the

---

[21] Ibid., 452, 453, emphasis in original.

pus-filled bulbous of everyday human interaction as, somehow, meaningful.

The next steps in this parallel journey occur in the years 1897–1901. In a command performance, Royce was invited back to the University of California, Berkeley, in 1895, in order to defend his Absolute Idealism against critics, especially the gifted American philosopher, George Holmes Howison. The invitation was accepted by Royce with enthusiasm, for he enjoyed the prospect of returning home to California as a representative of his Brahmin nest at Harvard University. He met more opposition than he anticipated, however, as Howison, still smarting over being bypassed by Royce for the Harvard appointment, went on the attack. In a perceptive critique of Royce's position, Howison asks rhetorically:

> *Whose* omniscience is it that judges the ignorance to be real?—*whose* absolute experience pronounces the less organised experience to be really fallacious? Well,—whosesoever it may be, it is certainly acting in and through *my* judgment, if I am the thinker of that argument; and in every case it is *I* who pronounce sentence on myself as really ignorant, or on my limited experience as fallacious. Yes,—and it is *I* who am the authority, and the only direct authority, for the connexion put between the reality of the ignorance or of the fallacious experience on the one hand and the reality of the implicated omniscience on the other.[22]

Royce begins to see cracks in his Absolute Idealism as the antidote for an understanding of systemic evil. In response to Howison, he pleads that his

---

[22] Royce, *The Conception of God* (found in 'The City of God, and the True God as Its Head'. Comments by Professor Howison, 108–109). It may be of significance here to reflect on the idiosyncratic events which brought Royce to Harvard University instead of at the time the more deserving Howison.

The biographers of Howison point to the irony of this reversal of roles for Howison and Royce. They cite James in a letter to Thomas Davidson of August 1883, that 'Royce has unquestionably the inside track for any vacancy in the future. I think him a man of genius, sure to distinguish himself by original work.' They add, however, that James goes on to remark: 'But when I see the disconsolate condition of poor Howison, looking for employment now, and when I recognize the extraordinary development of his intellect in the past 4 years, I feel almost guilty of having urged Royce's call hither. I did it before Howison had returned, or at least before I had seen him, and with my data, I was certainly right. But H. seems now to me to be quite a different man, intellectually, from his former self; and being so much older, ought to have had a chance, which (notwithstanding the pittance of a salary), he would probably have taken, to get a foothold in the University.'

John Wright Buckham and George Malcolm Stratton, *George Holmes Howison* (Berkeley: University of California Press, 1934), 70.

critic does not realize that the individual and the particular are not obliterated by the Absolute, which, although transcendent, does not destroy its components.[23] In *The Conception of God,* Royce makes a valiant effort to defend his position, even though he is aware that Howison and others have struck a deadly blow against him, for he cannot account for the irreducible character of particulars, especially persons and personal acts. It is not irrelevant that in 1898, Royce publishes his moral and social existentially sensitive essays on Good and Evil, inclusive of commentaries on Job, Bunyan, and the relation between self and social consciousness.[24] Yet, Royce, stung by the criticism at Berkeley, devotes his Gifford lectures on 'The World and the Individual' to a resolution of his difficulty in maintaining a fidelity to the personal, acting, willing self, while yet holding to a principle of final accountability as found in the existence of an Absolute Mind. In the 'Preface' to the published version of his Gifford lectures on *The World and the Individual,* Royce plots his course as a response to the earlier objections of Howison and, increasingly, William James.

> While this central matter regarding the definition of Truth, and of our relation to truth, has not essentially changed its place in my mind, I have been doing what I could, since my first book was written, to come to clearness as to the relations of Idealism to the special problems of human life and destiny. In my first book the conception of the Absolute was defined in such wise as led me then to prefer, quite deliberately, the use of the term Thought as the best name for the final unity of the Absolute. While this term was there so defined as to make Thought inclusive of Will and of Experience, these latter terms were not emphasized prominently enough, and the aspects of the Absolute Life which they denote have since become more central in my own interests. The present is a deliberate effort to bring into synthesis, more fully than I have ever done before, the relations of Knowledge and of Will in our conception of God. The centre of the present discussion is, for this very reason, the true meaning and place of the concept of Individuality, in regard to which the present discussion carries out a little more fully considerations

---

[23] See Royce, 'Professor Royce on His Critics', *The Conception of God,* 333, where he objects to Howison's 'failure to comprehend that self-consciousness and the unity of consciousness are categories which inevitably transcend, while they certainly do not destroy individuality'.

[24] In my view, Royce's 1895 essay on 'Self-Consciousness, Social Consciousness and Nature', in *Studies of Good and Evil,* is a forerunner to the work of the American philosopher George Herbert Mead. In fact, Mead's book on *Mind, Self and Society,* reflects the original table of contents in Royce's papers, as a task to be done.

which appear, in a very different form of statement, in the 'Supplementary Essay', published at the close of *The Conception of God*.[25]

In this massive and complex work of metaphysics and epistemology, Royce attempts to work out a strategy for dealing with one of the most stubborn of all philosophical questions, known to the ancients as that of 'the one and the many'. Do we begin with an experience of many singles, particulars and put a conceptual blanket over them, so that they be one? If so, does this principle of unity exclude significant individual characteristics, such that the unity be a sham, a mere gathering of the obvious? Or do we begin with an intuition of unity and come serially to distinguish particularity, by accrued sense experience? If so, is this grasp of unity to be trusted? Is it the same for all persons? Are the resulting singulars truly distinctive or are they only figments of a roving imagination which is bored with the principle of unification? These rhetorical questions mask the philosophical *dramatis personae* from Heraclitus and Parmenides to Quine. Intermediate pauses with the thought of Plato, Aristotle, Scotus Erigena, Aquinas, Duns Scotus, Descartes, Spinoza, Leibniz, Kant and Hegel only prepare us for the recent debate as carried on by Bergson, Whitehead, Russell, James, Heidegger and, of course, by Royce.

Speaking now only of Royce, he takes the position of an epistemological voluntarist, which is to say that for him particulars exist precisely because they are the constituency of the Absolute. A particular, that is a person, an individual self, is as it is, precisely because in its purpose as being, it fulfils the portion of reality necessary to a realization of the Absolute as all that has been, is or can be. In a clever turn of phrase and idea, Royce holds that the particular is particular for the reason that the Absolute is a realization of all particulars. In his analysis of the conception of being as found in the meaning of ideas, Royce writes:

> ... first, *the complete fulfilment of your internal meaning*, the final satisfaction of the will embodied in the idea, but secondly, also, *that absolute determination of the embodiment of your idea as this embodiment would then be present,—that absolute determination of your purpose, which would constitute an individual realization of the idea.* For an individual fact is one for which no other can be substituted without some loss of determination, or some vagueness.[26]

As he hinted in his 'Preface', Royce now makes the will a knowing probe of the self. Ideas become neither copies nor representations nor even intuitive flashes, but rather probes which carry the self into uncharted and rich areas of potential meaning. This voluntarism has a pragmatic tone and the influence of William James is beginning to be felt on the formerly

[25] Royce, *The World and the Individual,* I, ix–x.
[26] Ibid., I, 338–339.

impervious Absolute Idealist conceptual hide of Royce. Yet, the time for capitulation to the pragmatic and totally empirical/experiential approach is not yet present for Royce. He thinks that he has one last card to play, and among recent philosophers he is one of the few who could play it; that is, a formal logical and mathematical resolution of the problem. Stated simply, Royce's difficulty is how can you have an Absolute, an infinite series and still have a *bona fide* individual, self, or particular. His metaphysical effort to resolve this has been herculean, yet he is not satisfied with the result, nor should he be. Perhaps logic and mathematics holds the key. Under the influence of Charles Sanders Peirce and the early twentieth-century mathematical explorations of the infinite, Royce makes one last-ditch effort to ground his Absolute without simultaneously destroying the individual person in all of his/her distinctive and unrepeatable experiences.

Paradoxically, Royce looked to logic as the way to provide a still more voluntaristic, constructive character to human inquiry. In this effort, Royce was prescient for he grasped the little-known character of modern logic as a method for 'building' versions of the human quest rather than as a form of denotation of that already in place. Even Morton White, no champion of Royce or of his approach to philosophy, cites him as a forerunner of the twentieth-century revolution in logic.

> For Royce was more than a metaphysical soothsayer, more than a philosopher of religion and of loyalty to loyalty: he was also a logician and a philosopher of science. He was one of the first American teachers of philosophy to recognize the importance of research in symbolic logic and to encourage its study both for its own intrinsic intellectual importance and as a tool. Some of his pupils, like C. I. Lewis and H. M. Sheffer, became distinguished Harvard contributors to this subject and founders of one of the most influential centers of logic in the twentieth century.[27]

Despite the many logical and mathematical byways taken by Royce in his attempt to forge a new logic, known to him as 'system sigma', Royce had his eye on the problem which had vexed him from the beginning, namely, the possibility of an individual or particular if, in logical fact, there is an infinite system. It is intriguing that Royce hoped to show that modern logic and the modern logician proceeds from a world which is 'empirical'.[28]

Royce filled hundreds of pages with logical notations, most of them on behalf of an original system, in an effort to fuse his developing philosophical empiricism and his recent pragmatic sensibility, with that of his long-

---

[27] Morton White, 'Harvard's Philosophical Heritage', in *Religion, Politics and the Higher Learning* (Cambridge: Harvard University Press, 1959), 53.
[28] See McDermott, *Royce*, II, 787. Originally in Josiah Royce, *The Principles of Logic*, Arnold Ruge (ed.) (London: Macmillan Company, 1914).

standing commitment to Absolute Idealism. By 1913, in his work on *The Principles of Logic,* Royce capitulates to a pragmatic grounding of the Absolute. Clearly anticipatory of the work of W. V. O. Quine, Royce clings to the Absolute only in a functional way, and as a result of successful reporting or activity. In the last section of *The Principles of Logic* on 'The Logical Genesis of the Types of Order', Royce makes his last, valiant effort to preserve both an empirical and constructive epistemology and a doctrine of Absolute Truth.

> *In brief, whatever actions are such, whatever types of action are such, whatever results of activity, whatever conceptual constructions are such, that the very act of getting rid of them, or of thinking them away, logically implies their presence, are known to us indeed both empirically and pragmatically (since we note their presence and learn of them through action); but they are also absolute. And any account which succeeds in telling what they are has absolute truth. Such truth is a 'construction' or 'creation', for activity determines its nature. It is 'found', for we observe it when we act.*[29]

In the meantime, with the other hand/person, as it were, Royce was continuing his social philosophical writings. In 1908, he published *Race Questions, Provincialism and other American Problems,* which was a volume of sermonic essays. That on 'Provincialism' is still viable, for Royce put his finger on a serious dilemma in the pedagogy of culture. Surely we cannot be closed off from other cultures, persuasions and ideas, if we are to achieve a human community in the fullest sense, as, for example, in Royce's vision of the 'beloved' or 'great' community. Yet, Royce warns us as paraphrased, that to love the world and detest one's brother or sister is to be a hypocrite. For Royce, community is a flowering of deeply and integrally held commitments to one's local environment. The underpinning of the attempt to structure a community is what Royce details as loyalty. In 1908, the same year as his publication of *Race Questions, Provincialism and other American Problems,* and in the midst of his intense personal work on logic and mathematics, Royce publishes his book on *The Philosophy of Loyalty.*

Actually, the misunderstandings of Royce's doctrine of loyalty are easily traceable to the fact that his critics read only that work or, at best, knew little of Royce's philosophical work and vision. In fact, *The Philosophy of Loyalty* is vintage Royce, being an attempt to justify personal experience as an anticipation of eternal meaning. I must grant that Royce's phrasing is not always sufficiently cognizant of the short-sighted opponent and, therefore, his doctrine of loyalty is often subject to critical abuse. He

[29] See McDermott, *Royce,* II, 813. Originally in Royce, *The Principles of Logic.*

writes, for example, that loyalty is 'The willing and practical thoroughgoing devotion of a person to a cause'.[30] The uninitiated will immediately challenge on behalf of the obvious fact that some causes are worthy and others are not worthy. It is not until some 300 pages later that Royce also writes: 'Loyalty is the will to manifest, so far as is possible, the Eternal, that is, the conscious and superhuman unity of life, in the form of the acts of an individual Self'.[31]

The second text merely opens the first text, in a way that Royce, in 1908, takes for granted, that is, all personal acts take their meaning from a more expansive context, one which casts approving or disapproving light on their intentionality. In obvious terms, if one is 'loyal' to an evil cause, there is no self-transcendence and no commitment to the other person or persons. Consequently such activity is not loyalty for Royce but rather self-aggrandizement and, indeed, disloyalty to the potential for personal growth. To the contrary, loyalty to a cause, *de facto,* is a commitment to an idea, event or person, which forces upon the human self a willingness to transcend the narrow boundaries of self, be they preservation, reputation or success. In a paraphrase of an earlier text in *The Religious Aspect of Philosophy,*[32] Royce sees loyalty as an activity whose eternal end-in-view renders the temporal act meaningful, even though confusion may reign as to what one is to do or believe at any given time. So much does Royce believe in this possibility of the capacity of human life to transcend the pitfalls of seductive allegiance, that he insists, with the passing of time, the eternal fragrance will make itself felt among the thorns and vicissitudes of the daily demands. Royce sees a unity of persons who so believe in this hidden, but palpable capacity of the loyal to experience the eternal. On behalf of this spiritual loyalty, he writes:

> Moreover, that which I have called the cause of all the loyal, the real unity of the whole spiritual world, is not merely a moral ideal. It is a religious reality. Its servants and ministers are present wherever religious brotherhood finds sincere and hearty manifestation. In the sight of a perfectly real but superhuman knowledge of the real purposes and effective deeds of mankind, *all the loyal, whether they individually know the fact or not, are, and in all times have been, one genuine and religious brotherhood.* Human narrowness and the vicissitudes of the world of time have hidden, and still hide, the knowledge of this community of the loyal from human eyes. But indirectly it comes to light whenever the loyalty of one visible spiritual community comes, through any sort of tradition, or custom, or song or story, or wise word or noble

[30] Royce, *The Philosophy of Loyalty,* 16–17. McDermott, *Royce,* II, 861.
[31] Royce, *The Philosophy of Loyalty,* 357. McDermott, *Royce,* II, 996.
[32] See Royce, *The Religious Aspect of Philosophy*, 289. 'We go to seek the Eternal, not in experience, but in the thought that thinks experience'.

deed, to awaken new manifestations of the loyal life in faithful souls anywhere amongst men.[33]

Up to this point, Royce kept the two aspects of his thought and person in a tolerable and creative relationship. Yet, surely he knew that despite his conceptual brilliance, the gnawing intractability of human suffering could not forever be 'transcended' by a philosophical protocol, however logical it might seem to its polymathic author. Consequently, in 1913, Royce publishes his attempt at bridging his two parallel approaches to the problem of suffering, namely, *The Problem of Christianity.* This book is somewhat mistitled, for it is not so much about Christianity as it is about the Pauline doctrine of the beloved community, a notion inspired by Jesus, but hardly representative of the history of Christianity except for an occasional Benedictine or Franciscan monk.

The most important aspect of Royce's book is his utilization of Peirce's doctrine of signs, converted by Royce into a method of interpretation. Royce finally gives way in his fealty to the language of Absolute Idealism and begins to speak more of the 'community', in process, than of the Absolute. Royce, despite his prodigious knowledge, or maybe because of it, was a learner. Peirce had stung him by giving faint praise to the publication of *The World and the Individual,* saying that it was a good effort given that the author knew no logic.[34] Royce responded by making an effort to understand the logic of Peirce, despite its complexity and comparative unavailability in published form. One cardinal tenet of Peirce's logic did become accessible to Royce, that of the doctrine of third term mediation. For every A in relationship to B, there is needed a third, interpretive term C. Royce converts this triadic logic into a doctrine of interpretation, wherein protagonists in an otherwise communal setting take it upon themselves to listen to a third party, one who has the sense of both missions, both allegedly viable and praiseworthy, so as to render a *vade mecum,* for purpose of amelioration. Royce details the 'world of interpretation' as follows:

> We all of us believe that there is any real world at all, simply because we find ourselves in a situation in which, because of the fragmentary and dissatisfying conflicts, antitheses, and problems of our present ideas, an interpretation of this situation is needed, but is not now known to us. *By the 'real world' we mean simply the 'true interpretation' of this our problematic situation.* No other reason can be given than this for believing that there is any real world at all. . . .
>
> In brief, then, the real world is the Community of Interpretation which is constituted by the two antithetic ideas, and their mediator or interpreter, whatever or whoever that interpreter may be. If the inter-

---

[33] Royce, *The Sources of Religious Insight,* 279–280.
[34] See Kuklick, *The Rise of American Philosophy,* 376.

pretation is a reality, and if it truly interprets the whole of reality, then the community reaches its goal, and the real world includes its own interpreter. *Unless both the interpreter and the community are real, there is no real world.*[35]

What then can be rendered significant by interpretation? Surely Royce has the intention of bequeathing a way to build a truly human community. To this end he offers these conditions for the existence and well-being of a community.

The *first* condition upon which the existence of a community, in our sense of the word, depends, is the power of an individual self to extend his life, in ideal fashion, so as to regard it as including past and future events which lie far away in time, and which he does not now personally remember. That this power exists, and that man has a self which is thus ideally extensible in time without any definable limit, we all know. . . .

The *second* condition upon which the existence of a community depends is the fact that there are in the social world a number of distinct selves capable of social communication, and, in general, engaged in communication.

The *third* of the conditions for the existence of the community which my definition emphasizes consists in the fact that the ideally extended past and future selves of the members include at least some events which are, for all these selves, identical. This third condition is the one which furnishes both the most exact, the most widely variable, and the most important of the motives which warrant us in calling a community a real unit.[36]

If we look carefully at these three Roycean conditions for the existence of a community, rather than being simply a human conglomerate, a thread appears throughout. One could call it transcendence, or reaching or getting, going beyond oneself, but however the description it is clear that Royce expects us to enter into a form of interpretation so that our jealously guarded turf, beliefs, commitments and assertions are at the very least, subject to the viewpoint of another, distant, although concerned participant. This process does not end in any form of closure, for Royce holds that we always have the possibility of 'an endless wealth of new interpretations'.[37] The building of the human community becomes for Royce nothing less than the meaning of the world, in the most profound sense of 'meaning', as in metaphysics. Royce writes:

Metaphysically considered, the world of interpretation is the world in which, if indeed we are able to interpret at all, we learn to acknowledge the being and the inner life of our fellow-men; and to understand the

[35] Royce, *The Problem of Christianity*, 337 and 339.
[36] Ibid., 253, 255 and 256.
[37] Ibid., 294.

constitution of temporal experience, with its endlessly accumulating sequence of significant deeds. In this world of interpretation, of whose most general structure we have now obtained a glimpse, selves and communities may exist, past and future can be defined, and the realms of the spirit may find a place which neither barren conception nor the chaotic flow of interpenetrating perceptions could ever render significant.[38]

Royce wrote the above text at the dawning of a great calamity, the First World War, a conflict which was to begin the erosion of confidence in the classical values of Western civilization.[39] In failing health and enormously depressed by the sinking of the *Lusitania* in May of 1915, Royce nonetheless clung to the possibility of rebuilding a sense of community. To that end, in 1916, the year of his death, Royce published a paper on 'The Hope of the Great Community' in the prestigious *Yale Review*. At the very end of his successful but deeply troubled life, Royce wrote:

... The citizens of the world of the future will not lose their distinct countries. What will pass away will be that insistent mutual hostility which gives to the nations of to-day, even in times of peace, so many of the hateful and distracting characters of a detached individual man. In case of human individuals, the sort of individualism which is opposed to the spirit of loyalty, is what I have already called the individualism of the detached individual, the individualism of the man who belongs to no community which he loves and to which he can devote himself with all his heart, and his soul, and his mind, and his strength. In so far as liberty and democracy, and independence of soul, mean that sort of individualism, they never have saved men and never can save men. For mere detachment, mere self-will, can never be satisfied with itself, can never win its goal. What saves us on any level of human social life is union. ...[40]

It is fitting that we have a discussion of the philosophy of Josiah Royce in this international setting, characterized as it is by an effort to reach out and transcend our parochial sentiments by sharing the wisdom of American philosophy with a culture from whence it originated, England. On this matter of classical American philosophy, it has been too long detached from other cultures, for it has much to learn and much to teach. I appreciate the opportunity for both experiences, here in the great city of London.

[38] Ibid., 294.

[39] In 1914 Royce attempted to structure a programme of indemnification for victims of the burgeoning war. This effort of Royce, although receptive of little support, is a remarkable anticipation of the type of international activity found in the present United Nations. See Josiah Royce, *War and Insurance* (New York: Macmillan Company, 1914).

[40] Royce, *The Hope of the Great Community*, 51–52.

Does American Philosophy Rest on a Mistake?

BRUCE KUKLICK

When I write about 'American philosophy' in this paper, I refer not to the practice of philosophizing in a certain geographic area during a certain time. Rather I mean a scholarly field defined by certain conventions, standard arguments, and major works. I hope primarily to show that that area of inquiry is befuddled. I also want to suggest, however, that it may be unhelpful to try to write about the practice of philosophizing in a certain geographic area—the continental United States—in anything like the way scholars now write about it.

The paper has two parts. I first sketch the conventional view of American philosophy and suggest its substantive weaknesses. The second part is more theoretical. I diagnose the weaknesses of the conventional view as philosophical history. The problem here is the same problem that plagues most work in the history of philosophy; the history of *American* philosophy is merely a special case. Moreover, this second part analyzes the troubles of the conventional view when it links thought to culture. These troubles also simply illustrate issues that arise when historians of philosophy try to join texts and contexts. But American philosophy is a peculiarly good example, for the 'Americanness' of American philosophy disturbs commentators in a way that the 'Englishness' of English philosophy, or the 'Finnishness' of Finnish philosophy does not.[1]

* * *

Surveys of American philosophy treat the same canonical figures. Although scholars dispute how these figures are to be interpreted, they

---

[1] The substantive issues raised in this essay are treated at length in my *Churchmen and Philosophers: From Jonathan Edwards to John Dewey* (New Haven: Yale University Press, 1985), where extensive citations can be found. Pp. 301–302 of that work cites the series of methodological articles in which I have raised issues similar to the ones raised in this essay. *Churchmen and Philosophers*, as well as my *The Rise of American Philosophy: Cambridge, Massachusetts, 1860–1930* (New Haven: Yale University Press, 1977), contains biographical and bibliographical references that will aid the reader in examining the works and lives of the thinkers I have mentioned in this essay.

agree on who is to be interpreted. Canonical histories begin with Jonathan Edwards and his Puritan background and then move to the Massachusetts religious liberals who attacked Calvinism and to the Founding Fathers, represented by Franklin, Hamilton, Jefferson, and Madison. Thus, the first step in these histories is tracing the movement from evangelical religion to liberalism in both politics and religion. Thereafter politics vanishes as the evolution of religious liberalism continues from Boston Unitarianism through Concord Transcendentalism—Ralph Waldo Emerson and Henry Thoreau; then to the writers of the American Renaissance—Hawthorne and Melville—where the literary concerns of the Transcendentalists are translated into fiction. William James is next seen as the heir to Emerson's views and the foreshadower of those of John Dewey, the quintessential twentieth-century liberal.

The canon stresses thought that is seen to anticipate the secular values of many contemporary intellectuals. Present liberal scientific ideals in America are traced through a triumphal succession of eighteenth- and nineteenth-century figures. Edward's paradigmatic ideas are seen rapidly to yield to a democratic spirit that substitutes pragmatic science for superstitious religion.[2]

Knowledgeable readers will note that my canonical history is an ideal type and eliminates idiosyncrasies in individual scholarship. The history is best reflected in reading lists and syllabi for undergraduate courses in the United States where the demands of simplicity are often overriding. For more sophisticated audiences, for example, the novelists, 'easy' reading, go by the boards, as Charles Peirce, the founder of pragmatism, is inserted. In the rush from religion Emerson is sometime made the successor of Franklin, circumventing even the 'corpse cold' liberalism of Boston Unitarianism. In professional philosophical circles, distancing themselves from theology quickly takes philosophers from Edwards, Franklin, and Emerson to what is called the Golden Age of American philosophy. To James and Dewey are added not only Peirce, but also Josiah Royce, George Santayana, and George Herbert Mead.

The canonical history has three serious problems, the first of which I call the problem of consistency. Edwards and Dewey were formal system builders, but in the time between them radically different sorts of minds are studied. Franklin and the Transcendentalists, self-conscious popularizers, disdained systematic rumination. The men of the American

---

[2] See, for example, Paul Conkin, *Puritans and Pragmatists* (New York: Dodd, Mead, 1968); Morton White, *Science and Sentiment in America* (New York: Oxford University Press, 1972); and Elizabeth Flower and Murray G. Murphey, *A History of Philosophy in America*, 2 vols (New York: G. P. Putnam's, 1977); and finally Murphey's explicit criticism of his own work, 'Toward an Historicist History of American Philosophy', *Transactions of the Charles S. Peirce Society* **15** (1979), 3–18.

Renaissance wrote fiction. The Founding Fathers were interested not so much in the metaphysics of the social order as in the application of political ideas. In short, conventional histories lack the consistency of studies of Greek naturalism, British empiricism, or German idealism, or other accounts of philosophical traditions.

This problem is implicitly recognized in two divergent justifications given for the field of American philosophy. Europeans often comment that it results from the requirements of mass undergraduate education and the inevitable popularity of American studies in the United States. A ragtag and ill-assorted group of 'thinkers' is created and some 'thought' teased out of them. American scholars often accept part of this critique but assert that in a democratic and pluralistic society, formal thought—perhaps barren in any case—is not all important. Gifted 'representative men' who, like Franklin and Emerson or James, express the deepest concerns of an entire culture may also be significant.

A second problem with the canon is its continuity. The standard history fails to link its parts. It does not clarify the ambiguous and complicated relation between religion and politics in the late eighteenth century.[3] Moreover, the novelists have only a slight connection to other areas of intellectual inquiry. Emerson did not give birth to James; if anyone did it was the French philosopher Charles Renouvier. And as I hope it can be shown, James did not give birth to Dewey.

The third problem is the problem of Boston. The critical aspects of canonical history focus on south-eastern Massachusetts: the rise of Boston's religious liberals and Unitarians after the Great Awakening, the elaboration of the thought of the Concord Transcendentalists and of the Cambridge pragmatists. South-eastern Massachusetts may have been the centre of philosophical life in the eighteenth and nineteenth centuries, but we must recall that many of the most influential expositors of standard views have had Harvard connections. Harvard professors Barrett Wendell and Josiah Royce gave expression to the canonical history at the turn of the century. Their successors, Perry Miller, F. O. Matthiessen, and Morton White also taught there. Wendell, Matthiessen, Vernon Louis Parrington, Van Wyck Brooks, and Murray Murphey were all undergraduates at Harvard.[4]

[3] On this serious issue there is a substantial literature that begins with Alan Heimert's *Religion and the American Mind from the Great Awakening to the Revolution* (Cambridge: Harvard University Press, 1966).

[4] For Wendell see *A Literary History of America* (New York: Charles Scribner's Sons, 1900); and for Royce, 'William James and the Philosophy of Life', in *William James and Other Essays in the Philosophy of Life* (New York: Macmillan Co., 1911). Miller's most important works in this connection are his *The Life of the Mind in America from the Revolution to the Civil War* (New York: Harcourt, Brace, and World, 1965), and his anthology *American*

I suspect that the canon reflects more Harvard's dominance of the academic world in the United States in the late nineteenth and early twentieth centuries, when the canon was established, than the truth about the eighteenth and nineteenth centuries. During this long period Cambridge was idiosyncratic, more religiously liberal than other intellectual centres. Thinkers in Boston were not interested in systematic thought. From Samuel Willard's *Complete Body of Divinity,* posthumously published in 1726, to John Fiske's *Cosmic Philosophy,* of 1874, Cambridge did not produce a single systematic effort.

Students of the canon have found in it a usable past: a heroic tale of liberation from pre-modern ideas and the growth of spiritual autonomy. But if this is the chronicle of Harvard, it should not be mistaken for the chronicle of America. Neither should the gaps in the narrative go unnoticed, nor should we accept the doubtful wisdom of treating as a unified whole an amalgam of theology, cultural criticism, politics, fiction, and speculative musings.

Let me sketch one different story. The work of Jonathan Edwards inspired the ruminations of two generations of gifted Calvinist thinkers in the colonies and new nation. The theologians involved included Joseph Bellamy, Jonathan Edwards the younger, Stephen West, John Smalley, Asa Burton, Nathan Strong, and Moses Hemmenway. The two most important of these men—Samuel Hopkins and Nathaniel Emmons—were the leaders of what was known as the New Divinity movement, the first and most creative stage of a 125-year-long religious tradition in trinitarian Congregationalism called the New England Theology. In the late eighteenth and early nineteenth century the New Divinity, under the leadership of Hopkins and Emmons, curbed the power of the religious liberals. With its institutional locus at Yale, where almost all of its worthies had been educated, and centred in the Connecticut Valley, the New Divinity made liberalism a local, Boston, phenomenon. Although the establishment of the Harvard Divinity School about 1815 ensured the survival of Unitarianism as a denomination, the liberals were isolated and soon ringed by a formidable array of Calvinist institutions of advanced learning. Andover Seminary had been founded in 1808 because of Harvard's inclinations, the Princeton Seminary in 1812, Yale in 1822, Hartford in 1832, and Union in 1837, as well as many others.

Thought: Civil War to World War I (New York: Rinehart and Company, 1956). Matthiessen's fame rests on *American Renaissance* (New York: Oxford University Press, 1941). White's and Murphey's synthetic works are cited above. Parrington wrote *Main Currents in American Thought* (New York: Harcourt, Brace and Co., 1927–30); Van Wyck Brooks, most prominently, *The Flowering of New England 1815–1865* (New York: E. P. Dutton and Co., 1936); Curti, *The Growth of American Thought* (New York: Harper and Brothers, 1943).

The focus was still at Yale, however, and in the 1830s the Congregational Yale Divinity School produced a creative successor to Hopkins and Emmons, Nathaniel William Taylor. While the appraisal of intellect may not be the first task of the historian of ideas, Taylor is clearly the most talented systematic thinker in America between Edwards and Dewey. His ruminations gave birth to what was castigated as the New Haven Theology. Taylorism, as it was also called, was the next major phase of the New England Theology, after the New Divinity.

In the forties and fifties, it is true, further elaborations of the New England Theology display a falling away in sustained achievement. Even the sympathetic observer, I think, cannot help but evaluate the developments as more akin to the growth of astrology than astronomy. The lack of vitality suggests that professionalism—here exhibited by American divinity—need not be progressive. The divines were insular and ignored European currents of thought. They were inbred and hired only within the narrowest of circles. Most important, they dismissed the challenges science posed to their enterprise and, consequently, also the possible answers to these challenges.

In the middle third of the century reigning ideas were modified by a heterogeneous group of preachers, gentlemen of leisure, and men on the periphery of the academic system. These thinkers were innovative, as the divinity school ministers were not, but they were not positioned to formulate, and were usually not interested in formulating, systematic thought. Emerson is to us the most famous of these seers, but the group included people like James Marsh of the University of Vermont in Burlington, John Williamson Nevin and Philip Schaff of the Mercersburg Seminary in western Pennsylvania, and William Torrey Harris, leader of the St. Louis Hegelians. From the perspective of the trinitarian Congregational philosophy of religion we have been examining, the most influential was the Hartford minister, Horace Bushnell.

Unlike his professional peers Bushnell interested himself in German thought, and used it to reconstruct an orthodoxy threatened by perplexing problems. A student of Taylor's, Bushnell defended the Calvinist essentials of depravity and grace, the fall, the natural sinfulness of man, and the need for redemption. Yet Bushnell made Christological concerns central in his Calvinism; he brought God and man together unlike the followers of Edwards. He also gave a role to historical concerns, in dramatic contrast to the ahistorical individualism of New England religion.

Within Congregational circles there were two successive responses to Bushnell, the first conservative, the second more radical. The first in the fifties and sixties inspired a modest renaissance in formal Calvinist thought; the second in the seventies and eighties brought about the end of the tradition.

The first response was that of Henry Boynton Smith of Union Theological Seminary, the leading New School Presbyterian, heavily influenced by Congregational theology, and Edwards Amasa Park of Andover, the leading Congregational theologian of his era. Both Smith and Park were interested in German ideas, and soberly took up Bushnell's ideas in an academic setting. They emphasized his historic Calvinist affirmation, and not his dismissal of some of the conundrums central to the American Congregational tradition.

Both of these men were swept aside by the 'New Theology' movement of the 1880s and 1890s. Led by a group of Park's students at Andover, the new theologians used Bushnell to undercut Calvinist ideas. They downplayed his traditionalism and stressed his iconoclasm. At Andover the new theologians, known as the Andover Liberals, drove Park's journal, *Bibliotheca Sacra,* to Oberlin, Ohio, and founded their own magazine, *The Andover Review.* The young turks also saw to it that Park's successor there was not Park's hand-picked choice but one of their own. Well past seventy and in retirement, Park fought his ungrateful students tooth and nail, but by the late 1880s Andover Calvinism in the tradition of Edwards had been replaced by the distinctive doctrines of the New Theology known as 'Progressive Orthodoxy', the precursor of genuine liberal theology in Congregationalism.

Look at my tradition: Jonathan Edwards, Samuel Hopkins, Nathaniel Emmons, Nathaniel William Taylor, Horace Bushnell, Henry Boynton Smith, Edwards Amasa Park, and the Andover Liberals, a tradition that takes us from Calvinism to liberalism in Congregational theology.

The last part of this story does contain a revolution. But the overthrow of Park by the Andover Liberals turned out to be a palace coup, for at the same time theology of whatever description was giving way to philosophy as the speculative science sanctioned by crucial legitimating communitites on the east coast. The end of the nineteenth century was the period of the rise of the modern university system in the United States, the growth of disciplinary scholarship outside of divinity, and the emergence of a host of secular, scientifically orientated creeds that come into existence in response to Charles Darwin's *Origin of Species.* In this intellectual environment theology was unable to prosper, and it lost its hold on the literate, upper-middle class public. Philosophy came to command the respect of this public at the expense of theology. Philosophy departments attracted the money, talent, and social support that had previously been devoted to theology. At Harvard President Charles Eliot built 'the great department' that a European of the stature of Bertrand Russell recognized as 'the best in the world'.[5] In the nineties—the same time—Andover Seminary went into

[5] Russell, *Autobiography,* Vol. 1 (New York: Little, Brown, and Co., 1967), 326.

radical decline, and shortly thereafter merged with Harvard. At Princeton James McCosh asserted the primacy of philosophy over theology after the dominance of the Princeton Seminary over the college for well over fifty years. At new universities like Chicago philosophy became pre-eminent while divinity was relegated to a secondary status.

This is the context in which it is appropriate to account for the career of John Dewey. Dewey was born into an orthodox Congregational Calvinist family in Burlington, Vermont. The most formidable influence on his life was his mother who often made old-fashioned fear and degradation the core of religious life. Dewey's religion was also shaped by the work of the Congregational minister in Burlington. Lewis O. Brastow, who later taught at the Yale Divinity School, enunciated in Vermont a popular blend of evangelical beliefs similar to what was being propagated by the Andover Liberals. Dewey underwent a conversion experience when he was in his early twenties, taught Congregational Sunday School, and was an active church member until he went to teach at the University of Chicago in his mid-thirties.

Dewey had two academic mentors. H. A. P. Torrey, the professor of philosophy at the University of Vermont, and George Sylvester Morris, of Johns Hopkins, where Dewey took an early doctorate in philosophy. Both Torrey and Morris had been Congregational students of Henry Boynton Smith at the Union Seminary; but both had given up the Congregational ministry—Torrey actually left a pulpit—for careers in academic philosophy. Both were philosophic defenders of a Protestant Christianity based on German thought, and Dewey their student took up their concerns.

As a philosopher of religion Dewey believed that the New Theology of the Andover Liberals had an inadequate philosophical base. In its attachment to Bushnell, Andover had not fully escaped the careful logical categories of Edwardsean Calvinism. In particular Progressive Orthodoxy had no compelling way of disputing the older Calvinist dualisms between God and man, and the natural and the supernatural, although the progressives did denigrate these dualisms. The German thought on which Andover had fallen back, Dewey believed, was still too dualistic. Hegel relied on a dichotomy between absolute and individual spirit—between God and man—and Kant distinguished between the phenomenal and noumenal worlds—nature and the supernatural. Dewey wanted to reconstruct German thought on anti-dualistic lines and thus provide a solid philosophic base for progressive orthodoxy. Indeed, much of his early writing appears in the *Andover Review,* the journal that had replaced Park's *Bibliotheca Sacra* at Andover.

Commentators have regularly noted that the young Dewey was a Hegelian, and while this is a bit of a distortion it is near enough to the mark. What they have neglected to note is that Dewey's 'Hegelianism' promoted a philosophy of religion designed to fortify the latest developments in Trinitarian Congregationalism. What Dewey was doing had little to do with the pragmatism of Charles Peirce and William James. Dewey was a disciple of Morris at Johns Hopkins, and avoided Peirce, believing that Peirce's 'formal' logic typified just the sort of dualism that had to be avoided. While Dewey did find much in James's *Principles of Psychology,* the book appeared in 1890, after Dewey's own position had been formulated, and James had previously poked fun at Dewey's ruminations.

In the 1880s Dewey argued that we could not separate God and man, absolute and finite spirit. God *was* only as individual selves realized him; the dynamic evolution of self-consciousness in human beings in history was God. Dewey also denied a cleavage between the natural and the supernatural, phenomenal and noumenal. The two worlds were one; spirit was in nature; nature was a symbol of spirit. The physical world evolved into the spiritual; it had spiritual potential in it. Nature *became* moral and religious.

In both of these attacks on philosophic dualisms Dewey developed his own philosophical dialect, a German teleological vision of Darwinian science. But in the late eighties and early nineties he abandoned the language of German idealism for a more scientific vocabulary. Instead of talking about the union of man and God, Dewey spoke of the intrinsic meaningfulness of experience and the ability of men, using the scientific method, to uncover greater and greater syntheses of meaning. Rather than writing of the human realization of God, Dewey wrote of science progressively increasing human harmony and tranquillity through the growth of meaning.

Dewey also ceased to write of the connection between the natural and the supernatural worlds. Instead, he wrote that the scientific method had previously been applied to nature but could now be applied to the social world. The spheres of nature and morality were of a piece, and the method perfected in physics could be used in the arena of culture. Thus, questions about nature and supernature were transformed.

At this point I hope it is clear that Dewey's concerns of the early 1890s are the recognizable ones of 'our' Dewey. One way to construe these changes is cosmetic, as changes in rhetorical strategy. The issues for Dewey in the late seventies and early nineties were the same; the mode of expressing them altered. Why did Dewey alter his linguistic strategy? In part, like most other American intellectuals, he was captured by the ideal of applied science. He was only the most prominent among American thinkers who read Darwin in a benign way that promoted a new way of thinking about man and the world. In part Dewey was also a man on the make. He knew that systematic theology was no longer a sure route to success. He wanted to be a respectable theoretician in his culture, and this desire meant coming to terms with science. Whatever we make of this mix of motives, it is well to remember that Dewey did not *merely* change his language. He was also a creative genius. In casting the problems of the philosophy of religion in a new set of formulas, he shifted the axis on which intellectual problems were conceived. He had begun his career by intending to shore up Andover liberalism. The changing milieu in which he wrote meant that he came to maturity as the founder of modern thought.

Commentators argue that Dewey naturalized German thought by a stress on the concrete growth of cultures and the interaction of organisms in their environment. Dewey's 'instrumentalism' is a hard-headed, tough-minded creed that grounds the hope for a scientific politics; it is a mature philosophy of social science. What is more important, however, is that Dewey began his professional life as a certain sort of philosopher of religion. Although he shifted the contours of thought in the United States, his philosophy bore the tell-tale marks of his older interests. The locus of the divine shifted from the supernatural to the natural, and science could be applied to what was formerly supernatural. But there was still a godly residue in things. Edwards believed that man was redeemed only through grace. For Dewey man was still redeemed, but the instrumentality was the ostensibly areligious technique of science.

In the twentieth century science served what in the nineteenth century was clearly a divine purpose. In effect the theoreticians of social science functioned as the theologians of another age had done. Dewey provided the grammar for a common faith in an era when old-time religion was no longer compelling for intellectuals. To say Dewey was the chief exponent of post-traditional liberalism is unnuanced; he rather transformed religious concerns into a new language acceptable to his contemporaries because it allowed them to avoid ancient problems and look at new, but also because it gave them a creed to live by.

*   *   *

The standard 'history of American philosophy' is confused because the story in narrates is not a genuine history—the figures it brings together are part of a dialogue only in the minds of recent scholars. Moreover, the story is not about 'America' but about Boston; and because the material it covers is not 'philosophy' either in our present or any past definition. But the other account I have given of the links between Edwards and Dewey is not 'the history of American philosophy' either. *It* is a history of some aspects of Trinitarian Congregational theology and an explanation of how it lost its intellectual dominance in New England. That is, I do not think there is any way we can rescue the endeavour of 'American philosophy'.

To explain its confused nature we must examine more theoretical issues. The first concerns the history of *philosophy* as philosophers conceive it. The second concerns the *history* of philosophy as historians conceive it.

Bruce Kuklick

Philosophers customarily display an interest in their past, but their motives are rarely pure. The works of illustrious predecessors are often simply pillaged to find argumentation that supports some contemporary idea, allowing the pillager not only to use the argumentation but also the prestige of the predecessor—witness the interest of some phenomenologists in William James. On the other side, if arguments can be attached to thinkers despised in certain circles, more recent exponents of the same sorts of doctrines can be dismissed by a procedure of philosophical guilt by association—witness the way some contemporaries have their views castigated as evidencing the foundationalism of C. I. Lewis. These uses of the past are none the less honourable. Philosophers are trained to find out which speculative positions are true, which notions sound. When they study their history, they relentlessly approach it with a view to learning which ideas are justifiable over the long haul, which beliefs stand up to present scrutiny, which texts are now worth reading. The focus is the cogency and relevance of a past practitioner's argument. We learn that a now-deceased speculator has something to say about a problem that is of interest today. Or that his writing can be reconstructed to cast light on a problem of current importance. A. J. Ayer's work on American pragmatism—it is a form of suborning perjury—exemplifies the way thinkers no longer able to defend themselves can be used for a present purpose when their inquisitor is ruthlessly talented.

Philosophers' predilections in thinking about the past often result in misconstruing the intentions of the men they write about. Philosopher-historians are less interested in their subjects than in the present, and so are more prone to get their subjects wrong. But my chief complaint now is not this sort of 'presentism', but the presentism involved in simply deciding *who* is to be studied.

Philosophers write histories of philosophers whom they or others think are great. R. G. Collingwood taught us long ago that historical narratives are answers to questions. Initially, in the United States, scholars asked: what past American thinkers are great?; and: how are they connected to what interests us now? More recent scholars, confronted with an acceptable canon, have even further reduced interrogative complexity. They ask only: how are the conventionally great thinkers related to what interests us now?; why do *I* think that Edwards or Emerson or Royce is great?

These questions avoid all variety of exploration of past ideas in exchange for learning what a small coterie of philosophers thinks is 'worthy' in past thinking. The questions are not *wrong*; they just rest on a feeble inquisitiveness. Instead of asking: why is Edwards important for American philosophy? why not ask: how did various groups of intellectuals use Edwards in the late eighteenth and nineteenth centuries? Instead of asking: what is Franklin's pragmatism?, why not ask: why did Franklin exercise such a hold on twentieth-century American literary critics?

Instead of asking: what did Emerson think? why not ask: why did Nathaniel William Taylor drop completely out of sight less than thirty years after he was the most influential thinker in the United States?

Part of the reason that American philosophy is confused is that philosophers are flat-footed in the questions they ask. The other reason is that scholars of American thought are over-eager to link ideas to society.

In discussions of American philosophy it is still popular to speak of the American mind, and clichés about the practicality of American ideas, the quest for community, the self-conscious concern for national identity, and similar ideas still come tripping off the tongues of scholars. Such notions might be true, but the evidence does not bear them out. One can, to be sure, pick out some prominent Americans and urge that certain peculiarities dominate their work. Philosophical commentators interested in the canon usually do this, for example, with men like Franklin, Emerson, and James. But this sort of arbitrary selection tells us little about national character, as historians have recognized for some thirty years. Moreover, even within the canon it is hard to defend the generalizations. Jonathan Edwards's concerns are those of a Calvinist divine, not of an American. The liberal religious thinkers like Unitarian William Ellery Channing are as unconcerned with their Americanness as Emerson is concerned with his.

If we go to the immediate outskirts of the canon, things get much worse. Chauncey Wright is often cited as the father of the pragmatists, but one will search his writing in vain for even a glimmer of interest in material that is not connected to Wright's attempt to construct a philosophy of science congruent with Darwin's biology. The most influential American philosopher, Charles Peirce, is widely recognized as the 'inventor' of pragmatism. Some scholars have recently ransacked his writings to discover a few paragraphs indicating his interest in American life, but to understand him serious students also soon immerse themselves, as Peirce himself did, in the technicalitites of scholastic realism, logic and mathematics, and late nineteenth-century metaphysics and epistemology. American philosophy in the last fifty years is also infertile ground for getting at the American character. What is 'American' about C. I. Lewis or W. V. Quine?

Thinkers outside the select Boston few, of course, are even more problematically fitted into an American mould. The ministers in Edwards's tradition in the eighteenth and nineteenth centuries are defined by their professional commitment to the study of theology. The nineteenth-century college philosophers, numerically the largest group of thinkers in the United States, are conspicuously absent in studies of American philosophy despite the fact that at the time they were as much a part of philosophical life as, say, Oxbridge was in Britain in the quarter of a century after World War II. The American academicians were about as 'American' as the Oxbridgeans are 'English'. How American are John

Witherspoon, Princeton's eighteenth-century realist president; Old Calvinist William Hart, a foe of Edwards's followers; Johann B. Stallo, the leading Cincinnatti philosopher of science in the nineteenth century; George Herbert Palmer, the most politically powerful philosopher of Harvard's Golden Age; Irwin Edman, the enormously popular Columbia philosopher of the twentieth century; Pittsburgh's Wilfrid Sellars, our contemporary?

It is often urged that certain common philosophical themes are characteristically American. For example, pragmatism—in some loosely defined sense—is usually a prime candidate. But pragmatism has a much shorter tradition than the realistic or the idealistic one in America; and there is no good reason for lighting on it, as opposed to the other two. The most formidable candidate certainly is that of the Augustinian tradition that has been defined by divines before Edwards, Edwards and his followers, Princeton in the late nineteenth and early twentieth centuries, and then Richard and Reinhold Niebuhr. This tradition commands the allegiance of millions of Americans today. Will anyone stand up for fundamentalism?

A more serious candidate for giving thematic unity to American philosophy is the connection between the individual and the community that one can extract from thinkers like Edwards and that is, indeed, manifest in the work of some important late nineteenth-century speculators. It is first well to remember that such a theme could not be uniquely or distinctively American. The Greeks were consumed by the question; so were the British idealists, from whom many of the Americans picked up their ideas. The irony is that the idealism that gave life to the quest for community that some commentators believe defines American thought is the same sort of idealism that commentators have overlooked in Britain when they discuss British empiricism.

But the quest for community will not do as an American theme. It is a function of the metaphysical commitment to various idealist-tinged doctrines. It is not present in figures unpersuaded of idealism. One cannot find the idea in Princeton's famed realist James McCosh, still writing in the latter part of the century; in Arthur O. Lovejoy, a very powerful thinker even at the turn of the century; or William P. Montague, the Columbia realist.

Perhaps although there is really nothing quintessentially American about American thought, it is true that American philosophers have *thought* there was, and can be distinguished by their self-conscious regard for what they construe as their Americanness. This is an interesting idea, but a little reflection will show that it is associated with the Golden Age of American philosophy, 1890 to 1910, its coming, and its aftermath. During this period Emerson was elevated to his status as a 'representative' thinker, and his musing about the American character celebrated; and the students of the speculators of the Golden Age occasionally retained some of the interests of their mentors, although many did not.

The self-consciousness was, I believe, a reflection of America's growth as a great power that Europe had at last to take notice of. With recognition as a great power went intellectual recognition. For example, after importing second-rank Scottish philosophers to America for well over 100 years, the United States sent Royce and James to give the Gifford lectures in Scotland at the end of the nineteenth century. This sort of recognition prompted the *angst* about the American character that one does find in many philosophers of the Golden Age, but one hardly finds it elsewhere. Where is the self-consciousness of Donald Davidson, Saul Kripke, or David Lewis today? Where is the self-consciousness of Laurens Perseus Hickok, the most creative American academic philosopher of the mid-nineteenth century? Of theologian Bennet Tylor, the most conventional Edwardsean in the nineteenth century? Of Yale's Noah Porter, perhaps the most typical mind among the nineteenth-century collegians?

Traditions of thought have existed for periods of time in America; they have, although it is *very* hard to sort them out, been linked to assorted institutions, and other non-intellectual variables. There is a long tradition of pragmatism at Harvard; Congregational Calvinism produced a distinctive system of divinity. During a period of institutional malaise from 1830 to 1880 a vital group of preachers, amateurs, gentlemen of leisure, and men of letters were a vigorous force in intellectual life in New England and the old North-west. Academic philosophers in the nineteenth century shared certain Scottish epistemological concerns. In the twentieth century positivism had a great influence fuelled by the flight of many philosophers from Hitler. But none of these exemplary traditions has much to do with the meaning of America. 'National character' may be critical to the study of ideas in America, but so far no one has shown this to be the case.

Once philosophers have a canon of great American thinkers, they feel compelled to justify their inclusion in the canon. So scholars have asked: Why did America give rise to Edwards and Emerson? What is American about them? How is Franklin similar to James? That is, the other difficulty that frustrates canonical history is asking these sorts of follow-up questions the answers to which, as I have tried to suggest, are inevitably inadequate.

In 1912 H. A. Prichard wrote an essay, 'Does Moral Philosophy Rest on a Mistake?', from which I have taken the title of this paper. Prichard argued that his subject was the result of trying to answer 'an improper question'. The questions that have generated the history of American philosophy are not improper. It is not conceptually misguided to ask: Who are the great thinkers in America?; or the connected question: What makes these great thinkers American? It is rather that these questions are at best not very interesting, at worst silly. This essay is a plea that we ask better questions.

Jonathan Edwards

HANS OBERDIEK

I. Preface

For nearly a century and a half after his death, Jonathan Edwards remained America's greatest philosopher. His rigorous, systematic vision coupled with a synthetic, creative imagination were unrivalled until the appearance of that great triumvirate of pragmatic philosophers—C. S. Peirce, William James, and John Dewey—at the close of the nineteenth century.

Throughout his life Edwards was recognized by supporters and detractors alike as a man whose sermons, essays, and books had to be confronted, for there was no more powerful intellect in the Colonies. That he devoted himself to the support of strict Calvinist doctrines which were generally on the defensive served only to make him a more formidable opponent. And decades after he died, he continued to be widely read. His monumental treatise on the *Freedom of the Will* was required reading well into the mid-nineteenth century at leading American universities; his essay on *The Nature of True Virtue* was still being discussed as late as 1889; and his profound study of the psychology of religious life contained in his book on *Religious Affections* was read avidly late into the nineteenth century as well. 'New England theology', or 'Edwardseanism', as it was sometimes called, was a direct legacy of the preacher from Massachusetts. His indirect legacy—not always one he would have relished—may be found in Whitman's *Leaves of Grass,* Emerson's essays, and the gradual separation of secular and religious ethics.

II. Introduction

In 1758, three months after assuming the presidency of Princeton University, or Princeton College as it was then known, Jonathan Edwards died of a smallpox inoculation. Nearly all of his previous fifty-four years had been spent in New England during a vital period in pre-Revolutionary American history. After graduating from Yale, Edwards succeeded his eminent grandfather, Solomon Stoddard, in the influential parish of Northampton, Massachusetts. Nearly a quarter of a century later, dismissed by his congregation, he removed himself to Stockbridge (Massachusetts) where, for six years, he ministered to the Indians. Far removed from civilized intellectual life, Edwards none the less wrote two of his finest works, *Freedom of the Will* (1754) and *The Nature of True Virtue* (1755). He left Stockbridge only after being prevailed upon by the Trustees of Princeton, who saw in him a champion of their strict Calvinist views. Edwards accepted the presidency reluctantly—after turning down several posts in Scotland which would have given him the leisure to write—on the condition that he would be given time to complete a long envisaged project, the *History of the Work of Redemption*. But, as we know, death intervened, and prevented him from completing any of his remaining projects. Upon learning that he was dying, his physician wrote, Edwards at first appeared agitated, wondering why God would have called him to Princeton only to end his mission virtually before it began; he soon became reconciled to his fate, however, and died at peace with himself and his family and secure in his faith.

From the time he preached an invited sermon in Boston in 1731 until his death twenty-seven years later, Edwards dominated New England theological and ecclesiastical thought. And to do so in that time and place was to dominate thought, for religion and the religious life were central to colonial New England. Many would have trembled, for instance, on reading, let alone hearing, his most astonishing sermon, 'Sinners in the Hands of an Angry God'. That sermon, preached at the outset of the Great Awakening in 1741, admonishes us to think of ourselves as suspended over the pit of hell like a spider over a fire, only temporarily saved from everlasting torment by God's will. Yet Edwards is so much more than a hellfire preacher. Certainly his reputation in his own day, and in ours, extends far beyond what he said in the pulpit.

Not only was Edwards widely read by his contemporaries (and, I might add, by his contemporaries in Britain, especially Scotland, as well), but he participated actively in the leading theological, ecclesiastical, and therefore political controversies of the day. We must remember that in Colonial America no sharp distinction was drawn between Church and State: quite the reverse. Which brand of religion to mix with politics was hotly disputed, but not that religion and politics should not be mixed at all: to engage in theological and ecclesiastical controversies was inherently political.

Indeed, Edwards' rejection of his grandfather Stoddard's ecclesiastical innovation regarding church membership led his congregation in Northampton to remove him from his powerful pulpit. The congregational system of New England counted as 'visible saints' only those parishoners who had undergone a profound conversion experience, reported it to the congregation, and were accepted by the congregation as part of the 'church'. It was assumed, in the beginning, that the children of saints would themselves experience conversion in due course and become members. As time went on it became obvious that this assumption was false. By 1662 an accommodation known as the 'Half-Way Covenant' permitted the children of saints to bring their own children to baptism upon 'owning the covenant'. While this did not bring them church membership, it did keep alive the hope that they would become converted and it kept both them and their children under church authority. The inherent instability of that accommodation showed itself quickly, and less than twenty years later Jonathan Edwards' influential grandfather, Solomon Stoddard, effectively overthrew the principle underlying covenant theology—namely, that only those converted could be members of the church—and replaced it with the theological claim that the sacraments, now open to everyone who was not 'openly scandalous', were 'converting ordinances'; that is, means of bringing about conversion. As a consequence, Stoddard reaped five huge 'harvests' over the next forty years. Edwards never liked the idea of the Half-Way Covenant and abhorred the results of the innovation of his distinguished and revered grandfather. His determination to return to the theory and practice of the early seventeenth century was not only a futile effort to turn back the clock, but would have had the practical and political effect of denying church membership, and therefore political power, to the vast majority of his own congregation. Edwards' audacious attempt was bound to fail; a lesser, though perhaps wiser, man would not even have dared to try.

Because many of his fellow divines regarded him as a reactionary—and their numbers grew as time passed—Edwards' views were frequently attacked, though seldom directly, as he preached and published orthodox Calvinism as sanctioned by the Synod of Dort in 1619. The attacks, indeed, are less interesting than the counter-attacks they swiftly, vehemently, and effectively provoked. For in every case Edwards was far superior in intellect and eloquence to his adversaries, though they often had the weight of both public opinion and power, both secular and ecclesiastical, on their side.

Those who know Edwards through his fire and brimstone sermons will also know that he was a leading figure in the Great Awakening, that cataclysmic spiritual revival that swept through the Colonies in 1740 led by the youthful English preacher of dubious standing, George Whitefield. Edwards himself had instigated the first phase of it six years earlier in 1735 when he inspired an awakening on a smaller scale. When Whitefield arrived in Northampton, Edwards welcomed him to his church and his home, actively supported Whitefield's work, and defended the Awakening throughout his life. Although he came to deplore its excesses, he never abandoned its central message: that our only hope for a salvation which we do not deserve is through a regenerative gift of divine grace.

Yet despite the obvious truth that Jonathan Edwards participated *in* eighteenth-century American thought and culture—indeed, helped shape its contours—it seems to me that he was never truly *of* it, at least not in the manner of most of his fellow Americans, great or humble. The most salient truth about Edwards, I believe, is that his life was primarily and intensely an *interior* one, a life of the mind and affections, not a life of action. His own struggles were all inner struggles, struggles against his own felt unworthiness, struggles to resolve the paradoxes of a hard theology, and struggles to make clear to himself how the truths of Newton, Malebranche, and Locke could be made consistent with—even provide unshakeable grounds for—Calvinism. Edwards' influential but erratic biographer, Perry Miller, wrote of him in a book entitled *Errand in the Wilderness*. That title makes my point nicely. As a Christian citizen, as a minister, as an intellectual, Edwards could not and would not shirk his responsibilities. But they were in the nature of errands, of burdensome tasks (however vital), which took him away from his own true vocation: the intense mental and spiritual struggle to close with God.

Edward's errand was made more difficult by the uncomfortable fact that he had one foot firmly and irrevocably planted in the strict Calvinism of at least a century past—even his grandfather Stoddard was considered lax, at least in ecclesiastical matters—and his other foot equally well-planted in the emerging modernity of Newton and Locke, the neoplatonism of Henry More, and the Scottish aestheticism of Hutcheson and Shaftesbury. Needless to say, this is not an enviable position! Yet rather than letting it mire him in a welter of confusion and contradiction, Edwards found the challenge it presented invigorating: with eloquence and analytic rigour he applied his commanding intellect in defence of a moribund theology in light of a science and philosophy which had yet to seep into the consciousness of leading American thinkers.

Edwards' errand ended in failure. It did so not because of the bankruptcy of his ideas, though his ideas were attacked on all sides, but largely because America was becoming increasingly confident, even proud, of herself as self-making and self-saving. She was developing little patience for a voice, however incisive, that declared, in no uncertain terms, that even the greatest are worthless, depraved, destined to damnation, and utterly dependent on God's grace for their salvation. Men who thought of themselves as self-made and who were beginning to think about their political distinctness, if not independence, had little time for a preacher who insisted that God's glorification was our chief duty and that we are utterly dependent upon him for everything of value and hope.

Perhaps it is not surprising that interest in Edwards has increased markedly in the last few decades, for fewer and fewer Americans express, let alone feel, the kind of self-confidence found in Walt Whitman, Ralph Waldo Emerson, Andrew Carnegie, John Dewey, and Carl Sandburg. More and more Americans are beginning to believe that which Edwards never doubted: that good works cannot earn salvation—or even put much meaning into one's life without some transcendent commitment.

My subject is Edwards the philosopher. As a philosopher, Edwards is rich in argument, influence and affinities. Yet it must never be forgotten that he was first, foremost, and above all, a theologian. I mean by this not only that his interests and publications were primarily theological, but that he, like his medieval predecessors, regarded philosophy as the handmaiden of theology. In short, Edwards never permitted a philosophical doctrine to compromise his theology. However much he believed that reason was a gift of God to be used to discern his Word, he never subscribed to the overweening importance Enlightenment figures, such as his contemporary, Benjamin Franklin, or Thomas Jefferson granted to reason. Reason must always serve revelation and be checked by it. In reading Locke and others, then, Edwards was driven to amend, ignore, or rebut where necessary to make their philosophy consistent with his fundamental theological commitments. This is not to say that he bastardized those he read, any more than Aquinas bastardized Aristotle. Rather, he self-consciously *used* them for his own purposes without (deliberately, at any rate) distorting what they said. When and where he disagreed with them, he said so.

But if, for Edwards, philosophy is the handmaiden of theology and if his theological interests were primary, does it make sense to talk about Edwards the philosopher at all? I think it does, for although his philosophy and theology are thoroughly integrated, the former can be distinguished from the latter and assessed for its cogency. No harm will be done, provided that one guards against thinking that one has understood the entire body of his work.

Because of the primacy and centrality of his theology, Edwards' philosophy will be approached through it; in that way enough stage-setting can be provided to make sense out of the philosophical plot unfolding on centre stage.

III. God's Sovereignty

There can be little doubt that a conviction in the absolute and unconditional sovereignty of God serves as the cornerstone of Edwards' entire thought, both theological and philosophical. Not only does it provide support for his unwavering belief in predestined grace and damnation, but it provides support for his Berkelean idealism and his rigidly deterministic account of freedom and responsibility. His preoccupation with God's sovereignty can be felt on virtually every page he wrote and every sermon he preached.

After resisting the doctrine of God's sovereignty with 'cavils and objections', it eventually struck Edwards with such force and clarity that it became the central element in his transformation from a sincere would-be

Christian to a regenerated, born-again Christian. Edwards relates his conversion, which occurred when he was still a youth, in his *Personal Narrative,* written when he was about forty:[1]

> From my childhood up, my mind had been full of objections against the doctrine of God's sovereignty, in choosing whom he would to eternal life, and rejecting whom he pleased; leaving them eternally to perish, and be everlastingly tormented in hell. It used to appear like a horrible doctrine to me. But I remember the time very well, when I seemed to be convinced, and fully satisfied, as to this sovereignty of God, and his justice in thus eternally disposing of men, according to his sovereign pleasure.... God's absolute sovereignty and justice, with respect to salvation and damnation, is what my mind seems to rest assured of, as much as of any thing that I see with my eyes; at least it is so at times. But I have often, since that first conviction, had quite another kind of sense of God's sovereignty than I had then. I have often since had not only a conviction, but a delightful conviction. The doctrine has very often appeared exceedingly pleasant, bright, and sweet. Absolute sovereignty is what I love to ascribe to God.

It is this doctrine—which most moderns find utterly nasty, gloomy, and bitter—that informs so much of Edwards' thought. If we are to understand him rightly, therefore, we must explore this 'sweet and glorious doctrine' in greater detail.

Christians have generally celebrated God's omnipotence, but Calvin and Edwards championed the essential *arbitrariness* of God's power, his inalienable, incontestable *right* to save or condemn whomever he pleases. In describing God's power as arbitrary, of course, I mean arbitrary from the human point of view. Edwards never doubted that God has his fully sufficient reasons for everything he ordained; it is just that we necessarily remain in the dark as to why he pre-destines some souls to heaven and others to perdition. Edwards' defence of God's absolute right to save and condemn whomever he pleases for whatever reason he pleases has an understandable root: how can God be glorified to the highest if he is somehow tied to man's petty requirements? Edwards' first influential sermon, delivered at the request of the leading churchmen of Boston, hammers hard at those who would limit God in any way. His opening

---

[1] Jonathan Edwards, *Personal Narrative*, in C. H. Faust and T. H. Johnson (eds), *Jonathan Edwards* (New York: Hill and Wang, 1962), 58–59. This anthology, originally published in 1935, remains the best available. In addition to extensive selections from many of Edwards' major works and sermons, it contains a solid introductory essay and a good, though somewhat dated, bibliography. Hereafter F & J.

paragraph sets the tone, and justifies his title: 'God Glorified in Man's Dependence'.

> There is an absolute and universal dependence of the redeemed on God. The nature and contrivance of our redemption is such, that the redeemed are in every thing directly, immediately, and entirely dependent on God: They are dependent on him for all, and are dependent on him every way (F & J, 92).

The grace of God in giving us Christ, Edwards continues, is utterly free; he was under no obligation whatever to do so.

> And it is from mere grace that the benefits of Christ are applied to such and such particular persons. Those that are called sanctified are to attribute it alone to the good pleasure of God's goodness by which they are distinguished. He is sovereign, and hath mercy on whom he will have mercy (F & J, 94).

Edwards clearly wishes to distance God from his lowly and undeserving creation. How is this to be done? The elevation of God beyond the reach of any binding covenant with man, beyond the reach of any rights-claims that we might make against God is one way.

Another way, which Edwards also employs with great effect, emphasizes the depravity natural to us. Because of original sin, everyone has a natural propensity to evil, a propensity that inexorably leads one to sin. That sin, 'The Justice of God in the Damnation of Sinners', makes clear, 'being a violation of infinite obligations, must be a crime infinitely heinous, and so deserving of infinite punishment' (F & J, 113–114). Such is God's sovereign power and right, Edwards explains, '... that he is originally under no obligation to keep men from sinning; but may in his providence permit and leave them to sin' (F & J, 117).

It is as if Edwards thought that the distance between God and man could be increased by alternately raising God and lowering man. His keen sense of man's utter depravity comes clear in his *Narrative of Surprising Conversions,* accounts and reflections resulting from Edwards' first 'harvest' of 1735. There he describes those, such as four-year old Phebe Bartlet, whose conversion fills her with smug pride at the same time as it leads her to wallow in despair about the state of her soul. He described the conversion of a 'pious, bashful' woman of Northampton in similar terms:

> ... I went up to see her & found her Perfectly sober & in the Exer[c]ise of her Reason, but having her nature seemingly overborn & sinking, and when she could speak Expressing in a manner that cant be described the sense she had of the Glory of God, and Particularly of such & such Perfections, & her own vnworthiness, her Longing to Lie in the dust, sometimes her Longing to Go to be with Christ, & crying out of the Excellency of Christ, & the wonderfullness of his dying love; ... She

has since been at my House, & continues as full as can hold, but looks on her self not as an Eminent saint, but as the worst of all, & vnworthy to Go to speak with a minister; but yet now beyond any Great Doubt of her Good Estate (F & J, 79–80).

But if God's sovereignty, and with it man's original sin and natural depravity, serves as the cornerstone of Edwards' thought, surely divine grace is its complementary pinnacle. God's 'efficacious, determining grace' alone transforms some into living saints, overriding their natural depravity. When this happens, man does nothing; God does everything. Again, Edwards celebrates God's majestic sovereignty: 'It is manifest', he writes at the opening of *Efficacious Grace,* 'that if every men are turned from sin, God must undertake it, and he must be the doer of it; that it is his doing that must determine the matter; that all that others can do, will avail nothing, without his agency' (F & J, xcv). Man, as we shall see, is moved by his heart, his affections; but only God can lift the burden of sin from one's heart to let it respond virtuously to God's glory.

Here arises a paradox. If I am powerless to effect my own salvation—indeed, if my fate has been destined from the moment of creation—why should I *seek* salvation? And why should any minister warn me that I face Hell if God has already determined that it is, or is not, my ultimate destiny? Edwards never resolved the paradox satisfactorily. We all have the power to strive for our salvation, but in the end our salvation is a freely bestowed gift. He occasionally suggests that an earnest religious life *prepares* one for salvation, but clearly this will not do. 'How can a preparation that has no inherent connection with salvation be considered a preparation?'[2] Indeed, Edwards himself grants, at least by implication, that preparation is not necessary when he says 'We ought now to love all, and even wicked men; we know not but that God loves them'.[3]

Another attempt to resolve the paradox begins with the premise that God concerns himself with the soul of each and every individual. He requires of some that they strive mightily to prepare themselves for salvation; of others he does not. He requires of some that they undergo an intense conversion; of others he does not. Of course, one distressing consequence of this way out shows itself in the Great Awakening: people desperately tried any reasonable strategy which just might be what will have won them the gift of grace. It is as if each of us were given a unique combination lock: most are given locks that can never be opened, and the rather few who do possess a lucky lock try frantically to discover the correct combination, knowing all the time that it has been

[2] Clyde A. Holbrook, *The Ethics of Jonathan Edwards: Morality and Aesthetics* (Ann Arbor: University of Michigan Press, 1973), 19.

[3] Jonathan Edwards, 'The Justice of God in the Damnation of Sinners', *Works,* S. Austin (ed.) (Worcester: 1808), IV, 293.

determined that it shall be found or not—and, worse, never knowing in this life whether the current combination has been hit upon, for the lock will not be opened, if it be opened at all, until judgment day.

Needless to say, this resolution of the paradox does nothing to reassure anyone, nor, or course, is it its purpose to do so. It can and did, however, engender an enormous frenzy of disparate action and emotion. A dynamic preacher, by vividly describing the terrors of Hell, thus motivates his flock to seek salvation, for it may be that unless one seeks—and the preacher preaches—neither will have been saved! How far this provides a rational solution to the paradox is doubtful; how far it succeeded in driving people to seek salvation, history makes clear.

IV. Idealism

Edwards' commitment to God's absolute and unconditional sovereignty paves the way for him to defend a strong form of determinism with equanimity, as we shall see presently. But it also enables him to push towards the idealism of Bishop Berkeley—and for similar reasons. Like Berkeley, Edwards welcomes the conclusion that the world and everything in it exists in the Divine Mind because that further evidences God's splendid omnipotence.

Despite diligent efforts, scholars have been unable to uncover any direct evidence that during his formative years Jonathan Edwards read, or even heard of, Bishop Berkeley's idealism. They have sought such evidence because of the striking affinities between the two. Like Berkeley, Edwards exploits inherent weaknesses in Locke's epistemological dualism between primary and secondary qualities and the resultant doctrine that our knowledge of and the very existence of the world outside our minds must be inferential.

Locke, it will be recalled, argued that there are three sorts of qualities in bodies. First, there are real or primary qualities: solidity, extension, figure, number, motion and rest. These, Locke claimed, exist in objects whether observed or not and our perception of them gives us an accurate idea of the object. The dimensions of this sheet of paper, for instance, are what they are, whether or not anyone notices, and its dimensions are real properties of it. Secondary qualities, on the other hand—such as colours, sounds, tastes, odours, and tactile sensations—are merely *powers* to produce sensations in us and do not accurately represent qualities in objects. This same sheet of paper appears white and crackles when wrinkled, but neither its colour nor sound—nor scent, feel, and taste, for that matter— are in the object *as* colour or sound; *nothing* in the object *resembles* the experienced colour. Rather, the paper has *powers* enabling it to *appear* white to normal observers in normal circumstances. Finally, Locke distinguished a third quality; namely, the power in one object to effect changes in another. This sheet of paper has the power to reflect light, yet it would be a mistake, Locke argued, to regard the light which it reflects as a quality of the paper.

Edwards, who devoured Locke while a student at Yale, dismantles this dualism by showing that it leads straight to idealism, an idealism he happily embraces for reasons just mentioned: namely, it makes God's power central to the world's being and our knowledge of it.

Edwards' argument is as simple as it is elegant. Beginning with Locke's conclusion that objects are no more coloured than pins are pained, he maintains that figure cannot be a real property either, for it is nothing more than the termination of colour. *Resistance* alone, Edwards insists, can belong to body. Resistance, he argues, is solidity; and the termination of resistance, with its relations, is figure; and the communication of resistance through space is motion. Solidity, figure, and motion—all primary or real qualities for Locke—are therefore nothing but *modes* of resistance. Consequently, resistance alone exists out of mind. Nor is this quite true either, for when nothing is actually resisted, nothing exists but the mere *power* of resistance.

Edwards then argues—brilliantly, I think—that this power must be in some mind as an idea. For what is resisted? It would be absurd to say that resistance is resisted, so we must conclude that resistance is a mode or property of an idea. There are, after all, regular succession of ideas such that they may move, stop and even rebound. 'The world', Edwards concludes in his youthful *Notes of the Mind*, 'is therefore an ideal one; and the Law of creating, and the succession of these ideas is constant and regular' (F & J, 28).

This insightful argument is neater, though less elaborate, than Berkeley's more famous defence of subjective idealism. Both reject Locke's notion of causality and adopt instead the French philosopher Malebranche's occasionalism. Briefly, that view holds that A is the cause of B only in the sense that the occurrence of A is the occasion for the occurrence of B. Although no real connection obtains between A and B, scientific activity and its resultant laws can continue because scientific laws simply record God's determination to have B follow A given the appropriate occasion. Except when he wished to produce a miracle, God shows a steady determination to order the world in a regular and discoverable way.

This again serves to glorify God. Not only are freezing temperatures the occasion for the formation of ice, but striving for salvation may (in some cases) be the occasion for receiving God's grace. Just as freezing temperatures do not, as it were, force water to change into ice, so religious observance and good works generally do not force God to grant one entrance into his kingdom. One may be the occasion for the other . . . if God so pleases.

200

Edwards never abandoned the idealism of his youth, and yet never argued for it publicly. He knew that it would be subject to misunderstanding and, like other matters which he believed would only confuse non-philosophers, kept it private. His elegant argument in favour of idealism has much to be said for it, provided one does not question its basic presuppositions concerning ideas, minds and powers. As we know, each of these was trenchantly criticized by David Hume in his *Treatise of Human Nature* published in 1739 and later in his *Enquiry Concerning Human Understanding*. The former 'fell still-born from the press', as Hume put it, and was not known to Edwards; the latter may have been known to him, as was Hume's name, but it appears that Edwards took no philosophical notice of it. And that is a great pity, for it would have been intriguing to see how Edwards would have met Hume's sceptical challenge.

V. Freedom, Determinism and Responsibility

If Edwards rejects Locke's dualism, Locke's positive influence on Edwards shows itself in Edwards' discussion of free will, which could not have taken the shape it did were it not for his acceptance of Locke's attack on scholastic faculty psychology. Until Locke, most philosophers regarded the mind as if it were composed of distinct faculties operating within it very much as distinct organs operate with the body. Typically, reason, will and desire were identified as those mental faculties that determined one's character and actions. Typically, too, philosophers assigned reason the office of directing the will which, in turn, controlled, or tried to control, the passions. Will assumed special importance when man was under consideration as an active being, for the will was thought to cause one to choose to act as one did. But if my will causes me to choose to do this or that, what causes my will to will what it does?

Locke, and Edwards after him, believed that this way of thinking breeds needless confusion and perplexity, as surely it does. By abandoning faculty psychology in favour of a view that sees the mind as a unity acting as a whole, we can still distinguish different mental activities—such as thinking, imagining, willing, and desiring—without requiring that we think of them as substantial parts of the soul interacting causally. True, Edwards does often refer to the will as if it were a faculty, presumably because most of his contemporaries had not yet abandoned the older psychology. Although he uses the older language, however, he is never taken in by it.

As Edwards characterizes 'will', it is not a faculty but the *power* of choice; it is, indeed, choice itself. This characterization of will as choice has clear advantages and profound implications. There is no puzzle, for instance, about how 'faculties' interact causally or normatively. By defining will as choice, moreover, Edwards cuts through endless discussions concerning the will's 'freedom'. Under the old faculty psychology, the will was buffeted about, either by reason or desire or some combination of the two. Those who postulated a will 'free' from the casual or normative bondage of either reason or desire, seemed as though they were celebrating a will whose choices were simply arbitrary, occurring willy-nilly.

Edwards' conception of will stops certain discussions even before they begin. If the 'will' is understood as choice itself, then clearly it is not the kind of entity that can be free *or* determined, since it is not an entity at all. Further, once we abandon the idea that the will is a quasi-substance, we must abandon the notion that the will is either a cause or an effect, let alone both.

Edwards' specific targets are the Arminians, that loosely knit group of theologians, many of them British, united mainly in their attempts to soften the harsh tenets of orthodox Calvinism, particularly those tenets regarding original sin, predestination, and irresistible grace. None of his chief antagonists—Daniel Chubb (1679–1747), Daniel Whitby (1638–1726), and especially Isaac Watts (1674–1748)—was an Arminian in any strict sense of that term, but that did not stop Edwards from applying this odious term to them: any *hint* of laxity was sufficient to lay this dreaded heresy at one's feet. Concerning the subject of freedom, Arminians failed to see that their allegiance to faculty psychology and defence of free will leads them into absurdity after absurdity. Contrary to Edwards, the Arminians think of freedom as having three essential characteristics. First, will has the power of self-determination. Second, will has the property of *indifference,* where that is understood as a power to choose y even though one has already chosen x; that is, one's will is free to do x only if it is in one's *power not* to do x. Finally, Arminians maintain that there is no fixed and certain connection, known or unknown, with some prior gound of an act of will—the will is wholly contingent.

Edwards blasts the Arminans for failing to grasp the implications of their thread-bare psychology. As he rightly points out, Arminians are committed to the absurd position that the will is both a cause and an effect of itself.[4]

> To talk of the determination of the will, suppose an effect [viz. the will or choice], which must have a cause. If the will be determined, there is a determiner. This may be supposed to be intended even by them that say [as the Arminians do], the will determines itself. If it be so, the will is both determiner and determined; it is a cause that acts and produces effects upon itself, and is the object of its own influence and action.

Yet clearly, ridding ourselves of faculty psychology alone cannot quite so neatly dispose of the age-old question of human freedom: freedom of

[4] Jonathan Edwards, *Freedom of the Will*, Paul Ramsey (ed.) (New Haven: Yale University Press, 1957), 141. Hereafter cited as FW.

choice remains a genuine question, for if our choices are caused, then it seems that freedom and responsibility are illusions. Edwards knows this, and to see how he meets this challenge we must inquire into his views more deeply.

Edwards begins his positive defence of strict determinism by stating that the strongest motive causes us to choose as we do. By strength of motive Edwards means its tendency to move the mind—the only restriction imposed on what can serve as a motive is that it must be apprehended by the mind at the time of choice. This masquerades as an empirical claim about human motivation, but surely it must be understood as definitional; otherwise it is simply false. After all, we often have the experience of acting contrary to those desires and considerations which *feel* strongest. To reply that this only shows that what feels strongest is not strongest simply begs the question. Edwards' claim must therefore be understood as providing us with a definitional truth.

Edwards' second claim is also definitional: 'the will always is as the greatest apparent good is':

> ... whatever is perceived or apprehended by an intelligent and voluntary agent, which has the nature and influence of a motive to volition or choice, is considered or viewed as good (FW, 142).

And 'good' here means 'agreeable' or 'pleasing'. It follows that everyone chooses to do which appears most agreeable or pleasing to one, everything considered and under a certain description. Obviously, a trip to the dentist is neither agreeable nor pleasing. If however, we understand the decision as more agreeable and pleasing in prospect than the prospect of an excruciating toothache, then—by definition—one who chooses to visit the dentist *must* have found the trip more agreeable than the alternative and, conversely, one who procrastinates *must* have found the envisaged ordeal less agreeable than the risk of suffering a toothache in the future. Notice that one does visit the dentist *because* it is good; rather, by definition, one's choice *reveals* that one regards it as good. More pointedly, one cannot deliberately choose what one regards as evil, at least at the time of choice, for what one regards as evil, one does not choose. People do make evil choices, of course, but that is because they are moved by wicked motives.

Yet if Edwards' first two claims are definitional, how can they be used to generate a position regarding human freedom and responsibility? We have seen that choosing the greatest apparent good is analytic for Edwards, as is his claim that the strongest motive determines, i.e. causes, our choices. What is not analytic or definitional is the further inquiry into why some people are motivated as they are. And here Edwards offers several reasons: the apparent nature and circumstances of an object which make it appear desirable or undesirable; the degree of difficulty in satisfying our desire for the object; the consequences of succeeding or failing in satisfying our desire; the probability of success; and the strength, clarity, and liveliness of our idea of the object. As we shall see presently, the last consideration is of first importance.

But first we must get clear on Edwards' views concerning freedom and necessity. We begin with the latter, and here we must follow Edwards in distinguishing among various sorts of necessity. Philosophical and metaphysical necessity are, he says, nothing different from certainty.

Moral and natural necessity, on the contrary, have nothing to do with either philosophical or metaphysical necessity. The latter are either propositional or metaphysical dependencies; for instance, '2+2=4' is philosophical necessity; 'Judas betrayed Christ', however, is a metaphysical necessity because it occurred in the past, and cannot be changed.

Moral and natural necessities, on the other hand, are both concerned with causality, not analytic or metaphysical dependency. Edwards spells out the difference between the two nicely:

> ... by 'moral necessity' is meant that necessity of connection and consequence, which arises from such moral causes, as the strength of inclination, or motives, and the connection which there is in many cases between these, and such certain volitions and actions.... By 'natural necessity', as applied to men, I mean such necessity as men are under through the force of natural causes; as distinguished from what are called moral causes, such as habits and disposition of the heart, the moral motives and inducements (FW, 156–157).

From this pair of distinctions there follows another pair between moral and natural inability. Again, Edwards is his own best spokesman:

> We are said to be *naturally* unable to do a thing, when we can't do it if we will, because what is most commonly called nature won't allow of it, or because of some impeding defect or obstacle that is extrinsic to the will; either in the faculty of understanding, constitution of body, or external objects. *Moral* inability consists not in any of these things; but either in the want of inclination; or the strength of a contrary inclination; or the want of sufficient motives in view, to induce and excite the act of will, or the strength of apparent motives to the contrary (FW, 159).

Strictly speaking, Edwards adds, the word 'inability' denotes natural inability only, for 'a man can't be truly said to be unable to do a thing, when he can do it if he will' (FW, 162). Chains, stupidity, and paralysis are examples of natural inabilities: they prevent one from doing what one desires. Lust, apathy, and selfishness are examples of moral inabilities: they *seem* to prevent one from doing what one thinks one desires. In the latter instance, however, the inabilities are only apparent: if one truly desired to do what one should, nothing stands in the way but oneself. As

Edwards puts is, 'Therefore, in these things to ascribe a nonperformance to the want of power or ability, is not just; because the thing wanting is not a being able, but a being willing' (FW, 162).

Freedom, or liberty, Edwards understands as the power to do what one pleases: 'Or in other words, his being free from hindrance or impediment in the way of doing, or conducting in any respect, as he wills' (FW, 163). Freedom, in short, consists in the ability to do what one wants to do. Here Edwards departs from Locke and chooses instead to follow Hobbes and join with Hume. Like them, Edwards argues that how one came to choose as one does has no bearing on the question of freedom: one is free just in case one can do what one pleases.

Edwards' argument is ingenious. He believes that every event, and every substance, is brought into being and substained by a series of continuing acts of God. He thus firmly believes that every voluntary human action is caused. We must remember, however, that causal relations are not necessary connections for Edwards; rather, each element in the causal chain is but an occasion for God to choose another element to follow. And this does not lead Edwards to doubt that man is 'free'—at least in one ordinary sense of that slippery term: a man is free if and only if his choices are effective. That is, just in the case that his choosing to do something in a certain context is an occasion for the occurrence of another thing. He is not free, however, if his choices are—for whatever reason— ineffective; that is, if one's choice to do x with the intention of 'bringing about' y does not in fact lead God to use the occasion of one's willing x to bring about y. To put the matter in eighteenth-century terms, Edwards accepts liberty of spontaneity but rejects the Arminian notion of liberty of indifference. Edwards will have nothing to do with so-called 'contra-causal' freedom.

But what means this freedom? And how does freedom, understood as Edwards does, leave room for moral responsibility? Edwards has a clear and firm answer to both questions. 'Freedom' does not presuppose an open future for individual agents. The choices of Christ, for instance, were fully free, despite the fact that he could not have chosen evil. Of course, nothing prevented Christ from choosing evil, unless we think of his character as somehow preventing him from doing evil. And surely Edwards is correct in holding that one would speak paradoxically were one to say that Christ was prevented from choosing evil acts by his saintly character, for in an importance sense, one *is* one's character.

Similarly, Edwards argues, Christ deserves our praise for his extraordinarily virtuous life even though everyone—that is everyone in Edwards' audience—grants that Christ could do no wrong. And in saying that Christ deserves our praise, Edwards is saying that Christ is *morally responsible,* certainly praiseworthy, for his good life. For everyone, Christ included, is responsible for the kind of person he is, even if the kind of person he is finds its ultimate cause in God's choices. How is this possible? Again, we find Edwards developing an ingenious, if specious, argument.

Edwards rejects any proposal linking freedom to the suspension of deterministic dictates of God. It may be said of someone, of course, that he had the ability to do otherwise *if he had chosen otherwise,* but not that, given his character, he *could* have chosen otherwise. And it is this doctrine so many find obtuse if not barbaric. How can I be held responsible for having the sort of motives that lead me to make the choices I do unless I have the sort of self-determining power over my motives? Is it not both unjust and cruel to tell someone in the moral dock that he is being sentenced to eternal damnation for being the sort of person he is, even though he had no self-determining power to alter himself?

'Responsibility' has many uses in English, and Edwards seizes on one of them, a use not uncommon in Anglo-American law, to blunt this charge. In particular, a necessary condition for an attribution of responsibility in this sense is that the accused is at least the mediate author of the act in question. Thus, Judas, not Thomas, is responsible for betraying Christ because is was he, not Thomas, to whom the act of betrayal must be attributed. Now surely it is fitting to blame Judas for his betrayal, for it was a monstrous thing to have done. But in blaming him, we are clearly finding fault *with* him because of a fault *in* him. Judas, so the story goes, was moved to betray Christ because of a base motive, a motive that provides us with good reason to believe that it evidences a trait expressing at least some of Judas' central beliefs, attitudes and emotions. His action flows from his motive which, in turn, expresses his character; because his character is blameworthy, so is he. Consequently, in morality as well as in law, Judas is liable to punishment: he is fully responsible for his awful deed.

The law concerns itself primarily, though not exclusively, with actions that contravene its dictates. God, on the other hand, concerns himself equally with those who transgress his ordinances in spirit as well as in action. Judas betrayed Christ in action, and is justly punished for it, but God metes out just punishment to whose who betray him only in their hearts. One's feelings, attitudes and fantasies belong to one just as much as one's actions; in God's eyes, as it were, the latter are only the tip of the iceberg.

But why is Judas, or anyone, responsible for his traits, if those traits are not within his control? The law, after all, has rather different aims in determining responsibility than morality. Unless one has the ability to alter one's beliefs, attitudes, emotions and actions, freedom—and hence *moral* responsibility—is illusory, and it is this which I believe the Arminians clumsily grasped.

Freedom, contrary to Edwards, does involve the capacity, which is a power, to do otherwise: one is free to do x only if one has the ability not to *do x,* not to *think x,* not to *feel x,* given the opportunity to do so. Edwards' position rests on a venerable, though confused, philosophical doctrine: namely, that one's purposes, intentions and motives stand in causal connection with bodily actions just as do colliding billiard balls. But in fact purposes, wants, intentions and motives are not separately identifiable apart from the actions, feelings, and attitudes they allegedly cause.

Edwards' argument succeeds against the Arminians principally because they, like he, presuppose an untenable account of intentional verbs coupled with a dubious Newtonian determinism. The Arminians' mistake lay in denying essential elements of the picture, a mistake Edwards brilliantly exploits. Had they rejected the picture, they would have avoided Edwards' relentless *reductio* against them. They can hardly be blamed, however, for the deep confusion in the position of both was a commonplace throughout the eighteenth century, and its diagnosis and cure rests on philosophical developments growing out of the later work of Wittgenstein, a good two centuries after Edwards' death.

VI. Beauty and Excellence

Edwards' commitment to the doctrines of original sin, eternal torment for the damned, man's natural depravity, predestined grace, and God's awful sovereignty finds its happier complement in his equal, though less well known, commitment to God's excellence, or spiritual beauty. Obscurity, sadly, envelops his account of excellency, and it is only when we turn to his discussion of beauty that we learn that excellence itself is a kind of beauty.

In *Notes on the Mind* Edwards maintains that excellency resembles harmony, symmetry, proportion, and equality, for where these relationships obtain there is more beauty than otherwise. 'All beauty', he continues, 'consists in similarness of identity of relation', so that if two things are not in porportion, we find them deformed, because being itself is a kind of proportion (F & J, 33). Indeed, the greater the disproportion, asymmetry, or inequality, the more contrary to being something is, and the more it approaches nothingness. Conversely, the more harmony exhibited by something, the greater its being and agreeableness: 'Agreeableness of perceiving being is pleasure, and disagreeableness is pain' (F & J, 33). Excellency can then be formally defined as 'The Consent of Being to Being, or Being's Consent to Entity [i.e. to positive existence]' (F & J, 35). When this consent is of minds towards minds, as it is for humans interacting with one another or with God, it is called *love*; when it is of minds towards things, it is called *choice*.

Beauty, though certainly not identical with excellence, occupies a central place in Edwards' thought. Although an aesthetic category, his discussion of it sheds light not only on excellence, which is spiritual and moral, but on the nature of true virtue, or Christian morality.

Beauty is either natural or spiritual. The former, natural beauty, is but a shadow of the latter and consists of 'a mutual consent and agreement of different things, in form, manner, quantity, and visible end or design; called by various names of regularity, uniformity, symmetry, proportion, harmony' and 'uniformity in the midst of variety'.[5] The difference between the two kinds of beauty is important because unregenerate man, and some animals for that matter, are capable of recognizing secondary or natural beauty, for many creatures can recognize the beauty in flowers or in bodies. We are pleased when we see beautiful objects because we perceive the consenting relations between their parts or between them and other objects. Beauty is not so much a property of things, then, as it is constituted by relations between and among things or their parts. We are framed in such a fashion as to recognize these beautiful relations when we perceive them and be pleased by them.

Spiritual or primary beauty differs from natural beauty in its *moral* nature. That is, the object of spiritual beauty must be other minds, not other things, and the nature of the relations which makes them beautiful, or excellent, consists in their 'concord and union of mind and heart'.[6]

> The true beauty and loveliness of all intelligent beings does primarily and most essentially consist in their moral excellency or holiness. . . . 'Tis moral excellency alone, that is in itself, and on its own account, the excellency of intelligent beings: 'tis this that gives beauty to, or rather is the beauty of their natural perfections and qualifications (RA, 298).

Primary or spiritual beauty, then, consists in a general consent of minds to minds. Indeed, it is the neo-platonic model on which the natural beauty of sensible things is mere shadow and image. In so far as we can understand divine excellence at all, it must be in terms of spiritual beauty. The centrality of beauty is assured when Edwards remarks that 'God is God, and distinguished from all other beings, and exalted above 'em, chiefly by his divine beauty' (RA, 275). Spiritual beauty, he continues, is that 'wherein the truest idea of divinity does exist' (RA, 275).

This emphasis in Edwards on beauty may come as something of a surprise, given notions regarding his gloom and doom sermons. But Puritanism in his day stressed the significance of immediate experience, and this stress must have been reinforced by his reading of Locke, who champions experience as the way to knowledge. Further, as the world is

---

[5] Jonathan Edwards, *The Nature of True Virtue*, William K. Frankena (ed.) (Ann Arbor: University of Michigan Press, 1960), 28. Hereafter cited as TV.

[6] Jonathan Edwards, *Religious Affections, Works*, op. cit, II, 257. Hereafter cited as RA.

God's ideal creation, it would be more surprising were Edwards not to find it beautiful. Unregenerate men, of course, find deformity in the world, but this, Edwards explains, is only because they cannot see the whole. He himself, we will recall, could not see the beauty in God's omnipotent sovereignty until his conversion, and in later life he came to believe that no one was truly born again unless he could see the beauty in predestined divine grace or the eternal damnation of the unsaved, including unsaved infants. Put another way, Edwards essentially adopts and then adapts Leibniz' solution to the problem of evil—namely, that this is the best of all possible worlds.

VII. True Virtue

Edwards' reflections on morality are scattered throughout his writings and sermons, but the most systematic account occurs in *The Nature of True Virtue,* his only substantial non-polemical work, written among the Indians at Stockbridge. In it, he distinguishes true virtue from natural or secondary virtue; shows that Shaftesbury and Hutcheson—and by extension Hume—were mistaken in not recognizing the difference; and provides an explanation of the way in which we are moved to embrace or reject God. Indirectly, the essay helps explain, if not fully justify, Edwards' belief in the compatibility of hard determinism and moral responsibility.

All virtue is a kind of beauty, but not all virtue is true virtue. Specifically, the recognition of *primary beauty* alone characterizes moral agents and their relations and it alone is the mark of true virtue. As secondary beauty is found in all kinds of beings and their relations, most especially in natural man but in beasts as well, to identify it with true virtue is a deep confusion, for it confuses shadow with substance. And this is just the charge that Edwards levels against Hutcheson and Shaftesbury. All beauty, Edwards agrees, consists in unification amid diversity, but proportion or harmony alone is not primary beauty and hence not true virtue.

Unregenerate man, however, is not devoid of morality, for everyone is equipped with a natural conscience: ' . . . natural conscience, if the understanding be properly enlightened, . . . concurs with the law of God, and is of equal extent with it, and joins its voice with it in every article' (TV, 68). Further, everyone has a sense of natural justice, which is simply the notion that certain actions are fitting or unfitting. And finally, these two notions of natural conscience and natural justice are conjoined with a natural love of consistency, so that we are morally offended, for instance, whenever anyone makes an arbitrary exception on one's own behalf.

Natural man may thus lead a life which parallels that of one possessing true virtue to a high degree. But there is one crucial difference between the two. On judgment day, 'when sinners shall be called to answer before their judge, and all their wickedness, in all its aggravations, brought forth and clearly manifested in the perfect light of that day' *both* the man with grace and the man without will recognize the justice of God's judgments and actually join with God in condemning their sins (TV, 72). Only redeemed man, however, will feel *repentance*; natural man will feel only *remorse*. The repentant man has sinned and knows he has done so; but because of grace, he at the same time hates sin and loves holiness. Natural man, on the other hand, would only feel remorse; that is, he would see what a *fool* he had been and accept punishment, but 'without abhorring malevolence from a benevolent temper of mind, or without loving God from a view of the beauty of his holiness', for, Edwards concludes, 'These things have no necessary dependence one on the other' (TV, 74).

Natural man at his best, in short, would be like a deaf person who learned to read music and even came to have an understanding of when a musical composition was discordant, for such a person could avail himself of reason and determine the proper relationship among notes. But such a person would not be truly musical. For that, his ears would have to be unstopped, so that he could *hear*. Throughout his writings, like the Cambridge Platonists to whom he is so deeply indebted, Edwards uses metaphors of sight and illumination to similar effect. Further, just as one who is deaf or blind is unlikely to have his affections stirred by sounds or colours, so natural man is much less likely to follow God's law than is reborn man. For reborn man will be drawn towards God's beauty as one who is truly musical is drawn towards beautiful music; its attraction, though resistible because we are never whole, will nevertheless have a strong pull. The person of true virtue will feel this pull and respond appropriately to it. Those born deaf do not have it within their power to hear, and consequently do not have it within their power to grasp the substantial beauty of music; they can only chase after shadows. Similarly and more profoundly, all of us are born sinners and lack the power to love God with all our heart: only if God lifts the deadening burden of sin from our hearts can we sense the true beauty of God and be drawn towards it. True virtue, then, is an affair of the heart: it is true love, yet it is not within our power to *feel* or *sense* the beauty of God unless he chooses to bestow his grace upon us. Natural man can *know* of God's existence and of his power, justice and benevolence, and may even feel that he *ought* to be attracted to him, but this would be as pathetic as one who was stone deaf knowing *about* the sublime beauty of a Beethoven quartet, feeling he ought to love it, yet never hearing even a single note of it.

Edwards' metaphors rest on neoplatonic metaphysics, found in his day at Cambridge, and the need, common to most eighteenth-century thinkers, to show that self-love does not necessarily lurk behind every human action. Even natural man loves others than himself, though Edwards is quick to point out that love of others proceeds, in the end, from the principle of self-love. That we possess what Hume was to call a 'sentiment of humanity', however, should not mislead us into confusing enlightened self-interest with true virtue: 'The reason why men are so ready to take these private affections for true virtue, is the narrowness of their views; and above all, that they are so ready to leave the divine Being out of their view ...' (TV, 87). But Edwards does not despise self-love, even conceding that, so far from being useless in the world, 'it is exceeding necessary to society' (TV, 89). At the same time, because of its partiality self-love 'may make man a common enemy to the general system', even if one's private affection extends to a system embracing millions (TV, 89). In short, no Humean sentiment of humanity or Benthamite utilitarianism amounts to true virtue.

Benevolence and virtue are not unconnected, however. Both the excellency of God and true virtue are, as we have seen, primarily affairs of the heart, not cold objects of reason, so it not surprising that benevolence, which is a loving union of heart with the well-being of others, should have a prominent place in Edward's ethics. Indeed, Edwards states that 'True virtue most essentially consists in *benevolence to being in general*' (TV, 3).

> Love of benevolence is that affection or propensity of the heart to any being, which causes it to incline to its well-being, or disposes it to desire and take pleasure in its happiness (TV, 6).

As we can do nothing to further God's well-being, the most and the least we can do is to take pleasure in his happiness. And we are to do so, not principally because he himself is benevolent, but simply because he possess the greatest share of existence.

It is important to stress this metaphysical basis of Edwards' ethics, for without it, there is little to distinguish it from Hume's anti-rationalism and morality of sentiment. Like Hume, Edwards grants that moral distinctions are not derived from reason and that morality is more a matter of feeling than of thought. Unlike Hume, however, being draws us towards it as if it were a magnet. Hume did not have to face the prospect that his view would lead to a hopeless relativism because he imagined that we are enough alike so that what you feel anyone would feel; our experience of twentieth-century horror and indifference makes that empirical assumption less plausible. Edwards avoids relativism because he believes that a transcendent being draws us towards him: the attraction lies not so much in us for each other, as it is in Hume, but in each of us for God. The holocaust and other horrors are then to be explained because God has not enabled us to see him clearly; consequently, we wallow in our selfishness and are attracted to lesser being.

Although based in metaphysics, Edwards' ethics has definite social implications. There is, in fact, a double grounding for an activist social morality. Anyone who possesses true virtue will be moved to seek the well-being of his fellows and to desire and take pleasure in God's happiness. And as we know, the New Testament tells us that God so loves man that he gave his only begotten son to die for our sins and that we are to love our neighbours as ourselves. Anyone desirous of God's happiness, therefore, would necessarily seek the well-being of those whom he loves.

There are yet more particular implications of Edwards' metaphysically based social philosophy. The tired charge often levelled against Protestantism, that it glorifies the rights of individuals at the expense of communities, cannot fairly be directed at Edwards. That it cannot may be traced to his neo-platonism. We have seen that one being is superior to another because it has greater being; indeed, the more being, the greater its existence. Just as organic wholes have greater being than the atoms comprising them, so do communities have greater being than the individuals constituting them. Organicism, however, threatens to submerge the individual completely. Edwards' social philosophy assuages that fear because his neo-platonism is joined by his Protestantism. Communal life is necessary because it is only within communities that we are able to grow in love and to exhibit love. And for just that reason, God cares about the moral texture of communities. But his first love is for the individual, and the least individual, because he, like the greatest, possesses a soul; everyone must be loved.

Edwards' delicately balanced social morality was never properly understood or appreciated by his immediate audience. Those who saw that it was grounded in metaphysics either ignored its social implications altogether or rejected them because it cut against the grain of Enlightenment individualism. Those who saw its stress on duties of benevolence either read that as a rejection of concern with the purity of one's own heart or as a form of utilitarianism. Indeed, if Edwards has had any effect on the subsequent development of American moral thought it would be in the emergence of utilitarianism as a prevalent, if not dominant, mode of moral thinking—a development he would surely have abhorred.

VIII. Influences and Affinities

New England theology, or 'Edwardseanism', survived well into the nineteenth century in America. Its influence can still be felt today, albeit in forms that Edwards himself could hardly recognize. Perhaps enthusiasm is not a peculiarly American trait, but Edwards lent his considerable powers of intellect and persuasion to its furtherance. And that sort of enthusiasm survives today in evangelical churches throughout the United States. What contemporary forms of it lack, and I would suggest were lacking for the most part in Colonial America as well, was Edwards' secure grasp of its limitations. For however much Edwards stressed that religion was a matter of the heart or affections, he himself could not help inquiring into the grounds of things. His understanding of beauty, for instance, led him to grasp that disharmony, disproportion and excess are deformities of what would otherwise be an expression of true belief and true virtue. Nor was Edwards a 'fundamentalist' as that term is now abused. True, he took the Bible literally, but it was informed by his typology, which saw in the Bible analogy after analogy, and prevented his reading of the Bible from generating into a crude literalness. Further, there was not, for him, any clash between science and religion because he saw in science further evidence of the elegant simplicity with which God constructed the world. Of course, he did not have to face the considerable challenge Darwinism posed a century later, but my suspicion is that his objections would have been more deep and more sophisticated than many that were raised by leading thinkers of the time.

Perhaps Edwards' greatest influence lies in his aesthetics. For it is there that he reflects and reinforces a tradition which, at least in the West, is peculiarly American. For Edwards celebrates the beauty found in nature, especially its unity in diversity. And that theme, I would suggest, runs throughout American art and letters. Whitman's magnificent *Leaves of Grass*, of course, epitomizes the tradition, but it is found as well in Ralph Waldo Emerson, Emily Dickinson, and Robert Frost. Fiction, too, concentrates on the balance, proportion, and symmetry of nature, where everything has its place and where everything has its compensation.

Unlike Europe, where fine art occupies a prominent place, in America architecture, painting, sculpture, and music are far less important. Partly, of course, frontier life did not provide opportunities for the development of such luxuries. And, of course, there are exceptions: Thomas Jefferson's home in Monticello is but one example. Yet in the main I believe that Americans, for better or worse, have always in the main got their aesthetic sustenance from nature and its intricately simple beauty.

If Edwards' errand ended in failure, it did not end in tragedy. Throughout his life he defended his beliefs with integrity, insight, and passion. We might be tempted to say that he was fighting a losing cause, but that is only because we believe that certain battles end certain wars. Edwards did not.

Edwards was not, of course, beyond self-deception. He did think that the Great Awakening was likely to bring in the millennium imminently, even if not in his own lifetime. But he never deceived himself about the difficulty of his errand or its significance. It was, for him, enough to fight the good fight.

C. I. Lewis

SUSAN HAACK

Biographical note: Clarence Irving Lewis was born in 1883 in Stoneham, Mass., the son of a shoemaker. He received his BA from Harvard in 1905, taught first English in a Massachusetts high school and then English and philosophy at the University of Colorado, Boulder, returning to graduate school at Harvard in 1908, and receiving the PhD in philosophy in 1910. He taught philosophy from 1911 to 1920 at Berkeley, and from 1920 to 1953 at Harvard. *A Survey of Symbolic Logic* was published in 1918; *Mind and the World Order* in 1929; *Symbolic Logic* (with C. H. Langford) in 1932; *An Analysis of Knowledge and Valuation* in 1946; *The Ground and Nature of the Right* in 1955; *Our Social Inheritance* in 1957; *Values and Imperatives* (ed. J. Lange) in 1968; and *Collected Papers* (ed J. D. Goheen and J. L. Mothershead) in 1970. He died in 1964.[1]

Introduction

Lewis, according to Kuklick, was 'a private person', of 'unsparing honesty and . . . utter dedication to the rational pursuit of truth'. He was, Kuklick continues, 'equally uncompromising in what he expected of his readers, and as a result wrote for and lectured to a tiny group of scholars'.[2] I hope that—since I occasionally find myself borrowing from him and frequently find myself arguing with him—I may count myself as one of the 'tiny group of scholars' for whom Lewis wrote. And perhaps, by arguing with him again here, I may persuade some of you of the enduring interest of his work.

Lewis's work spans most of the central areas of philosophy: metaphysics; logic; theory of *a priori* knowledge; theory of empirical knowledge; theory of valuation; ethics and social philosophy. Lewis conceived of philosophy as concerned, not, like the sciences, to discover new phenomena, but, rather, to find a clear and coherent account of familar phenomena. The legitimate business of metaphysics, in particular, is, according to Lewis, not to speculate on ontological and cosmological questions that can ultimately be decided, if they can be decided at all, only by science; it is, rather, to reflect on the question of what system of

---

[1] Sources: P. A. Schilpp (ed.), *The Philosophy of C. I. Lewis* (Open Court, 1968); B. Kuklick, *The Rise of American Philosophy* (Yale University Press, 1977).

[2] Kuklick, 561.

categories would be the most adequate to order our experience.[3] Our choice of categories is rationally made, according to Lewis, on pragmatic grounds. Granted our choice of concepts, we have *a priori* knowledge of analytic truths; for such truths are, in at least a weak sense, man-made— they are true in virtue of relations among our criteria for the applicability of concepts.[4] Lewis's pragmatic theory of *a priori* knowledge was also informed by his work in formal logic. Lewis was an influential critic of the logic of *Principia Mathematica*. *PM* used a formalization ('⊃', referred to as 'material implication') of 'if ... then', which is truth-functional; it is sufficient for the truth of '$p \supset q$' that q be true, or p false. Lewis urged that this conditional was too weak, and should be replaced by a stronger conditional ('⇒', referred to as 'strict implication'; '$p \Rightarrow q$' means 'necessarily, $p \supset q$'). Lewis's logic of strict implication was to become the basis of modern modal systems.[5] This formal work contributed to Lewis's reflections on the epistemological status of alternative logics. Knowledge of logical truths, according to Lewis, like knowledge of analytic truths generally, though not infallible, is independent of experience. Synthetic knowledge, knowledge of how the world is, on the other hand, is possible only by means of experience; and Lewis's theory of empirical knowledge elaborates a foundationalist structure in which experiential beliefs form the basis of our knowledge of the world.[6] Valuation, according to Lewis, is a form of empirical knowledge; evaluative judgments are no less true or false, no less testable, no less objective, than descriptive judgments. 'Valuation', for Lewis, is broadly conceived; it covers logical, epistemological and aesthetic evaluation. Questions of ethics, however, according to Lewis, are not straightforwardly to be classified as questions of evaluation; because they include questions concerning justice, desert and distribution, they cannot be answered by appeal to empirical facts alone.[7]

[3] C. I. Lewis, *Mind and the World Order* (Charles Scribner's Sons, 1929), Ch. 1.

[4] C. I. Lewis, 'A Pragmatic Conception of the *A Priori*', *Journal of Philosophy* **XX** (1923), 169–177, reprinted in *Reading in Philosophical Analysis*, H. Feigl and W. Sellars (eds.) (Appleton–Century–Crofts, 1949), 286–294; *Mind and the World Order*, Ch. VII, VIII, IX; *An Analysis of Knowledge and Valuation* (Open Court, 1946), Book I; 'Autobiography' in Schilpp, 14.

[5] 'Modal' logics are those with operators representing 'necessarily' and/or 'possibly'. See C. I. Lewis, 'Implication and the Algebra of Logic', *Mind* **XXI** (1912), 522–532; 'The Calculus of Strict Implication', *Mind* **XXIII** (1913), 240–247; 'The Issues Concerning Material Implication', *Journal of Philosophy* **XIV** (1917), 350–356; *A Survey of Symbolic Logic* (University of California Press, 1918).

[6] C. I. Lewis, *Mind and the World Order*, Ch. IX, X; *An Analysis of Knowledge and Valuation*, Book II.

[7] C. I. Lewis, *An Analysis of Knowledge and Valuation*, Book III; *Values and Imperatives*, J. Lange (ed.) (Stanford University Press, 1968).

I shall not attempt a comprehensive study of Lewis's entire philosophy, but will concentrate on his theory of empirical knowledge. My main theme will be that Lewis's theory fails in ways which are particularly instructive because they point us away from an atomistic, foundationalist approach, and towards a holistic theory of the kind I have dubbed (since it includes elements of coherentism as well as foundationalism) 'foundherentist'.[8] But since my arguments will also lead me to question the distinction between the *a priori* and the empirical, they will also bear, indirectly, on Lewis's theory of mathematical and logical knowledge.

Lewis was old enough to have been taught by James and Royce; young enough, on the other hand, to have influenced Quine and Goodman. Perhaps it would not be too fanciful to see Lewis, with his pragmatic theory of *a priori* knowledge and his foundationalist theory of empirical knowledge, as trying to accommodate something of each of James's and Royce's approaches.[9] Certainly it would not be fanciful at all to see, in what I have to say in this lecture, a continuity with themes from Goodman and Quine. Indeed, some of you, no doubt, will have noticed already that my theme has strong affinities with the thrust of Quine's arguments in 'Two Dogmas' and 'The Pragmatists' Place in Empiricism';[10] I should, indeed, be content if this lecture succeeds in filling in some significant details in one corner of that larger canvas.

Statement of Strategy

Lewis's account of the role of experience in empirical knowledge rests on three crucial theses:

(1) One's apprehension of what is 'given' to one in sensory experience (i.e, of what one sees, hears, etc.) is absolutely certain.
(2) Unless there were such absolutely certain apprehension of the given, no empirical knowledge would be possible.
(3) The justification of one's (justified) beliefs about the world always derives, directly or indirectly, from these absolutely certain apprehensions of the given.

I believe that all these theses are mistaken, and that the attribution of an

[8] S. Haack, Theories of Knowledge: An Analytic Framework', *Proceedings of the Aristotelian Society* **LXXXIII** (1982–83), 143–157.

[9] Cf. Lewis, 'Autobiography', in Schilpp, 9ff.

[10] W. V. O. Quine, 'Two Dogmas of Empiricism' (1951), in *From a Logical Point of View* (Harper Torchbooks, 1952); 'The Pragmatists' Place in Empiricism', in *Pragmatism: Its Sources and Prospects,* Philip M. Zeltner (ed.) (South Carolina University Press, 1981), 21–39.

absolutely privileged status to apprehensions of sensory experience is *not* the appropriate way to represent how experience contributes to our knowledge. The appropriate way to do this is, rather, by means of a theory which is *naturalistic*, i.e. centrally concerned with the ways in which one amplifies and modifies one's beliefs in response to experience, and consequently focused on beliefs which are *prompted by* experience rather than on beliefs which are *about* experience; which is *fallibilistic*, i.e. denies that any beliefs are absolutely privileged; but which at the same time is *inegalitarian*, i.e. allows that that some beliefs are prompted directly by experience gives them a *prima facie* credibility; and which, however, since it allows that this *prima facie* credibility may be defeated by other evidence of a more theoretical kind, allows for *mutual support*, rather than insisting that justification be one-directional. (Fallibilism, Inegalitarianism and Up-and-Back-ism *define* 'foundherentism' in my terminology.)

I shall be arguing that the difficulties in Lewis's theory are precisely such as to point towards the sort of theory I defend. My critical strategy will be simple: after a summary of salient features of Lewis's account, I shall argue, in turn, against each of the three theses spelt out above. The interaction of my critique of Lewis with my defence of an alternative theory is a little more complicated; but the threads will be drawn together in a brief concluding section.

Goodman, of course, has argued against the first of these three theses, and Reichenbach, in the same famous symposium, against the second as well.[11] Though I think Goodman and Reichenbach were largely correct in their conclusions, I do not think they were fully convincing in their arguments; and I also think that it is the falsity of the third thesis that is most important in showing us the way forward. So I hope that something in what I say will be illuminating even to those already familiar with the work of Lewis's other critics.

Summary of Lewis's Theory[12]

Lewis characterizes knowledge as 'belief which not only is true but also is justified in its believing attitude' (*AKV*, p. 9). He acknowledges that this is

---

[11] N. Goodman, 'Sense and Certainty', *Philosophical Review* **61** (1952), 160–167; H. Reichenbach, 'Are Phenomenal Reports Absolutely Certain?', *Philosophical Review* **61** (1952), 147–159. Cf. also I. Scheffler, *Science and Subjectivity* (Bobbs-Merrill, 1967), Ch. 2; R. Firth, 'Lewis on the Given', in Schilpp, and Lewis's reply; M. Pastin, 'C. I. Lewis's Radical Foundationalism', *Noûs* **9** (1975), 407–420.

[12] My sketch of Lewis's theory is intended simply to supply the background necessary for the critical commentary in the following sections. For this reason

an idealization of ordinary usage, to which however, since he regards it as vague and even inconsistent, he feels no obligation to be strictly faithful. The central concern of Lewis's theory of knowledge is to give an account of the structure of justification—of how a person's beliefs can come to be sufficiently justified to count as knowledge. I say 'sufficiently justified' to indicate that Lewis takes justification to come in degrees, and that he does not require that a belief be conclusively justified in order to qualify as knowledge.

'Our empirical knowledge', Lewis writes, 'rises as a structure of enormous complexity . . . all parts of which rest, at bottom, on direct findings of sense' (p. 171). The basis upon which all warranted empirical beliefs ultimately rest is apprehensions of immediate (i.e. current and uninterpreted) sensory experience, of how things presently appear to one. Such apprehensions are not often formulated linguistically, and indeed are not easy so to formulate; but they may be reported by means of what Lewis calls the 'expressive' use of language, as in, for example, 'I now see what looks like a sheet of white paper in front of me'. The expressive use of language is to be understood precisely as intended to restrict what is said to how things *appear*; as opposed to how things *actually are*, which is represented by what Lewis calls the 'objective' use of language, as in, for example, 'There is a sheet of white paper in front of me'. The foundation of empirical knowledge lies in 'what remains if we subtract, in what we say that we see, or hear, or otherwise learn from direct experience, *all that could conceivably be mistaken*' (pp. 182–183). Here we have thesis (1): apprehensions of what is given to one in sensory experience are absolutely certain.

We suppose, though, that we have knowledge of how things actually are. How could such knowledge be possible? A judgment to the effect that, for example, there is a sheet of white paper in front of me, is, according to Lewis, equivalent in meaning to an infinite set of judgments to the effect that if I were to open my eyes and look directly ahead, I would see what looks like a sheet of white paper in front of me, that if I were to reach out my hand directly in front of me, I should touch what feels like a sheet of paper, . . . etc., etc. Lewis calls judgments of the latter kind 'terminating

---

I have kept my account as neutral as possible. This has meant that, at certain points, I have papered over (what I regard as) cracks in Lewis's theory. These points will be sorted out later. I shall base what I have to say about Lewis's theory of empirical knowledge largely on his account in *An Analysis of Knowledge and Valuation* (and page references in the text will be to this book). Lewis comments in his 'Autobiography' on the ways in which this book improves on the treatment given in *Mind and the World Order* (Schilpp, 17–18).

judgments', because they can, he believes, be decisively verified or falsified by experiential test (pp. 203ff.). Lewis's schema for reports of terminating judgments is: Given S (initial sensory conditions), if A (apparent action on my part), then E (experience of mine) will result. Judgments about how things are Lewis calls 'non-terminating judgments'; this is because they cannot be conclusively verified, since we can never be in a position to check all of the inexhaustibly many terminating judgments that each non-terminating judgment has as consequence, nor can they be conclusively falsified. Non-terminating judgments, being concerned with how things actually are, are linguistically represented in objective language. But, though they cannot be decisively verified or falsified, non-terminating judgments may be rendered more or less probable by favourable or unfavourable terminating judgments. It is through the mediation of terminating judgments that our apprehension of how things appears to us, which is certain, is to render our beliefs about how things actually are probable enough to constitute knowledge.

However, the way in which apprehensions of experience verify or falsify terminating judgments, which in turn confirm or disconfirm non-terminating judgments, is complicated by a feature which has not, so far, been given prominence. What has been stressed, up till now, is that these are apprehensions purely of what is given in experience, uncontaminated by any element of interpretation. What needs stressing at this point is that these are apprehensions of the experience being had *by the person having the experience, at the time of the experience.* The idea is that a person's apprehension of the experience *he* is having, *at the time he is having it,* is absolutely certain. But whatever plausibility this idea has scarcely extends to a person's judgments about the experience *someone else* is having, or to his judgments about the experience he had *at some earlier time.* So each person's knowledge depends, ultimately, on *his present* experiences (including his experiences of others' reports of their judgments) (p. 335). But a person's knowledge of the world, though it derives ultimately from his apprehension of his present experience, is mediated by his beliefs about his past experience, i.e. by memory. It is not, then a straightforward matter of apprehensions of one's present experience verifying or falsifying terminating judgment which in turn raise or lower the probability of non-terminating judgments. A person's empirical knowledge rests ultimately only on his apprehensions of his present experience, which are certain, but often more immediately depends on his memory of his past experience, which is fallible.

However, Lewis argues, though memory is fallible, the fact that one seems to remember having had a certain experience gives a *prima facie* credibility to the belief that one had the experience. And when, in addition, one's memories hang together, their agreement raises their initial credibilities. Lewis's technical term for what I have called 'agreement' or 'hanging together' is 'congruence'. A set of statements is congruent if it is consistent, and such that the probability of any one of its members would be raised by the truth of any of the others, and hence also by any evidence which raises the probability of the others (pp. 338, 345ff.). Lewis illustrates this concept by the example of a number of witnesses, none of them, individually, particularly reliable, who all, without collusion, tell the same story; evidence that the story told by any one of them is true raises the probability that the others' statements are also true. Congruence, according to Lewis, is a pervasive feature of empirical knowledge. The probability of a belief the initial credibility of which is too low for it to count as knowledge can be raised by congruence with other beliefs initially no more credible than itself to the point where it does count as knowledge (pp. 347–348). And, more particularly, congruence solves the problem about the dependence of much of a person's empirical knowledge on his memories of his earlier experience. For when a person's memories are congruent with each other, their congruence reinforces the initial presumption in their favour, and raises the probability of his beliefs about his past experiences sufficiently for them to make his beliefs about how the world is, which they support, probable enough to constitute knowledge (p. 354).

Lewis is at pains to distinguish his concept of congruence from coherence, which he understands as requiring that a set of statements be both consistent and comprehensive. A coherence theory of empirical knowledge, he argues, cannot be adequate; for *any* contingent belief could belong to *some* consistent and comprehensive set of beliefs (pp. 339ff.). But Lewis is certainly not offering a congruence theory of empirical knowledge instead; the congruence of a set of beliefs, he stresses, is no better guarantee of its credibility than its coherence. Congruence can raise the probability of beliefs, but only if those beliefs already, independently, have some initial probability.

So, unless something were absolutely certain, Lewis argues, nothing could be even probable (pp. 186, 235): here we have thesis (2). Beliefs may be rendered probable by the support of other beliefs, which are themselves rendered probable by the support of yet further beliefs, . . ., and so on. But unless there is, eventually, something which is certain, which 'stands fast without support' (p. 333), none of one's beliefs will be genuinely probable, but at best probable relative to some further ground.

Congruence can raise antecedent probabilities, but without the ultimate support of something certain there would be no antecedent probabilities to be raised. 'However important this relation of congruence in the building up of our structure of empirical beliefs', Lewis argues, 'the foundation stones which must support the whole edifice are still those items of truth which are disclosed in given experience' (p. 353). Any belief a person holds which is probable enough to count as empirical knowledge must get its support, not necessarily wholly, but at least in part, from his apprehensions of his immediate experience, which are absolutely certain. Here we have thesis (3).

Critique of Thesis (1)

A serious examination of the claim that apprehensions of what is given to one in experience are absolutely certain obviously requires both a precise understanding of what counts as an 'apprehension of what is given in experience' and a clear account of what is meant by 'certain'. Unhappily, Lewis is far from clear or unambiguous on either of these points; but the formidable task of sorting out what he means cannot be shirked.

It turns out to be best to begin with Lewis's notion of certainty. Apprehensions of experience are variously described as 'immune from error' (p. 183), 'conclusively true' (p. 204), 'completely assured' (p. 243), 'indubitable' (p. 179), and 'incontestable' (p. 262). My conjecture is that there are, basically, two notions of certainty in play, the first concerned with truth, the second with justification. According to the first conception—which I shall refer to as 'T-certainty'—apprehension of experience is certain because it is impossible that it be mistaken. According to the second—which I shall refer to as 'J-certainty'—apprehension of experience is certain because it is impossible that the subject be unjustified in his apprehension.

I think Lewis believes that apprehensions of experience are certain in both senses. Lewis's critics have tended to concentrate on T-certainty;[13] but I see two reasons for giving equal if not greater weight to J-certainty. The first reason is that Lewis's argument that something must be certain if any knowledge at all is to be possible makes much better sense if one understands 'certain' as 'J-certain' rather than 'T-certain'. The argument, in essentials, is that if any belief is to be genuinely justified by the support of further beliefs, those further beliefs must themselves be justified, and that, if an infinite regress is to be avoided, there must, as ultimate grounds, be something which is justified but not justified by the support of further beliefs. This seems to be an argument that something must be J-certain. It is not even plausible as an argument that something must be T-certain; that it rests on something which could not be false would not show a belief to be justified (for one may unjustifiedly believe something that could not be false). The second reason is that Lewis's account of the role of beliefs about one's past experience makes much better sense if 'certain' is understood as 'J-certain' rather than 'T-certain'. Lewis argues that, once an experience is past, it ceases to be 'available' to one as it was when it was

---

[13] Including Reichenbach in 'Are Phenomenal Reports Absolute Certain?' and Goodman in 'Sense and Certainty'.

present, that the certainty of one's apprehension of experience runs out, as it were, as time passes. Since justification is temporally dependent in a way that truth is not, this argument is more plausible with respect to J-certainty than with respect to T-certainty.

Lewis is, of course, aware of the distinction between truth and justification, and aware that it is possible to believe, unjustifiedly, something which happens to be true ('what is affirmed may happen to be true, but if the one who affirms it lacks a justifying ground of his assertion, then his commitment may be a fortunate one but is nevertheless ... not knowledge'). But he does claim that 'there is no distinction of these two dimensions' in the case of apprehension of the given (p. 254). I shall take this as indicating that the justification involved in J-certainty must be full or conclusive justification, and hence truth-guaranteeing; in other words, that Lewis takes J-certainty to imply T-certainty. In what follows, both the claim that apprehensions of experience are T-certain, and the claim that they are J-certain, will come into question.

Another distinction will also be needed before I can turn to the question of what Lewis means by 'apprehensions of experience'. Something is T-certain if it could not be mistaken, J-certain if it could not be unjustified. I shall say that something is *trivially* T-certain if it could not be mistaken *or correct*, and *trivially* J-certain if it could not be justified *or unjustified*; and that something is *substantially* T-certain if it could not be mistaken *but must be correct*, and *substantially* J-certain if it could not be unjustified *but must be justified*. It is clear that the epistemologically interesting interpretations of thesis (1) are those which take it to claim that apprehensions of experience are substantially T-certain and/or J-certain, not those which take it to claim that apprehensions of experience are trivially T-certain and/or J-certain. For the point of insisting on a certain foundation is precisely the idea that *bona fide* knowledge should rest on something guaranteed to be true, or guaranteed to be justified.

What is it that, according to Lewis, is certain?—'apprehensions of experience'—but what are they? Let me start by distinguishing between:

(i) An experience (e.g. my seeing what looks like a sheet of white paper in front of me).
(ii) A judgment about one's experience (e.g. my judgment that I now see what looks like a sheet of white paper in front of me).
(iii) A report about one's experience (e.g. 'I now see what looks like a sheet of white paper in front of me').

It is quite clear that (iii) does not qualify as an 'apprehension of experience' as Lewis uses that phrase; he is careful to stress that though one's *apprehension* of experience is certain, one's *report*, which may be verbally mistaken or insincere, is not. But I am afraid that there is serious ambiguity about whether 'apprehensions of experience' refers to experiences, or to judgments about what is given in experience. There is a passage, though a rather ambiguous passage, in which Lewis apparently denies that apprehensions of experience can be identified with judgments about experience (p. 183);[14] but there are also passages where Lewis indicates that apprehensions of experience are linguistically represented by *statements*, such as 'I now see what looks like a sheet of white paper', which implies that they *are* judgments (p. 179). The best strategy will therefore be to argue that neither experiences nor judgments about experience qualify as certain in an appropriate sense.

My seeing what looks like a sheet of white paper in front of me (the experience) could not, to be sure, be false, neither could it be unjustified. But then it could not be true, either, nor could it be justified. Experiences, in short, are trivially T-certain and trivially J-certain; but they are not substantially certain in either sense.[15]

The question of whether any judgments about what is given in experience are substantially T- or J-certain is trickier, because of the problems involved in figuring out just *what* judgments about experience Lewis could have in mind. It is clear that for something to count as a judgment about 'what is given in experience', it must be about what is given in the experience of the person making the judgment at the time the judgment is made. I shall turn in a moment to the question of what the restriction of the content of the judgment purely to what is 'given in experience' amounts to. But first I want to consider the restriction of the content of the judgment to the experience of the person making the judgment at the time the judgment is made.

'I now see what looks like a sheet of white paper in front of me' represents a judgment of the appropriate kind; but, though I am Susan Haack, and though it is now 1.15 on 11.11.84, 'Susan Haack at 1.15 on 11.11.84 sees what looks like a sheet of white paper in front of her' does not represent a judgment of the appropriate kind. (Lewis frequently uses formulations of the first, never formulations of the second, kind. And while it is at least understandable why Lewis should suppose that the sort of judgment represented by the first kind of formulation is certain, there seems to be no plausibility in supposing that the sort of judgment represented by the second kind of formulation is certain.) So it is necessary to distinguish between the judgment expressed by 'I now see what looks like a sheet of white paper in front of me', uttered by Susan Haack at 1.15 on

[14] My thanks to K. Schwartzberg for drawing this point to my attention This also seems to be how Lewis approaches the matter in *Mind and the World Order*.

[15] Goodman, in 'Sense and Certainty', 161–162, makes what is essentially the same point, though not, of course, using my terminology of substantial versus trivial certainty.

11.11.84, and the judgment expressed by 'Susan Haack at 1.15 on 11.11.84 sees what looks like a sheet of white paper in front of her'. This can be done if judgments are characterized, not as being about a certain thing (person, time, or whatever) *simpliciter*, but as being about a certain thing *as presented in a certain manner*. The relevant class of judgments can then be characterized as: judgments about the experience of the person making the judgment, *qua* person making the judgment, at the time at which the judgment is made, *qua* time at which the judgment is made.[16]

So the claim that judgments about what is given to one in experience are substantially T-certain could be rather more precisely represented as:

(IT) Necessarily (if a person believes at a certain time, of himself, *qua* person making that judgment, at that time, *qua* time of that judgment, that Φ of that person at that time, then Φ of that person at that time).

And the claim that such judgments are substantially J-certain could be represented as:

(IJ) Necessarily (if a person believes at a certain time, of himself, *qua* person making that judgment, at that time, *qua* time of that judgment, that Φ of that person at that time, then that person is justified in believing of himself, *qua* person making that judgment at that time, *qua* time of that judgment, that Φ of that person at that time).

One is told that the judgments in question concern only the 'presented content' of sensory experience; only what is 'sensorily given' to one, not the 'interpretation' one places upon it; that they concern only appearances, without commitment as to how things actually are, being no less certain in cases of hallucination than in ordinary perception; that, if they are to be represented linguistically, it must be by means of the expressive, not the objective, use of language (e.g. p. 179). This is still not as clear as one might like; but the best way to proceed seems to be to work on the basis of the suggestion that the judgments in question concern appearances only.

Although Lewis makes a quite elaborate argument to show that there must be *something* which is certain, he offers scarcely any argument at all to show that judgments about what is given to one in immediate experience have this privileged status. It may be that he relies on the idea that, since a judgment purely about what is given is free of any element of interpretation, it is sure to be free, also, of any element of *mis*interpretation. In the absence, however, of any argument that there *are* judgments which

---

[16] To make the '*qua*' precise, we can use the method introduced by Burdick in 'A Logical Form for the Propositional Attitudes', *Synthese* **52** (1982), 185–230.

involve no interpretation of one's experience, this is inconclusive. At one point Lewis hints that the certainty of judgments about the given results simply from the fact that such judgments are defined to be what is left when one 'subtracts' from judgments about the world 'everything that could conceivably be mistaken' (p. 183). But Lewis cannot seriously be taken to be defending the thesis that judgments about what is given to one in experience are devoid of content. 'I now see what looks like a sheet of white paper in front of me' is not empty; it is certainly not logically impossible that it be false. Indeed, this statement is not even logically weaker than 'I now see a sheet of white paper in front of me'; with appropriate lighting conditions, the former could be true and the latter false, *or* the latter true and the former false. The claim, if it is to have any plausibility at all, must be conditional, as in (IT) and (IJ): it is impossible that a person should be mistaken (IT), or unjustified, (IJ) if he makes a certain sort of judgment. Nothing Lewis says amounts to a conclusive, or even persuasive, argument for either (IT) or (IJ).

This, of course, does not show that (IT) or (IJ) is false, only that Lewis has not established them. Nevertheless, I think that (IT) and (IJ) *are* false. Consider the ophthalmologist's test in which the client is presented with a fan of lines each of equal thickness:

and asked whether the lines all look of the same thickness, or whether the lines on the left, in the centre, or on the right, look thicker. (If no astigmatism is present the lines will look, as they are, of equal thickness; but if there is astigmatism, some lines will look thicker than others.) Now, it is not uncommon for patients to hesitate, and to be unsure which, if any, lines look thicker. Furthermore, patients are routinely asked this question more than once (looking through the same lens), *to allow for the possibility of mistake*. It is acknowledged that there is, for example, a possibility of 'wishful thinking'—that the client's judgment that the lines now look of the same thickness may be influenced by his desire to believe that this correction is, at last, the right one. Suppose that a client reports that the lines look to him of equal thickness, and then, very shortly afterwards, looking through the same lens at the same diagram, that the lines on the left look thicker. It is possible to say that the way the lines look actually changes, even over a brief period, perhaps as a result of abnormal muscular adjustment; but if this is the case, other tests should confirm it. Because the stimulus and the lens are the same, and the time between the two reports short, it is taken to be likely that the lines look the same to him throughout, and that one of the reports is mistaken.[17]

From what Lewis says in response to Goodman, it seems likely that his reaction to this sort of case would be to point out that it is compatible with what has been said to insist that, if a person reports at one time that the lines look of the same thickness, and shortly after that the lines on the left look thicker, then the way the lines look must have changed.[18] And indeed, as I remarked earlier, it is. But this is not a decisive reply; for it is also compatible with what has been said to allow that one of the person's reports may have been mistaken. Certainly, I think, cases of this sort make the claim that such mistakes are inconceivable implausible in the extreme.

If (IJ) implies (IT), (IJ) is, of course, also false. But it will be prudent to look directly at (IJ). Recall that according to Lewis one may be more or less justified in believing something, and someone who makes a judgment concerning what is given in his own experience at the time of judgment is, inevitably, fully justified in this judgment. Consider, now, a patient taking the astigmatism test just described. Suppose our patient had reason to belive that he is more suggestible than average (perhaps he has been told this about himself after taking part in a psychological experiment). Suppose further that the ophthalmologist is not being too careful about how he phrases his questions; and that, when the patient is looking through what the ophthalmologist thinks is probably the correct lens for him, what he says is, 'There, that should do it, they all look the same thickness now, don't they?' The patient promptly judges that the lines do, indeed, all look the same thickness. But, though he surely has some justification for this, it seems doubtful that he is fully justified in doing so.

Thesis (1), I conclude, is false.

Critique of Thesis (2)

If Lewis were right in holding that, unless something were certain, no belief would be even probable, so that there could be no *bona fide*

[17] Opthalmologists distinguish between what they call 'objective' and what they call 'subjective' vision tests. Tests where the optician directly examines the patient's eyes are called 'objective'; tests where he asks the patient for reports on how things look to him are called 'subjective'. Objective tests are used to confirm the results of subjective tests, as well as the other way round. Subjective tests are standardly repeated, to check on possibly mistaken reports by the patient. See H. Asher, *Experiments in Seeing* (Basic Books, 1961), Ch. 10. Both Goodman and Reichenbach make the point that phenomenal beliefs must be consistent with other beliefs; Reichenbach mentions the danger of wishful thinking.

[18] C. I. Lewis, 'The Given Element in Empirical Knowledge', *Philosophical Review* **61** (1952), 173.

knowledge, the argument of the previous section would indicate a sceptical conclusion. Fortunately, however, as I shall argue in this section, he is not.

The essential message of thesis (2) is that no empirical knowledge would be possible unless apprehensions of the given are, as Lewis claims, absolutely certain. Lewis's usual way of expressing thesis (2), however, appeals to the notion of probability; and so do his arguments for it. 'If anything is to be probable', Lewis writes, 'then something must be certain' (p. 186). This raises the question of what Lewis takes to be the connection between knowledge and probability. He uses the notion of probability, I think, in two ways. When he speaks of probability in a non-relative sense (as 'the belief that P is probable to such-and-such degree'), he is referring to the rational credibility, warrant, or, in short, justification of the belief in question. It is in this sense that knowledge requires probability, since, to constitute knowledge, a belief must be sufficiently justified, i.e. probable to an appropriate degree. But Lewis also apeaks of probability in a relative sense (as, 'the belief that P is probable to such-and-such degree on the basis of the belief that Q').[19] Interplay between the non-relative and the relative notions of probability plays a key role in Lewis's arguments for thesis (2).

Thesis (2) is to be taken, I suggest, as saying that if anything is to be sufficiently probable in the non-relative sense, something must be certain. I think that in this context 'certain' must be understood to mean 'J-certain'. J-certainty is, of course, a limit case of probability in Lewis's non-relative sense of probability; a belief which is J-certain is justified to the highest possible degree and in a way which is not relative to any further belief. So thesis (2) becomes: unless something is J-certain, i.e. conclusively justified, and not relative to any further beliefs, no belief can be sufficiently justified to count as knowledge. This makes it apparent that Lewis needs to establish *two* things: that some beliefs must be *conclusively* as well as *non-relatively* justified.

Here are two passages in which Lewis is arguing for thesis (2):

> ... Proximate grounds of the probable or credible need not be certain: it will be sufficient if these are themselves genuinely credible. If 'P' is credible on ground 'Q', then the credibility of 'Q' assures a lesser degree of credibility than if 'Q' were certain. But if the credibility of 'P' rests on the credibility of 'Q', and that of 'Q' on 'R', and so on; and if in this regress we nowhere come to rest with anything that is certain; then how can the credibilities spoken of ... be genuine, since each in turn is relative to a ground, and no ultimate ground is given? Unless there is eventually some termination of this series of supporting grounds; in

---

[19] *An Analysis of Knowledge and Valuation*, Ch. X, is devoted to a discussion of the concept of probability; but the distinction which concerns me is actually clearer in Ch. XI.

something which stands fast without support; will not the whole edifice of empirical knowledge come tumbling down? (p. 333).

If what is to confirm the objective belief and thus show it probable, were itself an objective belief and hence no more than probable, then the objective belief to be confirmed would only probably be rendered probable. Thus unless we distinguish the objective truths belief in which experience may render probable, from those presentations . . . of experience which provides this warrant, any citation of evidence for a statement about objective reality, and any mentionable corroboration of it, will become involved in an indefinite regress of the merely probable—or else it will go round in a circle—and the probability will fail to be genuine (p. 186).

Neither passage seems to say more than this: if someone believes that P on the basis of his belief that Q, then the degree to which he is justified, relative to his belief that Q, in his belief that P, will depend on how justified he is in his belief that Q, and how probable P is given Q. For someone to *know* that P, however, he must be sufficiently justified in believing it, not just sufficiently justified in believing it relative to his belief that Q. So genuine knowledge is impossible unless some beliefs are justified in a way which is not dependent on other beliefs. If the belief that P depends on the belief that Q, and the belief that Q on the belief that R, . . ., and so on without end, the original belief will never achieve more than relative justification; only if the chain ends with some belief which is justified independently of other beliefs could the original belief count as knowledge. But this shows at most that some beliefs must get some justification otherwise than from the support of other beliefs, not that any beliefs must be conclusively so justified.

Some critics have thought that Lewis really has in mind an argument about what I will term the 'dilution of justification'.[20] I have not been able to find this argument explicit in Lewis's text; but it will be instructive to glance at it anyway. The product of two probabilities less than 1 will be smaller than either; the product of infinitely many probabilities less than 1 will be zero. So if one belief rests on another, which is itself only probable to some degree relative to the further belief on which it rests, which is in turn only probable to some degree relative to the further belief on which it in turns rests, . . ., then, if this goes on without limit, the belief at the head of this chain will have no justification at all; its justification will have been so 'diluted' that there is nothing left. This is supposed to show that the chain of justification must come to an end with beliefs which are J-certain.

[20] E.g. Reichenbach in 'Are Phenomenal Reports Absolutely Certain?'; see also J. Van Cleve, 'Probability and Certainty; an Examination of the Lewis/Reichenbach Debate', *Philosophical Studies* **32** (1977), 323–334.

But the claim is that if the series were without limit, *and* all the probabilities were less than 1, the probability of the belief supposedly being justified by the support of all the further beliefs in the series would dwindle to zero; and to avoid this conclusion it is sufficient to deny either part of the antecedent, and not necessary to deny both. If the series is not infinite but comes to an end, the beliefs with which it ends do not have to be fully justified, only justified to some degree. In short, this also establishes at most that there must be beliefs which have some justification independently of the support of further beliefs, and not that these beliefs must be conclusively so justified.

In fact, it is clear that Lewis himself is obliged to admit that this is all that is required. Lewis allows that justification comes in degrees, and that it is not necessary, for a belief to count as knowledge, for it to be fully justified. And, as the first sentence of the first passage quoted allows, if a person believes that P on the basis of his belief that Q, then if P is probable given Q and he is justified to some degree in believing that Q, then he is justified to some degree in believing P (he will be less justified in believing that P than he is in believing that Q, at least unless P is probable to degree 1 given Q; but he will nevertheless be justified to some degree). So far as I can see, there is nothing to exclude a person's being sufficiently justified in believing something to count as knowing it, even though the further beliefs upon which this belief of his ultimately rests are less than completely justified.[21]

Indeed, given that, according to Lewis, mutual relations of support can raise probabilities—i.e. that beliefs which are not, in themselves, sufficiently justified to count as knowledge may achieve that status by means of their congruence with other beliefs no more privileged than themselves—it is not even necessary for him to require that the 'basic' judgments have whatever degree of justification is needed to count as knowledge. Lewis insists that congruence cannot, so to speak, make something out of nothing, only more out of less; but this requires only that some beliefs have *some* initial degree of justification.

Thesis (2), I conclude, is also false.

Critique of Thesis (3)

According to Lewis, apprehensions of experience do not depend for their justification on any beliefs about the world, but any justified belief about the world derives its justification, ultimately, from apprehensions of experience. Justification, in short, is essentially one-directional. At least, this is the official theory. But difficulties in the official theory, which Lewis himself acknowledges, tempt him to compromise the one-directional pic-

---

[21] Cf. Goodman, 'Sense and Certainty', 163.

ture of justification. He pretty much resists the temptation; but I shall argue that it is, in fact, irresistible.

The support given to objective judgments (as, 'There is a doorknob in front of me') by apprehensions of the given (as, 'I now see what looks like a doorknob') is supposed to be mediated by terminating judgments (as, 'Given that I now see what looks like a doorknob, if I were to appear to reach out my hand, I would touch what feels like a doorknob'). The problems I want to discuss all arise, in one way or another, from Lewis's account of the nature of terminating judgments, and their role in justification. Terminating judgments have the form 'Given S (sensory cue), if A (apparent mode of action), then E (predicted experience)'. 'S', 'A', and 'E' concern appearances only, i.e. are representable in expressive language. The conditional is irreducibly subjunctive, i.e. it is to be understood as 'Given S, if it *were* the case that A, it *would be* the case that E'. (Interestingly, Lewis concedes that it would be no more satisfactory to represent the conditional by his strict implication than by the material or formal implications of *Principia Mathematica*.) Because of the irreducibly subjunctive character of the conditional, a terminating judgment does not concern only a single occasion on which a sensory cue is given, but makes a claim about all possible such occasions. This includes occasions on which the sensory cue is given to a person other than oneself, past occasions on which the sensory cue was given to oneself, and possible-but-not-actual occasions on which the cue might have been given to oneself or someone else (pp. 203ff.). But it is only one's apprehension of *one's own, actual, present* sensory experience which is supposed to be privileged.

The first issue I want to look at concerns Lewis's account of the role of one's past experiences. The verification/falsification of a terminating judgment depends, not only on judgments about how things *now* sensorily seem to one, but also on judgments about how things sensorily *seemed* to one on earlier occasions; it relies on memory. Memory, Lewis admits, is fallible. But, he argues, there is an initial presumption in favour of the truth of (apparent) memories, and this initial credibility can be raised by congruence. The trouble with Lewis's response is that it vacillates between two different pictures, one of which seems roughly right but obliges one to give up one-directional justification, and the other of which preserves one-directional justification, but is plainly wrong. Let me explain.

Why should there be an initial presumption in favour of the truth of apparent memories? The natural answer, which Lewis seems at one point (p. 336) to give, is that this presumption derives from beliefs to the effect that if it seems to a person that he remembers having had such-and-such experience, then, more likely than not, he *did* have such-and-such experience. (Just how true this is, or in just what sorts of cases it is true, is a question I need not pursue here.) But this sort of belief is of course an objective belief. So to allow that the *prima facie* credibility of apparent memories has to be based upon beliefs of this sort requires justification to go back as well as up.

Lewis almost admits as much (p. 338), but then draws back (p. 339). He thinks that he preserves the essentially one-directional character of justification because he appeals to congruence rather than coherence; for he insists that congruence can only raise the degree of justification of a belief if it is already justified to some degree, and that a belief can only get this initial justification by means of the support of apprehensions of experience. (One might make the point vivid by saying that Lewis thinks of congruence as, so to speak, only earning interest on money that all must come, originally, from the one source.) But it is just false that, if beliefs to the effect that at such-and-such a past time it sensorily seemed to one thus and so have, as Lewis claims, a *prima facie* credibility, it is in virtue of their being supported by beliefs to the effect that it now sensorily seems to one so and thus. One does not normally infer how things sensorily seemed to one in the past from how things sensorily seem to one now (and one wouldn't be remembering a past experience if one did). Lewis seems, as I said, to acknowledge this earlier on, but he becomes so preoccupied with the differences between congruence and coherence that he apparently forgets it.

There are also, I think, two other factors that confuse him here. The first is that one's correctly remembering having had such-and-such sensory experience logically requires that one had such-and-such sensory experience, and that Lewis rarely marks the distinction between memory and apparent memory. The second is that a judgment to the effect that one remembers having such-and-such sensory experience is itself a judgment about one's present experience, though not one's present sensory experience, and that Lewis is apt to fudge the distinction between judgments about one's sensory experience, and judgments, more generally, about one's experience. It is only because of these confusions, I think, that Lewis fails to see that memory judgments could acquire an initial credibility for congruence to raise only in an up-and-back, and not in a one-directional, structure of justification.

The second issue I want to look at concerns Lewis's account of the logical relations between terminating judgments and, on the one hand, the apprehensions of the given which are supposed to verify and falsify them, and, on the other, the objective judgments which they are supposed to confirm or disconfirm.

I begin with the claim that apprehensions of experience conclusively verify and falsify terminating judgments. I take this to mean that an apprehension of one's experience (a) is itself certain, and (b) is sufficient to establish the truth/falsity of a terminating judgment. I have already argued against (a); it is (b) that concerns me here.

Terminating judgments are to be construed as subjunctive, not material or formal conditionals; i.e. the claim they make is that in any possible instance in which such-and-such a sensory cue is given, if it appeared that such-and-such action were taken, such-and-such experience would eventuate. The terminating judgment has the form: for all possible instances, if it were the case that S and A, it would be the case that E. It entails but is not entailed by the formal conditional: for all actual instances in which S and A, E. Now, one may be (or may put oneself) in a position to determine that in a particular instance such-and-such a sensory cue is given and such-and-such an action apparently taken, and that in this instance such-and-such experience eventuated. But it should already be apparent that Lewis is wrong to claim that such a positive test could conclusively verify a terminating judgment. At the very best, a single positive instance would confirm the terminating judgment to some extremely modest degree. (Indeed, given that it is a matter of one positive instance of an unrestricted generalization, even this is debatable.) It should also be apparent, however, that the question of falsification is not symmetrical. One negative instance *is* sufficient conclusively to falsify a terminating judgment. For the terminating judgment entails the corresponding formal conditional, though it is not entailed by it. If sensory cue S_i is given, A_i apparently taken, and experience E_i does not result, it must be false that in all possible instances in which S, if it were the case that A, it would be the case that E. So judgments about one's immediate, present, sensory experience can conclusively falsify terminating judgments, but not conclusively verify them.

I turn next to the claim that terminating judgments confirm/disconfirm objective judgments. This claim is based on Lewis's account of the 'sense-meaning' of objective statements. The sense-meaning of an objective statement, Lewis explains, 'is exhibitable in some set of terminating judgments' (p. 211). This apparently means that any objective judgment strictly implies and is strictly implied by some set of terminating judgments. I shall represent this by: $O \{\Leftrightarrow\} \{T_1, \ldots, T_n\}$. The set of experiential consequences of each objective statement is according to Lewis, inexhaustible (p. 180), so presumably $\{T_1, \ldots, T_n\}$ is not finite. (This account represents Lewis's version of the Pragmatic Maxim of Meaning, accordance to which the meaning of a statement is to be given by its 'pragmatic' or 'experiential' consequences.) It is in virtue of this relationship of mutual entailment, Lewis thinks, that objective judgment can be confirmed or disconfirmed by terminating judgments.

But Lewis's account of the relation between objective judgments and terminating judgments runs into the mirror image, so to speak, of the difficulty just discussed for his account of the relation between terminating judgments and apprehensions of experience. This time, it is his account of the effect of negative instances that gives trouble. Recall that the claim is that $O \Leftrightarrow \{T_1, \ldots, T_n\}$, and that the truth of any of the T_i confirms, and the falsity of any of them disconfirms, O. Given that O *entails* $\{T_1, \ldots, T_n\}$, however, this latter claim is obviously mistaken; the falsity of any of T_1, $\ldots$, T_n would not merely *disconfirm O*, it would *conclusively falsify* it.

This time, however, Lewis realizes, in due course, that something is wrong. At this stage he shifts to a new account of the relation of terminating judgments to objective judgments (pp. 231–232). According to the revised account, this relation, formerly characterized as mutual entailment, is to be mutual probabilification. Lewis shifts to the revised account, he says, rather than accepting the conclusion that objective judgements can be conclusively falsified by the failure of a single terminating judgment, because 'direct inspection of cognitive experience' indicates that this is the proper course. He spells out what he has in mind by discussing a case in which (as he puts it) seeming to see a doorknob in front of me, I reach out my hand, but fail to grasp a doorknob. One of the terminating judgments which on the original account is entailed by the objective judgment that there is a doorknob in front of me is thereby falsified. But I would not, Lewis allows, thereby be obliged to conclude that the objective judgment is, likewise, false: I might more reasonably conclude that my co-ordination is not all it might be (p. 232).

Lewis's comments on this case seem, in essentials, plausible. But he seems not to realize just how radical their consequences are. For what, examined closely, they indicate, is this. No terminating judgment follows from an objective judgment *by itself*; further assumptions are always required. (In the case Lewis discusses these further assumptions include beliefs about my ability to reach out my hand accurately in the direction of a seen object, the reliability, in this instance, of my vision and sense of touch, etc.) The failure of the terminating judgment, then, implies only that *either* the objective judgment is false, *or* these further assumptions are false; and only in so far as these further assumptions are themselves probable does it disconfirm the objective judgment. (The point of Lewis's discussion is presumably that to the extent that it is improbable that it looks as if there is a doorknob there when there is not, it is probable that when it seemed to me that I reached out my hand in the direction of the seen doorknob, I did not really do so.) And the further assumptions involved will not, generally, be themselves exclusively experiential— typically they will concern such matters as the conditions of perception, the incidence of *trompe-l'oeil* pictures in the vicinity, etc., etc. And the conclusion to which this points is that experiential beliefs and beliefs about the world are *interdependent*.

It is the question of falsification of objective judgments that directly prompts Lewis to modify his theory and to compromise its one-directional character. But a closer look at his remarks about verification reveals that a similiar pull is at work there. For Lewis realizes that, granted only that O

$\Leftrightarrow \{T_1, \ldots, T_n\}$, the confirmation afforded to O by any of the T_i will be so slight, given the infinity of the set, as to be practically negligible. (And on the revised account, less still.) The serious confirmation afforded to O by the verification of one of the T_i, he then explains, results, rather, from the *im*probability of the T_i given not-O. (If there is no doorknob in front of me, it is rather improbable that, given that I see what looks like a doorknob, when it seems to me that I reach out of my hand, I will touch what feels like a doorknob.) What this amounts to is: if not-O, then, given certain further assumptions, not-T_i. Verification of T_i improves the probability of O to the extent that those further assumptions are themselves probable. Once again, the further assumptions will not, generally, be themselves purely experiential.

'[D]irect inspection of cognitive experience', by Lewis's own admission, makes an up-and-back picture of mutual support among experiential and objective beliefs more plausible than the one-directional account that Lewis officially offers. Thesis (3), I conclude, is false.

But it will be worthwhile to linger long enough to show that Lewis can achieve a *desideratum* to which he attaches considerable importance— avoiding phenomenalism—only by giving up the one-directional picture; for this will lead naturally to some more positive remarks, in the last section, about experiential versus objective beliefs. Lewis's requirement that terminating judgments be construed as subjunctive and not material conditionals (which was what gave rise to the trouble over their verification) is motivated by his belief that in this way he can avoid phenomenalism (pp. 214ff.). In virtue of his original account of the sense-meaning of objective statements, however, Lewis commits himself to the view that statements about physical objects are reducible to statements about experience—and thus, in the usual meaning of that term, to phenomenalism. Requiring the conditional to be subjunctive only means the reduction is one which relies on an appeal to possible as well as to actual experiences. Why, then, does Lewis believe his account to be realist? I think the explanation is this. On a realist view (as Lewis understands it) there are physical objects which we can experience, but which exist independently of our experience of them. This idea is expressible, Lewis suggests, in the form 'If such-and-such observation should be made, so-and-so would be experienced (and this is true even if observation is not made)' (p. 126). And so, he concludes, his insistence on a subjunctive conditional makes his account safely realist. But, in fact, his conditional is not of the right kind; it is subjunctive, all right, but its antecedent concerns, not the test *actually* made, but the test *apparently* made. It is, for instance, '(Given that I see what looks like a doorknob in front of me) *if it were to seem to me that I reached out my hand directly ahead*, it would seem to me that I touched a doorknob'; not '(Given that I see what looks like a doorknob in front of me) *if I were to reach out my hand directly ahead*, it would seem to me that I touched a doorknob'. (If the difference is not clear, perhaps it will become so if I point out that Lewis's subjunctive conditional could be true even if there were no doorknob, provided the illusion to which I was subject was sufficiently systematic.) Lewis is very careless about how he expresses the 'A' part of his terminating judgments, more often than not writing 'If I were to do A' rather than 'If it were to seem to me that I do A'; no doubt it is because of this sloppiness that he wrongly believes that adopting a subjunctive conditional will enable him to avoid phenomenalism. (Cf. my 'as he puts it' on p. 234 above.)

So long as Lewis sticks to the original account of the relation between objective judgments and terminating judgments, he is committed to phenomenalism. Once, however, he shifts to the revised account—the account which admits mutual dependence—he avoids this commitment. There is, the revised account concedes, no way to isolate the experiential content of a single objective judgment, taken by itself.

Empiricism Without Theses (1)–(3)

Lewis thinks that empiricism—acknowledgment of the crucial role played by experience in our knowledge of the world—obliges one to accept a foundationalist theory in which absolutely privileged beliefs about sensory experience are the ultimate basis for all our empirical knowledge. I have argued, against Lewis, that beliefs about one's immediate experience are not absolutely privileged, i.e. not T-certain or J-certain; and that it is not necessary, in order that empirical knowledge be possible at all, that there be such absolutely privileged beliefs. (This is the fallibilist strand of my argument.) Rather, I have argued, the beliefs that Lewis thinks are absolutely privileged get their justification, like the rest, in part from experience and in part from the support of other beliefs. (This is the 'up and back' strand of my argument.)

However, I agree with Lewis that sensory experience *is* crucial to our knowledge of the world, though I disagree with him about how this crucial role is played. Though all beliefs, according to me, depend for their justification partly on experience and partly on the support of other beliefs, some get relatively more of their justification from experience and relatively less of their justification from other beliefs. (This is the inegalitarian strand of my argument.) Some beliefs are, so to speak, relatively but not absolutely privileged. The most privileged, according to me, are those beliefs most directly prompted by experience, which depend most on experience and least on other beliefs. And these are generally not beliefs about one's experience, but beliefs about the world—'There's a sheet of white paper', not 'I now see what looks like a sheet of white paper', which, according to me, is relatively theoretical. (These are the naturalistic and physicalistic strands of my argument.)

In a sense, I think, I may justifiably claim to be, not only no less, but actually *more* of an empiricist than Lewis. For the very arguments that lead me to reject his foundationalist theory of empirical knowledge also lead me to be sceptical of the distinction between empirical and *a priori* knowledge which he takes for granted. Lewis distinguishes linguistic meaning (the implication relations among sentences) from sense meaning (the relations between sentences and experiences) (p. 37). His theory of sense meaning is, in effect, an attempt to characterize, atomistically, the experiential content of sentences. My critique of that theory—of Lewis's account of the relations between expressive judgments and terminating judgments, on the one hand, and terminating judgments and objective judgments, on the other—suggests a more holistic picture which undermines the sense meaning/linguistic meaning distinction. Or, to put the point in another way: all one's beliefs connect both with experience and with other beliefs; and just as none are entirely free of the rest, none are entirely free, either, of experience.

Of course, to make this point out with due care would be a large task indeed, and not one I can undertake here. But it is worthwhile to point out that there are strong affinities between my critiques of Lewis's theory of sense meaning, and Quine's critique, in 'Two Dogmas', of atomistic reductionism. My comments in the last paragraph are intended in the same spirit as Quine's observation that the two dogmas of 'Two Dogmas' (i.e. atomistic reductionism and the analytic/synthetic distinction) are 'at root, identical'.[22]

Lewis, indeed, is one of the philosophers whom Quine criticizes in 'Two Dogmas'. But Quine also mentions Locke, Hume, Tooke, Bentham and Carnap as all belonging to the same admirably empiricist, but regrettably atomist, tradition. This observation puts me in a position to make, by way of postscript, a tiny contribution to an issue to which Professor Singer has asked his lecturers to give attention: the question of what, if anything, is distinctively American about the American philosophers they discuss. One might count Pragmatism as, so to speak, a characteristically American contribution to the empiricist tradition, as one might count Logical Positivism as a characteristically Viennese contribution. Lewis describes himself, and is usually classified, as a Pragmatist; so it is here that one might look for an answer to Professor Singer's question. (There are, indeed, some notable contrasts between Lewis and, say, Peirce; for example, between Lewis's insistence on distinguishing cosmological speculation, which he regards as illegitimate for philosophy, from 'reflective metaphysics', which he regards as legitimate, and Peirce's insistence that only 'scientific' metaphysics' is meaningful. But Lewis certainly is like other Pragmatists in important ways; for instance, in stressing the connec-

[22] W. V. O. Quine, *From a Logical Point of View*, 41.

tion between knowledge and action ('knowing is for the sake of doing' (p. 3)); and, as I have already observed, in his account of the relation between objective judgments and terminating judgments, his version of the Pragmatic Maxim of meaning.) However, from the point of view of the epistemological issues that have concerned me here, Pragmatism and Positivism are, I think, very much alike.[23] The criticisms I have made of Lewis's foundationalism could also have been made, *mutatis*, of course, *mutandis*, of, say, Carnap's.[24] (It might be pointed out that Peirce seemed, at least sometimes, to appreciate the need for a less atomistic, more holistic approach in epistemology; it might also be pointed out that Neurath did, too.) In short, from the point of view of the issues I have taken up, I see nothing more distinctively American in Lewis's philosophy than his description (p. 264) of our empirical knowledge as 'an Empire State Building made out of toothpicks'.

---

[23] Lewis discusses the relations between Pragmatism and Positivism in 'Logical Positivism and Pragmatism' (1941) in *Collected Papers*, J. Goheen and J. L. Motherhead, Jr (eds) (Stanford University Press, 1970), 92–112; cf. his reply to W. H. Hay in Schilpp.

[24] R. Carnap, *The Logical Structure of the World* (1982), trans. R. A. George (Routledge and Kegan Paul, 1967).

The Moral Individualism of Henry David Thoreau

DAVID L. NORTON

Henry Thoreau boasted that he was widely travelled in Concord, Massachusetts. He was born there on 12 July 1817, and he died there on 6 May 1862, of tuberculosis, at the age of forty-four years. In 1837 he graduated from Harvard College, and in 1838 he joined Ralph Waldo Emerson, Margaret Fuller, and others in the informal group that became known as the New England Transcendentalists. The author of four books, many essays and poems, and a voluminous journal, he is best known for the book *Walden* and the essay 'Civil Disobedience', and for the circumstances attending these two milestones in American thought and literature.

In 1845, at the age of twenty-eight, he removed himself by two miles from Concord to live alone for two years in a cabin he had built on the edge of a pine woods beside Walden Pond, There he completed first drafts of his books *A Week on the Concord and Merrimack Rivers* and *Walden,* wrote some lectures for the New England Lyceum circuit, kept his journal, and refined the skills of observation and meditation on nature that were to earn him recognition as a leading American naturalist and forerunner of the conservation and ecological movements. But most of all, there he led his life as he chose to live it, and he chose to live it in search of himself. The two years beside Walden Pond were given by Thoreau to the task of self-discovery.

Early in the second year, on a trip to the Concord shoemaker, Thoreau was arrested for refusing to pay his poll tax (a Massachusetts head tax on all males between the ages of twenty and seventy). His single night in jail was made famous by his essay, 'Civil Disobedience', which strongly influenced Mohandas Gandhi, and stands as one of the most provocative pieces in Western literature on the relations of the individual and the state.

In Thoreau's case the philosophy and the life are so closely connected that it is impossible to speak of one without the other. This is so because Thoreau believed *example* to be the best teaching and the ultimate test of philosophy. For this reason he is little inclined to the *argumentation* that today is the leading characteristic (some would say the sole preoccupation) of philosophy. He said of his own time, 'There are nowadays professors of philosophy, but not philosophers. Yet it is admirable to profess because it was once admirable to live. To be a philosopher is not merely to have subtle thoughts, nor even to found a school, but so to love wisdom as to live in accordance with its dictates, a life of simplicity, independence, magnanimity, and trust. It is to solve some of the problems of life, not only theoretically, but practically.'[1] For Thoreau 'philosophy' was not deserving of the name if it did not directly or indirectly deal with the vexed problems of ordinary life, and the true test of a philosophy was not its ability to deflect counter-arguments invented *in abstracto*, but the experiment of living upon it with close attention to the results.

Thoreau himself was engaged at experimentation lifelong, thereby exhibiting in himself a trait that has prominence in the American character. Likewise his individualism, his independence, his insistent emphasis upon rebirth and re-beginning, and his endorsement of what may be termed the 'principle of multiple chances' are features of what have been recognized worldwide, whether with favour or disfavour, as the distinctive American character, and accordingly Thoreau's philosophy is distinctively American. It is possible, of course, that this limits its relevance. But it is no less possible that it thereby expresses aspects of human nature generally that 'the American experience' notably manifests, and can contribute to the self-understanding of mankind at large.

My thesis is that all of these traits combine in Thoreau's answer to what was for him the central question of philosophy, namely, 'What constitutes a worthy life for the human being?' But as I am obliged by the clock to limit my remarks I shall concentrate on what surely is Thoreau's most striking characteristic—his independence.

The United States began with a Declaration of Independence which was presumably once and for all, but Thoreau embodied that beginning in his own re-beginning by declaring his own independence, and by doing so every day of his mature life. It is instructive to notice what he declared his independence from.

His first public declaration was made at the age of twenty-three, when he refused to pay a church tax, and filed a statement with the selectmen of Concord, saying, 'Know all men by these presents, that I, Henry Thoreau, do not wish to be regarded as a member of any incorporated society which I have not joined'.[2] And he informed the selectmen that if they would provide him with a list of all the societies he had never joined, he would sign a specific denial of membership in each one of them.

He declared his independence of Concord and its residents by moving into the cabin he had built at Walden Pond and living there for two years. To emphasize the point he announced from there, 'I live in the angle of a leaden wall, into whose composition was poured a little alloy of bell metal.

[1] Henry D. Thoreau, 'Economy', *Walden,* J. Lyndon Shanley (ed.) (Princeton: Princeton University Press, 1971), 14–15.

[2] *The Writings of Henry David Thoreau*, 'Walden' edition (Boston: Houghton, Mifflin, 1906), IV, 374–375.

Often, in the repose of the midday, there reaches my ears a confused *tintinnabulum* from without. It is the noise of my contemporaries.'[3]

He declared his independence of conventional possessions and of such public utilities as railroads, mail service, telegraph, and newspapers, contending that our possessions possess us instead, and a person ought to travel light. 'If you are a seer', he says, 'whenever you meet a man you will see all that he owns, ay, and much that he pretends to disown, behind him, even to his kitchen furniture and all the trumpery which he saves and will not burn, and he will appear to be harnessed to it and making what headway he can.'[4]

Provoked by his government's complicity in slavery and its conduct of an unjust war on Mexico, Thoreau not only declared his independence of it but turned the tables and proclaimed the state's dependence on him. 'There will never be a really free and enlightened State,' he argues, 'until the State comes to recognize the individual as a higher and independent power, from which all its own power and authority are derived, and treats him accordingly.'[5]

Doubtless this is enough to establish independence as Thoreau's most conspicuous characteristic, but it is only the beginning.

In religion he declared his independence of the deep-rooted Calvinism of New England, and especially its doctrine of Original Sin, by insisting upon man's aboriginal innocence and the responsibility of each individual to recover it.[6] And though he remained a theist of a sort, he declared his independence of God by announcing, 'If by trusting in God, you lose any particle of your vigor, trust in him no longer'.[7]

He violently declared his independence of tradition as such, saying, 'Old deeds for old people, and new deeds for new', and 'Age is not better, hardly so well, qualified for an instructor as youth, for it has not profited so much as it has lost.' Or again, 'One generation abandons the enterprises of another like stranded vessels'.[8]

---

[3] *Walden*, 'Conclusion', 329.

[4] *Walden*, 'Economy', 66.

[5] Henry D. Thoreau, 'Resistance to Civil Government', in *Reform Papers*, Wendell Glick (ed.) (Princeton: Princeton University Press, 1973), 89. The essay is better known as 'Civil Disobedience', the title it received in a collection of Thoreau's essays published four years after his death, and I have used that title in the body of the text.

[6] An excellent study of this is R. W. B. Lewis, *The American Adam* (Chicago: University of Chicago Press, 1955), especially Ch. 1 and 2.

[7] Henry D. Thoreau, *Journal*, John C. Broderick (gen. ed.) (Princeton: Princeton University Press, 1981), I, 235. I have modified punctuation in the interest of readability. Idiosyncratic punctuation in the *Journal* was modified by Thoreau himself when preparing *Journal* segments for publication.

[8] *Walden*, 'Economy', 8, 9, 11.

David L. Norton

And he even declares his independence of his past self, and advises us to do likewise. This is the meaning of his celebration of 'morning' in *Walden*. 'The morning', he says, 'which is the most memorable season of the day, is the awakening hour. Then there is least somnolence in us . . .'[9] Morning is his great symbol of rebirth and re-generation, though he often uses such images as the moulting of birds ('Our molting season, like that of the fowls, must be a crisis in our lives'[10]) and the sloughing of skins by reptiles. For Thoreau, morning is the opportunity of a fresh start, and to this effect he quotes an Eastern sage: 'Renew thyself completely each day; do it again, and again, and forever again'.[11]

More than anything else it is Thoreau's insistence on personal independence that has induced some readers to dimiss him as a crank. Indeed, one of his contemporaries, a man named Isaac Hecker, grumbled that he was so 'consecrated' a crank that he 'would rather be crank than president'.[12]

But Thoreau was not a crank but a philosopher (and if the categories sometimes overlap, I want to show that they do not so, at any rate to the detriment of philosophy, in Thoreau's case). We can see this if we avoid hasty misconceptions and find the true place of independence in Thoreau's conception of worthy living. He is not recommending a solitary and self-sufficient life. He indeed advocates solitude, not, however, as a way of life, but as instrumental to the self-discovery that he takes to be the responsibility of every person. In the beginning, as he says, 'We belong to the community',[13] by which he means we are creatures of the community and do the community's bidding for we know no other. With self-discovery we come into possession of a principle for guidance from within ourselves. Yet we are not severed from the community but belong to it no less, though in a different sense. For now we begin to contribute to the community, not according to its dictates, but out of ourselves. 'Use me then', Thoreau says, 'for I am useful in my way, and stand as one of many petitioners, from toadstool and henbane up to dahlia and violet, supplicating to be put to my use, if by any means ye may find me serviceable.'[14] Indeed, he may seem almost to retract his individualism when he says, 'I have no private good, unless it be my peculiar ability to serve the public. This is the only individual property.'[15] Yet it glints in the phrase, *'my peculiar ability* to serve the public', as also in 'I am useful *in my way'*. Each person is meant to

[9] *Walden*, 'Where I Lived and What I Lived For', 89.
[10] *Walden*, 'Economy', 24.
[11] *Walden*, 'Where I Lived and What I Lived For', 88.
[12] *Journal*, I, 587.
[13] *Walden*, 'Economy', 46.
[14] Henry D. Thoreau, *A Week on the Concord and Merrimack Rivers*, Carl F. Hovde, William L. Howarth and Elizabeth Hall Witherell (eds) (Princeton: Princeton University Press, 1980), 287.
[15] *Journal*, I, 393.

242

be useful, not for any or every purpose, but in his or her distinctive way, and is responsible for discovering and perfecting that way. To discover and perfect our way is what Thoreau refers to as 'our business'.[16]

We begin to understand Thoreau's 'independence' aright when we recognize that, having achieved it, he uses it to re-establish relations with everything he has divorced himself from, but in new terms. Here is the crucial and profound death and rebirth of which Thoreau's morning rebirths are reaffirmations. 'Not until we are lost', he says, 'in other words, not till we have lost the world do we begin to find ourselves, and realize where we are and the *infinite extent of our relations*.'[17] The world that we must lose is the inherited world which has conferred a self upon us, but the self we discover newly relates us to the world in original terms.

The tradition Thoreau castigates is mindlessly inherited tradition, and he extricates himself from it in order to choose himself and thereby choose his meaningful tradition. Likewise the identity he leaves behind is the identity conferred upon him by his inherited tradition, and he does so in the interest of self-discovery and self-identification. And subsequently the distance that he each morning places between himself and the self he has been is not to deny responsibility for his previous self, but to exercise the responsibility of self-criticism in the interest of moral growth by choosing what of his prior self he will continue to identify with.

But is it possible to thus separate ourselves from these things that sociology and psychology tell us are constitutive of the persons we are— from society and convention and government and tradition—even though the separation be only provisional and for the purpose of re-establishing our relations upon a new footing?

It has been said that to move the world one must have a place to stand and to provide the fulcrum for one's lever. Thoreau's standing-place is his presupposition that all persons by the nature of personhood are innately invested with unique potential worth. He terms this unique potentiality a person's 'genius', and regards it as that person's 'reality' or true self, which his actual self may or may not reflect. In childhood one's distinctive potentially is merely latent, and children are dependent upon parents and teachers not only to learn the language and beliefs of their community, but for their very identities. But subsequent to childhood, in the stage of life we term adolescence and for which Thoreau employed the metaphor of the 'spring' of life, some inklings of an identity beneath the conferred identity of childhood are felt, and it is in this 'season' of life that responsibility for self-discovery appears. According to Thoreau self-discovery can only occur experimentally, and it consists in the discovery, not of an idea of

[16] E.g 'Life Without Principle', in *Reform Papers*, 159.
[17] *Walden*, 'The Village', 171. (My emphasis.)

ourselves, but of what 'rightfully attracts'[18] (and rightfully repels) us. In short our 'genius' or innate self subsists as a system of preferences and aversions. The difficulty is that our childhood enculturation has been a training in what to prefer and to disprefer, and therefore self-discovery must work its way beneath our layers of enculturation. It is to indicate this that Thoreau employs the imagery on one hand of 'husks' and 'rinds', and on the other of digging and burrowing. Thus, 'My instinct tells me that my head is an organ for burrowing', or again, 'Let us settle ourselves, and work and wedge our feet downward through the mud and slush of opinion, and prejudice, and tradition, and delusion, and appearance . . . til we come to a hard bottom'.[19]

This 'hard bottom' is our genius, which sets for each of us the moral work that is, according to Thoreau, our first responsibility—the work of progressively actualizing our distinctive potential worth. When Thoreau says, 'Let everyone mind his own business, and endeavor to be what he was made',[20] it is this primary moral business that he is referring to. It is by no means a selfish business for by attending to it we actualize in the world objective worth, which is to say it will be of worth, not alone or primarily to the person who actualizes it, but to others as well. 'Just so sacred and rich as my life is to myself', Thoreau says, 'so it will be to another.'[21] Indeed, Thoreau identifies the life lived according to its genius as the foundational form of gift-giving, and says, 'Be sure that you give men *the best* of your wares, though they be poor enough, and the gods will help you lay up a better store for the future'.[22]

But it is difficult business, and not least because everyone who has the scantiest acquaintance with us thinks they know better than we what we ought to be doing. This is the obstacle of convention, and Thoreau presents it in the form of an anecdote. 'There is a coarse and boisterous money-making fellow in the outskirts of our town, who is going to build a bank-wall under the hill along the edge of his meadow. The powers have put this into his head to keep him out of mischief, and he wishes me to spend three weeks digging there with him. The result will be that he will perhaps get some more money to hoard and leave for his heirs to spend foolishly. If I do this, most will commend me as an industrious and hard-working man; but if I choose to devote myself to certain labors which yield more real profit, though but little money, they may be inclined to look on me as an idler.'[23]

[18] *Walden*, 'Conclusion', 330.
[19] *Walden*, 'Where I Lived and What I Lived For', 98, 97–98.
[20] *Walden*, 'Conclusion', 326.
[21] *Journal*, I, 390.
[22] Ibid., 230.
[23] 'Life Without Principle', *Reform Papers*, 156.

But the greatest difficulty is that of discovering one's genius, or innate self. Some thinkers have gone so far as assert its impossibility on the ground that the self, whose business it is to know other things, cannot for that very reason know itself. But this is pure sophistry, for it first says what the self is, and then says that because this is what it is it cannot be known for what it is. The difficulty as identified by Thoreau has already been mentioned. It is that the innate preferences and aversions that characterize the true self have been overlain by the trained preferences and aversions of dependent childhood. These trained preferences and aversions constitute a conferred identity, and the independence that Thoreau so vigorously sought is independence of this conferred identity in order to realize his innate identity, thereupon to re-establish relations with the world. To meet this difficulty Thoreau devises a carefully articulated strategy of self-discovery. Each of its elements is associated with a key word in Thoreau's writings. 'Genius' is one of them, and 'morning' is another, but no less important are 'simplicity', 'economy', 'solitude', 'nature', 'innocence', and 'reality'. We shall direct our attention to these key terms, endeavouring to uncover Thoreau's meaning and to exhibit their interrelations.

Solitude, for example, is a clear feature of Thoreau's strategy, and typically he gave it colourful exemplification in his own life by retreating to Walden Pond for two years. (On the question of why Thoreau distanced himself just a short two miles from Concord, Stanley Cavell notes that 'It was just far enough to be seen clearly'.[24]

But solitude is for Thoreau a purely instrumental value, not an intrinsic one, nor is it the intractable human condition. We find no hint in his writings of existentialism's lament (or self-congratulation) at being 'doomed to solitariness'. The function of solitude is to still the voices of others in order to hear one's own inner voice, and the need for it lies in the fact that one's own voice, in the beginning, is tentative and timid, hence impossible to hear in the self-confident clamour of the social world. But physical solitude is neither necessary nor sufficient for the instrumental solitude that self-discovery requires. It is not sufficient because we internalize the voices of others and, it may be, take them with us wherever we go. This is the substance of Thoreau's complaint at Walden of the bell-metal in his composition that resonates to the noisy tintinnabulum of his contemporaries. And Thoreau recognizes that it is not necessary in his observation that the 'really diligent student in one of the crowded hives of Cambridge College is as solitary as a dervish in the desert'.[25]

Thoreau's ingenuity appears in his advice that instrumental solitude can be found in novel experience. Novel experience is experience with respect to which we have not been preconditioned—trained in what to think and

[24] Stanley Cavell, *The Senses of Walden* (New York: Viking Press, 1972), 11.
[25] *Walden*, 'Solitude', 135.

feel—in our dependent years. It therefore affords us what Thoreau means by recovered 'innocence'—not moral innocence, but innocence of convention in a return to our nature. It is a return because of course our nature was with us in the beginning of our lives, subsequently to be overlaid by convention. But in the beginning we were unable to recognize or enact it. By contrast our return to our nature subsequent to our enculturation is marked by our abilities to recognize and enact ourselves. It is true that these abilities are themselves partly the products of enculturation, but this does not catch Thoreau up in contradiction as some critics have supposed.[26] Rather it demonstrates that Thoreau did not foolishly oppose all convention, but only certain conventions, namely those conventions that induce individuals to falsify their natures.

Novel experience elicits from us novel responses, and these novel responses provide the materials amid which we can profitably seek what 'rightfully attracts' (and rightfully repels) us.

When my younger brother reached adolescence he took up three avid interests at approximately two-year intervals. The first was photography, the second was bowling, and the third was weight-lifting. Abstractly considered, it would be hard to find a relation among the three, but they are alike in that no one in our household had the least acquaintance with any of them, and they thus afforded my brother novel experience, untrodden ground for exploration, effective solitude.

Thoreau cannily refines the technique of novelty by his use of constructive imagination. Imagination is the antidote to the parochialism of habituation in conditioned perceptions and conditioned responses; it is our capacity to exchange perspectives upon the world and ourselves, perceiving things in novel aspect. It is what enables Thoreau to say, 'The aspects of the most simple object are as various as the aspects of the most compound'.[27] And it is the lack of the incorporation of imagination into daily life that Thoreau bemoans when he says, 'Our limbs indeed have room enough but it is our souls that rust in a corner. Let us migrate interiorly without intermission, and pitch our tent each day nearer the western horizon . . .'[28] It will be evident that Thoreau follows the Romantics, and especially such of the English romantics as Blake, Coleridge and Wordsworth, in attributing to imagination the ability to apprehend truth, but Thoreau remains an individualist, and in consequence truth remains perspectival, each person's truths differing from others' and, ideally, complementing the truths of others. But what Thoreau may be said to

[26] Beginning with James Russell Lowell, 'Thoreau', in *Thoreau, A Century of Criticism*, Walter Harding (ed.) (Dallas: Southern Methodist University Press, 1954); see p. 52.
[27] *Journal*, I, 310.
[28] Ibid., 119.

have done for the Romantic imagination is to have provided it with solid practical application, namely to the problem of self-discovery.

The advantage of imagination with respect to the task of self-discovery is that it obviates the need to go in search of novelty by casting the familiar in novel light. Thus Thoreau, as a master of constructive imagination, adventures continuously on home ground, where others somnambulate. Who but he could say, for example, that 'One value of even the smallest well is, that when you look into it you see that the earth is not continent but insular. This is as important as that it keeps butter cool.'[29] He puts the same capacity to work in connection with a farm he proposes to buy when he expresses pleasure at 'the gray and ruinous state of the house and barn, and the dilapidated fences', because they 'put such an interval between me and the last occupant'.[30] And this capacity is on full display in 'Civil Disobedience', when he cites the advantages afforded him by his night in jail. 'It was like traveling into a far country, such as I had never expected to behold, to lie there for one night. It seemed to me that I had never heard the town clock strike before, nor the evening sounds of the village . . . It was to see my native village in the light of the Middle Ages, and our Concord was turned into a Rhine stream, and visions of knights and castles passed before me. They were the voices of old burghers that I heard in the streets. I was an involuntary spectator and auditor of whatever was done and said in the kitchen of the adjacent village inn—a wholly new and rare experience for me. It was a closer view of my native town. I was fairly inside of it. I had never seen its institutions before . . . I began to comprehend what its inhabitants were about.'[31]

This last citation affords concrete illustration of the relation of imagination to the 'economy' to which Thoreau gives so much emphasis. 'Economy' has several levels of meaning in Thoreau's usage, but at the deepest level it means, in Thoreau's terms, 'to affect the quality of the day'.[32] Living worthily entails the conservation of value, and this requires of us the ability to recognize the possibilities of value-actualization that each day, indeed each hour and moment present. What the jail episode shows is that even the most conventionally unpromising situations afford such opportunities. If they do not do so when viewed conventionally, then imagination can be called upon to reveal their hidden possibilities. In sum, there are no axiologically barren situations to the imagination that can disclose their multiple aspects.

One of Thoreau's persistent detractors, James Russell Lowell, says of Thoreau's writing style that he 'turns common places end for end, and

---

[29] *Walden*, 'Where I Lived and What I Lived For', 87.
[30] Ibid., 83.
[31] 'Resistance to Civil Government', *Reform Papers*, 82.
[32] *Walden*, 'Where I Lived and What I Lived For', 90.

fancies he makes something new of them'.[33] Thus Lowell displays his blindness to the important work that Thoreau assigns to imagination.

Earlier we noted Mohandas Gandhi's expressed indebtedness to some of Thoreau's writings, and especially to 'Civil Disobedience'. When Gandhi was jailed he turned to his writing, and thanked his captors for the relief from distraction that jail provided him. When writing materials were denied him he thanked his captors for the opportunity to discourse with fellow prisoners, persons whom he otherwise would not have met. And when he was placed in solitary confinement, he thanked his captors for the opportunity to meditate. Had he been executed, surely his voice would have been audible from the beyond, thanking his executioners for the move that assured victory for his cause.

But we have departed from Thoreau's strategy for self-discovery and are speaking of the life that is lived on the basis of self-discovery. We can conveniently return to the strategy by looking for the place of 'economy' in it.

In the 'Economy' chapter of *Walden*, Thoreau says, 'My greatest skill has been to want but little'.[34] On the strength of it Thoreau found that he could sustain himself by working just six weeks in the year, thereby conserving time and energy for his 'business', which at this time was the business of self-discovery. But economy in Thoreau's deepened meaning has a more direct bearing upon self-discovery, for together with learning to want but little we must learn to want the right things. In this interest he admonishes us to 'Simplify, simplify'.[35] His meaning of simplicity here is absence of complexity, and the reason for his admonition is that complexity obscures and distracts. His supposition is that prior to self-discovery our wants are conventional wants and our possessions are conventional possessions, and he proposes to us the experiment of seeing what we will be better off by doing without. The ignorant omnivorousness that wants everything and proclaims itself as entitled to anything as anyone else is the product of ignorance of self, and is debilitating. When by experiment we discover what, among our possessions and wants, we are better off without, we have taken a step toward self-discovery; we are learning what we have advertently or inadvertently identified with, at cost to ourselves. And at the same time we will be clearing the ground for discovery of our true needs, which consist in those things that are required for the actualization of our distinctive genius. The principle here is 'no waste of potential value'; do not desire or own things whose potential values you cannot actualize, or whose potential values you can only actualize at cost to your self-actualization. The discovery of our true needs is self-discovery.

[33] James Russell Lowell, 'Thoreau', in Harding, *Thoreau, A Century of Criticism*, 47.

[34] *Walden*, 'Economy', 69.

[35] *Walden*, 'Where I Lived and What I Lived For', 91.

In this connection Thoreau amusingly twits the person who has an extensive wardrobe by pointing out that no item of clothing is worn often enough to acquire the virtue of conforming to the owner's body.[36] (I think here of us men who teach ourselves to sit carefully in our newly pressed trousers, deftly plucking at each knee to preserve the crease. Thus we dance to the tune of our dry-cleaners. I leave women to enumerate their comparable concessions.) Of course clothing is cited by Thoreau in part symbolically: it is the activities that compromise our lifestyle that must fit, and what they must fit is not our bodies but that innate potentiality for character of a certain sort that Thoreau terms our genius.

In Thoreau's strategy we have related 'economy' to 'simplicity' in the meaning of 'absence of complexity'. But simplicity has for Thoreau a second meaning that connects it to 'Nature', namely as 'absence of duplicity'.

By 'Nature' Thoreau oftenest refers to the phenomena of the world exclusive of man and his effects. Thus he says, 'I love nature partly *because* she is not man, but a retreat from him. None of his institutions control or pervade her.'[37] In this usage he is contrasting nature's 'simplicity' (which he sometimes terms 'innocence') with the duplicity of human beings. Distinctively, man is the being who can and regularly does misrepresent himself. In him there is a slip-plane between surface and depth, appearance and reality, such that the face he presents to others is as likely to belie as to express his inner state. Against this trees, rivers, clouds, lakes, flowers, and animals present themselves exactly for what they are. (It is not nature that deceives us, but we who deceive ourselves if we suppose that the stick which appears bent in the water will appear the same way out of the water.)

With respect to self-discovery, when a person is seeking the truth in himself it is honest company he should keep, and he will find it in nature. His tutelage in integrity will be found in the kinship with nature that Thoreau expresses when he says, 'Every little pine needle expanded and swelled with sympathy and befriended me'.[38] This is not hollow sentimentality but advantageous insight. Nor is it sentimentality when Thoreau ascribes 'innocence' to 'the fox, and skunk, and rabbit'.[39] Is he heedless of 'nature, red of tooth and claw'? Does not the fox prey on the rabbit? To be sure, but what Thoreau notices is that the fox does not prey on the rabbit under the guise of serving the rabbit's true interests. By his use of the term 'innocence' Thoreau means simplicity in our present sense. He cannot be

---

[36] *Walden*, 'Economy', 21–22.

[37] Journal entry for 3 January 1853, cited in Walter Harding, *The Days of Henry Thoreau* (New York: Alfred A. Knopf, 1965), 329.

[38] *Walden*, 'Solitude', 132.

[39] Ibid., 129, 131.

supposed to attribute moral virtue to Nature, for the condition of choice is lacking. But there is moral virtue in a human being who, by choice, overcomes his duplicitousness and achieves the simplicity we term integrity.

Critics have charged that the so-called 'nature-worship' of the Romantics is parochial, for the Romantics knew only a tamed and domesticated nature. By the time of Blake, Coleridge, and Wordsworth, England was a veritable park, and if the New England of Thoreau was not quite such, nevertheless it was nature in a form congenial to man. The implication is that the Romantics would have been totally disabused of their nature-workship, and indeed terrified, by the fetid tropics, the scorched Sahara, and the Arctic wastes. But I see no reason to suppose that this would be the case with Thoreau. It was not at bottom nature's beauty or benignity that attracted him, but—to repeat—her simplicity in the meaning of absence of duplicity. And this trait is no less evident in the Arctic, the desert, and the jungle. Some critics to the contrary notwithstanding, Thoreau is not the boy who pitches his tent in the back garden and runs for the house with the first rumblings of the thunderstorm.

It remains to speak briefly of the meaning of 'reality' in Thoreau's usage. 'Be it life or death', Thoreau says, 'we crave only reality. If we are really dying, let us hear the rattle in our throats and feel cold in the extremities; if we are alive, let us go about our business.'[40] Thoreau equates reality with nature, but this is a second and different usage of the term 'nature' in which human beings are included. Our nature is our innate self or genius, which is obscured by convention. Our recovery is effected in self-discovery, which is the discovery of our inmost nature, and for this, as previously noted, we require—or at least can be aided by—the honest company of nature, understood as the phenomena of the world exclusive of human beings and their effects, and therefore without duplicity. For human beings the reality of being alive is going about our business, which is first of all to discover ourselves as the distinctive individual we *in potentia* are, and thereafter to live in truth to ourselves, progressively actualizing our potential worth.

Thoreau is here relying upon the ancient Stoic and Epicurean distinction between nature and convention, *phusis* and *nomos*. It is man's nature to design for himself his patterns of living, and by living them in a sense to generate his own nature. But Thoreau terms the nature that man creates for himself by living the patterns of life that he designs, a 'second nature'.[41] Beneath it is his original nature, consisting in the innate genius or distinctive potential worth of each individual. The 'second nature' that we create

[40] *Walden*, 'Where I Lived and What I Lived For', 98.
[41] *Walden*, 'Economy', 12.

for ourselves ought, according to Thoreau, to express and perfect our original, given nature, but is as likely to falsify it.

If we were to supply examples of what Thoreau means by falsification, one of them might be the Victorian suppression of sexuality, which, according to studies of the period, produced in many individuals a repression of their own sexuality such that in some cases they became unaware of its existence.

Another ready example would be the traditional role-training of male and female children, aimed at preparing girls for a domestic and maternal life, and boys for making their way in the world. As is well known, many women today hold that such channelling, while certainly a form of development, is so constricted as to warp their natures and be fulfilling for only a few. Meanwhile boys are taught that to become men they must repress a wide range of feelings, and the suggestion today is that they are thus alienated from some feelings which are essential to full humanness.

Thoreau himself identified the conventional meaning of work as a serious falsification of nature, terming it 'one of the most extensive systems of counterfeiting that the world has seen'.[42] He offers in evidence that work is widely regarded as an unpleasant necessity which most persons would avoid if they could, and which most persons engage in solely for extrinsic rewards, i.e. for money. But in Thoreau's conception human beings are by nature active, and productively so, and the deepest intrinsic rewards of living are to be found in the work that is the right work for the given individual to do. The reason that many people envisage paradise as idle dalliance is that they have never experienced intrinsically rewarding work, and the reason in turn that they have not is that, historically, no attention has been given to the problem of matching individuals to the kind of work that each finds intrinsically rewarding to do. (To be sure Plato gave priority to just this problem in *The Republic*, but it is a utopian vision that has not found historical embodiment.) When the kind of work people as individuals do is left to chance, or to dire necessity, or (on the inspiration that launched the economic individualism of the modern world) to exclusively economic opportunity, the number of persons who discover their meaningful work will be so small as to have no effect upon the conventional understanding.

It is true that man is by nature the convention-making animal, but this does not dissolve the *nomos/phusis* distinction if we retain the idea that by nature persons have particular moral jobs to do, for conventions may then be judged according to whether they facilitate or obstruct this work. It is also true that every aspect of any 'second nature' that man may create for himself is the actualization of what was antecedently a possibility in man's nature, and so 'natural' in that sense. But all possibilities are not to be

---

[42] 'Life Without Principle', *Reform Papers*, 163.

actualized by any individual but rather particular possibilities are to be actualized by each, and convention, which is generalized habit, is incapable of making the particular determinations. By convention we do what is done by everyone, which is to say, by no one in particular; but according to Thoreau 'our business' is in the case of each of us a particular business, and must be found out for ourselves.

Evil possibilities indeed subsist in every person, but are no one's destiny. Initially all persons are, as Plato and Aristotle said, 'lovers of the good', and the evil will is a reactive phenomenon. When the initial aspiration to worthy living is thwarted, whether by the world or the individual's own ignorance or incapacity, it can be transformed into a pervasive resentment or hatred that speedily corrodes the initial enterprise. It was to empower the initial aspiration against this danger of corruption that Thoreau laboured to cultivate individual resourcefulness. *In extremis* his aim is apparent in his words, 'Tumble me down, and I will sit/Upon my ruins, smiling yet'.[43] Or in milder speech and circumstance, 'If we be quiet, and ready enough, we shall find compensation in every disappointment'.[44]

I have concentrated on Thoreau's strategy of self-discovery rather than his political views, or the social implications of his conception of personhood, or his prescription for living subsequent to self-discovery, because I believe that what is most original in his contribution to the problem of worthy living lies there. To the reader who remains unconvinced of Thoreau's basic premise, that all human beings possess innate genius, or in his words that 'There is a solid bottom everywhere', I will offer an anecdote told by Thoreau. 'We read that the traveler asked the boy if the swamp before him had a hard bottom. The boy replied that it had. But presently the traveller's horse sank in up to the girths, and he observed to the boy, "I thought you said this bog has a hard bottom". "So it has", answered the latter, "but you have not got half way to it yet."'[45]

For biographical material I am indebted (with all who study Thoreau) to Walter Harding, *The Days of Henry Thoreau* (New York: Alfred A. Knopf, 1965).

Suggested Reading in Thoreau

First *Walden*, which is Thoreau's literary masterpiece and contains much of his philosophy, his naturalism, and his close observation of unusual

[43] *Journal*, I, 98.
[44] *Journal*, I, 56.
[45] *Walden*, Conclusion', 330.

personalities. Then, perhaps, *A Week on the Concord and Merrimack Rivers*, and the splendid philosophical essay on work, 'Life Without Principle'. It is against this background that 'Civil Disobedience' can be properly understood. Then, it may be, such of Thoreau's masterful nature essays as 'Walking', 'Autumnal Tints', and 'Wild Apples'. And time spent with the *Journal* will markedly deepen the reader's understanding of Thoreau and his ideas.

The definitive scholarly edition of Thoreau's complete works is presently being published by Princeton University Press, with seven volumes (including much of the above) issued. Many of the important writings (though none of the *Journal*) are included in an inexpensive paperback, *The Portable Thoreau*, edited by Carl Bode, published in the US by Viking Press and in England by Penguin Books.

Stanley Cavell's book, *The Senses of Walden* (New York: Viking Press, 1972) is a sensitive and insightful study of the book *Walden* and of such of its leitmotives as rebirth and regeneration, and moral necessity. But its identification of Thoreau with the Hebrew prophets Jeremiah and Ezekiel seems strained to me. And whereas to Cavell, Thoreau was first of all a writer bent upon the 'redemption of language', I perceive him as above all bent upon the redemption of life through experiments in living.

American Legal Philosophy

RICHARD TUR

The critical legal studies movement has undermined the central ideas of modern legal thought and put another conception of law in their place (R. M. Unger, 'The Critical Legal Studies Movement', *Harvard Law Review* **96** (1983), 561, 563).

[W]hat we are witnessing is the birth of a distinctive form of legal discourse (B. A. Ackerman, *Reconstructing American Law* (London, 1984), 3).

Given statements like these about current developments in intellectualizing about law in America it is an exciting time to look at American legal philosophy. Given the ferment in the law schools and the volume of literature in the law journals it is also a difficult task confidently to extract the main lines of current thought and adequately to assess the significance of current intellectual movements. American lawyers are inclined to point out that there is no such thing as 'American law'. Rather, in addition to Federal law and the Supreme Court's jurisdiction there are some fifty jurisdictions each with its own Constitution, Legislature and Supreme Court and consequently diversity rather than uniformity is the rule. Equally, the very idea that there is some single, coherent and widely accepted theory of law deserving description as 'American legal philosophy' obviously begs all manner of significant questions.

None the less, through British eyes, a specifically American form of intellectualizing about law has long been apparent. This is widely known as American Realism and is, perhaps, widely misunderstood. The crucial point about American Realism is that '. . . there is no school of realists . . . no group with an official or accepted or even with an emerging creed . . . there is however a *movement* in thought and work about law'.[1] The common point of departure for members of the movement is '. . . skepticism as to some of the conventional legal theories, a skepticism stimulated by a zeal to reform, in the interests of justice, some court-house ways'.[2] I propose to take American Realism as the focal point for discussion, tracing its development out of earlier intellectualizing about

[1] K. Llewellyn, 'Some Realism About Realism', *Harvard Law Review* **44** (1931), 1222, 1234.
[2] J. Frank, *Law and The Modern Mind* (New York, 1930; English edn, London, 1949), Preface.

255

law and its relationship to general philosophical ideas abroad at the time. I shall try to give expression to the concerns of some leading participants in the movement and, finally, I shall try to locate current American jurisprudentializing in relation to this central movement. Current intellectualizing about law can be grouped roughly as follows: (1) Economic Analysis of Law;[3] (2) Critical Legal Studies;[4] (3) Constructivism,[5] although this list is not intended to be exhaustive.

I should add, by way of caution, that my treatment of the authors, movements and ideas referred to is necessarily impressionistic and simplificatory. To survey intellectualizing about law in America over the last 100 years in so limited a space of time forces one to occupy the high ground, to leap from one mountain peak to another and temporarily to disregard the rugged terrain over which a more painstaking explorer would move. Fortunately much of the landscape has been fairly fully mapped already by such explorers.[6] What I omit by way of detail is, therefore, readily available to those whose interest in American legal philosophy may be excited by the overview I present.

The starting point in my story is with the theories that America inherited along with the common law. 'English law was the only law that post-Revolutionary American lawyers knew anything about.'[7] That meant, above all, Blackstone's *Commentaries on the Laws of England* (1765–69). Blackstonian jurisprudence is a form of *a priori* rationalism and he represented the common law as an absent-minded achievement of perfected reason. Law, on this model, is a closed logical system admitting of water-tight syllogistic reasoning from major premises given in 'the immutable laws of nature'.[8] Historically, Blackstone's thought profoundly

[3] See R. Posner, *The Economic Analysis of Law*, 2nd edn (London, 1977); R. Posner, *The Economics of Justice* (London, 1981).

[4] See D. Kairys (ed), *The Politics of Law* (New York, 1982); R. M. Unger, *Knowledge and Politics* (New York, 1975); R. M. Unger, *Law in Modern Society* (New York, 1976); R. M. Unger, 'The Critical Legal Studies Movement', *Harvard Law Review*, **96** (1983), 563–675; A. Hunt, 'Critical Legal Studies: A Bibliography', *Modern Law Review* **47** (1984), 369–374.

[5] See B. A. Ackerman, *Social Justice in the Liberal State* (New Haven and London, 1980); B. A. Ackerman, *Reconstructing American Law* (Cambridge, Massachusetts and London, 1984).

[6] See W. E. Rumble, *American Legal Realism* (Ithaca, New York, 1968); W. Twining, *Karl Llewellyn and the Realist Movement* (London, 1973); T. Campbell, 'Adam Smith and the Economic Analysis of Law', in V. Hope (ed), *Philosophy of the Scottish Enlightenment* (Edinburgh, 1984), 133–156; D. Beyleveld and R. Brownsword, 'Critical Legal Studies', *Modern Law Review* **47** (1984), 359–369.

[7] G. Gilmore, *The Ages of American Law* (New Haven and London, 1974), 19.

[8] Blackstone, *Commentaries*, Bk I, 167.

influenced American law. His conception of the relationship of natural rights and positive law is embodied, albeit in a secularized form, in the Bill of Rights, and his style of thought was wholly congenial to the early American lawyers. Indeed, Blackstone's thought is not without relevance even today in understanding movements in intellectualizing about law.[9] None the less, for all its attractiveness at the highest level of philosophical abstraction, the theory simply did not fit the facts of legal systems in general and even of the English legal system of Blackstone's own day. Hegel remarks that 'when philosophy paints its grey in grey, then has a shape of life grown old'.[10] Arguably, Blackstone's account of English law was less a descriptively accurate construction but more a conservative attempt to freeze law in its contemporary shape in the face of dramatic and explosive social change brought about by the Industrial Revolution. If, indeed, the common law was the perfection of reason it should be preserved immune from reform because reform could only impoverish and diminish the perfect.

The only credible alternative to Blackstonian iusnaturalism in play at the time was what today we would certainly call Benthamite positivism but which in the history of legal ideas was primarily associated with John Austin. Positivism differed from iusnaturalism in that it presupposed no immutable natural laws nor any natural and imprescriptible rights. Bentham thought such to be 'nonsense on stilts'.[11] Law for these positivists was not intrinsically moral by nature and the most pernicious laws were still laws enforced by judicial tribunals.[12] Thus positivists looked to the pedigree of law and not to its context as a means to identify law. Bentham and Austin regarded the commands of the sovereign as law and proposed tests for the identification of the sovereign. It is well known that Austin had difficulty in identifying *the* sovereign even in the English legal system and that he entirely failed to locate sovereignty in the American legal system. Indeed the central notion that in every legal system there is an identifiable sovereign, one or number, indivisible and legally illimitable appears in historical context as a prescription borne of Bentham's evangelical zeal for codification rather than as an accurate description even when Austin (let alone Bentham) wrote his seminal work. In this, at least, I agree with Professor Posner who remarks that Bentham, in conscious opposition to

[9] See R. Posner, *The Economics of Justice*, Ch. 2; D. Kennedy, 'The Structure of Blackstone's Commentaries', *Buffalo Law Review* **28** (1979), 209; N. MacCormick, *Legal right and Social Democracy* (Oxford, 1982), Ch. 7.

[10] *Philosophy of Right*, trans. T. M. Knox (Oxford, 1952), 13.

[11] J. Bentham, 'A Critical Examination of the Declaration of Rights', in *Bentham's Political Thought*, B. Parekh (ed.), (London, 1973), 269.

[12] J. Austin, *The Province of Jurisprudence Determined* (first published in 1832; London, 1955), 184–185.

the common law, 'urged that all political power be vested in the House of Commons to expedite the translation of popular preferences, which he assumed would coincide with the greatest happiness principle, into legislative reform'.[13] Thus, 'finding the [existing] English system an obstacle to his ideas, he proposed to sweep it away and substitute a system in which power might be dangerously concentrated in a single branch'.[14]

Yet for all the radical and polemic opposition to Blackstone's jurisprudence emanating from Bentham and his intellectual followers, there were salient features in common. First, both schools of thought agree that law is primarily a matter of *general* rules. Secondly, although Benthamism radically separated the law as it is from the law as it ought to be, the Principle of Utility was taken as *the* criterion of good law and even (in John Austin's phrase) 'the index to God's will'.[15] Given the conviction that utilitarianism provided a rational and objective science of legislation (that is a science of values) intellectualizing about law would involve deductive reasoning from the principle of utility as major premise and statements of fact as minor premises to produce reform proposals as conclusions. Indeed had Bentham's obsession with codification ever been fulfilled the result would have been remarkably similar to the Blackstonian edifice with the significant substitution of the 'scientific' and immutable principle of utility for the 'metaphysical' and immutable laws of nature.

Finally, both approaches were not dissimilar as to the judicial role. Blackstone's judges were engaged in a declaratory exercise, stating what the common law is and always has been and they had no separate law-making function. Bentham roundly condemned 'Judge & Co.' who, in his view, made law for us as we would make law for our dogs, that is, wait until something bad occurs and then beat the beast for it.[16] John Austin revealed a rare touch of independence when he observed that judges made law better than legislatures.[17] Generally, however, Austin regarded judges as applying the sovereign's commands to particular facts and not as independent law-makers. Indeed, Austin regarded judicial law as indirectly the sovereign's law on the fictitious basis that what the sovereign permits, he commands. Ideally, however, in the Benthamite reconstruction of the legal universe judges would have no significant role to play, all questions being exhaustively pre-determined by the utilitarian code. Bentham's notion was that a clear and comprehensive code would conduce to every man being his own lawyer and therefore to a diminution of the 'sinister interest' of lawyers and the arbitrary whim of judges. If Bentham revered

---

[13] R. Posner, *The Economics of Justice*, 38.
[14] R. Posner, op. cit., 40.
[15] J. Austin, op. cit., 87.
[16] J. Bentham, *Works* (Bowring edn), V, 235.
[17] J. Austin, op. cit., 191.

Plato, it was not as the author of the *Republic* but as the author of the *Laws*.[18] Bentham's ideal judge would, in Montesquieu's phrase, be 'but the mouth which pronounces the words of the law'.[19] Taking these tendencies all in all, *both* Blackstonian and Benthamite theories fostered 'formalism', that is the view that law is a matter of logically precise deduction. Thus, together with the common law of England, America inherited the formalist notions inherent in the thought of the great intellectualizers of English law.

It would be wrong, however, to give too significant a place to the legal 'formalism' inherited from the intellectual tradition of English law. Other influences were at work. In economics, for example, *laissez faire* ruled. Philosophically that involved a highly formalist approach favouring *a priori* reasoning, logic and mathematics as against the empirical and experimental study of social phenomena. In legal education, the first Dean of Harvard Law School, Langdell, elected in 1870, adopted the notion that law is a 'science' but by this was meant that there is but one true law which, once discovered, endures, and that the appropriate mode of intellectualizing about law was the pursuit of 'fundamental legal doctrines' which Langdell believed to be 'much less [in number] than is commonly supposed.'[20] These 'fundamental legal doctrines' which could be gleaned from the study of the cases provided the basic propositions from which legal truths could be deduced. Langdell and his followers, however, were highly selective in the cases they relied on, taking the view that 'the vast majority are useless, worse than useless, for any purpose of systematic study'.[21] Such a cavalier attitude to the data of the law must strike a modern observer as radically unscientific and it could be sustained only by virtue of assuming general principles whose truth was prior to and independent of the data. These principles were to include Freedom of Contract, Private Property and Fault Liability, writ large and conceived of as absolutes. The case method, pioneered by Langdell, was, sadly, more sham than science and, just as Blackstone's account of law did not fit the facts of his day, so Langdell's so-called science of law simply ignored the diversity, flexibility and variety of American law as it actually was at the time.

The dominance of formalism in jurisprudence, economics, philosophy and legal education bred a uniquely American reaction which, without aspiring to too much philosophical precision, we may refer to as 'pragmat-

[18] In the *Republic*, Plato celebrates the intuitionistic judge who does justice without justice being susceptible of precise statement in rule or principle; in the *Laws*, he celebrates the opposite extreme, that is, the mechanical jurisprudence of a nomocracy.
[19] Montesquieu, *De l'esprit des lois* (1748; Vedel edn, Paris, 1964), Bk XI, Ch. 6.
[20] C. C. Langdell, *Cases on Contract* (Boston, 1871), Preface.
[21] Ibid.

ism'. James caught the central notions of the approach when he observed that it is a '... perfectly familiar attitude in philosophy, the empiricist attitude, but it represents it ... both in a more radical and a less objectionable form than it has even yet assumed; ... [it] turns away from abstractions ... bad *a priori* reasons, from fixed principles, closed systems and pretended absolutes. [It] turns towards concreteness, facts; ... [it] means the empiricist temper regnant and the rationalist temper sincerely given up ... it does not stand for any results ... it is a method only.'[22] The spirit of this American philosophy, born in the revolt against formalism, is intensely *practical*.

Put these observations into jurisprudential mood and at once one encounters the most significant American legal intellectualizer, Mr Justice Holmes. He stands like a colossus above all that follows in American legal philosophy.[23] Admire or despise him, one cannot ignore his contribution. Even Professor Gilmore, an unsympathetic commentator,[24] brackets *The Common Law* (1881) with Cardozo's *The Nature of the Judicial Process* (1921) as 'the two most celebrated books in the history of American jurisprudence'.[25] The pages of his seminal article, 'The Path of the Law' (1897) published in the *Harvard Law Review* are more thumbed and tattered than those of any other article I have read. One should not, of course, imagine that what came to be known as 'American Realism' sprang ready-armed from these works. None the less, several of the central concerns of the later participants in the Realist Movement were expressed first and forcibly by Holmes. He rejected the absolutes of the natural lawyer and with it the Blackstonian approach. He rejected the Austinian notion of sovereignty as ill-adapted to the complexities of the federal constitution and he regarded Langdell as 'the power of darkness [who] is all for logic and hates any reference to anything outside it'.[26] For Holmes, 'the life of the law has not been logic; it has been experience'.[27] He held that 'general propositions do not decide particular cases'.[28] In short, he opposed the idea that law was an ideal entity embodying *a priori* values and principles which were susceptible of syllogistic reasoning to conclusions. He thought that prophecies of what the court will do in fact is what law is about and he was more interested in what the court will decide than in the abstract arguments or deductions presented by the traditional approach.

[22] W. James, *Pragmatism* (New York, 1907), 51.
[23] W. Twining, op. cit., 15–16.
[24] G. Gilmore, op. cit., 49: 'The real Holmes was savage, harsh, and cruel, a bitter and lifelong pessimist ...'.
[25] G. Gilmore, op. cit., 75.
[26] *Pollock–Holmes Letters*, 2 vols (Cambridge, Massachusetts, 1942), I, 17.
[27] O. W. Holmes, *The Common Law* (first published in 1881; M. D. Howe edn, Boston, 1963), 5.
[28] *Lochner* v *New York* (1905) 198 U.S. 76.

He regarded history as an experiment in practical reasoning rather than as a source of unquestioned authority. 'It was revolting', he thought, 'to have no better reason for a rule than that it was laid down at the time of Henry IV'.[29] Thus, as for Gaius and later, Tribonian, history was not only a key to understanding but also a repository of the obsolete and the historically given might properly be subjected to rational criticism.[30] Holmes sought to show that 'the teaching of the common law is a lesson in philosophy—a lesson in the tentative and experimental character of judgment'.[31]

Holmes emphasized the sterility of a jurisprudence that ignored social, economic, psychological and moral conditions which provided the life-blood of the law. He moved the study of law from a rationalist, syllogistic enterprise to an empirical and experimental endeavour. However, the British Empiricists and their jurisprudential cousins such as Bentham, Austin and Mill were simply not empirical enough. Thus, for Holmes, the first requirement of a sound theory of law was that it should fit the facts. Indeed, law should correspond with 'the actual feelings and demands of the community, whether right or wrong'.[32] Thus, in the last resort, the arbiter of ultimate choice could only be force: 'I believe that force, mitigated so far as may be by good manners is the *ultimata ratio*'.[33] 'Society', he thought, 'rested on the death of men' and therefore he shrank from 'the moral tone'.[34] None the less, 'the law is the witness and external deposit of our moral life. Its history is the history of the moral development of the race'.[35] Thus Holmes was no amoralist. Nor should we too readily believe that Holmes opposed *theory*. Although he preferred to leave 'twisting the tail of the cosmos' to his friend, James, he asserted that 'we have too little theory in law' and expressed the view that 'the world is governed more today by Kant than by Bonapart'.[36] Indeed, the Kantian influence upon and dimensions of American pragmatism would provide a lecture in itself.[37]

Nor can we be certain as to the influence of pragmatism upon Holmes. Certainly there was a high degree of coincidence between his thought and the major tenets of pragmatism. Certainly, too, Holmes was profoundly

[29] O. W. Holmes, *Collected Legal Papers* (London, 1920), 187.
[30] T. Honore, *Tribonian* (London, 1978), 246–256.
[31] M. D. Howe, in O. W. Holmes, *The Common Law*, Introduction, xix.
[32] O. W. Holmes, *The Common Law*, 36.
[33] *Pollock–Holmes Letters*, II, 36.
[34] *Pollock–Holmes Letters*, I, 385.
[35] O. W. Holmes, 'The Path of the Law', *Harvard Law Review* **10** (457) (1897), 459.
[36] O. W. Holmes, 'The Path of the Law', *Harvard Law Review* **10** (457) (1897), 478.
[37] See Richard Tur, 'The Kelsenian Enterprise' in *Essays on Kelsen,* Tur and Twining (eds), (Oxford, forthcoming).

interested in philosophy and, indeed, had to be 'kicked into law by his father'.[38] Certainly he knew many of the pragmatists, such as James and Peirce, very well indeed and they were all members of the oddly named 'Metaphysical Club'. Holmes therefore moved in the intellectual company of those who 'sharpened British empiricism with skepticism and strengthened it with science'.[39] Holmes's own mind may, however, have contributed as much as it received in these early days of pragmatism and his legal philosophy may well have anticipated themes later to be more fully developed by pragmatist philosophers. Thus Dewey wrote in 1924 what was virtually a commentary on Holmes's aphorism that the life of the law had not been logic but experience.[40] Dewey's point was that by 'logic' Holmes obviously meant syllogistic logic and that by 'experience' he might be understood to have meant what the pragmatists thought 'logic' to be, namely 'an empirical and concrete discipline'. Syllogistic logic, according to Dewey, implied that for every case that might arise, there is a fixed, antecedent rule at hand and it tends, where accepted, to lead to what Pound aptly called 'mechanical jurisprudence' and to an obsessive concern with certainty.

Another influence upon Realism is to be found in the work of Gray. Although he was primarily an orthodox property lawyer, Gray gave more emphasis to the non-logical elements in law-making, such as personality, political sympathy and economic theory than was usual within the analytical school. Further, Gray, uniquely among analytical jurists, regarded statutory rules as being merely sources of law and not law themselves.[41] This scepticism as to rules was to be echoed and developed in realism which exhibited a decisionist rather than a statutory emphasis as to the nature of law which, at least in the early phase of the movement, tended to place courts at the centre of the jurisprudential universe. Not all the inheritors of the realist tradition embraced such extreme rule-scepticism and Cardozo, for example, criticized Gray's conception of law as 'only isolated dooms'[42] nor, for that matter, did the mature realists concentrate solely on the role of judges. Llewellyn, for example, broadened the focus from judges to judges, legislators and administrators and even to officials

[38] M. D. Howe, in O. W. Holmes, *The Common Law*, Introduction, xii.

[39] M. D. Howe, in O. W. Holmes, *The Common Law*, Introduction, xiii.

[40] J. Dewey, 'Logical Method and the Law', *Cornell Law Quarterly* **10** (1924), 17.

[41] J. C. Gray, *Nature and Sources of the Law* (New York, 1931) sections 276, 366, 369.

[42] B. Cardozo, *The Nature of the Judicial Process* (New Haven and London, 1921), 126; and see Tennyson, *Aylmer's Field*, describing the law 'a wilderness of single instances'.

in general.[43] None the less, the emphasis on particular decisions and the radical scepticism about rules inherent in Gray's jurisprudentializing significantly influenced the realist movement.

Realism attained a self-conscious identity as a result of a controversy sparked off by Pound's article, 'The Call for a Realist Jurisprudence' (1931)[44] when Llewellyn and Frank, believing themselves to be the target, jointly penned a response, published under Llewellyn's name,[45] identifying themselves as Realists, though paradoxically denying the existence of any Realist 'School', and criticizing Pound quite savagely for misunderstanding the nature of their concerns. Indeed the antipathy had been prefigured in an earlier article by Llewellyn which had commented unsympathetically on Pound.[46] In Llewellyn's articles one can find a catalogue of the central concerns which moved him and his colleagues. First, there is no Realist 'school'; Realism is 'a *movement* in thought and work about law'. Secondly, Realism conceives of law as in flux, as a means to social ends and it conceives of society changing faster than law. Thirdly, Realism *temporarily* divorces 'is' and 'ought'. It is not primarily a philosophy of values and it seeks to find out what law is and to judge law and the evolution of law not through any conformity to absolute values but by its effect. Fourthly, Realism distrusts legal rules as accurate descriptions of what the law is. Rather it treats generalized predictions of what the courts will do as central. It distrusts abstractions and overly ambitious generalizations and prefers to group cases and legal situations into narrower and more particular categories than the traditional method employed. Realism therefore exhibited a particularizing tendency which called for 'sensitivity to the nuances of the particular' and for 'situational sense'. It denied that legal rules, traditionally conceived, were *the* heavily operative determinants of decisions and it espoused a study of the personal elements in judicial decision making in contradistinction to the method of the water-tight deductive syllogism. Consequently, the nature of the judicial process contemplated was such that rules did not determine decisions and that judges, rather after the manner of Plato's philosopher-kings, intuit their decisions and subsequently rationalize them. Hence the hunch-judge of American jurisprudential folk-lore. Even this had been anticipated by Holmes who, having stated that general propositions do not decide particular cases, went on to explain that 'the decision will depend upon a judgment or intuition more subtle than any articulate major premise'.[47]

[43] K. Llewellyn, 'Using the New Jurisprudence, *Columbia Law Review* **40** (1940), 581.
[44] *Harvard Law Review* **44** (1931), 697.
[45] *Harvard Law Review* **44** (1931), 1222.
[46] *Columbia Law Review* **30** (1930), 431.
[47] *Lochner* v *New York* (1905) 198 U.S. 76.

Frank was even more sceptical.[48] He regarded Realists as either rule sceptics or fact sceptics. He thought that the rule sceptics were still in psychological bondage to the illusion of certainty and he pressed through to the point that radical uncertainty is an inherent feature of fact. Thus, even if one could identify and isolate clear and certain rules, the problem would remain as to ascertaining whether or not the fact situation contemplated by the rule was present. Frank couched his discourse in psychological mode, seeing in the commitment of analytical jurisprudence to certainty, a child-like desire for security and certainty. His ideal was the 'completely adult lawyer' which, for Frank, was exemplified by Holmes. Frank, more than any other participant in the Realist movement, generated an interest in fact-finding techniques, evaluation of prejudice, psychology of witnesses and the like. He thought that others suffered from too much attention to appellate courts and that the proper focus for attention was the trial court; he chided his colleagues for attending too much to jurisprudence and not enough to 'juriesprudence'.[49] Frank's hunch-judge was, perhaps, too unconstrained by legal rule or concept to be acceptable even to other Realists as a plausible figure. Llewellyn, in particular, came to defend rationality in appellate decision-making against what he called 'a crisis in confidence which packs danger' and argued that the work of appellate courts all over the country is 'reckonable'.[50]

Indeed, the meaning of rule scepticism is itself controversial within the tradition. It can mean either total scepticism as to the *existence* of rules or it can mean doubt as to the capacity of rules exhaustively to determine decisions. As one tends to one or the other extreme one is radically iconoclast or merely 'realist'. Certainly, the tendency has been to adopt the middle way between radical and iconoclastic rule scepticism and obsessive rule-fetishism.[51] So, too, with values. Although the movement has been profoundly empiricist and although it has separated fact and value, it came as with Frank and Llewellyn, to be increasingly concerned with justice and social values. Realists *are* frequently criticized for ignoring the normative character of legal rules and for seeking to substitute for this a wholly 'scientific' (or 'external') regularity which would reduce law to fact without remainder. No doubt, some of the practitioners of what I regard as 'decadent' Realism, for example Judicial Behaviouralism or Jurimetrics, took their scientific empiricism to such extremes thereby justifying description (and implied criticism) as 'gastronomic jurisprudes'. None the less, later Realists, for example the mature Llewellyn, took all proper

---

[48] J. Frank, *Law and the Modern Mind*.
[49] J. Frank, *Law and the Modern Mind*, Preface.
[50] K. Llewellyn, *The Common Law Tradition* (Boston, 1960), 178–181.
[51] H. L. A. Hart, *The Concept of Law* (Oxford, 1961), Ch. VII.

cognizance of the normativity of legal rules,[52] thereby justifying my description as a 'realist jurisprudent'.

I turn now to a brief assessment of Realism. It combines positivism and sociology, that is to say, it is concerned with the law as it is but also with the effect of society upon law. In its early phase, at least, it centred attention upon the judge and stressed the notion that law is what judges decide. This emphasis is often explained (and debunked) by commentators (and critics) by the circumstance that, in America, judges are very important[53] and that they were particularly important in the development of the law at the time the early Realists wrote their seminal works. Again, critical commentators sometimes seize upon the point that American judges, being elected (though this is not universally the case), are less trustworthy than, say, their English counterparts and are therefore more open to observation, scrutiny and criticism. It is, indeed, true that the American legal system was 'young' and characterized by judicial creativity when the Realists first wrote and this golden age of the American judge remained a powerful feature of American legal thought. The divergent and separate common law systems of the American states provided, at the time, more than sufficient evidence for the centrality of the judicial role. Indeed, judicial 'activism' remained a significant feature of the American legal system[54] and this, in part, explains the continuing hegemony of Realist thought-ways over the American legal mind. Reactions, comments and criticisms of this general kind have been widely received as showing that American Realism is a uniquely American phenomenon of merely geographical and historical interest. I reject this perspective on American Realism if it implies that it is of no relevance outside America or that it is of no relevance in America today.

To develop only the second of these points, I turn now to recent American legal philosophy. First, there is the Economic Analysis of Law which is associated with Professor Posner and the Chicagoans, from 1960 or thereby.[55] I see this as a pre-Realist revivalist movement. The basic notions are that wealth maximization is an ethical as well as an economic value and that the common law exhibits (albeit absent-mindedly) substantial conformity to the monolithic value of wealth maximization. This movement applies the theories and empirical methods of economics to law allowing law to be understood and, where necessary, improved by

[52] K. Llewellyn, 'The Normative, the Legal and Law Jobs', *Yale Law Journal* **49** (1940), 1355.

[53] Cf. the Roman legal system; see J. P. Dawson, *The Oracles of the Law* (Ann Arbor, 1968), 100; 'Instead of making their judges monumental figures, it seems that the Romans hid them in caves'.

[54] G. Gilmore, op. cit., 142, n. 48.

[55] See R. Posner, *The Economic Analysis of Law*, 2nd edn (London, 1977); R. Posner, *The Economics of Justice* (London, 1981).

reference to economic efficiency. The approach is therefore descriptive in that it purports to discover the value of wealth maximization immanent in the common law and normative in that it criticizes such law as is not economically efficient as being wrong-headed and in need of reform. Consequently, the movement distrusts statutory and commends common law.

The approach might, at first blush, suggest at least a partial identity of interest with Realism. After all, did not Holmes, himself, emphasize the importance of economics for the student and practitioner of law? However, to a Realist, such a movement must appear primitive. In Realist eyes it is a return to that type of formalism against which battle was joined in Realism's formative years. The Chicagoans are committed to a rationalist, deductive, mathematical account of law and although they could pray Holmes in aid as an oath-helper for the relevance of economics, doubtless Holmes would have been concerned with real world economics rather than the economics of the perfectly rational optimizer living in an hypothetical universe defined by the posit of zero transaction costs. The ideological thrust of the movement is as obvious as its methodological poverty. Even if (and it is a large 'if') the common law had been perfectly in harmony with wealth maximization and economic efficiency, a great deal of legal materials nowadays are legislative or administrative and there is no obvious reason why economic efficiency should be taken as its moving principle. There are, indeed, some obvious reasons why economic efficiency should *not* be taken as the moving principle behind legislative and administrative intervention. In England, the law limited the operation of the free market in order to protect vulnerable groups.[56] In America, the Supreme Court abandoned freedom of contract as an absolute[57] and imposed affirmative duties pertaining to equality.[58] It is therefore implausible that American law can be explained *solely* in terms of economic efficiency. Nor is it clear to many critics of the Economic Analysis of Law why it *ought* to be.

The second movement which excites attention is in every sense the polar opposite of the Economic Analysis of Law. I turn to the Critical Legal Studies Movement. It, I believe, can be located as Realism revivified. Perhaps such a revivification was long overdue in that Realism, which had originally perceived itself and had been perceived as being iconoclastic and radical had become manicured, conservative and uncritical. No one can claim privileged insight into the fundamental nature of the movement.

[56] See T. Honore, *The Quest for Security: Employees, Tenants, Wives* (London, 1982).

[57] *Lochner* v *New York* (1905) 198 U.S. 76.

[58] *Brown* v *Board of Education* (1954) 347 U.S. 483; and see Richard Tur, 'Justifications of Reverse Discrimination', in *Law Morality and Rights*, M. A. Stewart (ed) (Dordrecht, Boston and Lancaster, 1983), 259–294.

None the less, one can turn to what those associated with the movement themselves say in order to assess and locate the movement. Professor Kairys, in introducing a collection of essays by participants in the movement, seeks to identify some of its chief concerns.[59] These include, first, that the movement is profoundly 'anti-formalist' and this is further explained as invoking the notion that the judicial process is not a matter of water-tight syllogistic deduction. Secondly, although law is not value-neutral, any vulgar Marxist model of ideological superstructure is emphatically rejected in an attempt to escape what is described as a 'crippling choice between liberal theory and mechanical, determinist forms of Marxist-Leninism.'[60] Thirdly, modern America does not fulfil the constitutional promise of genuine public participation in law-making and government and therefore violates the first principle of democracy. All of this, together with other concerns which Professor Kairys mentions, is summarized as 'a continuation of the Realists' project'.[61]

Professor Roberto Mangabeira Unger is another significant commentator.[62] It would be dangerous to claim that Unger is a fully paid-up, card-carrying member of the Critical Legal Studies Movement and it would be entirely wrong to regard his recent, extensive and elaborate article as a definitive statement of the movement's concerns. Indeed, Unger candidly denies that he is attempting to describe the movement. Rather, he sees himself as making a series of proposals about the direction in which the movement might develop. These 'proposals', however, might be taken as approximating to the movement's concerns. For present purposes I draw attention to the following five points. First, Unger states that the Critical Legal Studies Movement builds on two sceptical ideas, namely 'anti-formalism' and 'anti-objectivism'. Secondly, he sees a need for *constructive* criticism. That involves recognizing legal discourse as discourse concerning the basic terms of social life without reducing such discourse to the ideologies of dogmatic conservatism or visionary revolution. Thirdly, Critical Legal Studies exhibits (or ought to develop) a specific method. That method involves taking existing legal materials seriously and recognizing their normative claims. But such materials, though recognizably normative, exhibit contradictions and disharmonies. Out of these contradictions and disharmonies one is exhorted to (or participants in the movement are described as) build(ing) deviationist doctrines. For the traditional lawyer, 'doctrine' determines outcomes of controversies. Unger appears to advocate the development of a critical, but constructive,

[59] See D. Kairys (ed), *The Politics of Law* (New York, 1982).
[60] D. Kairys, op. cit., 16.
[61] D. Kairys, ibid.
[62] R. M. Unger, 'The Critical Legal Studies Movement, *Harvard Law Review* **96** (1983), 563–675.

approach to 'doctrine' in order to incorporate flexibility into law. This is an exciting invitation: the 'good' lawyer, student, practitioner or professor, should seek to produce unorthodox conclusions by orthodox methods from orthodox (i.e. recognizably normative) materials. This means developing, through immanent critique of legal principles and counter-principles, rules and counter-rules, new and changing doctrine. The shadow of Kuhnian 'paradigm shifts' is cast over Unger's treatment of law as exhibiting much 'routinization' and occasional 'revolution' but no serious philosopher of law, schooled at the knee of Holmes, for whom philosophizing about law could not amount to much until one had soaked oneself in the details, could long withhold assent. Fourthly, all this leads to views about law and the Constitution. Prevailing hierarchies and immanent tendencies of the state to fall into the hands of 'factions' are to be resisted by use of liberating deviationist doctrine. Thus, in 'public' law the Critical Legal Studies Movement tends (or ought to tend) to secure 'empowered democracy'. Fifthly, all of this taken cumulatively leads to what Unger refers to as 'super-liberalism', that is a society in which no current social arrangement is taken for granted or as permanent. Nothing is permanently beyond nor immune from criticism and reform. Law is not naturally given; current arrangements are hostage to re-assessment of reasons and that which is currently a social necessity is not to be deemed either a natural nor a logical necessity.

Of course, many latter day authors have sought to give their ideas the gloss of historical or traditional legitimacy and, perhaps, the views of those who speak for the Critical Legal Studies Movement should be received with caution. None the less, it is remarkable how closely the views expressed by Kairys and Unger correspond with the main themes and concerns of Realism. One difference, and it may be more of degree than kind, is the actively political stance of the movement and its concerns with constitutional issues. That, however, may merely reflect developments in political structure and therefore in the way in which law impinges upon social life rather than any real difference in cast of mind or philosophical approach as between the earlier Realists and the current Critical Studies Movement. It is not unrealistic, therefore, to see in the movement a revivification of Realism. Even the Realists' emphasis on intuition or situational sense finds a ready echo in the views of at least one prominent member of the movement.[63] This prized possession of the Realists, their crafty situational sense and intuitive grasp of the right and the just is one of the major points of difference between both Realism and its Critical successors on the one hand and, on the other, the third contemporary

---

[63] See D. Kennedy, 'Form and Substance in Private Law Adjudication', *Harvard Law Review* **89** (1976), 1985; D. Kennedy, Legal Formality', *Journal of Legal Studies* **2** (1973) 351.

American movement in legal intellectualizing, namely Constructivism. I classify this movement in thought as Realism transcended and rejected.

This third movement is represented by Professor Ackerman who might be understood both theoretically and politically to adopt a middle position between the two movements in thought already discussed.[64] Ackerman criticizes the Economic Analysis of Law writers for their adoption of a limited, simplified and artificial methodology, though he agrees with them that economic analysis is important for the post-Realist lawyer. Indeed, Ackerman criticizes the Critical Legal Studies Movement because of its continuing the staunch Realist hostility to formalism in all its guises and for its continued glorification of intuitionism. If that means that the Critical Legal Studies Movement has no (or very little) time for the formal analyses of economics, statistics and computer modelling then (for Ackerman) so much the worse for Critical Legal Studies. Ackerman's post-Realist lawyer will have to be competent in such formalist disciples if he is to survive. There are, he says, increasing numbers of experts other than lawyers with important things to say about the terms of social life and lawyers must adapt their conversational idiom or fall into irrelevance.

Ackerman seeks to explain the enduring phenomenon of Realism by tracing the impact of the New Deal upon the conversational idiom of lawyers. Prior to the activism brought about in the wake of the New Deal it was at least possible to talk in a formal idiom with Free Contract, Private Property and Fault Liability as the major categories of abstract thought. Until about fifty years ago, it was possible for lawyers to regard state intervention as extraordinary and the common lawyer was able to navigate happily on the open sea of 'private' law, leaving the few 'public' law islands strictly alone. But, as Ackerman points out, slowly, perhaps, but surely and permanently the islands increasingly occupied territory once solely the preserve of the common lawyer. Such a revolution could not but affect the conversational idiom of lawyers. It was increasingly difficult to pretend that the grand abstractions of the common law as taught by Langdell, for example, could provide explanatory or predictive general principles for all this entirely new law-stuff. The explosion in legislative and administrative law materials put the conversational idiom of the common lawyer under considerable strain. Just at the time when the wilderness of single instances had been 'scientifically' reduced to a comprehensive and rational set of principles, the law-stuff of the New Deal threatened significant, perhaps total, deconstruction. The proud attempts of the Restatement Movement could not avail in such a new and hostile climate. The new law-stuff revealed that any attempt to produce a perfect map of the law must fail. Indeed, the Realists ridiculed such attempts as a grand illusion, perhaps

---

[64] B. A. Ackerman, *Reconstructing American Law* (Cambridge, Massachusetts and London, 1984).

resulting from deep psychological insecurity. Given that a perfect legal landscape was an unrealistic aspiration, the Realists urged that the business of lawyers was to concentrate on the real aspects, be they political, economic, psychological or moral in actual disputes. The focus of attention was to be the particular aspects of cases rather than the pursuit of grand overarching generalizations. Thus Free Contract was reduced to 'contracts'; Private Property to 'property'; and Fault Liability to 'liability'.

The effect of this move was that the legal profession could go on using their cherished categories, albeit in radically diluted form. Realism therefore did not undermine traditional categories. Rather it preserved them through particularization. Given that law became much wider than merely the common law and that it embraced legislative and administrative law-stuff, the traditional form of highly abstract generalization was no longer able to cope. But the new insights of the Realists that the common law was much more subtle than hitherto recognized; that the high abstractions were to be radically particularized by Realists, sensitive to the nuances of the particular; and that low order generalizations were legitimate provided that they were built up painstakingly and *a posteriori* rather than grandly assumed *a priori* allowed traditional law-talk to continue. Consequently, Ackerman can classify Realism as ultimately a conservative movement. By the method of particularism, Realists could even accommodate at least some of the new law-talk. Thus Doctrine gave way to 'doctrines'. In Contract one stopped talking of Consideration and started to talk of 'consideration *and* unconscionability'; in Tort, Negligence became 'negligence *and* strict liability'. Thus the lawyer's enterprise was to be conceived of as the sensitive formulation of highly particular rules and a realistic refusal to generalize beyond the particular contexts which gave them their meaning. Thus the Realists provided for the continuity of traditional legal discourse by virtue of their scepticism about abstractions and their confidence in intuitionist adaptation to the new values inherent in the activist state.

Ackerman believes that American law has not yet made good its activist promise and that in order to meet the challenges posed by social and political life lawyers must now transcend Realism. First, legal thought must go beyond particularized fact-patterns in order that 'statements of fact' relate individual conflicts to the systematic structured tensions of social life. Thus, for example, it is one thing for a Realist judge to intuit an injustice to a particular tenant at the hands of a particular landlord and perhaps in order to do justice to imply a term into the particular contract. It is entirely another, Ackerman believes, seriously to face up to the structured inequalities of the landlord–tenant relationship. Facing up to that problem reveals the inadequacy of the particularized intuitions of justice and the particularized statements of fact canvassed by the Realists. Not only fact, but also value calls for a restatement if the Constructivist aspiration is to be realized. Here, Ackerman insists that lawyers must go beyond the intuitionist approach in order to test activist interventions. His solution is to construct a theory of justice out of the fundamental principles of American Constitutional Law. The theory is developed at length in his *Social Justice in the Liberal State* (1980). The fundamental principles require (i) 'comprehensive legal dialogue'; (ii) (a) no claim to moral insight intrinsically superior to that of others, and (ii) (b) no claim to intrinsic superiority over others. These principles reflect the Due Process, the Free Exercise and the Equal Protection Clauses of the American Constitution and conjoin in such a way as neither to affirm nor repudiate free-market efficiency. Rather, they combine to produce a 'conditional affirmation of market freedom', that is, conditional upon rights to education and fair shares of economic power. This, in turn, leads to a 'basic structure of undominated equality'.

Such, then, are some of the dominant movements in intellectualizing about law in America today. All can be related to and understood in the light of American Realism. The exciting aspect of the developments, whatever differences they exhibit is the manner in which law and legal discourse is linked to social and political concerns. Today's lawyer can no longer stand aloof from central issues such as social justice and democracy nor can he isolate himself from arguments and reasons of a social or political nature. Further, at least two of the three movements discussed appear to agree that legal discourse cannot be reduced without remainder to an uncritical rehash of the dictates of monolithic ideologies, be they of the right or of the left. The fundamental challenge held out by current American legal philosophy is that of transcribing the opposition of free-market economics and collectivist tendencies. Neither has been chosen by the American people and the lawyer's business is progressively to articulate the terms of social life implicit in the social choices already made. How significant a difference there is now between Unger and Ackerman is unclear. Both seek to take the law as it is, normatively given, as a basis for future development. One seeks 'empowered democracy', the other seeks 'undominated equality'. Though he once pronounced liberalism bankrupt,[65] Unger now proposes a *liberal* or a 'super-liberal' reconstruction of society.[66] If Unger has shifted his ground, there may be hope for something of a *rapprochement* between Critical Legal Studies and Constructivism. Only time will tell whether a better form of liberal democracy emerges. The ferment in the law schools and in the legal journals is evidence, however, of a deep discontent with the traditional terms of legal discourse and of a desire radically to reconstruct society and the law.

[65] See B. A. Ackerman, op. cit., 103, n. 32, commenting on R. M. Unger, *Knowledge and Politics* (New York, 1975), 1–144.
[66] R. M. Unger, 'The Critical Legal Studies Movement', *Harvard Law Review* **96** (1983), 563, 602.

I hope that I have made out my claims that it is an exciting time to look at American legal philosophy and that American Realism remains relevant in that it assists in organizing and explaining current concerns of those who take law as central to their theoretical and practical endeavours. I am conscious that in this lecture I have left many issues unstated and that significant jurists (such as Pound), judges (such as Cardozo) and philosophers (such as Morris Cohen) have found no place in my discussion. I am aware, too, that I have not discussed the Rights and Principles School[67] nor sought to locate it in relation to American Realism. I hope, however, that my selective treatment of American legal philosophy provides a coherent picture of the central concerns of American lawyers and legal philosophers over the last 100 years and that, selective as it is, the lecture provides an introduction to major issues in the subject.

Select Bibliography

O. W. Holmes, 'The Path of the Law', *Harvard Law Review* **10** (1897), 457.

K. Llewellyn, *Jurisprudence: Realism in Theory and Practice* (Boston, 1962).

J. Frank, *Law and the Modern Mind*, 2nd edn (London, 1963).

W. E. Rumble, *American Legal Realism* (Ithaca, New York, 1968).

W. Twining, *Karl Llewellyn and the Realist Movement* (London, 1973). 'Talk About Realism' (Dewey Lecture, 1984), *New York University Law Review* (1985) (forthcoming).

R. Posner, *The Economics of Justice* (London, 1981).

D. Kairys, *The Politics of Law* (New York, 1982).

R. M. Unger, 'The Critical Legal Studies Movement', *Harvard Law Review* **96** (1983), 561.

B. A. Ackerman, *Reconstructing American Law* (London, 1984).

---

[67] See R. M. Dworkin, *Taking Rights Seriously* (London, 1977).

The Philosophical Background of the American Constitution(s)

ANDREW J. RECK

I

The Constitution of the United States was constructed by men influenced by fundamental ideas of what a republic should be. These ideas hark back to the ancient philosophers and historians, and were further articulated and developed in modern times. From time to time scholars have sought to collect and reprint selections from- the classical, biblical, and modern sources upon which the Founding Fathers fed. Remarkably, however, the best anthology of these sources to understand the republican idea that undergirds the Federal Constitution was prepared on the eve of the Constitutional Convention by John Adams, a signer of the Declaration of Independence, then in London as American envoy to Great Britain and eventually the second President of the United States. I refer to Adams' *A Defence of the Constitutions of Government of the United States of America, against the attack of M. Turgot, in his letter to Dr. Price, 22 March, 1778.*

This work appeared in three volumes, the first in early 1787, the second later the same year, and the third in 1788.[1] The second volume treats the history of republics, and the third, while continuing the history of republics, offers a critique of the political theory of Marchamont Nedham. The first volume will occupy our attention today.[2] It is the volume that is anthological in character and presents translations, selections, and paraphrases from the classical and modern sources of the republican idea. Indeed, a study of Volume I of *A Defence* discloses how John Adams used the doctrines of the philosophers and the lessons of history to sketch the republican idea behind the American constitutions. Printed in London in early 1787 and immediately the same year in New York and Philadelphia,

---

[1] In 1794 Adams published a revised edition of *A Defence*, and Charles Francis Adams, with even more radical revision, republished it as volumes IV, V, and VI in *The Works of John Adams, Second President of the United States*, edited by Charles Francis Adams, 1850–56 (reprinted Freeport, NY: Books for Libraries Press, 1969). Subsequent references to *The Works of John Adams* are to the 1969 reprint of the Charles Francis Adams' edition.

[2] The edition cited in the present paper is John Adams, *A Defence of the Constitutions of Government of the United States of America* (New York: H. Gaine, 1787). All page references given in the text are to this edition.

it was, according to Charles Francis Adams, John's grandson and editor, 'much circulated in the [American Constitutional] convention [of 1787], and undoubtedly contributed somewhat to give a direction to the opinion of the members'.[3] While influencing the delegates to the Constitutional Convention of 1787 may not have been Adams' purpose, his work contains the sort of philosophical opinions and analyses of the histories of republics which reverberated in the debates at the Convention,[4] and outside and beyond the Convention its impact was profound. In a letter to John Adams, Thomas Jefferson, to cite but one leading eighteenth-century republican revolutionary, wrote: 'I have read your book with infinite satisfaction and improvement. Its learning and its good sense will, I hope, make it an institute for our politicians, old as well as young.'[5] And as the authoritative Adams' biographer, Page Smith, has reported:

> The influence of the *Defence* in America was considerable. By the standards of its day it was a best seller, appearing in a number of editions, widely read and hotly debated. . . . The *Defence* enjoyed an inevitable pre-eminence by virtue of the fact that for a good many years it had the field to itself. It was the first extensive examination by an American of the nature of government.[6]

The foil for Adams' composition of *A Defence* was a letter written by Anne Robert J. Turgot (1727–81), French economist and statesman, to Richard Price (1732–91), Welsh philosopher, whose pamphlet *Observations on Civil Liberty and the War with America* (1776), had identified him as a sympathizer and supporter of the American side in the war for independence. Turgot had criticized the constitutions of the American states for having failed to collect 'all authority into one center, that of the nation', and for having established, instead, 'different bodies, a body of representatives, a council, and a governor'. Turgot accused the Americans of imitating 'the customs of England . . . without any particular motive'. For while in England a House of Commons and a House of Lords may be necessary 'to balance these different powers' in order to check 'the enormous influence of royalty', no such equilibrium is required in 'republics founded upon the equality of all the citizens' (pp. 1–2). Against Turgot's criticisms Adams undertook to justify in the American republics where all citizens are equal just the sort of constitutional governmental structure that

---

[3] *The Works of John Adams*, Vol. IV, 276.

[4] See 'Debates in the Federal Convention of 1787 as reported by James Madison', *Documents illustrative of the Formation of the Union of the American States* (Washington: Government Printing Office, 1927), 109–745.

[5] 4 July 1787, in the Adams Papers at the Massachusetts Historical Society, quoted in Page Smith, *John Adams*, Vol. 2 (New York: Doubleday and Company, Inc., 1962), 699.

[6] Page Smith, op. cit., Vol. 2, 700.

Turgot condemned. Adams' use of a letter nearly a decade old to compose almost frantically *A Defence* had been triggered by the spread of unicameralism in America, and perhaps in particular by the prestige his fellow republican, Benjamin Franklin, had lent to the unicameral movement by supporting it in Pennsylvania. While in composing *A Defence* Adams clearly had in mind the states' constitutions, he was nevertheless also aware of such events in America as Shays' rebellion,[7] which were moving many leading politicians in the direction of a strong federal system.

Although he was at the time employed in practical affairs as American minister to Great Britain, Adams sequestered himself in his library and hastily composed the first volume of *A Defence* in the form of fifty-five letters: the first dated 4 October 1786, the last 21 December 1786, all with the heading Grosvenor Square. The letters, written at the pace of nearly one a day, were ostensibly addressed to his son-in-law, William Stephens Smith. Enclosed by a long preface and a brief postscript, both written in January 1787, the letters constitute the 1787 version of *A Defence*, Volume I. The haste with which the work was written is evident in the looseness of organization, the repetitiveness, the errors of translation and attribution. None the less, the work, unlike Adams' *Thoughts on Government* (1776), which expresses the same republican political philosophy, is a major source book for the philosophical background of the American constitution(s). It is also a minor masterpiece in republican philosophy, and a singular essay articulating some fundamentals of American political ideology. Although most of the volume is devoted to an analytical survey of the governmental constitutions of republics—democratic, aristocratic, and monarchic—I shall focus on Adams' excerpts from and discussions of the philosophers and the philosophical historians. Adams sought to enlighten readers about the formation of the governments of the American states, about which little was known, and to show that the men who erected them were not inspired by the gods, but merely used

> ... reason and the senses. . . . [N]either the people, nor their conventions, committees, or sub-committees, considered legislation in any other light than ordinary arts and sciences, only as of more importance (p. xvi).

They studied the histories of nations and examined the theories of political thinkers, comparing historical realities with theoretical conceptions, and inquiring

> ... how far both the theories and the models were founded in nature, or created by fancy: and, when this should be done, as far as their

---

[7] On Shays' rebellion and its role in the movement toward a federal constitution stronger than the Articles of Confederation, see *Encyclopedia of American History*, R. B. Morris (ed.) (New York: Harper & Row, 1976), 137–138.

circumstances would allow, to adopt the advantages, and reject the inconveniences of all ... As the writer was personally acquainted with most of the gentlemen in each of thirteen states, who had the principal share in the first draughts, the following letters were really written to lay before the gentleman to whom they are addressed, a specimen of that kind of reading and reasoning which produced the American constitutions (pp. xvi–xvii).

For students of philosophy it is interesting and illuminating to consider the philosophers and philosophical historians Adams elucidated as having influenced the men who framed the American constitutions. What may be observed in Adams' work is the relevance of philosophy to public affairs, manifest in the contributions of great thinkers to the formation of the public philosophy that shapes and explains American institutions. This is not to say that American institutions or American constitutions are the mere applications of European ideas. On the contrary, in regard to constitutions the Americans were innovators who originated the mechanism of constitutional conventions to express the sovereignty of the people when erecting governments over themselves, and in regard to the constitution of the United States the Americans departed from the republican tradition when they established a federal republic which extended over a vast territory, embraced thirteen republics, and was constructed to generate and include other republics within the American continent and beyond. What may also be observed in Adams' work is a feature that characterizes American philosophy, whether public or academic—namely, its openness to ideas from elsewhere and its assimilation of these ideas as it makes up its own mind.

In *A Defence* Adams presented the theories of the philosophers and the philosophical historians neither in a logical nor a chronological order. Listed chronologically, they are: Plato (427–347 BC), Aristotle (384–322 BC), Polybius (205–123 BC), Cicero (106–43 BC), Machiavelli (1469–1527), Harrington (1611–77), Algernon Sidney (1622–83), Locke (1632–1704), Montesquieu (1689–1755), Hume (1711–76), and Price (1723–91). Except for Cicero, I will consider each in chronological order.

II

Cicero figures prominently in the Preface. Here Adams was engaged in the task of defining what a republic is, and he looked to Cicero, whose authority, in Adams' words, 'should have great weight', because 'all the ages of the world have not produced a greater statesman and philosopher' united in one person (p. xix). Adams quoted at length in Latin several passages from the fragments of Cicero's *De Re Publica*. These passages take the term 'republic' to mean, in the first sense, 'the thing (or property) of the people', or 'the public property', or, to use an equivalent English word, 'the commonwealth'. The most notable quotation from Cicero (p. xix), as rendered into English, is:

> ... a commonwealth (*res publica*) is the property of a people (*res populi*). But a people is not any collection of human beings brought together in any sort of way, but an assemblage of people in large numbers associated in an agreement with respect to justice and a partnership for the common good.[8]

Adams also approved Cicero's thesis that the ideal constitution for a republic be a mixed government, one in which the elements of monarchy, aristocracy, and democracy are interwoven to compose a balance. Then, in the second sense of 'republic', it is understood to be a government of laws rather than of men. Where there is no mixture, there is no balance, and, as a result, government is a matter of will and pleasure instead of laws.

Since Adams did not have at hand Cicero's text as it is available today, he apparently did not know that Cicero, following Polybius, had portrayed the Roman republic as the embodiment of the ideal, mixed constitution, and, also like Polybius, had correlated organs of the Roman government with the principles of monarchy, aristocracy, and democracy—viz. the consuls representing the monarchic principle; the senate, the aristocratic principle; and the tribunes, the democratic principle.

For Adams it was not Rome but Great Britain, with Commons, Lords, and King, which had best realized the ideal mixed constitution, and which had even surpassed the ancient model in regard to the enduring stability and the preservation of democracy within the constitution. The British, he contended, had 'blended together the feudal institutions with those of the Greeks and the Romans; and out of all have made that noble composition, which avoids the inconveniences and retains the advantages, of both' (p. xxiii). Whereas the ancients had defined the three pure types of polity and three deviant types, and had established that a mixture is the best type (although this mixture may be designated monarchic, aristocratic, or democratic, depending upon which element is most secure or prevails), it was the moderns, principally the British and the Americans, who had discovered three additional principles that guarantee free government. These principles are:

> Representations, instead of collections of people—a total separation of the executive from the legislative power, and of the judicial from both— and a balance in the legislature, by three independent, equal branches ... (p. iv).

Hence Adams' direct answer to Turgot was that the American states, instead of being criticized, should be praised for following the British

[8] Cicero, *The Republic* I, xxv, in *De Re Publica, De Legibus*, trans. by C. W. Keyes (Cambridge: Harvard University Press, 1977), 65.

Andrew J. Reck

model of a mixed constitution. Whereas the British constitution had developed historically, Adams declared, 'the United States of America have exhibited, perhaps, the first example of governments erected upon the simple principles of nature' (p. xv).

III

Adams lauded Plato for having 'given us the most accurate detail of the natural vicissitudes of manners and principles, the usual progress of the passions in society, and revolutions of governments into one another' (p. 186). Letter XXXIV focuses on two parts of Plato's political theory as expounded in the *Republic* and consists mainly of translated excerpts and paraphrases. The first part is taken from Book IV; here Plato depicted 'his perfect commonwealth, where kings are philosophers, and philosophers kings' (p. 186). The second part is taken from Book VIII, continuing into Book IX, where Plato sketched the four degenerate types of polity and the sociological and psychological genesis of each. Throughout Plato correlated type of polity with kind of human being.

Adams found much in Plato's ideal polity to commend it: happiness pervades the whole and 'the laws govern' (p. 187). The state is one and not divided into factions; members are ranked according to merit; education is public, supplementing the laws in producing 'the virtues of fortitude, temperance, wisdom and justice, in the whole city, and in all the individual citizens' (p. 187). It is, moreover, according to Adams' interpretation, a system in which the best individuals rise to serve as 'guardians of the laws', so that if there is one guardian surpassing all the rest, monarchy results, and if several, aristocracy.

Adams approved the correlation of type of polity with type of human nature (or in Plato's terminology, type of soul), and he observed that, although for Plato there is but one excellent constitution, or 'principle of virtue'—namely, the ideal commonwealth sketched above, there are four imperfect types, or vices, each correlated with a type of soul. Hence there are: (1) the ideal republic, (2) timocracy, (3) oligarchy, (4) democracy, and (5) tyranny. Adams retraced Plato's account of the sociological and psychological causes for the degeneration of the ideal republic through the various phases leading down to tyranny.

Adams portrayed Plato as a philosophical historian whose scheme of historic political change needs only to be fleshed out by an examination of the actual course of history. When this is done, it is seen that Plato 'has not exaggerated in his description of the mutability in the characters of men, and the forms of government' (p. 208). Plato 'drew his observations and reasoning' from Greece, and Adams applauded. For the history of Greece is like 'an octagonal apartment with a full-length mirror on every side, and another in the ceiling' (p. 209). Studying it is like seeing our images reflected from every angle, so that we see the distortions in our appearance produced by any distemper on our part, and proceed to correct them. As Adams summed the point up:

> A few short sketches of the ancient republics will serve to shew . . . that the *orders* (classes of men) we defend were common to all of them; that the prosperity and duration of each was in proportion to the care taken to *balance* them; and that they all were indebted by their frequent seditions, the rise and progress of corruption, and their decline and fall, to the imperfection of their orders, and their defects in the balance (p. 209).

IV

No particular letter treats Aristotle, and this is remarkable in view of Aristotle's undoubted influence on subsequent political theory. In Letter XXVI, where Adams quoted the statements of classical and modern writers on the nature of republics, he cited Aristotle, 'this great philosopher', on the subject, although the citations are without references. The first quotation presents Aristotle saying that 'a government where the *laws alone* should prevail, would be the kingdom of God'. The second reports Aristotle identifying 'order' with 'law', and states that 'it is more proper that law should govern, than anyone of the citizens' and, further, that 'if it is advantageous to place the supreme power in some particular persons, they should be appointed to be only guardians, and the servants of the laws' (p. 123).

The omission of Aristotle from the sort of examination accorded Plato is surprising, because Aristotle enunciated many of the fundamental themes of the republican idea Adams espoused. These themes backed by quotations from Aristotle are presented toward the end of Adams' history of republics in the third volume of *A Defence*, where, incidentally, Adams charged Aristotle with inconsistency for espousing the doctrine of natural inequality to exclude persons of the lower socio-economic classes from the exercise of their political rights.[9]

Perhaps Plato's precedence over Aristotle in *A Defence* springs from Adams' appreciation of the dynamics of the genesis of one type of constitution from another. Certainly Plato's socio-psychological explanation of the degeneration of polities in the moral terms of corruption and vice was a theme dear to the hearts of the Founding Fathers. In any event, it is noteworthy that in later editions of *A Defence* Plato is classified as an historian rather than as a philosopher.

[9] In *The Works of John Adams*, Charles Francis Adams (ed.), Vol. V (Boston: Charles C. Little and James Brown, 1851), 454ff.

10

V

Polybius logically and chronologically follows after Plato and Aristotle, but not in Adams' loose organization of his treatise. Polybius, a universal historian centering his attention on Rome, excelled at the kind of didactic historiography that engrossed the Founding Fathers. Adams concentrated on a fragment in Book VI of *The Histories*; the fragment reflects the influence of Aristotle, even though its subject is the Roman constitution. It opens with a discussion of the achievement of Lycurgus as lawgiver to Sparta in contrast to Solon as lawgiver to Athens. Whereas Solon's establishment of democracy did not long survive, Lycurgus' institution of a mixed constitution endured for centuries. Polybius confirmed the superiority of the mixed constitution by pointing to its complete realization in the Roman republic. While Adams agreed with Polybius on the merits of the mixed constitution, he did not concur in the judgment that Rome best exemplified the type.

Adams retraced Polybius' account of the degeneration of one polity into another, and also offered the fundamental argument for the mixed constitution as the guarantor of political stability. Adams emphasized that 'the generation and corruption of governments' stems from 'the progress and course of human passions in society' (p. 175). And he recorded the evolution (or devolution) of government from monarchy to kingly rule to tyranny to aristocracy to oligarchy to democracy back to monarchy, explaining the processes of change by reference to human features such as weakness and passions such as envy. 'This', Adams declared, 'is the rotation of governments, and this the order of nature, by which they are changed, transformed, and return to the same point of the circle' (p. 179). To this extent at least Adams merely copied Polybius:

> ... every form of government that is simple, by soon degenerating into that vice that is allied to it, must be unstable. The vice of kingly government is monarchy; that of aristocracy, oligarchy; that of democracy, rage and violence; into which, in process of time, all of them must degenerate ... (p. 168).

Adams differed from Polybius in refusing to concede that a pure type, no matter how brief the period, is without abuse of power. He suggested instead that 'perhaps it might be more exactly true and natural to say, that the king, the aristocracy, and the people, as soon as ever they felt themselves secure in the possession of their power, would begin to abuse it' (p. 180).

The remedy for the political instability manifest in the incessant circular change of polities was, for Polybius and for Adams, to be found in the

> ... government not of one sort, but ... [incorporating] all the advantages and properties of the best government; to the end that no branch

of it, by swelling beyond its due bounds, might degenerate into the vice that is congenial to it; and that, while each of them were mutually acted upon by *opposite powers*, no one part might incline any way, or *outweigh* the rest; but that the commonwealth, being equally *poised* and *balanced*, like a *ship* or a *waggon*, acted upon by *contrary powers*, might long remain in the same situation . . . (pp. 168–169).

Adams of course disagreed with Polybius' portrait of the Roman republic as the best constitution, but preferred instead the American constitutions. He turned the argument to use against Turgot's criticism of bicameralism. Adams espoused the doctrine of a natural aristocracy 'formed partly by genius, partly by birth, and partly by riches' (p. 137). He deemed it dangerous to assign all representatives, including the natural aristocrats, to a unicameral legislature. It would be an invitation to corrupt the election process by the infusion of the superior wealth of the aristocrats to secure their election so that 'rage and violence would soon appear in the assembly, and from thence be communicated among the people at large' (p.181).

VI

Machiavelli intrigued Adams. In the first volume of *A Defence* Adams concentrated on the Florentine's *Discourses on Livy*, and in the second volume on the *History of Florence* . He credited Machiavelli for grounding his philosophy of politics and of law upon the doctrine of man according to which 'all men are bad by nature . . .' (p. 129). What seems to be operative in Adams' thinking as in that of the other Founding Fathers on the natural depravity of man is the permanent deposit of Calvinism monitoring their embrace of the liberal philosophy of the Enlightenment. In the first volume of *A Defence* Adams was attracted to Machiavelli's discussion of the mixed constitution in Book I, Ch. 2 of the *Discourses*, whereas in Volume 2 he was engrossed by the historical record of Florence, which he viewed as a falsely acclaimed republic that suffered a relentless series of political disasters because it failed to establish a mixed constitution—the point Adams repeatedly belaboured Machiavelli for missing. In the passages from the *Discourses*, excerpted by Adams, Machiavelli is revealed to be a follower, almost a slavish follower, of Polybius, whose theory has already been expounded. This did not deter Adams from assigning the Florentine republican almost the highest rank among modern writers on politics. Let Adams speak:

The science of government has received very little improvement since the Greeks and Romans. The necessity of a strong and independent executive in a single person, and of three branches in the legislature

instead of two, and of an equality among the three are improvements made by the English, which were unknown, at least never reduced to practice, by the ancients. Machiavel was the first who revived the ancient politics; the best part of his writings he translated almost literally from Plato and Aristotle, without acknowledging the obligation; and the worst of the sentiments, even in his *Prince*, he translated from Aristotle, without throwing upon him the reproach. Montesquieu borrowed the best part of his book from Machiavel, without acknowledging the quotation. Milton, Harrington, and Sidney, were intimately acquainted with the ancients and with Machiavel. They were followed by Locke, Hoadley, etc. (p. 323).

VII

The high rank James Harrington occupies in Adams' list of republican authors is easy to understand. Harrington's *Oceana* (1656) was a visionary portrait of England as a classical republic and had served as a model for the constitutions of several American states. As J. G. A. Pocock, author of the pioneering reinterpretation of republicanism in the modern world, *The Machiavellian Moment* (1975), has observed, during the period of the Puritan revolution in England, Harrington was 'England's premier civic humanist and Machiavellian'.[10]

Adams quoted approvingly Harrington's distinction between 'government *de jure*' and 'government *de facto*'. Having distinguished 'ancient prudence' from 'modern prudence', Harrington linked 'government *de jure*' with the former, which he approved, and 'government *de facto*' with the latter, which he condemned. Thus he defined 'government *de jure*' as 'an art, whereby a civil society of men is instituted and preserved upon the foundation of *common interest*; or ... an empire of laws and not of men', and he defined 'government *de facto*' as 'an art by which some man, or some few men, subject a city or a nation, and rule it according to his or their private interest' (p. 124). For Harrington, interest is the mover of all governments, law proceeding from human will, and he had differentiated the interest of the people from the interests of a king or a party. Where private interest rules, it is a government of men and not of laws. Since the interest of the people is the public interest, 'where the public interest governs, it is a government of laws and not of men' (p. 124).

Adams devoted Letter XXX to a discussion of Harrington's political philosophy. He prefaced the discussion with a distinction between two kinds of principles: 'principles of authority and principles of power' (p.

[10] J. G. A. Pocock, *The Political Works of James Harrington* (Cambridge: Cambridge University Press, 1977), 15.

156). Virtues of the mind and heart, such as wisdom, prudence, courage, patience, temperance, and so forth are principles of authority, while the goods of fortune, such as riches, knowledge, and reputation, are principles of power. Among the principles of power Adams, following Harrington, ranked riches (or wealth) first.

Adams accepted as axiomatic Harrington's thesis (formulated succinctly by the latter's editor John Tolland) that 'empire follows the balance of property, whether lodged in one, a few, or many hands'; he deemed this discovery to be on a par with Harvey's discovery of the circulation of the blood (p. 157). By 'property' Harrington primarily meant land. Whoever owns the property reduces to a servile condition those who depend upon it for their livelihood. Harrington was most explicit about the link between the military and the ownership of property. His statement is graphic: '. . . an army is a great beast that has a great belly, and must be fed' (p.161). If the monarch owns all the land, then, as in Turkey, his empire is absolute monarchy, and the army will be loyal. If the few own the land, then there is a mixed monarchy, a Gothic constitution, with the power shared by the monarchy and nobility, as in Spain. If, in the third place, 'the whole people be landlords, or hold the lands so divided among them, that no one man, or number of men, within the compass of the few, or aristocracy over-balance them, the empire is a commonwealth' (p. 153). Where the farmer, who owns the plough, is ready to turn it into a sword in defence of his own, the security of freedom and the military defence of the commonwealth are greatest.

In linking political power to property ownership, Harrington contended that the former naturally depended on the latter. The so-called degenerate polities of tyranny, oligarchy, and anarchy arise when force is used to introduce and support governments not so naturally grounded; and these degenerate polities are, in Harrington's words, 'confusions . . . but of short continuance, because against the nature of the balance; which not destroyed, destroys that which opposes it' (p. 159).

Adams applied Harrington's theory to the American revolution.

> The balance of land, especially in New England, where the force [of fleets and armies] was first applied, was neither in a king or a nobility, but immensely in favour of the people. The intention of the British politicians was to alter this balance, frame the foundation to the government, by bringing the lands more and more into the hands of the governors, judges, counsellors, etc., etc., who were all to be creatures of the British ministry. We have seen the effects—the balance destroyeth that which opposed it (p. 160).

And Letter XXX concludes with Adams' reflection on America:

> In America, the balance is nine-tenths on the side of the people: indeed there is but one order; and our senators have influence chiefly by the

principles of authority, and very little by those of power . . . (pp. 166–167).

VIII

Algernon Sidney, found guilty of high treason and executed in 1683 on such evidence as his unpublished *Discourses concerning Government* (1698), was regarded by the Americans as a martyr for republicanism and liberty. The use to which Adams puts Sidney's doctrine is curious. At one point in *A Defence* Adams relied on Sidney to establish the linkage between liberty and law, and he quoted Sidney's definition of liberty as consisting in 'an independency on the will of another' or 'in being subject to no man's will' (p. 125).

But most of Adams' consideration of Sidney dwells on the English republican's negative views of democracy. Letter XXVIII, devoted to Sidney, opens with a reiteration of the three types of pure polity, and the judgment that

> . . . the wisest, best, and by far the greatest part of mankind, rejecting these simple features, did form governments mixed or composed of the three . . . which commonly received their respective denomination from the part that prevailed, and did receive praise or blame, as they were well or ill-proportioned (p. 146).

And he accepted Sidney's statement that 'the best governments of the world have been composed of monarchy, aristocracy, and democracy' (p. 146).

But most of Adams' quotations from Sidney are derogatory of democracy and laudatory of aristocracy as the dominant feature in the mixture. Sidney held, and Adams concurred, that governments wherein democracy dominates err more frequently than those wherein aristocracy prevails in regard to 'the choice of men, or the means of preserving that purity of manners which is required for the well-being of a people . . .' (p. 149) As for absolute monarchies, these are worse still than democracies, since the demogogues who propose to establish such tyrannies 'abhor *the dominion of the laws*, because it curbs their vices, and make themselves subservient to the lusts of *a man* who may nourish them' (p. 149).

IX

Locke, widely acclaimed as the philosopher of the American Revolution, received short shrift from Adams in *A Defence*. This brusque treatment may, indeed, startle those who rightly esteem the English philosopher to be a maker of the American political mind. It may even be construed as a sign of Adams' idiosyncracies, limitations or aberrations. However, Adams never denied Locke his place as a philosopher of natural rights, crucial to the struggle for American independence. But as the Americans moved from revolution to the establishment of constitutions, Locke receded from the centre of their attention. If Locke had, indeed, been the philosopher who most influenced Jefferson's composition of the Declaration of Independence,[11] he was certainly replaced by Montesquieu as the thinker who most profoundly affected the formulation of the American constitution(s). As Adams pointed out in the introductory remarks to his brief discussion of Locke, a philosopher, no matter how great his achievements in such fields as metaphysics, philosophy of mind, and moral philosophy, may fail utterly in the practical matter of making a constitution—'nay, he may defend the principles of liberty and the rights of mankind, with great abilities and success; and after all, when called upon to produce a plan of legislation, he may astonish the world with a signal absurdity' (p. 363). Such he deemed the case of John Locke. As a young man in the employ of Lord Ashley, Earl of Shaftesbury, Locke had assisted in the writing of a constitution for Carolina that had vested all power, executive and legislative, in the proprietors, and that, under this oligarchical sovereignty, had created orders of nobility based on the amount of land owned by the members distributed among the noble orders. Rhetorically Adams asked:

> Who did this legislator think would live under his government? He should have first created a new species of being to govern before he instituted such a government (p. 364).

From Adams' standpoint Locke's constitution had excluded the democratic element, so that, designed for an uninhabited colony, it would be too unpopular to attract men to live under it.

---

[11] The appreciation of Locke's influence on the Declaration of Independence has altered in the past decade. The classic study is, of course, Carl Becker's *The Declaration of Independence* (New York: Harcourt, Brace and Co., 1922). This study in the history of political ideas stressed the role of Locke in the formation of Jefferson's thought and expression. However, in the aftermath of the celebration of the bicentennial of American independence two books have appeared which have suggested that other thinkers were more influential than Locke. Morton White, *The Philosophy of the American Revolution* (New York: Oxford University Press, 1978), resurrects Jean Jacques Burlamaqui as the primary influence, and Garry Wills, *Inventing America, Jefferson's Declaration of Independence* (New York: Doubleday & Company, Inc., 1978), points to Francis Hutcheson.

X

Letter XXIX contains a translation of Montesquieu's *Spirit of the Laws*, Ch. vi, on the Constitution of England. That Adams translated without interjecting comment suggests that he wholly approved of the excerpt from Montesquieu. Here the French thinker established several points central to the structure of American constitutions. Foremost is the tripartite distinction of powers: legislative, executive in regard to foreign relations (executive power of the state), and executive in regard to internal laws and their applications (judiciary). The legislative power, Montesquieu continued, 'enacts temporary or perpetual laws, and amends or abrogates those that have been already enacted' (p. 151). The executive power of the state 'makes peace or war, sends or receives embassies, establishes the public security, and provides against invasion' (p. 151). The judiciary power 'punishes criminals, or determines the disputes that arise between individuals' (p. 151).

Secondly, political liberty requires the separation of these powers. Adams quoted Montesquieu's definition of the political liberty of the citizen as 'a tranquillity of mind, arising from the opinion each person has of his security'. It requires that the government under which he lives 'be so constituted, as that one citizen need not be afraid of another citizen' (p. 151). To fuse the powers would obliterate political liberty. For if the legislative and executive powers were combined, whether in a prince or in a senate, the upshot would be tyranny. Furthermore, to combine the judiciary with the legislative and executive powers would enable the judge to 'behave with all the violence of the oppressor'. When all the powers are embodied in the same body of officials, they uncheckedly might 'plunder the state by their general determinations' (p. 152), and, with the judiciary power in their hands, they might ruin every private citizen by their particular decisions.

Among other corollaries relating to free government as requiring the separation of powers, Montesquieu formulated a significant justification for a representative legislature and for the elections of representatives within fixed localities rather than at large. The doctrine that 'the legislative power should reside in the whole body of the people' is analogous to the accepted principle that 'in a free state, every man who is supposed a free agent, ought to be his own governor' (p. 155). However, it is impossible in large states and inconvenient in small ones for the people to legislate for themselves, and so they resort to representatives. Since representatives elected at large are less attentive to, or cognizant of, the wants and interests of a particular town or locality, 'it is proper, that in every considerable place, a representative should be elected by the inhabitants' (p. 155). Montesquieu, apparently with Adams' approval, considered the people collectively to be unfit to discuss the issues as ably as a body of representatives; he regarded this disadvantage in the people to be 'one of the greatest inconveniences of a democracy' (p. 155).

XI

Although Adams had approved of Sidney's caustic strictures on democracy, he criticized Hume for neglecting the democratic element in his 'Idea of a Perfect Commonwealth'. Adams' treatment of Hume in *A Defence*, like that of Locke, may strike the reader as naive. However much Adams appreciated and absorbed these two great philosophers in other respects, he was sharply critical of them as authors of constitutions. Perhaps some of his animus sprang from his egotistical sense of being a man of historically significant action instead of being a mere theoretician. But this reflection must be balanced by the consideration that he took theories so seriously that he studied them, expounded them, rejected some, adopted others, and digested and applied much. What probably stimulated his sharply critical evaluations in *A Defence* is that he focused strictly and narrowly on what these great British philosophers had presented as models for written constitutions.

The hierarchical structure of Hume's plan of government in his 'Idea of a Perfect Commonwealth' prescribes that the freeholders and householders in the counties elect county representatives and the county representatives elect county magistrates and senators. Then, the senators, who meet in the capital, exercise the whole executive power of the commonwealth; and the county representatives, who meet in the particular counties, possess the legislative power, except that the senate must first debate every new law and is empowered to break any tie. This plan, Adams declared, is defective in that it is 'a complicated aristocracy, and would soon behave like all the other aristocracies' (p. 368). For the senators would decide which laws the representatives would consider. Since the proposed laws would have to be debated in every county, there would be endless delays and confusions. Finally, Adams deemed as 'decisive' against Hume's plan of the ideal commonwealth two objections:

1. that it lets 'the nobility or senate into the management of the executive power'; and,
2. that it takes 'the eyes of the people off from their representatives in the legislature. The liberty of the people depends entirely on the constant and direct communication between them and the legislature, by means of their representatives' (p. 369).

Adams was emphatic about the dependence of republican government on popular representation, and he struck out against the intellectual elite in the Enlightenment who thought otherwise.

Americans in this age are too enlightened to be bubbled out of their liberties, even by such mighty names as Locke, Milton, Turgot, or Hume; they know that popular elections of one essential branch of the legislature, frequently repeated, are the only possible method of forming a free constitution, or of preserving the government of laws from the domination of men, or of preserving their lives, liberties, or properties in security; they know, though Locke and Milton did not, that when popular elections are given up, liberty and free government must be given up (p. 367).

XII

Richard Price is discussed in some depth in Letter XXVI. Adams accepted Price's distinctions concerning physical, moral, religious, and civil liberty; he even quoted Price's definition of civil liberty as

... the power of a civil society to govern itself, by its own discretion, or by laws of its own making, by the majority, in a collective body, or by fair representation. In every free state, every man is his own legislator. Legitimate government consists only in the dominion of *equal laws*, made with *common consent*, and not in the dominion of any men over other men (p. 120).

Here in Price's description of legitimate government is to be found the crux of the republic conceived as a government of laws and not of men.

Against Price's conception of civil liberty Turgot had raised the objection that even if a system of equal laws made with common consent were established, there would be no guarantee of civil liberty; the rights of the minority could well be trampled by the majority. So Turgot suggested that the notion of 'general interest', or 'public good', has to be added to the ideas of equal laws by common consent. Adams considered this device unnecessary. The issue as Adams perceived it pivots on the distinction to be drawn between law and liberty. The definition of a republic as a government of laws is not tantamount to the definition of liberty. Of course in a republic with a prominent democratic element the fondness of men for liberty would guarantee 'that, if the whole society were consulted, a majority would never be found to put chains upon themselves, by their own act and voluntary consent' (p. 126). Although law is distinguishable from liberty, Adams contended 'there can be no uninterrupted enjoyment of liberty, nor any good government, in society, without laws...' (p. 126). Hence the question is not to abolish laws but rather 'what combination of powers in society, or what form of government will compel the formation of good and equal laws, an impartial executive, and faithful interpretation of them, so that the citizens may constantly enjoy the benefit of them, and be sure of their continuance' (p. 126).

Adam's answer was the mixed polity, which separated the powers of government into a legislature, an executive, and a judiciary, and which further divided the legislature into two chambers. Thus the orders or classes of men would be checked in the pursuit of their interests from infringing upon the rights of others. Throughout the voluminous *Defence* Adams, like his fellow American patriots, was a vigorous advocate for the natural rights of mankind, but he was emphatic that their security required a framework of laws, a constitution grounded in the balance of the mixed polity and containing an explicitly formulated Bill of Rights. In this spirit he had, in 1779, framed a model for the constitution of the state of Massachusetts, the first chapter of which is 'A Declaration of the Rights of the Inhabitants of the Commonwealth of Massachusetts'.[12] It reiterated the liberties guaranteed by the Virginia Bill of Rights and reaffirmed the principles enunciated in the Declaration of Independence (for the institution of which Adams, as a member of the committee selected by the Continental Congress to draft it, stands second only to Jefferson). Adams' Declaration of Rights, was, with minor alterations, incorporated in the Constitution of Massachusetts, established in 1780.[13]

XIII

As justification for his theory of government, Adams appealed to a theory of human nature. He wrote:

> ... the first inquiry should be, what kind of beings men are? You and I admire the fable of Tristram Shandy more than the fable of the Bees, and agree with Butler rather than Hobbes. It is weakness rather than wickedness, which renders men unfit to be trusted with unlimited power (p. 127).

In this regard Adams offered a theory of passions. By nature, he argued, passions are unlimited; for if bounded, they atrophy. He pointed to three so-called aristocratic passions as central to the political process: love of gold, love of praise, and ambition. These passions come to dominate and absorb all the others, and they are so cunning that they wreak their effects while hidden from the sight of the men they drive. The remedy was to seek a balance through a system of checks. Adams explained:

> Men should endeavor at a *balance* of affections and appetites, under the monarchy of reason and conscience, within, as well as at a balance of power without. If they surrender the guidance for any course of time to

[12] *The Works of John Adams*, IV, 219–259.
[13] *The Political Writings of John Adams*, ed. with introduction, by George A. Peek, Jr (New York: The Liberal Arts Press, 1954), 93.

any one passion, they may depend upon finding it in the end, a usurping, domineering, cruel tyrant (p. 128).

Political power is similar to the passions from which it springs. If allowed to go unchecked, it results in tyranny. For absolute power is destructive in the same way that the domination of a single passion is.

Thus Adams' conception of human nature opened a narrow route of escape from the absoluteness of the Machiavellian–Calvinist judgment of universal badness or depravity. Adams' doctrine of human nature may best be elucidated by shifting from an exploration of his evaluation of his philosophical predecessors to an examination of his own views in works both earlier and later than *A Defence*. In his earliest published essay, which appeared in the *Boston Gazette*, 29 August 1763, Adams called critical attention to the principle of 'self-deceit', which he blamed for being the source of 'the greatest and worst part of the vices and calamities of mankind'.[14] Described as 'the spurious offspring of self-love', self-deceit, according to Adams, originates in the deeper human drive for self-esteem, the propensity of men to present themselves admirably in their own eyes and the eyes of others. A. O. Lovejoy, who singled out Adams as 'the principal American exponent' of the late eighteenth-century theory of man according to which reason is subservient to interests, passions, or will, has construed this theory to hold that self-deceit fosters rationalization and self-delusion, concealing or repressing true intentions.[15] Adams of course believed in the capacities of the greatest geniuses to penetrate to the truth and so escape from self-delusion; at least he was confident of his own abilities in this regard.

Later in his *Discourses on Davila*, published in 1790, Adams, while acknowledging benevolence as a characteristic of human nature, focused attention on emulation, the passion for distinction, the love of praise as 'a principal source of the virtues and vices, the happiness and misery of human life'[16] and 'that great leading passion of the soul'.[17] This desire for approbation, a passion unlimited and insatiable, he contended, overrides all others as the object for political philosophy and practical politics. It is, he declared, 'a principal end of government to regulate this passion, which in its turn becomes a principal means of government'.[18] Indeed, Adams was critical of the new American federal constitution, by comparison with the Roman constitution, for failing to grasp fully the significance of approbative emulation by conferring outward marks of distinction, such as

---

[14] 'On Self-Delusion', *The Works of John Adams*, III, 433.
[15] A. O. Lovejoy, *Reflections on Human Nature* (Baltimore: The Johns Hopkins Press, 1961), 33–34.
[16] 'Discourses on Davila', *The Works of John Adams,* VI, 234.
[17] Ibid., VI, 246.
[18] Ibid., VI, 234.

special garments and medals, for meritorious public service, although he was appreciative of the bicameralism and the tripartite separation of the branches of government as a regulation of the passions.

Obviously the framers of the United States Constitution were not as singleminded as Adams in regarding approbative emulation as the ruling passion in politics. They recognized as well the self-interest of economic groups or factions. Nevertheless, they concurred with Adams in appreciating what A. O. Lovejoy has aptly called 'the method of counterpoise—accomplishing desirable results by balancing harmful things against one another'.[19] It is the political and moral reflection of a conception of man that reverberates in the debates of the Constitutional Convention of 1787 and has found eloquent expression in *The Federalist*, Numbers 51 and 55, by James Madison.

> Ambition must be made to counteract ambition. The interest of the man must be connected with the constitutional rights of the place. It may be a reflection on human nature, that such devices should be necessary to control the abuses of government. But what is government itself, but the greatest of all reflections on human nature? If men were angels, no government would be necessary. If angels were to govern men, neither external nor internal controls on government would be necessary. In framing a government, which is to be administered by men over men, the great difficulty lies in this: You must first enable the government to control the governed; and in the next place, oblige it to control itself. A dependence on the people is, no doubt, the primary control on the government; but experience has taught mankind the necessity of auxiliary precautions.[20]

> As there is a degree of depravity in mankind which requires a certain degree of circumspection and distrust: So there are other qualities in human nature which justify a certain portion of esteem and confidence. Republican government presupposes the existence of these qualities in a higher degree than any other form. Were the pictures which have been drawn by the political jealousy of some among us, faithful likenesses of the human character, the inference would be, that there is not sufficient virtue among men for self-government; and that nothing less than the chains of despotism can restrain them from destroying and devouring one another.[21]

XIV

Philosophical historians of the American ideology have marked the period in which the federal Constitution of the United States was established as

---

[19] A. O. Lovejoy, op. cit., 39.
[20] *The Federalist*, Max Beloff (ed.) (Oxford: Blackwell, 1948), 51, p. 265.
[21] Ibid., 55, p. 287.

'the end of classical politics'.[22] The main thrust of this interpretation is that the Constitution of the United States, as explained in *The Federalist*, particularly Number 10 by James Madison, displays a preoccupation with the balancing of interests as foundational to the American republic, rather than a stress on virtue as commitment to the public good, upon which classical republicanism rests. John Adams' *Defence of the Constitutions of the Governments of the United States*, interpreted as an essay in classical republicanism blending aristocracy and democracy, has been rejected as 'already a historical freak'.[23]

However, *A Defence* reveals that Adams did not underestimate the role of interest in politics. He, along with the other Founding Fathers of the American republic, conceived good polity to consist in the balance or equipoise of competing interests. Virtue is a requisite of the politicians and statesmen who are needed to effectuate and sustain the balance, as it is also expected of the people who are depended upon to elect as their representatives and governors persons of superior virtue. The constitutions of the states and of the federal government were devised to implement this republican political philosophy. It assumes no radical dualism between interest and virtue, but rather a continuum; interests, brought into balance, are transmuted into virtue under the governance of superior leaders, natural aristocrats elected by the people. When, furthermore, it is remembered that the aristocracy Adams and even Jefferson cherished was never deemed to be hereditary and that the virtue they praised signified merit and ability, readily evidenced in wealth, the classical politics of virtue has survived and even dominates interest group politics.

Let me summarize what has been found in a study of Adams' *Defence*.

1. The ideas of the philosophers and the historians traced and examined by John Adams in *A Defence* make up the philosophical background of the American constitution(s).
2. Adams based his politics on the theory of man, and his theory is that man is by nature bad. Although reason is a check, man succumbs to his passions unless governed by laws. Human weakness verging on depravity, moreover, infects the rulers as well as the ruled, so that they, too, must be governed by laws.
3. Virtue is not antithetical to interest, but they may be opposed. On the contrary, interest is the motor of political action and virtue is the

---

[22] The phrase is from Gordon S. Wood, *The Creation of the American Republic 1776–1787* (Chapel Hill: University of North Carolina Press, 1969), 562, 606–615. It has been adopted also by J. G. A. Pocock, *The Machiavellian Moment: Florentine Political Thought and the Atlantic Republican Tradition* (Princeton: Princeton University Press, 1975), 523ff.

[23] Pocock, *The Machiavellian Moment*, 526. For a rival position, supporting Adams' viewpoint, see Paul Eidelberg, *The Philosophy of the American Constitution* (New York: The Free Press, 1968).

rational discipline that adjusts or harmonizes the interests and directs political action toward a shared—i.e. a public—good. Civic virtue has as its object the public good.

4. To be free, government must be popular; it must contain a democratic element. American constitutions incorporate the democratic element by means of their representative assemblies, the members of which are elected for short terms from fixed localities.

5. In any body of people there are some who excel in virtue, ability, or wealth. These constitute a natural aristocracy. They should be elected to a separate chamber of the legislature, and play a guiding role in law-making and in advising the executive. Property is indispensable to sound politics.

6. The executive should be strong, elected from the natural aristocracy, but empowered not only to execute laws and conduct foreign policy, but also to participate in the legislative process, particularly by means of the veto.

7. The judiciary should be separate from, and independent of, the legislative and executive branches.

8. A republic is a government of laws and not of men. That is not to say that a republic is essentially a free society. However, there is little hope for liberty except as secured within a framework of law.

9. A government of laws is impossible if one of the three ingredients—democracy, aristocracy, or monarchy—is absent from the constitution. For corruption results from the fact that the dominating principle—whether it be monarchic, aristocratic, or democratic—would have no check on its passionate interests.

10. All the teachings of the classical republicans converge to recommend a mixed constitution wherein balance—like the harmony of our passions and interests at the personal level—prevails.

11. The elements of the mixed constitution correspond to the three orders of men in every society: the high, the middle, and the low. Unless these orders are balanced, there is political instability, and history is a cycle of degenerating polities.

12. The ultimate image projected by John Adams and, I would suggest, reflected in the constitutions of the United States is that of a complex and delicate mechanism always in dynamic equilibrium. Originating in the speculations of the ancients, enriched by the reflections and experiences of the moderns, modified, implemented, and applied by our Founding Fathers, it has borne fruit in the constitutions of the United States, and these constitutions endure as the American experiment.

Two American Philosophers:
Morris Cohen and Arthur Murphy

MARCUS G. SINGER

It may be thought odd that these two philosophers should have been selected for discussion together. They had no special connection with each other. They were not personally close. They did not teach or write in the same place. Nor were their personalities at all similar. None the less there are similarities of thought and perspective that make the conjunction illuminating.

It may be thought even odder that these two philosophers should have been selected for discussion at all. After all, who today reads them, or has even heard of them? Very few. If they ever were in fashion, they are not in fashion now. But this situation results from ignorance, which this series aims to dispel. Remember, it was meant to be a revelation to the ignorant as well as an inspiration.

This last situation, however, reflects one point of similarity. Each of these philosophers was, during his working lifetime, about as famous in the American philosophical scene as it was possible to be, yet each immediately after his death dropped from sight and mind, providing a phenomenon that needs philosophical explanation. Each was a president of the American Philosophical Association, elected at a fairly early age; each was a Carus Lecturer; each was very often invited to speak at APA symposia, and attracted large audiences; each was known in the wider intellectual and cultural community, addressing conferences and contributing essays to publications not narrowly speaking philosophical or professional (though Cohen was in this way much more well known than Murphy). And there are a number of other points of similarity. Each was a great, even inspiring, teacher, in his own way (their ways were quite different). They each had large numbers of students on whom they made an indelible impression. Each in his own way somehow fit the popular picture of what a philosopher is or should be. Each is eminently quotable, and a book on the model of 'The Wit and Wisdom of . . .' series could be compiled from the writings of each (though this aphoristic quality is more characteristic of Cohen than of Murphy).

Both wrote philosophy (as Murphy described his own practice) 'in the present tense and with explicit reference to contemporary issues and doctrines'.[1] This, as Murphy immediately added, is a 'hazardous

---

[1] Arthur E. Murphy, *The Uses of Reason* (henceforth UR), p. v. The books of Cohen and Murphy cited within are cited by abbreviated titles; the keys are contained in the appended list of Sources (see *infra*, pp. 325–6).

enterprise', for the present of the writer is inevitably the past of the reader 'and will have lost something of its urgency and altered somewhat in emphasis and perspective with this change of temporal status'. And their reputations have suffered the consequences of so doing. They were, to put it another way, engaged much earlier in this century in a version of what has now come to be called 'applied philosophy' well before the activity was ever envisioned or even thought possible by so many other professional philosophers. Yet there is an important difference. Neither Cohen nor Murphy conceived of philosophy as so bifurcated. Each conceived of philosophy as essentially tied up with wider cultural concerns and having as its mission to articulate, clarify, and enlighten them. With Cohen this conception and this concern took the form of exhibiting, in the process of philosophizing on any subject, what he called 'the genuine interplay of practical issues and theoretic philosophy' (RN, xv). Although with Murphy it took a somewhat different form, he expressed basically the same idea when he said: 'philosophical scholarship is an instrument of research in an inquiry whose goal is wisdom, and wisdom, or the lack of it, is "in" a civilization not as books are in a library or earrings in the ears to which they are appended, but rather as order or confusion, sanity or fanaticism are in the purposes and behaviour of a growing mind' (RCG, 215).

On the other hand, both held that philosophy fulfilled its function not by being stretched into dealing with matters foreign to it but by dealing with the problems of philosophy, albeit in a humanly enlightening way. Cohen spoke disparagingly (in 1919) of 'the complacent assumption that only by absorption in some contemporary social problem can the philosopher justify his existence. The great philosophers, like the great artists, scientists, and religious teachers, have all, in large measure, ignored their contemporary social problems' (FL, 88).

> There are plenty of historic precedents to justify some skepticism as to the infallibility of the prevailing judgment on what is fundamentally important. Don't you now think the discovery of certain mathematical propositions by Archimedes to be more important than the siege and capture of Syracuse? They used to scorn Hegel for being concerned with his *Phenomenology* while the fate of Germany was being sealed at Jena almost at his very door. Yet history has shown the appearance of Hegel's unearthly book to have been of greater importance than the battle of Jena. The results of the latter were wiped out within seven years, while the results of Hegel's thought will for good or evil last for many years to come ... (FL, 87).[2]

---

[2] Again (in 1929): 'When the public at large is urging us, on the authority of our leading representative, Professor Dewey, to abandon the technical problems which occupy philosophers and to go back to the problems of men, it is

Murphy made the same basic point on a number of occasions. Here is a sample from one, where he is responding to P. A. Schilpp's allegations about 'The Abdication of Philosophy': 'Surely before we offer our collective wisdom to mankind on such an issue we should take care to see that what we have to offer is wisdom and not merely propaganda on axiological stilts' (RCG, 379).

> If doom is now as imminent as Professor Schilpp believes, we shall not be saved from it by a crash program in which philosophers raise their collective voice in warning. Even if we were to shout in chorus on Michigan Avenue, and perhaps make the front page of the *Chicago Tribune* in consequence, we should only add a little to the general clamor. But wherever there is a civilization worth preserving and men who care enough for truth to seek and live by it, there will be a need for philosophical inquiry and understanding. Plato's *Republic* and *Laws* did not save the Athenian State. Aristotle carried on business as usual in the Lyceum while the conquests of Alexander were making much of what he had to say about the *polis* politically obsolete. Kant's *Perpetual Peace* forestalled no wars and would hardly be remembered now if it had not been written by the man who also wrote the *Critique of Pure Reason*. Yet humanity would be poorer than it is today if these men had not done their distinctive work ... (RCG, 384).[3]

However, between these last two points of similarity there is a dialectical pull or tension which neither wholly resolved and which is only partly due to the fact that their different remarks were addressed to different audiences and different questions.

Three more points of similarity should be mentioned here. They both were rationalists (although only Cohen applied the label to himself). They were both liberals, who thought of liberalism as part and parcel of their philosophies and of philosophy as part and parcel of their liberalism (though this also is a misleading term requiring some definition). They both had a special interest in American philosophy and wrote voluminously and expertly on it. It is partly for this reason that I have referred to them as 'American philosophers'. They both wrote about

---

surely opportune to insist in all seriousness that we shall never help humanity very much by neglecting our own special task, the only task for which we are as philosophers properly trained. It is true, of course, that in science as in the arts technical problems tend to become too complicated, and it is often advisable to retrace our steps and to find a new path through our tangled difficulties. But the value of a new approach is to be tested by whether it enables us to see the old problems in a new light' (FL, 369; cf. p. 289).

[3] Cf. Murphy's 'Problems of Men', *The Philosophical Review* **56** (1947), 194–202.

philosophy, and about American philosophy, in relation to the American scene and against the background of the American tradition. It is important to note that merely being an American and a philosopher does not in any significant sense make someone an American philosopher (any more than being both Jewish and a philosopher makes one in any significant sense a Jewish philosopher). In the context of this series, on American philosophy, that is an important attribute of our two philosophers.

But I now must turn to telling you something about Morris Cohen, and after giving you a picture of Cohen I will give you a picture of Arthur Murphy. I deliberately use the word 'picture'—though 'sketch' would also have done—for there is no time for more than a picture, and every picture tends to distort. If one brought in details that are omitted, one could paint a different picture, and, as Cohen was given to pointing out, different pictures of the same subject can all be true, in their own way (though some to be sure can distort so grossly as to be false). But there is no time here for the sort of critical exploration that knits ideas together and is necessary for an adequate philosophical picture. My object on this occasion is only to provide you with an introduction to these two American philosophers.

I. Morris R. Cohen (1880–1947)

Morris Raphael Cohen lived from mid-1880 (perhaps 1881—the exact date is unknown) to January 1947. He was born in Russia, in the Jewish ghetto in Minsk, was brought to the United States in 1892 and lived on the lower East Side of Manhattan. After a while his family moved to Brownsville in Brooklyn, but the lower East Side is where Cohen had his spiritual and cultural home for years. This is where, apart from Russia, he came from and had his roots. And that he was Jewish, and a Jewish immigrant, is an important part of those roots. Yiddish was his mother tongue. He did not learn English until after he was twelve, which is when he first went to public school and first had active contact with non-Jews. He and his family lived in conditions of poverty and anti-Semitism which, however, were not, as they very likely would have been in Russia, life-threatening or hopeless.

To forestall misconceptions I should say right off that I was never a student of Cohen's, never met him, never laid eyes on him; though, as a boy growing up in New York City, I had heard about him. (I was a student of Murphy's, but more of that anon.)

Cohen was of slight stature, with a voice in the tenor range, and a dominating presence. After a paper at an APA meeting Cohen was always first off the mark starting a discussion. He had an acerbic wit, with a keen sense of humour, usually put to work only to illustrate a point. For example, a student in class 'launched an attack on the dogmatism of

Catholicism. To make the point that dogmatism is a personal feature not a logical consequence of a general position, Cohen simply went into a story (didn't make the point in general terms)—"I have a friend who is a Catholic priest and he says 'My religion compels me to believe there is a hell, but it doesn't compel me to believe anyone goes there'".' He gives 'no further argument, but goes on to the next question'.[4]

Cohen was for most of his life associated with the College of the City of New York (CCNY, or City College), first as a student, then as a teacher of mathematics (this for some eight years), and then, after a long and seemingly endless wait, as Professor of Philosophy, from 1912 to 1938, when he retired, aged fifty-seven, to concentrate on his writing and on some other projects of a practical character. New York was the centre of immigration in those days—it is, of course, where the Statue of Liberty is located—and City College, whatever the purposes of its original charter, was one of the institutions that served to facilitate the process of absorbing immigrants into American life. For residents of New York City it was tuition free, as part of the public school system, and it had very high admission standards. Only the very smartest and generally the poorest boys went to City College, and it was, I should add, solely an undergraduate institution. For almost all who went it was their only opportunity for higher education, and it was part of what America, as the advertised land of opportunity, had to offer. As Cohen described it, 'Social life, sports, social polish, and the other superficial attractions of American College life were neglected. . . . Those who chose City College did so only because its courses seemed to offer a key to a wider intellectual world. It was . . . the student body rather than the faculty that created the intellectual tone of the College. . . .' The students who went to City College were not only very bright but also intellectually eager with a passion for ideas and argument. 'It was hard for a teacher who was not a master of his subject to survive this sort of intellectual climate . . .' (DJ, 89, 90). This is of interest because it helps to explain Cohen's characteristic teaching method, which was an especially combative form of what he himself called 'the Socratic method' of question and answer, and his special style of philosophical writing.

In the time he was a student at City College, Cohen was also involved in various other educational activities with immigrants on the East Side. One of the great influences on him in this period was Thomas Davidson, an itinerant philosopher and teacher (Davidson was originally from Scotland, and played a role in the founding of the Fabian Society and the Aristotelian Society) who in 1898 came to teach at the Educational Alliance on the lower East Side. Davidson, who died in 1900 at the age of sixty, was an

---

[4] I owe this account, both in substance and in wording, to Abraham Edel, who handled discussion sections for Cohen for some seven years prior to Cohen's retirement from City College.

inspiration to Cohen. It was owing to Davidson's encouragement that Cohen came to realize that he had philosophical talent, and it was Davidson's example and teaching that helped form Cohen's philosophical ambitions and ideals. As Cohen tells it:

> the enthusiasm of . . . Davidson that influenced me most was the dream of an Encyclopedia of Philosophy that should do for the culture of the twentieth century what the Brothers of Sincerity did for the tenth, and Diderot and d'Alembert did for the eighteenth. This dream has dominated my whole intellectual life. All my reading somehow or other gets fitted into that scheme. And though I was never to realize that youthful ambition, it has given form to all of my fragmentary efforts at the statement of a philosophical position adequate to the understanding of the problems of modern civilization (DJ, 109; cf. SPS, 5–6).

This explains a lot about Cohen's philosophical practice and style. His range of knowledge was immense; he was often compared with Aristotle, in this respect at least, that he took all knowledge for his province, and almost gained it. Thus the great variety and sheer number of the different fields he wrote about, his vast knowledge of science and history and law, his moving about in his writing between one branch of philosophy and another with little regard for conventional boundaries. Thus also the scrappy character of so many of his writings and the unfinished state of so many of his projects.

Cohen went to Harvard in 1904 and got his PhD in 1906 with a thesis on Kant. While at Harvard he roomed with Felix Frankfurter, then a student of law and later on one of the most famous law professors in the United States, trusted adviser to President Franklin Roosevelt, and then Supreme Court justice. Cohen attributed his interest in legal philosophy to his friendship and discussions with Frankfurter. (I think it would have developed anyway, given his background and other interests, but that is something else.) His major teachers at Harvard were James and Royce (Santayana was then on leave), and in studying with James and Royce, Cohen found himself in the middle of the perennial dialectic that went on between them for so long. This also may help explain something about his philosophical outlook. But we should not exaggerate the importance of the Harvard connection. Cohen's connection with Columbia University, both before and after his Harvard stay, was even more extensive. Cohen attended classes at Columbia (in the days before Dewey arrived there) with, among others, Felix Adler and W. H. Sheldon and Frederick Woodbridge (a philosopher little read today and possibly unknown in Britain, but who was the guiding spirit behind Naturalism in American philosophy).

After he got his PhD Cohen went back to teaching mathematics in the high school department at City College. He could not get a position teaching philosophy anywhere (except for an unpaid one at Columbia) and it was six years before he was appointed to the Philosophy Department at City College. The explanation seems clear enough. He was Jewish, and not only that, he was an immigrant Jew, with a foreign accent, and from Eastern Europe besides. In the United States in those days, this sort of genteel anti-Semitism was especially pronounced, even open (though of course not talked about and not admitted). Jews, especially immigrant Jews from Eastern Europe, simply did not get to teach philosophy in the United States, the land of opportunity. In the colleges at large, which were almost invariably church founded and connected, the professor of philosophy was also both the president of the college and the college chaplain, a Doctor of Divinity. In the universities the role was not as rigid, but the position of professor of philosophy was still not available to Jews. It was just a matter of time before the barriers were down, but this did not occur generally until after World War II. Morris Cohen was the first (except for Felix Adler, the founder of the Ethical Culture Society—and one of Cohen's mentors—who had a special post as Professor of Ethics at Columbia University), and the most successful and prominent of this group. Cohen spoke of his appointment as Assistant Professor of Philosophy in July 1912 as marking the end, for him, 'of a long valley of humiliation' (DJ, 143). He was already, through his writings and his appearances at APA meetings, well known and highly regarded in the profession and also, I gather, respected if not feared for his caustic wit and dialectical ability.

The curriculum at City College provided few courses in philosophy itself, although the College offered a 'variety of courses in languages, literature, and science'. Cohen says:

> I therefore saw no adequate opportunity for teaching philosophy along traditional lines, and so I had to give courses in related subjects, hoping to bring philosophic insight to my students through courses on the nature of civilization, the philosophy of law, and the topics covered by Santayana in the last four volumes of his *The Life of Reason* (FL, 294).

Thus he abandoned the 'traditional attempt to teach philosophy as a self-sufficient body of learning, and instead' attempted 'to teach future scientists, lawyers, economists, and citizens to think philosophically about the problems of science, law, economics, and citizenship' (FL, 295). It may well have been this unusual teaching situation that led Cohen to write so much in what have since come to be called the 'philosophy-of' areas, in particular philosophy of law, philosophy of science, and philosophy of history (as well as philosophy of mathematics, philosophy of logic, and philosophy of civilisation). It may help us understand also why he took the aim of philosophy to be to trace out and examine the philosophical assumptions underlying other fields of thought and endeavour, such as law, science, politics, economics, history. He gave his students, and he gave his readers, the feeling that philosophical assumptions, and consequently philosophical inquiry, were inescapable no matter what one thought about. It is worth noting that he had an extraordinary number of students (all undergraduates) who went on to become well-known philosophers: Sidney Hook, Ernest Nagel, Herbert Schneider, Paul Weiss, Morton White, and Philip Wiener are just six of the best known. Cohen also became widely known, not just in the intellectual world of New York City, but in the country at large. (He was thought of, in the informed public mind that knew something about intellectual and cultural matters, alongside Dewey and Russell as one of the most famous philosophers of the day.) This was partly brought about by the amount and character of the writing he did for the general literate press, such as *The New Republic* and the *Nation*. When *The New Republic* was founded in 1914, Cohen was enlisted as one of its regular writers, and over the years to 1936 contributed some sixty-five pieces to it, articles and editorials, some of them on topics as recondite as Einstein's theory of relativity (on which he was recognized as expert), others on American philosophy, others on other philosophical subjects and current philosophical books. It was also, I think, brought about by his reputation in the New York area, which at that time seemed the centre of the cultural universe (at least in the United States). He had an effect on his students, and through them on the literate community of New York, that is sometimes hard to believe. He was easily the most famous and highly regarded teacher at City College if not in the whole city. And this not by soft soap but by astringent methods. It was not so much question and answer as thrust and parry, challenge and response. If the accounts I have heard are veracious, Cohen rivalled the fastest gun in the west with the quickest tongue in the east. In repartee it is hard to see how there could have been anyone much quicker. His students, very bright themselves, used to arrange surprise confrontations of ideas to see how fast and with what new argument he would react, much as the other Marx Brothers, in their vaudeville days, used to depart from the script in unexpected ways to test the quickness of Groucho's wit. Cohen stories abound. There is one that is also told about some other philosophers who became noted more for the severity of their criticism than for their substantive doctrines, such as Prichard. But it certainly applies to Cohen. As the story goes, Professor Cohen dies and presents himself at the gates of Heaven, where St Peter awaits to determine his credentials for entering. 'What did you do in life?' St Peter asks. 'I was a philosopher', says the shade of Cohen. 'All right, if you were a philosopher', says St Peter, 'say something profound.' 'Oh no, St Peter, you don't understand', says the S. of C. 'You say something profound, and I'll refute it.' A student is reported to have become exasperated at Cohen's practice of invariably, or so it seemed, responding to a question by asking another question. 'Tell me, Professor Cohen', the student said, 'why, why is it that every time someone asks you a question you respond with another question—why?' Professor Cohen: 'Why not?' There was a student who became unusually perplexed by the predicament of Descartes, and said, in an agony of perplexity, 'Professor Cohen, please tell me, do I exist? Please, prove to me that I exist'. Professor Cohen, looking around: 'Who's asking?'

Cohen set out to demolish the shibboleths of popular opinion, such as popular psychoanalysis, behaviourism, communism and dialectical materialism, and, in a word, any simple all-embracing formula. Indeed, he would sometimes seem to be arguing against both sides of what seemed superficially to be exhaustive and mutually exclusive alternatives on some matter, such as evolutionism and the doctrine of special creation, theism *and* atheism. Naturally students confronting him for the first time were shocked and dismayed, and often confused and upset by this assault on the opinions they had brought to college with them. When one complained about this negative assault on ideas and wondered why Cohen didn't supply any positive doctrines to take their place, Cohen retorted, it is reported, 'It is not recorded that Hercules was asked to do any more than *clean out* the Augean stables'.

There are a number of observations of Cohen's that I have always found of special use in my own teaching and thinking. Two in particular are these. In the first he is responding to those who belittle reasons and reasoning. 'We have no way of counting', he observes, 'all those who, though unwilling in the heat of argument to admit the force of their opponents' reasons, yet sooner or later are so affected by them as to use them against others' (FL, 8). In the second, in a discussion of teaching, he observed that 'the overcoming of intellectual obstacles is necessary to the growth of intellectual power, just as the overcoming of physical difficulties is necessary to the development of physical strength' (FL, 277).

In 1938 Cohen retired from City College (the student paper had a headline, when his retirement was announced, saying 'We won't let him!'). He then went to the University of Chicago, where he had graduate students for the first time, and was there from 1938 to 1941. (There was one lively time when Cohen, Russell, and Carnap were there together.) In 1942 he had a stroke from which he never fully recovered; his work as an active philosopher ceased, though he was able to put together collections of essays for publication in book form, aided by his son Felix, a philosopher of moment as well as a lawyer, and other members of his family; he died in January 1947.

Cohen published a very large number of essays and reviews—many of his reviews had the character of essays, in the manner of though not as long-windedly as Macaulay—in philosophical journals (thirty in the *Journal of Philosophy* alone), in popular journals of opinion (well over seventy here), and in law journals (at least twenty-four), others in books and other types of periodicals. Many of these essays were republished in book form.

His books include *Reason and Nature* (1931); *Law and the Social Order* (1933); *An Introduction to Logic and Scientific Method*, with Ernest Nagel (1934), one of most well-known and highly regarded logic texts ever produced; *A Preface to Logic* (1944); *The Faith of a Liberal*, a fairly large collection of essays on many topics (1946); and *The Meaning of Human History*, his Carus Lectures (1947). After his death a number of others came out (largely through the work of his son Felix), including his autobiography, *A Dreamer's Journey,* in 1948; *A Source Book in Greek Science*, edited with his former student Israel Drabkin (which was put together to establish Cohen's thesis that science was founded by the ancient Greeks and not by Bacon or even Newton) in 1948; and *American Thought* in 1954. Two others of consequence are *Studies in Philosophy and Science* (1949) and *Reason and Law* (1950). *Reflections of a Wondering Jew* (1950) illustrates another area of his interests. There were a total of fourteen (not counting the published Holmes–Cohen letters), but this was still far short of the number he had planned when he planned to write a philosophical encyclopedia adequate to the understanding of the problems of modern civilization. Still, when one reflects that through most of his career he had a twelve to fifteen hour teaching load, and in addition was both involved in the work of various organizations and also teaching at the New School for Social Research, the wonder is that he got any books at all written.

As a student of American philosophy, Cohen published a bibliography of the published writings of Peirce in 1916, the first such compilation to be made, and he edited the first collection of Peirce's writings in 1923 under the title *Chance, Love and Logic*. He was the first scholar to bring Peirce to the attention of the learned world and the philosophical community generally.

What was Cohen's philosophy? Cohen himself did not find it very easy to say, although he provided a number of nutshell summaries, and, abstracted from the context in which he developed it, by contrast with and in the light of opposing views on the subjects he dealt with, any simple statement of even his major themes is bound to be oversimplified and misleading. He called himself a realistic rationalist, also a logical realist. He held, following Peirce (and the early Russell), that universals are real, as logical relations, and are not only real parts of nature but exist. He qualified this by maintaining that there are different types or orders of existence. His main criticism of the New Realism of 1912 was that it was not realistic enough, in hedging on the existence of universals. On Cohen's view, when a mathematician proves an existence theorem, say that every equation of the nth degree has n roots, he proves the *existence* of these n roots not the nebulous subsistence of them; and, moreover, the manner in which mathematical and physical existences are determined is exactly the same, although they do not exist in the same way (SPS, 112–113). Cohen regarded nominalism as a vacuous error, having pernicious effects not only in metaphysics, but in logic, history, law, politics, and society. He was a rationalist, not in the *a priori* sense of deducing all of nature from a few postulates—for Cohen that was irrationalism—but in the sense of maintaining that the major role in science and inquiry generally was played by reason, in the form of critical intelligence using ideas and hypotheses as searchlights for discovering the truths of nature, and that inquiry always starts with an idea, not with facts. And he believed that what science discovered about the world was the truth about it, not merely the truth about some realm connected only in some nebulous way with the world we have to deal with in everyday affairs. He thus rejected the Kantian conception of a divide between the phenomena of nature and the noumenal *ding-an-sich*, not discoverable by us, as well as the conventionalism of Duhem and Poincaré. On Cohen's view, reason, working by the methods of science, is capable of discovering the nature of things as they are in themselves, and is doing this all the time, even though these discoveries are not certain but only probable and are liable to revision by further inquiry. At the same time, he did not think reason was capable of discovering the whole truth about the universe. In his view, the universe taken as a whole is an illegitimate totality, which cannot be known except piecemeal and in part (SPS, 16–18; cf. RN, 145–146). Here is an oft-quoted Cohen dictum: 'Our reason may be a pitiful candle light in the dark and boundless seas of being. But we have nothing better and woe to those who wilfully try to put it out' (RN, 165). (One would think that it would also be woe to the rest of us, as well as those who inadvertently put it out—but Cohen characteristically did not consider such alternatives when he was in the grip of epigrammatic fever.)

Cohen rejected the view, later elaborated by Russell (*The Scientific Outlook*, 1931, 74–83; cf. p. 75), that science is itself a source of scepticism about the external world and the world of nature and that (to quote Russell): 'our faith in the external world must be merely animal faith' (*Scientific Outlook*, 83). On Cohen's view, that something is an inference from present data in no way puts its existence or the reality of its inferred characteristics in doubt; Cohen maintained that all our knowledge is inferential, and that such an argument (as the one made by Russell) would undermine its own foundations. 'History as the knowledge of the past', he said, 'and indeed all knowledge, can be obtained only through inference'; 'the study of the past begins with the present', but 'the present can be understood only in terms of the past' (C&N, 324). The connecting thread is supplied by the system of propositions as a whole and by what Cohen often referred to as 'the threads of identity' running through perceptibly different phenomena which enables inquiry to connect them into a system. Thus: '. . . we perceive and master the flux of phenomena only when we see running through it the threads of identity' (C&N, 375; cf. RN, 225–

229). This, he believed, both requires and also helps establish the reality of relations and universals in general. Thus it was his view that philosophy of science, as the study of the distinctive methods and major results of the sciences, not only presupposes metaphysical ideas—as does every other human activity—but helps establish them. So he did not divorce his study of metaphysics from his study of science and the sciences, and this is one of the meanings of scientific method that his *Reason and Nature* is intended to teach. Through reason, he maintained, reasonably understood and applied, we discern the substance and the order and the reality of nature.

The idea Cohen was most noted for is what he called the principle of polarity. This is not easy to state accurately in short compass; in accordance with its own meaning it takes on different meanings and is also differently formulated in different contexts, and it is very far from being a simple principle. It has at least two main interpretations, one ontological, the other heuristic or regulative. Cohen applied this principle in nearly all of his works and in every area of philosophy. Here is one way he stated it, taken from just one of numerous contexts of discussion (1927):

> to make logic applicable to empirical issues, we must employ the principle of polarity. By this I mean that the empirical facts are generally results of opposing and yet inseparable tendencies like the north and south poles. We must, therefore, be on our guard against the universal tendency to simplify situations and to analyze them in terms of only one of such contrary tendencies. The principle of polarity is a maxim of intellectual search, like the principle of causality, against the abuse of which it may serve as a help. If the principle of causality makes us search for operating causes, the principle of polarity makes us search for that which prevents them from producing greater effects than they do ... it may be generalized as the principle, not of the identity, but of the necessary copresence and mutual dependence of opposite determinations (PL, 74–75).

At another time (1930), Cohen said this about it:

> The obvious value of the principle of polarity is in enabling us to avoid one-sided and interminable ... issues, and in making us more hospitable to the complexity of seemingly paradoxical facts such as that we rest alternately on our feet while walking or that we remain the same while growing ...
> ... The opposing considerations involved in all existences ... are different aspects which never become identical though they necessarily coexist (SPS, 13, 14).

Earlier (1915), Cohen had applied it thus:

> A good deal of the wisdom of life is apt to appear foolishness to a narrow logic. We urge our horse downhill and yet put the brake on the

wheel—clearly a contradictory process to a logic too proud to learn from experience. But a genuinely scientific logic would see in this humble illustration a symbol of that measured straining in opposite directions which is the essence of the homely wisdom that makes life livable (LSO, 193).

I would take this 'measured straining in opposite directions' as the dominant metaphor underlying Cohen's philosophical outlook. It was also a feature of his personality and of his teaching.

It may well be that Cohen's major philosophical contribution will be found to have been in philosophy of law, as has been suggested by a number of commentators, except for the fact that Cohen himself was so constantly stepping over these artificial boundaries. He never abided by traditional distinctions and boundary lines. Cohen was, however, certainly America's first and foremost philosopher of law. This is not to overlook the overriding importance of Holmes (with whom Cohen, incidentally, had a close association—Holmes regarded Cohen as his philosophical adviser and tutor). But Holmes was a lawyer with philosophical interests, not himself a philosopher in a technical sense. The best way to get an idea of Cohen's treatment of philosophy of law is to see the liberal outlook from which he approached it, as revealed in the Preface to *Law and the Social Order*:

> The meaning of law in the lives of men and women is a theme to which my earliest reflective thought was directed; for I could not help seeing the effects of legal rules and judicial decisions on the daily life of those nearest to me. . . . As the teaching of philosophy became my daily occupation, I found that legal material gave new and pointed significance to old issues in logic, ethics, and metaphysics. Sound methods and logical errors seem strikingly illustrated in the reasons courts give for their decisions, as well as in the writings of their critics. The craving for absolute moral distinctions and the confused effort to apply them to practical life—the source of so much of our spiritual grandeur and misery—appear nowhere more clearly than in the history of the law. And even the most elementary questions of metaphysics, such as the grounds of materialism and subjectivism, find revealing light thrown on them by a consideration of the nature of *things* in the law of property and of *will* in the law of contract. Law, philosophy, and social justice have thus become merged in an absorbing theme of reflection (LSO, v).

Although Cohen wrote voluminously in legal philosophy, he never finished a systematic treatise on the subject. What we have are collections of papers, and it would take a commentary to bring out the underlying unity of theme and purpose. Here I shall simply quote a few of his words to give you some of the flavour and incisiveness of his thought. In writing on 'The Process of Judicial Legislation' he observes that although finding and making, discovering and inventing, are usually poles apart, there are contexts in which they coalesce, as in finding and making an opportunity, finding and making time; the suggestion is that the distinction between finding and making the law is not as sharp as it has been supposed to be (LSO, 121). This is an application and illustration of the Principle of Polarity, and is only the beginning of the analysis he goes on to present. Again, he observes that the distinction between rights and duties, although often supposed absolute, can also coalesce. 'May there not be legal relations that can just as well be called rights as duties? Some of the very onerous rights of trustees come very near being of that type' (LSO, 179). This is meant to illustrate 'the difficulty of foisting an absolutely logical division upon the facts', and is another application of the principle of polarity. He defended a version of natural law theory when it seemed almost prehistoric; only recently has it come back into currency. All along he maintained the necessity of the ideals represented by natural law for understanding, interpreting, and changing positive law (RN, 401). In ethics as traditionally understood Cohen wrote little, and then mostly on method. However, he had insights here regarding method that may not be apparent to the untrained eye and which I have found useful in my own work. I have in mind in particular his discussion of the need to test general principles against judgments of particular cases and to test the judgment of particular cases against general principles, and on how this is done (e.g. in RL, 15); Cohen argued that this process need be neither circular nor question begging, and is analogous to the process of testing theories and discovering new facts in the sciences. But Cohen in the main treated ethics as subsidiary to philosophy of law, which he claimed 'is an indispensable part of any system of social ethics . . . Individual ethics', he claimed, 'seems to treat terms apart from their relations . . . the significance of most ethical issues becomes apparent only if they are writ large and made principles of social legislation' (RL, 129). Cohen's immersion in the philosophy of law gave him a unique vantage point for viewing the problems of philosophy, and for providing illuminating insights into the systems of the great philosophers. Thus he observed that 'the concept of law is fundamental to the whole body of Kantian thought, theoretic as well as practical. Not only is Kant's ethics decidedly legalistic . . . but his basic conception of nature is that of a system of laws . . .' (RL, 105).

A word about Cohen's liberalism. For Cohen there was a formal analogy between science and a liberal civilization, in that they are both self-correcting systems. He set out 'to rescue the word "liberal" from its association with *laissez-faire* economics, superficial politics, or mush-minded sentimentality, and . . . show liberalism as simply scientific method at work on human problems' (DJ, 159). But science was not, with Cohen, as it so often was with Dewey, a form of social gospel. Not only did he have deep knowledge of the sciences, but he did not identify what he tended to call 'scientific method' with the specific method used in any particular science. For him 'scientific method' meant rational method, and he tried close analysis of it in several works and in many areas. For Cohen the essence of liberalism is 'freedom of thought and inquiry, freedom of discussion and criticism' (FL, 118), not identification with any one political party or programme or social goal.

> To affirm a faith in liberalism may seem quixotic at a time when the word 'liberalism' is commonly associated either with an outmoded individualistic theory of economics or with a political trend that shuns clear thinking and seems to offer a special haven to those mushy-minded persons who, rather than make a definite choice between Heaven and Hell, cheerfully hope to combine the best features of each. But liberalism and liberal civilization may be conceived more generously. For my part I prefer to think of the liberal temper as, above all, a faith in enlightenment, a faith in a process rather than in a set of doctrines, a faith instilled with pride in the achievements of the human mind, and yet colored with a deep humility before the vision of a world so much larger than our human hopes and thoughts. If there are those who have no use for the word 'faith' they may fairly define liberalism as a rationalism that is rational enough to envisage the limitations of mere reasoning (FL, 437; cf. 452–453).

About Cohen's philosophy of history I shall say only this. If you read Cohen's *Meaning of Human History* from the standpoint of contemporary up-to-the-minute philosophy of history it may well seem disappointing, and it was negatively reviewed from this perspective. For the most part it does not deal with the problems agitating current practitioners, and where it does touch on them it is apt to appear, from that perspective, as somewhat superficial. (And similar things have been said about his philosophy of science, though I have not heard them said about his philosophy of law.) However, is that a sensible way to approach it? I think not. If you approach it from the standpoint of one who asks: What is history all about? What are the problems in the way of obtaining knowledge of history, how can we obtain such knowledge, and what lessons can we learn from history?—it takes on a fresh aspect and comes alive, even seems fresh and new. It is, on the whole, his most balanced book, the least polemical, the most constructive, and possibly the most underrated.

II. Arthur Edward Murphy (1901–62)

Horace Kallen once called Santayana 'our time's one laughing philosopher' (JP, v. 6(1), 2 January 1964, p. 35). Not so. Another was Bouwsma. Still another was Arthur E. Murphy. Murphy was a cheerful witty very funny man who was also a cheerful witty very funny philosopher. He was also a very serious philosopher with a deep sense of philosophy's urgency and importance both in itself, as the embodiment of inquiry, and in relation to the civilization in which it could flower and in which, in his view, it plays an essential role.

He was a short round man with twinkly eyes and a voice like a bell. He himself had an almost pixie quality, with a constant undertone of irony, and he rippled with humour. If you remember Joseph Welch, the Army attorney in the famous Army–McCarthy hearings, you will get some sense of what Murphy sounded like. He had a natural eloquence, and he spoke as he wrote and wrote as he spoke.

He spoke as he wrote and wrote as he spoke. But he wrote in long involved sentences with rounded periods and dependent clause within dependent clause. This often provided the effect that generated the humour. But it is also the source of the trouble so many people, especially students, have had reading him. His style is not the easiest to follow. You have to get the go of it. And there were philosophers who would never miss a Murphy performance yet did not read him much. For them the silver voice and the platform manner helped convey the ideas, and certainly provided the entertainment, and they could not get this from his writing in the same way.

He was born in September 1901 in Ithaca, New York, and died in Austin, Texas, in May 1962, at the age of sixty. At an early age, but not before he had had a chance to observe the filming of episodes of the *Perils of Pauline* in Ithaca's gorges—an event that helped develop his abiding love of motion pictures, even, as he put it, rather bad motion pictures—his family moved to California, where he went to Napa High School, and won the state debating prize. He earned both his Bachelor's degree and his PhD from the University of California, the latter in 1926.

Murphy's career was meteoric. He burst on the philosophical scene at the age of twenty-five with a paper with the provocative title 'Objective Relativism in Dewey and Whitehead', and that, together with some other papers he wrote at the same time developing the same theme, established him as a new force in American philosophy. Objective Relativism was the name of the doctrine he became associated with in the minds of those who knew anything at all about him, even though as he worked his way through it he later rejected it as unsound. His philosophical career was, for the time, unusual. He was one of the first of the itinerant professors. He taught a year at Berkeley, then he went to the University of Chicago for a year, then to Cornell for a year, then back to Chicago, this time for two years, 1929–31. While at Chicago he became associated with Mead, and he edited and brought to publication Mead's Carus Lectures, *The Philosophy of the Present*, after Mead died. Murphy then went to Brown University, in

Providence, Rhode Island, as a full professor at the age of twenty-nine—something as rare then as it is now. After eight years at Brown he went to the University of Illinois as head of the department, and thus began his career as an administrator and department builder. After six years at Illinois he went to Cornell as department head. He left Cornell after eight years to go to the University of Washington as department head, and after five years went to the University of Texas, in the same capacity, in 1958. He thus in a way re-enacted the saga of the mobile American. He lived in nearly every section of the country. He lectured all over, and served on various national committees and commissions, both philosophical and non-philosophical. He had charm, in abundance, and the gift of tongues. To follow out our Western analogy, we might say that he lived by the motto, 'Have tongue, will travel'.

I should say something about my personal relations with him. I was a student of his, as a graduate student at Cornell, 1948 to 1952, and we maintained contact, after a fashion, since. I co-edited a collection of his essays which was published in 1963, after his death; and I have in trust in my possession masses of his unpublished writings. But I did not develop my interest in Murphy as a result of being a student of his; I went to Cornell to study with him because I had heard about him and read his work—and then it turned out that most of my work at Cornell was done with other people. I had first heard about Murphy in the spring of 1946 when I came back to the University of Illinois after service in World War II; and I heard about him because students I met were still talking about his Honours' Day address, 'The Rewards of Learning', given as his swan song, so to speak, before leaving for Cornell. It made so much stir because it was taken, whether it was intended so or not, as an arch, subtle, clever, and very amusing attack on tendencies and ideas then, as now, prevailing with administrators and trustees at state universities and the legislators who would have to vote money to support them—in particular the state-supported and very large University of Illinois. Liberal arts students especially were very taken by it, and I even heard about it from some faculty members in liberal arts and sciences. I felt as though I had missed something. Then in a course in Theory of Knowledge I took with Fred Will, Murphy's recent book *The Uses of Reason* was studied the last few weeks of term. This led me to read some papers by Murphy, in particular, as I recall, his contributions to the Schilpp volumes on Moore and Dewey. And this, given that Max Black was also at Cornell, led me to the conclusion that Cornell, not Harvard, Columbia, Princeton, or Berkeley, was the place to go. It was.

The Uses of Reason (1943) was Murphy's first book, and the only one published in his lifetime. The collection of essays, *Reason and the Common Good*, came out in 1963. And his Carus Lectures, *The Theory of Practical Reason*, appeared in 1965 (edited by A. I. Melden). In about

1940 he completed a long manuscript—882 typed pages—on 'Contemporary Philosophy'. I do not know why he never published this 1940 manuscript. Perhaps he worked through it only to work out some ideas.[5] But the germs of his later philosophy are in it, including his critique of Objective Relativism, and ideas from it are apparent in *The Uses of Reason* and his papers of the 1940s. Murphy, though he published quite a bit, published comparatively little of what he wrote. There are a number of finished essays, unpublished, enough to make up another such collection, as well as portions of started but unfinished books he started earlier in life and then, for some reason not apparent, put aside. One of them, on 'Life and Philosophy', exists in several chapters only in holograph form, and was apparently started in the 1920s, when he was in his twenties. (Annex B provides a sample.)

Murphy's special knack was his ability, almost uncanny, to get directly at the heart of someone else's point of view and state in distilled form the essence of his thought. It was partly becaue I noticed this knack so early in my career that I went to study with him. I think I had some hope that I could learn how to do that too. What I discovered is that it is an ability that is not transferable, even by teaching. There are numerous samples available. Consider this, on *The Education of Henry Adams*: 'Adams was skeptical of the ideals embodied in his "education" because they had not fitted him for success in the modern world, and dissatisfied with the modern world because it did not conform to those ideals' (RCG, 231). For a capsule commentary on a recent philosopher of moment, and a philosopher important in the American tradition, consider this on the Santayana of *The Realms of Being* (1940):

> It was in Santayana's *Realms of Being* that free minds that had lost their faith in ideals found their most inpressive spiritual home. Mr. Santayana was certainly no liberal and his disillusionment with modern trends was of long standing. Since 1914 he had been as distant physically from the American continent as he had always been in spirit, and his more recent philosophical excursions into the realm of essence seemed to remove him even further from the main currents of contemporary thought. By the 1920s, however, this remoteness had come to stand in many minds for critical emancipation, and disillusionment with the modern was the latest and most fashionable substitute for wisdom. To such minds Santayana's nobly phrased philosophy was peculiarly persuasive. It offered a standpoint from which the disenchanted and hence 'free' spirit could with dignity surrender the 'realm of matter' to the arbitrary power and animal faith that would in any case control it and, with a respectful side glance at the unattainable immensities of the

---

[5] Some passages from this 1940 MS are reproduced *infra* Annex B.

realm of truth, proceed to find its proper satisfaction in the intuition of timeless essences. The spiritual victory thus achieved was indefeasible but attenuated. For essences are the sheer aesthetic surface of experience, accepted without interpretation or belief and enjoyed in consequence without any sort of intellectual risk or moral commitment. The detachment of the free mind from the cause of freedom and of the vocabulary of critical enlightenment from the use of practical reason here reaches its appropriate conclusion (RCG, 232).

As a commentator of this sort Murphy had no rivals. He flew where others trod. Perhaps as a consequence, it is as a commentator on the views of others that he is most often remembered by that decreasing number of people who do remember him. He wrote large numbers of reviews and studies of others' thought. But he was much more than a philosophically acute commentator on the views of others and on the foibles of his time and civilization. He had a philosophy, in particular a philosophy about philosophy, that should have a hearing or we are all the poorer.

It is difficult to resist the temptation to give you an account of Murphy's philosophy by reading to you segments from his writings, they are so rich with his distinctive style, personality, and humour, and consequently that is what I shall do. I see no other or better way in this setting of giving you a reliable account of the Murphyian philosophy, and I see no way at all of giving you a four-dimensional picture—a series of snapshots will have to suffice. The situation is brought about by the impossible commission given me by the person (I do not mean Professor Griffiths) who organized this series—and who is not to be found in the audience today—to give you a rounded developed and connected account of *both* Cohen and Murphy in the confines of one lecture, and all I have to say to that personage is that some day I hope to reverse the compliment by giving him a similar nearly impossible assignment.

First something about objective relativism, but only a bit, for, after all, Murphy did renounce the doctrine; we will then turn to the underlying or organizing idea of Murphy's philosophy, which is in turn illuminated by the reasons why he gave up objective relativism.

> The cat has many characters under many conditions. Each belongs to it in that context, and the cat would be a poor thing apart from its characters. They are relative to it, and it to them, and this objective relativity is the ultimate fact about nature, and about the cat.[6]

This passage, from Murphy's first philosophical paper, in 1926, gives the general idea of objective relativism. Murphy gave the name Objective

[6] Murphy, 'Ideas and Nature', in *Studies in the Nature of Ideas, University of California Publications in Philosophy,* Vol. 8 (Berkeley: University of California Press, 1926), 211.

Relativism to a view he found in both Dewey and Whitehead—already an anomaly—which was conceived of as both a metaphysical and epistemological answer to the problems posed by dualism. In Murphy's words:

> It attempts to unite two propositions which have uniformly been taken to be incompatible. (a) The objective facts of the world of nature and of reality are the very 'apparent' and relative happenings directly disclosed to us in perception. (b) In spite (or because) of such objectivity such happenings remain ultimately and inescapably relative. Such relativity is hence an ultimate fact about the objective world . . . (RCG, 50).

On objective relativism events are fundamental, 'the stuff of nature' (RCG, 56), and 'to events time does make a difference'. Objects are not basic, but 'are characters of events'; 'the relations of an event are internal, and it is precisely that fact which distinguishes it from an object' (53).

Now I doubt whether this severely abbreviated account will be transparently clear to everyone who comes across it. Those who are intrigued can readily go to the source to inquire further. For now we need simply note that Murphy, in 1927, did not put forward objective relativism as 'a complete and coherent philosophy as it stands' (66), but rather as the basis of a research programme that would have to 'justify itself in many fields', while 'the work in most of them has yet to be done'. For our purposes what is more pertinent is, as Murphy put it, what happened to objective relativism. To put it briefly, Murphy came to the conclusion that, at one level, the primarily logical or analytical level, objective relativism is enlightening in stressing 'the essentially contextual meaning or reference of statements' (68). (It is interesting that he cites 'a decisive statement by Morris Cohen [as giving] the text for this doctrine'—RN, 166.) But what happened is that objective relativism was generalized beyond the significant limits of its meaning and application, and led to such paradoxes as that 'everything truly is what it appears to be' (72), as for example that the railroad tracks when they appear to converge really do converge, so that all distinction between appearance and reality breaks down along with all distinction between veridical and delusive perception. This is sheer paradox, and in any case not a solution so much as an abandonment of the original problem of how to distinguish between appearance and reality. Murphy's later diagnosis, which he dubbed a melancholy one, is that the failure of objective relativism 'lay in its neglect of the consistent application of *contextual* principles', and, when this happened, 'the theory became just one of the "isms" and has shared their fate' (74).

What fate is that? It is the fate of being either gotten over and forgotten or of becoming one more term in an endless debate that cannot be settled because the parties have ignored the conditions of the problem that led to the view in the first place and have thus lost their conception of what disciplined philosophy is for. And this, as Murphy saw it, is what had happened in general in contemporary philosophy, in which 'the love of argument has supplanted the love of wisdom' (TPR, 368). It is this latter predicament that most troubled Murphy in reviewing the situation in philosophy.

This later philosophy is presented through the long analyses of recent and contemporary philosophical movements and problems in the manuscript of 1940, which, as I said, never got published. But a few of the key ideas in it did get presented, in a somewhat different setting, in *The Uses of Reason* of 1943. Although this is very much a wartime book, and one looking forward to the conditions of the future peace—as so many books were then—it presents a theory of knowledge, a theory of ethics, a social theory, a theory of philosophy itself and an argument to establish the primacy and the ultimacy of reason in all these endeavours. What Murphy tries to show in this book is the way reason works in various fields of human endeavour and how it justifies itself not as a source of *a priori* necessities but in its fruits and in its essentially organizing and clarifying capacity. Reasonableness, he argues, is not a matter of the origin or pedigree of ideas but rather one of their function and outcome, and the criteria appropriate to reasonable assessment in one field may be altogether inapplicable in another. This is the basic idea of what he calls contextual analysis. What contextual analysis chiefly insists upon is that,

> for philosophical purposes, meaning can reliably be assigned to terms employed, and to ideas for which they purport to stand, only by reference to some determinate use that is to be made of them in some discoverable context of inquiry or activity. Terms and ideas, abstracted from such specific contexts, may, of course, be assigned a new use and meaning, other than that which they elsewhere possessed. But apart from such specification of meaning those who employ the terms will confuse themselves and their readers interminably with loose talk without determinate content or foreseeable end (UR, 297).

The violation of contextual analysis occurs with

> the uncritical generalization of ideas which have an intelligible use and meaning somewhere but are by no means adapted to serve as guides to what is always and everywhere true and valid. To use such ideas 'philosophically' often means, for the uncritical, to spread them in all directions, though somewhat thinly, over the area of meaningful experience. If we hear of a theory of evolution that is valid in biology, we must have evolution everywhere, from anthropology to theology, until perhaps even a multiplication table that refuses to evolve will be set down in some quarters as a 'static' and vacuous sort of contrivance which the new 'Darwinism' in philosophy cannot tolerate. . . . It is in this way that the legitimate findings of the sciences become, through a popularization

which robs them of their specific contextual meaning, the idols of the market place for a reading public bent on keeping up with the times, and for those whose business it is to find sermons in stones, the vehicles of a new, if transitory, revelation. This is philosophy of a sort, but it is bad philosophy; for it assigns no new reliable sense to terms which it has stripped of their specific meaning and conduces rather to endlessly equivocal dispute with other pretenders to a similarly ubiquitous application than to knowledge of the world or of ourselves (UR, 296).

To use ideas philosophically, on Murphy's view, is 'to estimate their significance and importance from the standpoint of the rational organization of our experience as a whole' (UR, 297).

The aim of a reflective and responsible philosophy is to find the things worth taking seriously, the things to which the status designated by the terms 'real' and 'ultimately' can wisely be given, if not in virtue of their cosmic status—though this is usually a factor in the decision—at least in terms of their importance for human life and action (288–289).

To quote from the manuscript of 1940: 'the primary task of philosophy is to show how the various types of categories and criteria which, in their primary application, are the means by which we reasonably apprehend and evaluate the world, can be integrated in a working adjustment in terms of which we might say, with Aristotle and Santayana, that life at its human and attainable best, is reason in operation' (MS 1940, Ch. 1, 34–35). The bulk of Murphy's philosophic work from then on was an attempt to work this out in one philosophic area after another, dealing with the 'several types of categories and criteria'.

In theory of knowledge, Murphy's main criticism of epistemology is that it lays down in advance a conception of what knowledge *must be* and on the basis of that preconception proceeds to put aside, as not *really* 'knowledge', all sorts of things that we should ordinarily regard as knowledge, and which the philosopher outside the closet also inevitably regards as knowledge.[7] Perceptual observation, he observes, considered as a source of reliable information about ourselves and the world in which we live, has three important characteristics: (1) it is fallible, (2) it is corrigible, and (3) it is, considered as a self-correcting process, ultimate and fundamental, since there is no other way than it provides of finding out what we find out by its means (UR, 35–39). In response to the paradoxes of

---

[7] Murphy's best because most incisive account of this phenomenon, and also of contextual analysis, is in his 'Dewey's Epistemology and Metaphysics', in *The Philosophy of John Dewey*, P. A. Schilpp (ed.), Library of Living Philosophers, Vol. I (Evanston: Northwestern University, 1939), 195–196, 198. Cf. 'Two Versions of Critical Philosophy' (1938) and 'Moore's Defence of Common Sense' (1942), both reprinted in *Reason and the Common Good*.

advanced thinkers like Eddington and Russell, Murphy points out: 'If the
theories of physics really did cast doubt on the informational reliability of
perceptual observation, they would cast doubt also on their own empirical
foundations, and we should then have to ask what good reason there was to
suppose that what they said was factually correct' (UR, 41). This is an
instance of how Murphy clarifies what he calls 'the rational use of ideas in
the pursuit of truth', and this is one though not the only use of reason.

Another use of reason is what has been called, since Kant, practical
reason. Murphy took the basic problem of practical reason to be provided
by Hume's famous allegation that 'reason is and ought only to be the slave
of the passions'. Murphy defines 'practical reason' as 'the use of reason in
the organization of desires, and the adjustment of claims, in the pursuit of
goods judged to be desirable by methods held to be just and proper to that
end' (UR, 104). But I do not expect that bare statement to convey much
understanding. It is divorced from its context, and even in its context it is
difficult. Suffice it to say that Murphy proceeds to apply contextual
analysis, in what he calls 'the context of moral judgment', to determine
how, in response to Kant's question, reason can be practical, and in
response to his own conversion of Kant's question, how practice can be
reasonable. His discussion of this in *The Uses of Reason*, and in some
papers written in the early 1950s, turned out to be preliminary to the
inquiry of his Carus Lectures, which he entitled *The Theory of Practical
Reason*. It is intriguing that for quite some time he toyed with the idea of
entitling them 'An Inquiry Concerning Moral Understanding', for, as he
said in a letter, Hume, though he had all the wrong answers, asked all the
right questions. And Murphy's approach is more Humeian than Kantian
(though naturally more Murphyian than either); so far as I can see, the
bulk of what he takes from Kant is the concept of practical reason. This is a
book that it is very difficult to summarize, and impossible to summarize
adequately in the time I have left. I can, however, on the principle of
exposition adopted, give you some snapshots of it so that you can get a
glimpse of what it covers and how.

It was Murphy's view that common sense, in its moral variety, is
involved on our common moral life and is essential for there to be any
community, in and from which our ethical ideas and ideals take their rise
and to which they refer and which in turn they attempt to enlighten and
advance. Murphy held that the moral life is not a matter of the application
of an ultimate principle to the problems of conduct, and that this sort of
approach, so common in moral philosophy, eviscerates morality by turning what is essentially process in a context into a sort of game in which
everything that is morally relevant has been squeezed out in advance. As
was observed by A. I. Melden, in his Introduction to this work, it was
Murphy's conviction that 'good sense can be found in the common life
from which our philosophical inquiries take their departure and . . . it is

back to this common life, and with an increased understanding, to which our philosophy must return us'.[8]

But although it is back to our common moral life to which our philosophy must bid us return in order that we may grasp the distinctive features of our moral understanding . . . it is to that common life only in so far as it is in fact the achievement of reasonable men. Unless there were this rational pattern in our common way of life, there would be no discoverable reason which we could employ in our conduct . . .

. . . moral philosophy is not without its feed-back phenomenon: a successful disclosure of the rationality that is in our lives, whatever the area of human experience may be, inevitably contributes to it . . . (Melden, op. cit., xvii).

This accurately sums up the point of view that animates Murphy's theory of practical reason. As Murphy himself put it:

The world of action is a world of persons involved with each other in this shared activity that gives a practical structure and significance to their common life. It is as members of a community, as sharing and maintaining and in some cases rejecting or reconstituting the practices and standards of a way of life that men . . . act as persons. . . . The social environment is something outside the individual. The community is inside him, not spatially, physically, or biologically, of course, but practically and morally, in the sense that it is in his responsible participation in its shared concerns that he has being as a person . . . (TPR, 9–10).

The communities in which we thus learn and act are not idealized abstractions. They are the familiar, unideal, specific social groups in which we happen, without our own consent or preference, to have been born, or into which we move to make a living and to live a life. But they are social groups seen in certain light, the light . . . of practical understanding, as the ground and locus for those personal ties that make *moral* sense of what we do. There is a great deal more to being practically reasonable than this. . . . But without this basic grounding in that working understanding which is the stuff of our common lives this 'more' would make no moral sense . . . (TRP, 10–11).

Murphy regards this fact as the *'primary* fact', the essential starting and reference point, without and apart from which one can never understand what a moral reason, an ethical consideration, is.

That is a glimpse of the beginning. Here is a brief argument relative to the problem of moral diversity, and of what is known as ethical relativism, a problem on which Murphy had a point of view that is original and distinctive, and, oddly, unappreciated.

[8] A. I. Melden, Introduction to *The Theory of Practical Reason*, xi–xii.

Some of the allegedly 'deepest' problems of 'ultimate' right could practically be solved if moral busy-bodies, intent on rating all men's values on a scale that presuppose the preferential finality of their own, would mind their own business and let others solve, in their own way, the problems which are theirs, not ours. To make moral judgments at large about the Universe, or the ancient Greeks ... or the folkways of the Samoans, is for the most part simply not our business. The 'decisions' we are called upon to make are those that concern what we must do, where we are, and with the moral equipment which our own loyalties and reasons have supplied us. There is enough, and more, to keep us busy here. Moral diversity *becomes* moral disagreement only when the diversity itself is made a moral issue. And in nine cases out of ten, the part of plain good sense is *not* to make a moral issue out of it. But the tenth case remains to plague us and, in our times, it has unhappily become the model for all the rest. There are authentic practical conflicts that cannot in this way be resolved and the issues involved in them may become a source of moral conflict also ... (TPR, 338–339).

Now a glimpse of Murphy's conception of liberalism. According to Murphy, the demand that liberalism

makes is not primarily for free trade, or free labor or free competition, though these at times may serve its purpose, but for such freedom of the minds of men ... that they may explore the possibilities of cooperative social action and act responsibly as their judgment dictates. That kind of liberalism is an essential precondition for the effective use of reason in social action ... What takes its place is tyranny—the arbitrary exercise of irresponsible power—and the slavery, political or spiritual, which is its complement when men surrender the responsibility for making for themselves the decisions in terms of which their lives are to be determined. The freedom to make such decisions is not a peripheral accessory of a bourgeoise culture, to be weighed against the competing charms of security, national aggrandizement or 'charismatic' submission to a presumably inspired leader ... It guarantees the conditions under which and the area within which we act as morally responsible persons ... (UR, 198–199).

And, says Murphy, liberalism 'in this meaning ... is not a doctrine that has been outmoded, or is likely to be'.

In his consideration of American philosophy Murphy persistently tried to relate the problems of American philosophy to the problems of American civilization. He observed that 'the latest deliverances of contemporary anxiety need not be the final word of philosophical understanding'—a neat observation on existentialism taken *en passant*. And he also says this:

How can the idea of community be broadened to meet the requirements of a world society without losing its roots in local loyalties and traditional values? How can individual freedom, as actualized in responsible choice and judgment, maintain its claim to final value in a world of impersonal forces and organized group pressures? How can specialized knowledge find its fulfilment in practical wisdom and critical intelligence be brought into harmony with effective moral purposes? How can ideals be used, without special pleading and without illusion, to bring us into needed contact with realities we should never have discerned without them? These are still the basic questions that our civilization puts to our philosophy. The future of American philosophy and, in some measure, also, of American civilization, will depend on the answers that we give to them (RCG, 245–246).

One need not agree with this last claim to recognize that this is a large conception of philosophy.

III. Coda—American Philosophy

I think I have now explained the selection of these two American philosophers for presentation in this series, in a lecture that brings the series to a close—and, in a way, brings us back to the beginning. One thing remains to be considered. What happened to the reputations of Cohen and Murphy? There are of course two distinct phenomena here, and each needs to be explained in its own terms. Still, there are some factors that apply to both, and that may help explain the diminishing of some other philosophical reputations as well. And the explanation may tell us something about American philosophy and its growing separation from American culture and American civilization. Philosophy in America, as in Britain, largely through the influence of Russell and Moore, Wittgenstein and the positivists, and then of later writers such as Quine, has become in large part a highly technical study, with its own internal problems, special traditions, and mandatory vocabulary. In some ways it has become a special guild, and it apes in various ways the special sciences that it had traditionally been thought of as completing and unifying. Cohen spoke of this tendency as the exalting of technique over vision, and wrote about it often. (Of course, in his more technical writings he also contributed to it.) Murphy also wrote about it in many ways and in many contexts; it was the guiding concern behind his whole philosophy of philosophy.

Of course this tendency has always been endemic to philosophy. But it is one thing to ride with the tide, another to resist it, still another to encourage it as a positive virtue. (And of course it is still a different thing to complain about it from the outside, as is done by so many literary or culture critics, who confuse philosophy, the love of wisdom, with philodoxia, the love of opinion.) But I am not here talking about the technicalizing tendency of philosophy over the centuries. The tendency I am talking about is specific to this century, when for the first time it was thought a virtue to write philosophy in an artificial language. (The counterpart was in medieval times, when the mandatory language of learning was Latin. But Latin, though a dead language, was not an artificial and artificially perfect language. And Spinoza wrote in Latin.)

Russell in particular may have contributed to this situation by the separation he made between his philosophical writings and his writings on politics, economics, society, ethics. He regarded the latter as outside of philosophy properly so-called, and many of his professional readers came to agree with him, on this if so little else. The tendency was also hastened by the influence of positivism, now dead but ruling like a guiding spectre from the grave, in linking philosophy with logic and science and divorcing it from literature and ethics and cultural concerns.

Hence the Great Divide, which, especially post-Watergate and -Vietnam, so many professional philosophers have felt the need of bridging by establishing what is now called 'applied philosophy', accompanied by appeals to philosophers to subscribe to specialist journals in applied philosophy and attend conferences and write essays in this new supposedly relevant speciality. Of course, funding for such conferences is readily available from such institutions as the National Endowment for the Humanities and courses on such subjects are fruitful sources of students—which might provide us with the text for an application of the theory of the economic interpretation of academic history. But we need not go to some vulgarized version of Marx or Madison. Fashion and faddism are explanation enough. Emerson advised us to hitch our wagon to a star; its prosaic enactment seems to be, 'Hitch your wagon to the bandwagon of a star'.

For neither Cohen nor Murphy was there any such divide. Their writing is through and through permeated by a sense of practical import and of the philosophic basic of practice, to the point that those brought up on the current diet find it foreign food, an unseemly mixing of only separately digestible dishes. They appealed to and wrote for a wider community. Philosophy, in their philosophies, was not just for philosophers.

The professionalization of philosophy and the concomitant professionalization of philosophers has caused nearly all of us to lose sight of the original conception of our subject—and in accordance with that to act as though our characteristic defects are some higher form of health. And there are other outstanding philosophers of large conceptions who have entered that special section of oblivion reserved for those whom later generations put on a special shelf of honour but otherwise ignore: for instance, Dewey and Santayana, unread except by special coteries, and Whitehead (who should have been represented in this series) also. It is a strange period, in which Heidegger is treated as readable and worth reading, and Dewey and Whitehead not. But fashions change, and in our time very rapidly.

I have not been contending that either Cohen or Murphy was a great philosopher. Greatness is an interesting concept, is used often enough, even by philosophers, never examined. It is so hard to say what 'great' means in this context that I have not yet heard it said. Very few philosophers worth reading were *great*. (Plato, Aristotle, Kant, Descartes, Hume—who else belongs on that select shelf? Perhaps not even Descartes and Hume?—and that is sure to start an argument.) However, though not 'great', they were outstanding and still very worth reading, with distinctive and important things to say. Despite the contemporary references in their writings, they are likely to be worth reading for a long time to come. And, while I have no criterion for 'great' (at least I present none here), I have a criterion for 'worth reading'. A philosopher is worth reading if he is interesting, instructive, suggestive, and illuminating. On this criterion both Cohen and Murphy are worth reading, and they are entertaining besides. Each was carrying on, in his own way, the grand tradition in American philosophy.[9]

[9] I am grateful to Abraham Edel for useful information and suggestions about Cohen, and speculations about why his reputation went into eclipse. For similar information and ideas about Murphy I am indebted to A. I. Melden, Edmund Pincoffs, and Frederick L. Will. I am also grateful to H. S. Thayer for collecting and sending to me materials on or by Cohen available in the City College Library. In particular this enabled me to see the remarkable production (privately printed), 'A Tribute to Professor Morris Raphael Cohen, Teacher & Philosopher', published by 'The Youth Who Sat at His Feet' (New York, 1928), which records the speeches made and letters read at the testimonial dinner, attended by more than a thousand people, given for Cohen at the Hotel Astor on 15 October 1927, to celebrate the twenty-fifth anniversary of his joining the teaching staff of the College, which contains, besides Cohen's speech of response, essays on Cohen as a teacher by several of his former students, such as Sidney Hook, Ernest Nagel, and Paul Weiss. Although I had before heard about this banquet, it was only through seeing the book that I was able to realize what an extraordinary occurrence this whole thing was. And it occurred nearly eleven years before Cohen's retirement from the College.

Annex

I append here some further glimpses of the philosophies of Cohen and Murphy in the form of quotations from their writings that are either representative of their views or not so well-known instances of their insight. In the case of Murphy, the passages are all from unpublished writings, so they are bound to be somewhat less known than others. In the case of Cohen, the passage on metaphor provides a little known instance of his insight and interests.

A. *Quotations from Cohen*

1. On Metaphor:

... to eliminate all metaphors is impossible ... metaphors are not merely artificial devices for making discourse more vivid and poetical, but are also necessary for the apprehension of new ideas. ...

... metaphors are generally older than expressed analogies. ...

... Metaphors may ... be viewed as expressing the vague and confused but primal perception of identity which subsequent processes of discrimination transform into the clear assertion of an identity or common element (or relation) which the two things possess ... (PL, 85).

2. On Ontology:

The great objection to the ontologic interpretation of logical relations has been the fear that if this be granted, we shall be opening the gates to the deduction of empirical or factual determinations from *a priori* considerations. This, however, is a *non sequitur*. From that which is common to all possible transformations of objects, nothing can be legitimately deduced as to that which characterizes some particular sub-class such as specific physical objects. ...

... not only do all physical laws have reference to possibility but concrete statements about this or that physical object would be incomplete if we were to exclude reference to the possible. Facts are meaningless except as parts of a system; and science is possible and applicable to the actual world precisely because the actual world has repeatable patterns which can be abstracted and connected according to certain invariable relations. Real meaning, the nature of things, thus contains as one of its elements the logical invariants which hold of all possible transformations or of all possible objects ... (PL, 55–56).

3. On Relations:

... the abstract objects of thought, such as numbers, *law*, or *perfectly straight lines*, are real parts of nature (even though they exist not as *particular* things but as the *relations* or *transformations* of such particulars), so that none of the so-called fictions of science in any way falsifies its results ... (PL, 94).

4. On Logic:

Logic ... does not provide the food which sustains our intellectual life. That must come from our factual knowledge and insight. ... It is ... like the hydrochloric acid in our stomach that helps to digest our food. It is the antiseptic of our intellectual life which prevents our food from poisoning us. For the impressions we take into our minds will confuse us unless we order them according to some logical principle (PL, 182).

... whatever the opinions of philosophers, they must rely on the validity of logical reasoning to establish their position ... (SPS, 7–8).

5. The Laws of Nature:

The ultimate laws of nature are themselves contingent. They just happen to be. Any one law or reason from which they might all be derived (which is logically impossible) would itself be contingent, without any proof that it might not have been different. An infinite regress cannot eliminate contingency and the existence of a different world is always a theoretically significant alternative ... (SPS, 20).

6. On Science:

If we distinguish as we must between the verifiable truths of science and the fallible opinions of the individual scientist, we may define science as a self-corrective system. ... But ... the doubt and the correction are always in accordance with the canons of the scientific method, so that the latter is the bond of continuity.

One might draw a parallel in this respect between science and constitutional government. A constitutional government is one in which every particular law . . . can be corrected or abolished by constitutional means. This is not possible . . . in any form of dicatorship. In the latter you either accept the whole or else have to overthrow it all . . . (SPS, 50–51).

B. *Quotations from Murphy*

1. From 'Life and Philosophy'

This is the opening chapter of an unfinished unpublished book manuscript of the late 1920s or early 1930s, entitled 'Life and Philosophy', which exists only in holograph:

If a realistic observer from some remote region of space or time were set down in America today and asked to give an account of what he found here under the title of philosophy his report, I suspect, would be something like the following. Philosophy, in the first place, is a subject taught in Universities through the exposition, direct or at second hand, of certain standard texts of great dignity and, in most cases, of considerable antiquity. A sympathetic acquaintance with these works, as with the Bible and Greek mythology, is regarded as an important part of a 'humanistic' education and no one who is unable to appreciate polite references to them can really be at home in really cultivated society. Again, philosophy is a subject pursued by professors in their professional capacity under the title of 'research'. The problems with which such research is concerned are abstruse and technical, with special assumptions and a peculiar language which only the initiated can understand. This adds to the prestige of the researchers in university circles and qualifies the philosopher as a specialist who can speak with his colleagues in physics or biology on terms of real equality, since neither has one chance in ten of understanding what the other is saying. Finally, philosophy is a type of vague but edifying discourse on the 'meaning of life' offered with considerable popular success by the liberal clergy, by the more forensic scientists in their mellow moments, by evangelical psychoanalysts and, though more awkwardly as a rule, by professional philosophers themselves when the exigencies of the educational system require it. Such, our observer might conclude, is philosophy in America, and in large measure he would be right.

But not altogether right. For the realistic observer has a way of missing something essential in human activities though often hard to discern in their external manifestations—the spirit that is in them and by means of which they live. And he would see, if he looked more closely, that these secondary activities borrow such worth as they possess from a genuine urgency in human nature itself, an interest baffled today by the complexities of a world to which its own demands seem strangely incongruous but vital enough to maintain itself, though precariously and in reduced circumstances, even in such meager habitations as Dr. Will Durant has ironically offered as 'The Mansions of Philosophy'. Is it possible to work back from these externals of philosophy which today come so dangerously near to being the whole of it to the interest that supports them and to discern the conditions of its adequate expression? I believe that it is, and this book is an attempt to justify that belief. . . .

. . . The trouble with professional philosophy has not been its lack of popular success, but its actual irrelevance to the conditions of life . . . (Holograph MS, 'Life and Philosophy', c. 1930, Chapter One, 'What This Book is About', pp. 1–2, 10).

2. From MS *Contemporary Philosophy* (1940):

Murphy described this work as a 'study of what a philosophy in operation amounts to and what comes out of it' (Ch. 4, p. 6), and one dominant theme in its accounts of philosophical movements and 'speculations of the past fifty years' (Ch. 4, p. 83) (we can take this as going back at least to 1880) is that 'a philosophy develops and defines its position as the spokesman of an aspect of experience felt to be significant and fundamental, which the dominant philosophies of the period will not permit us to describe in language appropriate to its apparent nature' (Ch. 4, p. 7).

(a) Murphy on philosophy, or sound philosophy:

The correct [?] standpoint for philosophy . . . is simply that of the rational organization of experience, in which each element is seen for what, in its primary meaning, it reliably is, in which the possibilities of harmonious integration of its several aspects are explored without . . . distorting preconceptions which ... limit our awareness of their nature, and in which each candidate for philosophical preeminence is judged for what it might contribute to such an integrated whole (MS 1940, Ch. 9, p. 65).

(b) This helps explain one of his main themes:

... the objects we encounter and the meanings we apprehend and make use of in the course of our reliable commerce with the world in perceptual observation, in social cooperation, in scientific inquiry, are as 'real' as anything we shall ever find and ... a sane and responsible philosophy will acknowledge them as foundations on which it must build, if its constructions are to stand. The world doubtless contains very much more than this, and more that it would be good to know. But this at least is true, and a theory which substitutes for it, in its primary meaning, a more analytically or metaphysically eligible reality which its own stipulations have determined and thus, in the interests of speculative identification or critical precision, reduces the world to the limits of its preconceptions, will not provide a reliable working basis for philosophy, but will, on the contrary, tend to disorganize and distort our understanding of those basic elements in experience which it is the business of philosophy to set in order (MS 1940, Ch. 9, p. 1).

(c) And again on philosophy:

The standpoint of philosophy is that of the reasonable organization of experience, in which nothing humanly significant is needlessly omitted, nothing seen out of focus or blurred by a biased or one-sided interpretation, and nothing included as true or valid which, in spite of its emotional congeniality or plausibility, is found on the whole to produce such distortion and thus to impede the development of that comprehensive sanity which is the final fruit and justification of philosophical enlightenment. An acknowledgment of the adequacy and accuracy of 'common sense', or 'science', or any other activity will be soundly based only if it is made with a proper understanding of the place and function of that activity in a total human adjustment. Without this it remains equivocal in its implications and when confronted with problems or choices to whose determination its own methods are inappropriate, lapses into a dogmatism of the worst sort, identifying the limits of its own interests and preconceptions with the boundaries of significant discourse, reasonable belief, and acceptable procedure (MS 1940, Ch. 9, pp. 2–3).

(d) On Bradley, as another instance of Murphy's acute sensitivity:

'What must be and may be, that certainly *is*.' This was the rather dreary formula with which Bradley bolstered up his own doubts about his theory, doubts to which he returned again and again, with fine intellectual honesty, and which were never really set at rest. 'Must be'—because 'thought' (as interpreted by this theory) demands it and 'reality' (as so interpreted) will tolerate nothing less. 'May be', since what seems to fall outside it is, *if the theory is correct*, mere appearance whose factual ultimacy cannot stand against the theory. 'Is'—but only in a way we do not really understand, which rather appeases those sides of our nature which were committed in advance to a 'spiritual' conclusion, than raises our commerce with the world about us to the clarity, scope and rational coordination of philosophic wisdom (MS 1940, Ch. 2, p. 52).

(e) And on Santayana (the Santayana of *The Life of Reason*):

Santayana was able to find many virtues in reason, but he was never able to credit it with the simplest and most essential virtue of all, that of providing, on occasion, the plain truth about the world of nature (MS 1940, Ch. 9, p. 41).

Sources and Discussions

I. References to the works of Morris Cohen referred to herein are abbreviated as follows:

AT   *American Thought: A Critical Sketch*, Felix S. Cohen (ed.) (Glencoe: The Free Press, 1954).

DJ   *A Dreamer's Journey* (Boston: The Beacon Press; Glencoe: The Free Press, 1949). Contains a bibliography of Cohen's writings through 1948, almost complete though with a few inadvertent omissions, pp. 291–303.

FL   *The Faith of a Liberal: Selected Essays* (New York: Henry Holt and Company, 1946).

C&N   *An Introduction to Logic and Scientific Method*, with Ernest Nagel (New York: Harcourt, Brace and Company, 1934).

LSO   *Law and the Social Order: Essays in Legal Philosophy* (New York: Harcourt, Brace and Company, 1933).

MHH   *The Meaning of Human History* (La Salle: The Open Court Publishing Company, 1947).

PL   *A Preface to Logic* (New York: Henry Holt and Company, 1944).

RL   *Reason and Law: Studies in Juristic Philosophy* (Glencoe: The Free Press, 1950).

RN   *Reason and Nature: An Essay on the Meaning of Scientific Method* (New York: Harcourt, Brace and Company, 1931). There was a second edition (Glencoe: The Free Press, 1953), but if there are any changes they are inconsequential.

RWJ   *Reflections of a Wondering Jew* (Boston: The Beacon Press; Glencoe: The Free Press, 1950).

SPS   *Studies in Philosophy and Science* (New York: Henry Holt and Company, 1949).

In addition to the bibliography in DJ, there is a bibliography compiled by Martin A. Kuhn, *Morris Raphael Cohen: A Bibliography* (New York, 1957).

II. References to Murphy's books are abbreviated thus:

RCG   *Reason and the Common Good: Selected Essays of Arthur E. Murphy*, W. H. Hay and M. G. Singer (eds) (Englewood Cliffs: Prentice-Hall, Inc., 1963). Contains a bibliography of Murphy's writings, pp. 398–408.

TPR   *The Theory of Practical Reason*, A. I. Melden (ed.) (La Salle: Open Court, 1965).

UR   *The Uses of Reason* (New York: The Macmillan Company, 1943).

III. Discussions of Murphy's work are hard to find, tend to be scattered amongst discussions of specific topics in special contexts. There are numerous discussions of objective relativism (called by McGilvary and some others perspective realism) in various discussions of metaphysics and epistemology, and also some discussions of his critique of speculative philosophy, but very few accounts of Murphy's later philosophy. There is a commentary on his ethical theory by Konstantin Kolenda, 'In Defense of Practical Reason' in *Rice University Studies* **55**, No. 1 (Houston: Rice University, 1969). (Kolenda also reviewed *The Theory of Practical Reason* in *Man and World* 1 (1968), pp. 151–156.) But it is more important to read Murphy than to read about him, and the best source is *Reason and the Common Good* and the bibliography it provides. There is reason to think that some more things by Murphy will still appear.

IV. The best thing on Cohen that I have seen is by Abraham Edel, 'The Unity of Morris Raphael Cohen's Thought', *Transactions of the C. S. Peirce Society* **17** (Spring 1981), 107–127—sympathetic, critical, knowledgeable, philosophically aware, illuminating. Two other illuminating discussions are Arthur Smullyan's

'The Philosophical Method of Morris R. Cohen' and Philip Wiener's 'Cohen's Philosophical Interpretations of the History of Science', both in *Freedom and Reason: Studies in Philosophy and Jewish Culture in Memory of Morris Raphael Cohen*, S. W. Baron, E. Nagel and K. S. Pinson (eds) (Glencoe: The Free Press, 1951), 59–67 and 68–84. An interesting account of his legal philosophy is Ernest Nagel's 'The Dimensions of Cohen's Legal Philosophy', *Peirce Society Transactions* **17**, 98–106, and an interesting account of Cohen's metaphysics is in C. F. Delaney, *Mind and Nature: A Study of the Naturalistic Philosophies of Cohen, Woodbridge and Sellars* (Notre Dame: University of Notre Dame Press, 1969).

An adequate and philosophically capable full-length study of Cohen's philosophy is still to be written. A pretender to this position is David Hollinger's *Morris R. Cohen and the Scientific Ideal* (Cambridge, Mass.: MIT Press 1975). But only a pretender. It is useful for anyone interested in Cohen, and one can only admire the determination with which Hollinger has tracked down so many of Cohen's writings, even those in the obscurest journals, and interviewed so many of Cohen's associates and former students. Thus it is good to have the book available, if only for the sheer amount of information it provides. It is a considerable piece of research. But it is manifestly a book by a historian; it does not manifest any philosophical insight of its own. Like the revisionist historians to whom he is akin, Hollinger constantly looks for secret motives, secret missions, and secret treaties, and this is odd. All told, this is such a strange yet provocative book that some further comment here is justified. For it has considerable interest, and that is provided by its subject rather than its object.

Hollinger views Cohen from the perspective of philosophy that he acquired, presumably, in his student days, and, curiously, does not manifest any awareness of the frequency of changes in philosophical fashion, or how rapidly fashion shifted right after World War II, and again in the 1960s, any more than he manifests awareness of how an original and considerable philosopher can ride independently of the fashions even of his own time. Thus the book is written from the external point of view of the intellectual historian, rendering the judgment of a later generation—often confused with the judgment of history or of philosophy itself—on a considerable philosophical thinker who in that later generation is out of favour and out of mind. And it is philosophically broken-backed in two main ways: (1) its psychohistorical approach, and (2) its reliance on the opinions of others for its philosophical assessments. In interpreting Cohen, especially, this approach is most doomed to failure, for Cohen cuts across traditional boundaries so readily and so rapidly and calls on such a range of knowledge. The standard accounts of the different branches of philosophy do not provide a reliable standpoint for assessing him.

Hollinger's aim is to 'help us understand the differences between [Cohen's] age and ours' (p. ix), not to illuminate Cohen's philosophy (though he does do so on occasion) or to use Cohen's ideas and methods as a stimulus to philosophical thinking in its own right. I do not suggest that this aim is illegitimate. Only it is a historian's aim, not a philosopher's. And Hollinger seems to have no conception of the dangers of taking a philosophical remark out of its context, where it may be the answer to a specific question, and making it the vehicle of speculation or analysis (as though it must necessarily be interpreted as applying broadly); yet this is a danger especially pronounced with Cohen, so many of whose arguments were addressed to specific issues in specific contexts. But he seems also unaware, even in his reliance on authority, of the dangers of selecting evidence. Thus, to support his claim that Cohen was, by 1944, out of date, he selectively quotes a remark in Henry Aiken's review of *A Preface to Logic* (p. 125), and ignores the manifest fact that not only is Aiken's observation qualified ('If a considerable portion of Cohen's book is devoted to a flaying of dead issues, the greater part is nothing of the sort'— *New Republic* **112** (26 Feb. 1945), 307), but the review is overwhelmingly favourable. (Aiken closed with the observation that 'Of Cohen it may be said, what T. S. Eliot has said of Bradley, that he has an intense addiction to intellectual passion'.) To support an interpretation in this way is to suggest that it is somehow defective.

Consider the remark that 'Any thinker's work entails, obviously, an interaction between his psychological disposition and the forms of thought available to him' (p. 119; cf. p. xii). This is by no means obvious, even supposing it intelligible, but it is taken as an excuse for dealing more with Cohen's psychological disposition than his arguments. If we are dealing with a genuine thinker, however, there is much more involved than psychological disposition. There is his mind (not at all the same) and his talent and the philosophical problems that intrigue and animate him. No explanation solely in the terms presented can succeed in illuminating this. 'The forms of thought available to him' sounds portentous, but is really empty. No one's thought, as thought—as distinct from event—can be understood on this basis. But the remark also illustrates the incoherence of the psychohistorical method that animates this interpretation. On its terms Hollinger's own work 'entails an interaction between his psychological disposition and the forms of thought available to him'. But this does not tell us why Hollinger is determined to speak of Cohen constantly on the basis of emotive determinism, so that his account is couched throughout in terms of what Cohen 'wanted' to establish, 'desired' to prove, 'had a stake in' persuading people to believe. This makes Cohen out to be not a thinker but a propagandist, and we are not told, portentously or otherwise, why, or what 'a propagandist's work entails'. On this unremittingly psychohistorical approach arguments and ideas are omitted and validity and truth abstracted from, so that all that is left is causal interaction, or the watered down notion of influence. But the idea that one belief or intellectual event caused another itself claims to be true and backed up by arguments, though on its own terms this cannot be.

Hollinger claims that 'Cohen's role was to formulate, popularize, and reinforce certain suspicions about ideas more or less "accepted" in his day; when the intellectual traditions of his era were subsequently updated and revised, the weaknesses he had helped to identify were exactly those the new generation was most eager to assign to the realm of the "history of liberal thought"' (p. 248). There is some justice in this, but it can be put differently, and in a different light, so: Cohen's role was, in effect, to cast doubt on, if not to undermine, current and perennial shibboleths, and that is both what he set out to do and how he defined the role of the philosopher. Hollinger adds that Cohen's writings 'would never again . . . be endowed with the special social significance they carried in the 1910s, 1920s, and 1930s'. But that implies that they did carry special social significance. And it is to be noticed that there is no one like him now. It also overestimates the extent to which Cohen's writings, in their relation to contemporary problems, have actually dated. No doubt his discussion of the Bertrand Russell Case (1940) has dated, but his account of 'Why I am not a Communist' (1934) is not one whit more dated now than it was fifty years ago. And if his discussion of the Sacco–Vanzetti Case (1931) seems dated, that is only to a later generation that has allowed itself to forget what should never be forgotten. (All these can be found in *The Faith of a Liberal*.)

The purely external point of view of the intellectual historian (whether psycho or not) tends to squeeze the distinctive life out of ideas—no matter how illuminating it can be in the hands of a master—and needs to be supplemented by accounts from the internal philosophical point of view, on which ideas are treated as capable of truth and falsity and as elements of arguments. Thus, for all the historico-biographical merits of Hollinger's study, it needs to be supplemented by a capable philosophical account. Luckily Edel's essay is available for balance and a philosophical understanding Hollinger cannot provide. Thus Edel:

> Can we find a unity in Cohen's thought which will tie together his theme, his keynote ideas, his method of analysis? . . . I think there is a pattern to be found, and briefly stated it is this: Cohen grappled with nothing less than major intellectual problems that had and still have vital practical bearings. He helped to usher in directions of work that in later hands were to prove extremely fruitful. The stance he took—expressed in his principle of polarity—made him a philosophical arbitrator against philosophical extremism. The disadvantage of this role, and the principle of polarity itself, is that it usually operates within the formulation of issues that it is moderating (pp. 109–110).

There is insight here that no amount of psychohistorical or even historical analysis can match. And it can be done without looking for secret motives, secret missions, and secret treaties.

Bibliography and Postscript

Some of the lectures already contain suggestions for further reading. There follows a brief list of further items, divided into sections corresponding to some of the themes of the volume.

I. American Philosophy: Histories, Collections, Surveys

Anderson, Paul R. and Max H. Fisch, *Philosophy in America: From the Puritans to James, With Representative Selections* (1939).

Blau, Joseph L., *Men and Movements in American Philosophy* (1952).

Brodbeck, May, 'Philosophy in America, 1900–1950', in *American Non-Fiction, 1900–1950*, by Brodbeck, Gray and Metzger (1952).

Chisholm, R. M., H. Feigl, W. Frankena, J. Passmore and M. Thompson, *Philosophy* (1960) (in Princeton Studies on Humanistic Scholarship in America).

Cohen, Morris R., 'General Philosophy', Ch. 9 of *American Thought* (1954); a revision and expansion of Ch. 17, 'Later Philosophy', in *The Cambridge History of American Literature*, Trent, Erskine, Sherman and Van Doren (eds), Vol. III (1921).

Fisch, Max (ed.), *Classic American Philosophers: Peirce, James, Royce, Santayana, Dewey, Whitehead* (1951).

Flower, Elizabeth and Murray Murphey, *A History of Philosophy in America* (1977).

Kuklick, Bruce, *The Rise of American Philosophy: Cambridge, Massachusetts, 1860–1930* (1977).

Kurtz, Paul, 'American Philosophy', *Encyclopedia of Philosophy*, Edwards (ed.) (1967), Vol. I.

Mead, George Herbert, 'The Philosophies of Royce, James and Dewey in their American Setting', *International Journal of Ethics* **40** (1930).

Muelder, Walter G., Lawrence Sears and Anne Schlabach (eds), *The Development of American Philosophy: A Book of Readings* (2nd edn, 1960).

Murphy, Arthur E., 'American Philosophy in the Twentieth Century', in Curti (ed.), *American Scholarship in the Twentieth Century* (1953); also in Murphy, *Reason and the Common Good* (1963).

Reck, Andrew J., *Recent American Philosophy: Studies of Ten Representative Thinkers* (1964).

Reck, Andrew J., *The New American Philosophers* (1968).

Riley, Woodbridge, *American Philosophy: The Early Schools* (1907).

Riley, Woodbridge, *American Thought, from Puritanism to Pragmatism* (1915).

Rogers, Arthur Kenyon, *English and American Philosophy Since 1800* (1922).

Santayana, George, 'The Genteel Tradition in American Philosophy', *Winds of Doctrine* (1913).

Schneider, Herbert W., *A History of American Philosophy* (1946; 2nd edn, 1963).

Schneider, Herbert W., Max H. Fisch and Arthur E. Murphy, Symposium: 'One Hundred Years of American Philosophy', *The Philosophical Review* **LVI** (1947).

Smith, John E., *The Spirit of American Philosophy* (1963).

Townsend, Harvey G., *Philosophical Ideas in the United States* (1934).

Werkmeister, W. H., *A History of Philosophical Ideas in America* (1949).

White, Morton (ed.), *Documents in the History of American Philosophy, from Jonathan Edwards to John Dewey* (1972).

White, Morton, *Pragmatism and the American Mind: Essays and Reviews in Philosophy and American History* (1973).

White, Morton, *Science and Sentiment in America: Philosophical Thought from Jonathan Edwards to John Dewey* (1972).

Wiener, Philip P., *Evolution and the Founders of Pragmatism* (1949).

Winn, Ralph B. (ed.), *American Philosophy* (1955).

II. American Culture, Character, etc.

Bourne, Randolph, 'Trans-National America', *Atlantic Monthly* **cvxiii** (July) 1916 (also in *War and the Intellectuals*, Resek (ed.) (1964)).

Brogan, D. W., *The American Character* (1944).

Bryce, James, *The American Commonwealth* (1888).

Burlingame, Roger, *The American Conscience* (1957).

Cohen, Morris R., *American Thought* (1954), F. S. Cohen (ed.).

Commager, Henry S. (ed.), *America in Perspective: The United States Through Foreign Eyes* (1947).

Commager, Henry S., *The American Mind* (1950) ('The far from inarticulate major premise of my investigation is that there is a distinctively American way of thought, character, and conduct'—p. vii).

de Tocqueville, Alexis, *Democracy in America* (1835).

Erskine, John, *American Character and other Essays* (1918, 1927).

Gorer, Geoffrey, *The American People: A Study in National Character* (1948).

Laski, Harold J., *The American Democracy* (1948).

Lerner, Max, *America as a Civilization* (1957).

Low, A. Maurice, *The American People: A Study in National Psychology* (1909).

Maritain, Jacques, *Reflections on America* (1958).

Münsterberg, Hugo, *American Traits, From the Point of View of a German* (1901).

Münsterberg, Hugo, *The Americans* (1904).

Parkes, Henry Bamford, *The American Experience* (1947).

Perry, Ralph Barton, *Characteristically American* (1949).

Potter, David, *People of Plenty: Economic Abundance and the American Character* (1954).

Riesman, David, *The Lonely Crowd: A Study of the Changing American Character* (1950, 1960).

Rourke, Constance, *American Humor: A Study of the National Character* (1931).

Royce, Josiah, *California from the Conquest in 1846 to the Second Vigilance Committee in San Francisco: A Study of American Character* (1886).

Santayana, George, *Character and Opinion in the United States* (1920).
Siegfried, André, *America at Mid-Century* (1955) ('America is more American than it was some years ago, when it could be considered as a daughter of the old European continent who had not yet attained her majority. . . . We are studying a form of civilization rather than a country'—pp. v–vi).
Stearns, Harold E. (ed.), *Civilization in the United States* (1922).
Williams, Robin M., Jr, *American Society: A Sociological Interpretation* (1951).

III. National Character, Psychology, etc.

Bagehot, Walter, *The English Constitution* (1867; 2nd edn, 1872).
Barker, Ernest, *National Character, and the Factors in its Formation* (1927, 1948).
Dewey, John, *German Philosophy and Politics* (1915, 1942).
Emerson, Ralph Waldo, *English Traits* (1856).
Fyfe, Hamilton, *The Illusion of National Character* (1940).
Ginsberg, Morris, 'National Character', in *Reason and Unreason in Society* (1947).
Hingley, Ronald, *The Russian Mind* (1977).
Hume, David, *Essays, Moral, Political, and Literary,* 'Of National Characters' (1741).
James, William, 'German Pessimism', *Collected Essays and Reviews* (1920).
Mead, Margaret, 'National Character', in *Anthropology Today*, A. L. Kroeber (ed.) (1953).
Orwell, George, 'England Your England' (1940), in *The Collected Essays, Journalism and Letters* (1968), Vol. 2.
Orwell, George, 'The English People' (1944), in *The Collected Essays, Journalism and Letters* (1968), Vol. 3.
Santayana, George, *Egotism in German Philosophy* (1916, 1940).
Santayana, George, 'The British Character', in *Soliloquies in England* (1923).
Santayana, George, 'The Intellectual Temper of the Age', in *Winds of Doctrine* (1913).
Yutang, Lin, *My Country and My People* (1935).

IV. On Special Topics, Periods, Writers

Ayer, A. J., *The Origins of Pragmatism* (1968).
Frothingham, Octavius Brooks, *Transcendentalism in New England* (1876).
Gallie, W. B., *Peirce and Pragmatism* (1952).
Holmes, Oliver Wendell, *Ralph Waldo Emerson* (1884).
Knight, Margaret, *William James* (1950).
Lowell, James Russell, 'Thoreau', and 'Emerson, The Lecturer', in *My Study Windows* (1871).
Miller, Perry and Thomas H. Johnson, *The Puritans* (1938).
Miller, Perry (ed.), *The American Puritans* (1956).
Miller, Perry (ed.), *The American Transcendentalists* (1957).

Novak, Michael (ed.), *American Philosophy and the Future* (1968).
Perry, Ralph Barton, *Puritanism and Democracy* (1944).
Perry, Ralph Barton, *The Thought and Character of William James* (1935).
Pochmann, Henry A., *New England Transcendentalism and St. Louis Hegelianism* (1948).
Santayana, George, 'Emerson', in *Interpretations of Poetry and Religion* (1900).
Schneider, Herbert W., *The Puritan Mind* (1930).
White, Morton, *The Origin of Dewey's Instrumentalism* (1943).
White, Morton, *The Philosophy of the American Revolution* (1978).

V. Postscript: On 'National Philosophies'

The expression 'national philosophies' appears in the Index to *The Encylopedia of Philosophy* (ed. Edwards, 1967, Vol. 8, 493), to refer the reader to such articles as 'American Philosophy'. The following expressions accordingly appear in the index as titles of separate articles: American philosophy, British philosophy, Bulgarian philosophy, Chinese philosophy, Dutch philosophy, French philosophy, German philosophy, Hellenistic thought, Hungarian philosophy, Indian philosophy, Italian philosophy, Japanese philosophy, Latin American philosophy, Polish philosophy, Rumanian philosophy, Russian philosophy, Scandinavian philosophy, Spanish philosophy, and Yugoslav philosophy. (There are references to Greek philosophy and Roman philosophy, but no special articles on them.) Articles appear on Islamic philosophy and Jewish philosophy, but it is a matter of opinion whether these are designations of national philosophies or rather of movements or schools, as in 'Marxist philosophy'.

Philosophy is also discussed, of course, by reference to period rather than place or nationality, as in 'Medieval philosophy' and 'pre-Socratic philosophy'. Sometimes an adjective before the word 'philosophy' does not designate a nation or period or even a movement or school of philosophy, but indicates rather a type or style of philosophy, as in 'scholastic philosophy', 'empirical philosophy'. And an expression like 'pre-Socratic philosophy' can designate not just a period, but also a whole cast of thought characteristic of philosophers of that given period.

M.G.S.

Chronology

Jonathan Edwards, 1703–1758
Benjamin Franklin, 1706–1790
Ralph Waldo Emerson, 1803–1882
Henry David Thoreau, 1817–1862
Chauncey Wright, 1830–1875
Charles Sanders Peirce, 1839–1914
William James, 1842–1910
Josiah Royce, 1855–1916
John Dewey, 1859–1952
Alfred North Whitehead, 1862–1947
George Herbert Mead, 1863–1931
George Santayana, 1863–1952
Morris Raphael Cohen, 1880–1947
C. I. Lewis, 1883–1964
Arthur E. Murphy, 1901–1962

Notes on Contributors

James Campbell is Assistant Professor of Philosophy at the University of Toledo. Author of a number of articles on American philosophy, especially in the *Transactions of the C. S. Peirce Society*.

Susan Haack is Professor of Philosophy at the University of Warwick. Author of *Deviant Logic, Philosophy of Logics*, and of articles on philosophy of logic, epistemology, metaphysics, and American philosophy.

Peter Jones is Professor of Philosophy at the University of Edinburgh. Author of *Philosophy and the Novel* and *Hume's Sentiments*, and numerous articles on aesthetics, ethics, history of philosophy.

Bruce Kuklick is Professor of History at the University of Pennsylvania. Author of *Josiah Royce: An Intellectual Biography; The Rise of American Philosophy;* and *Churchmen and Philosophers: From Jonathan Edwards to John Dewey*.

John J. McDermott is Distinguished Professor of Philosophy and Medical Humanities at Texas A&M University. He has edited scholarly editions of the works of Royce, Dewey, and James, and is author of *The Culture of Experience* and *A Cultural Introduction to Philosophy*.

David L. Norton is Professor of Philosophy at the University of Delaware. Author of *Personal Destinies*, co-editor of *Philosophies of Love*, and author of articles in *Review of Metaphysics, Ethics, The Nation*, etc.

Hans Oberdiek is Professor of Philosophy at Swarthmore College and a frequent visitor to Oxford. Contributor to *Mind, Ethics, New York University Law Review*, etc.

Vincent G. Potter, SJ, is Professor of Philosophy at Fordham University. Author of *Charles S. Peirce on Norms and Ideals*. Contributor to *Thought, International Philosophical Quarterly, Transactions of the C. S. Peirce Society*, etc.

Andrew J. Reck is Professor of Philosophy at Tulane University. Author of *Recent American Philosophy, Introduction to William James*, and *The New American Philosophers*, and editor of *Selected Writings of George Herbert Mead*.

Marcus G. Singer is Professor of Philosophy at the University of Wisconsin, Madison. Author of *Generalization in Ethics* and editor of *Morals and Values*. His article 'Moral Issues and Social Problems' was published in *Philosophy* in January 1985.

T. L. S. Sprigge is Professor of Logic and Metaphysics at the University of Edinburgh. Author of *Facts, Words and Beliefs; Santayana: An Examination of His Philosophy; The Vindication of Absolute Idealism;* and *Theories of Existence*.

Notes on Contributors

Ellen Kappy Suckiel is Associate Professor of Philosophy and Provost of Kresge College at the University of California, Santa Cruz. She is the author of *The Pragmatic Philosophy of William James* and articles in various journals.

H. S. Thayer is Professor of Philosophy at the City College of the City University of New York. Author of *The Logic of Pragmatism* and *Meaning and Action: A Critical History of Pragmatism*; editor of *Newton's Philosophy of Nature* and *Pragmatism: The Classic Writings*.

Richard Tur is Benn Law Fellow at Oriel College, Oxford. Contributor to *Philosophical Quarterly, Journal of Applied Philosophy,* and various legal periodicals, and co-editor of *Essays on Kelsen*. His 'Dishonesty and the Jury' is in the 1984 volume of Royal Institute lectures.

Index

This index was compiled with the assistance of Michael F. McFall

Index

Bain, Alexander: influence on Peirce, 28, 33–5; on belief, 33–5; James' agreement with, 50

Bentham, Jeremy: 'nonsense on stilts', 257; positivism of, 257–9

Bergson, Henri: influence on James, 51, 60–1, 126; influence on Santayana, 126

Berkeley, George: Peirce's review of, 29; affinity with Edwards, 199–200

Bill of Rights, 257

Black, Max, 311

Blackstone, William: influence on American law, 256–7; Bentham's hostility to, 258

Blair, Hugh: *Lectures on Rhetoric,* 63

Bouwsma, O. K., 309

Bradley, F. H.: James' reaction to, 60; Murphy on, 325

British philosophical tradition, 22, 177, 179

Broad, C. D., 5–6

Brooks, Van Wyck, 179

Bushnell, Horace, 181

California: no philosophy in, 162

Calvinism, 65, 180, 202

Cambridge Platonists, 210

Cardozo, B. N.: *Nature of the Judicial Process,* 260; criticism of Gray, 262; mentioned, 272

Carnap, Rudolf, 19

Carnegie, Andrew, 194

Carus Lectures: Mead's, 93, 310; Cohen's, 295; Murphy's, 295, 311, 317–19

Cavell, Stanley: on Thoreau, 245, 253

C.C.N.Y., 299–303

Channing, William Ellery, 135

Cicero: and Hume and James, 65; Adams' use of, 276, 277

City College, 299–303

Clifford, W. K.: on Peirce, 26

Cohen, Felix S., 303–4

Cohen, Morris R.: on American thought, 11; on philosophy, 11, 296–7; affinities with Murphy, 295–8; as teacher, 295; and Dewey and task of philosophy, 296–7n, 308; interest in American philosophy, 297–8; characteristics of, 298–9; and Thomas Davidson, 299–300; career of, 300–3; and 'philosophy-of' areas, 301–2; wit,

302; Cohen stories, 302–3; writings, 303–4; and Holmes, 304, 307; realistic rationalist, 304; on New Realism, 304–5; existence theorems, 304–5; on conventionalism, 305; on nominalism, 305; on reason, 305; philosophy of science, 305, 306; metaphysics, 306; Principle of Polarity, 306–7; philosophy of law, 307–8; natural law theory, 308; on Kant, 308; liberalism, 308–9; philosophy of history, 309, reputation of, 320; discussions of, 326–9; on Hollinger on, 327–9; unity in thought of, 329; mentioned, 6, 272

Collingwood, R. G.: compared with James, 61; teaching of, 186

Constitution of the United States, 273–4

Constructivism, legal, 268–9

Contextual analysis, 314, 315–16

Critical legal studies movement, 266, 267, 268–9. *See also* Law

Critical Realism; *see* Realism, philosophic

Cultural generalizations, 12–15

Culture: relation to philosophy, 6, 12, 15; defined, 15

Darwin, Charles: influence on Peirce, 41; on Dewey, 74; mentioned, 182, 183

Davidson, Donald, 5, 189

Davidson, Thomas, 299–300

Declaration of Independence, 289

Descartes, 110, 120, 322

Dewey, John: Passmore on, ix–x; aim to reconstruct philosophy, 18; relations to James, 57, 75; influence of, 69, 89; Hegelian period, 70, 71, 154, 183; and Peirce, 70, 184; transition to instrumentalism, 72, 78–9; friendship with Tufts, 72; Laboratory School, 72; and Mead, 72, 92, 93, 95; central concern of, 72–3, 83; psychology of, 78, 87; influence of Darwin on, 74; early work of, 74–5, 184; theory of action, 74–6; on unit of behaviour, 77–8; critic of philosophy, 78; on reason, 78; on justification, 79; logic of, 79, 80–2; on experimental method, 79, 83; on reality, 80; on truth, 80; on knowing, 81–3; on ethics, 83–4; on democracy, 85–6; on education, 86, 87; on religion, 87–8; on culture, 88; Mead on, 108, 109; and Emerson, 148, 150; not given birth to by James, 179;

Index

Harvard: James and, 63; classical American philosophers at, 154; and idea of American philosophy, 179; not America, 180; Divinity School and Unitarianism, 180

Hegel, G. W. F.: *quoted*, 257; influence on American philosophy, 22; on Dewey, 70–3, 75, 154, 183–4; on Royce, 154; mentioned, 60, 183, 296

Heidegger, Martin, 322

Hickok, Laurens Perseus: 'most creative American academic philosopher of mid-nineteenth century', 189

Hitler, 189

Hobbes, 205

Hollinger, David: on Cohen, 327–9

Holmes, O. W., Jr.: and American legal thought, 260–3; and pragmatism, 261–2; Dewey on, 262; and Cohen, 304, 307

Hook, Sidney, 302, 322*n*

Hooker, Thomas: a founder of America, 155

Hopkins, Samuel, 180

Howison, George Holmes: criticism of Royce, 168; why not appointed to Harvard, 168*n*

Hume, David: and Peirce, 22; religious views and James', 55–6, 65; James on, 60; influence on James, 64; compared with Edwards, 205, 211; on government, 287; Adams on, 287; on reason and passions, 317; mentioned, 15, 57, 153–4, 211

Hutcheson, Francis: influence on Edwards, 194; Edwards on, 209

Huxley, Thomas Henry, 71

Idealism, 70, 72–3, 160, 166

Ideas: philosophical use of, 316

Induction: Mill and Whewell on, 32

Industrial Revolution, 257

Instrumentalism, 79

Intellectual history: difference from philosophy, 12, 185–6; first task of, 181; external point of view of, 329

James, Henry (brother of William J.): William James on, 47, 62*n*; mentioned, 7

James, Henry, Sr. (father of William J.): influence on William James, 44–5; character of, 45

James, William: in philosophical pantheon, 4; Royce on, 8; on nature of philosophy, 9–10, 46, 64; his pragmatism compared with Peirce's, 21, 36–41, 57–8; on Peirce, 24, 64; Peirce on, 31, 57, 64; influence of Mill on, 33; health of, 45, 46; on America, 45, 62; hostility to German philosophy, 46, 60; to academic philosophy, 46, 60; inspired by Scottish moralists, 46, 66; on habit, 47; on faith, 48, 50; on concepts as instruments, 48–9; and British empiricism, 48, 49, 50; and language, 49; on consciousness, 49–50; on metaphysical principles as expressions of aesthetic feeling, 50; on cause, 50; agreement with Bain, 50; on 'blooming, buzzing confusion', 51; on free will, 51; on education, 51; on ethics, 51; on Bergson, 51; dominant metaphor of, 52; on religion, 53–7; on 'tough-minded' and 'tender-minded', 57; on reality, 58; on truth, 58–9; pluralism of, 59; radical empiricism of, 59; influence of Hume on, 60, 64–5; compared with Collingwood, 61; on war, 61; place in American culture, 62; Ayer on, 64; on sentiment, 64; on professionalism, 66–7; influence on Dewey, 75, 179, 184; teacher of Mead, 91; Mead on, 108; teacher of Santayana, 118; relation to Royce, 119, 300; to Santayana, 126, 130; Santayana on, 125, 131; and Emerson, 141, 144, 150; arranged Royce's appointment to Harvard, 163; overlooked Howison, 168*n*; objections to Royce, 169; influence on Royce, 170–1; 'canonical figure', 178; teacher of Lewis, 217; friend of Holmes, 262; teacher of Cohen, 300; mentioned, *passim. See also* Pragmatism

Jefferson, Thomas: not founder of America, 155; compared with Edwards, 195; and Adams, 274; mentioned, 7, 289

Kallen, Horace: on Santayana, 309

Kant, Immanuel: influence on American thinkers, 22; specifically on Peirce, 22, 26; his term 'pragmatic', 39; Cohen on, 308; mentioned, 110, 183, 297, 317, 322

Index

James, 108; on Royce, 108, 109; on Dewey, 108, 109; on philosophy, 108–10 *passim*; on aesthetics, 108–9; on history, 109–10; on 'international-mindedness', 113; compared with Emerson, 149–50; as classical American philosopher, 154; relation to work of Royce, 169*n*; association with Murphy, 310; mentioned, 6. *See also* Pragmatism

Melden, A. I.: *quoted*, 317–18; mentioned, 311, 322*n*

Merchant of Venice, The, 16

Metaphysical Club, The, 22, 262

Mill, John Stuart: on study of national character, 15; as nominalist, 31; influence on Peirce, 31–2; on induction, 32; controversy with Whewell, 32; theory of belief disputed by Bain, 33; influence on James, 33

Miller, Perry, 179, 194

Montague, W. P., 188

Moore, G. E., 119, 320

Murdoch, Iris, *quoted,* 10

Murphy, Arthur E.: association with Mead, 93, 310; affinities with Cohen, 295–8; as teacher, 295; 'philosophy in the present tense', 295–6; on how wisdom is 'in' a civilization, 296; on philosophy, 296, 319–20, 321, 324; on American philosophy, 297–8, 319–20; objective relativism, 310, 312, 313–14; Honour's Day address, 311; on Henry Adams, 312; special knack of, 312; on Santayana, 312, 325; as commentator, 313; on reason, 315, 316–17; on contextual analysis, 315–16; on use of philosophical ideas, 316; epistemology, 316–17; on common sense, 317; on moral judgment, 317; theory of practical reason, 317, 318; on community and moral sense, 318, 320; on moral diversity, 318–19; liberalism, 319; reputation of, 320; on Bradley, 325; selections from unpublished writings of, 324–5; mentioned, 6

Murphey, Murray, 178*n*, 179

Nagel, Ernest, 302, 304, 322*n*

Nation, 302

National character: idea of, 6; involves cultural generalizations, 14; philoso-

phy as expression of, 15; doubts about, 187, 189

National philosophy: idea of a, 11

Naturalism, viii, 72, 300

Natural law theory, 308

Nevin, John Williamson, 181

New Divinity Movement, 180, 181

New England theology, 180, 181, 191, 212

New Realism; *see* Realism, philosophic

New Republic, The, 302

New Theology Movement, 181, 182

Nietzsche, Friedrich: similarities with Emerson, 147, 148

Nominalism: Peirce on, 29–30; Cohen on, 305

Objective Relativism, 310, 313–15

Ockham, William of, 29

Omissions, from this volume, viii

Paine, Tom, 7

Palmer, George Herbert: on Royce, 163; mentioned, 188

Parker, Theodore, 135

Parrington, Vernon, 179

Passmore, John, *quoted*, ix–x

Peirce, Charles Sanders: in philosophical pantheon, 4; view of philosophy, 18, 19; as working scientist, 21; continuity with Locke, Berkeley, and Hume, 22; recent recognition of, 22; interest of Frankfurt School in, 23; interest of German thinkers in, 23–4*n*; James' description of, 24; obscure style of, 24; *The Collected Papers,* 24; new chronological edition of, 24; Paul Weiss on, 24–5*n*; influence of Kant on, 26; Clifford on, 26; first formulation of pragmatic maxim, 27; on logic, 27–8; influence of Bain on, 28, 34; influence of Whewell on, 28, 32–3; system of existential graphs, 28; on norm of logical validity, 28; abduction, deduction, and induction, 28; on nominalist-realist controversy, 28–9; review of Berkeley, 29; realism of, 29; notions of truth and reality, 29; account of nominalism, 29–30; on reality and 'thing-in-itself', 30; categorial scheme, 30–1; account of realism, 30–1; on James, 31, 64; on continuum of inquiry, 35; 'pragmati-

344

Index